AS IT SEEMED
TO ME

AS IT SEEMED TO ME

Political Memoirs

JOHN COLE

Weidenfeld & Nicolson
LONDON

First published in Great Britain in 1995
by Weidenfeld & Nicolson

The Orion Publishing Group Ltd
Orion House
5 Upper St Martin's Lane
London WC2H 9EA

© 1995 John Cole

First published March 1995
Second Impression March 1995
Third Impression April 1995

A catalogue reference is available from the British Library

ISBN: 0 297 81529 6

Typeset by Selwood Systems
Midsomer Norton

Printed in Great Britain
by Butler & Tanner Ltd
Frome and London

To Madge and our sons –
Donald, Patrick, David and Michael –
for having lived cheerfully with
an obsessional.

CONTENTS

ILLUSTRATIONS

Nigel Lawson and Geoffrey Howe in conference: their resignations led to
  Margaret Thatcher's downfall [1]

The man they thought most likely to succeed [4]

Photographic credits:

[1] Hulton Deutsch

[2] Author

[3] The *Guardian*

[4] Hulton Reuters

[5] Syndication International

[6] Les Gibbard

INTRODUCTION

The title and subtitle of this book have been precisely chosen. These are *political* memoirs, not just memoirs, and not an autobiography. Nor are they a formal history of post-war British politics. Rather they are what the title implies: an account of events, at Westminster and beyond, as these appeared to me, at the time or shortly after. I have used my privileged access to leading actors in some of the more exciting events of the past half-century to give readers a flavour of what politics is like on the inside. Occasionally, a picaresque novel has seemed like a more suitable vehicle for the cast of intellectually subtle, amusing, or occasionally bizarre characters in the cast.

Most retiring ministers, including Prime Ministers, now write their autobiographies or memoirs. In these, they customarily try to establish their places in history. My advantage over politician authors is that, as an observer rather than a player in these great events, I have no place in history to worry about. Unlike them, I have been able to hear the frankest opinions about the characters, personalities, behaviour and policies of these politicians, from people in their own parties and beyond. The public will be surprised to know how thick are the walls which separate the cells at Westminster, how fallible the system of internal communication among the inmates.

There are advantages also in the perspective provided by a career in journalism and broadcasting which began just after the end of the Second World War; though I hope to have avoided at least some of the dangers in what my irreverent sons call 'Old Hand Syndrome'.

That perspective has provided the running theme of this book: the contrasting styles of politics represented by Harold Wilson's belief in pragmatism and Margaret Thatcher's addiction to ideology. These two Prime Ministers are only representatives, though colourful ones, of men and women in both parties who infuse their politics with varying amounts of those two ingredients, pragmatism and ideology.

Neither of these views of politics is specifically Conservative, Labour or Liberal. A belief in one or other may be found in every political party, and many politicians could not tell you whether they are pragmatists or ideologues. But I must now reach a conclusion which I would not have been free to declare when I was political editor of the BBC: that Lady Thatcher's 'conviction politics' has transformed the tone of British public life, and not for the better.

In my view, whatever her other claims to the gratitude of the nation, and despite her virtues of intelligence, hard work and drive, this propensity for enamelled certitude has reduced tolerance between the political parties, and even within them. Worse, it has led to a bitterness and rancour in the House of Commons which will outlive by many years her period as Prime Minister. All this is not to be laid to the account of one leader, however dominant. But it does seem to be a result of the modern version of political ideology.

This is not an argument for value-free politics, for mere political manoeuvring. Nor ought voters to be invited simply to decide that one party or another possesses unique ability to lead the country efficiently, without regard to the direction in which it is led. Of course political leaders must project a vision of the Britain they would like to see, and how they hope to create it.

Yet they must beware of an ideology, whether it be called monetarism, Marxism or political correctness, which turns into a guide to life, and absolves people from the bother of thinking. And they would do well to remember the words of Oliver Cromwell to those seventeenth-century ideologues, the General Assembly of the Church of Scotland: 'I beseech you, in the bowels of Christ, think it possible you may be mistaken.'

In writing this book, I relied heavily on notes of conversations, which I have kept since I arrived in London in 1957, with greater or less assiduousness, depending on which job I was doing at the time. In my years as a newspaper executive, these were dictated to a secretary, and then stored in a locked filing cabinet. In the more frenzied surroundings of the BBC office in the House of Commons Press Gallery, I typed them myself, in the few minutes available between returning from a lunch with a politician and descending into the Members' Lobby for the afternoon's news-gathering.

At the time I left the *Observer* for the BBC in 1981, there were so many files that I asked the managing director to fix a price for me to buy this cabinet. The archive swelled with greater speed during my BBC period, and had to be kept at home. For years, it has sat in our conservatory: a reproach to me, because I knew the more ancient of these notes would have to be sorted one day; a source of irritation to my wife, whose trailing plants only concealed inadequately this metal monstrosity. For this book, I have also drawn on my own writings in newspapers and elsewhere, and my broadcast scripts, when I could unearth these from the detritus of a lifetime.

My original purpose in keeping these notes was an immediate one. In the hectic world of Westminster, it could be difficult, when writing an article or script a week or more after meeting ministers or shadow ministers, to remember in detail what they said. Such information sometimes defies the memory even immediately afterwards. A colleague once confessed that he had often been tempted to write notes on the edge of the tablecloth, and buy it later from the head waiter. I was less ruthless than that in laying down this wine; but I trust it has matured with age.

The book enables me to tell stories I could not publish at the time, for a variety of reasons. Sometimes a politician revealed important information, but only when he or she knew it was no longer suitable for publication in a daily or weekly news outlet. For example, I would have been happy to know, in the early, ideological years of Ted Heath's government, that the man he defeated for the Conservative leadership had written a memorandum dissenting from the whole thrust of economic policy. But Reginald Maudling, isolated at the Home Office from the government's most crucial policy areas, loyally kept silent until Heath did his famous U-turn. Maudling was then proud to reveal to me the existence of this document. With even more subtle loyalty, he later used his suppressed memorandum as the basis for an article in *The Times*, to justify the government's change of course.

Similarly, it was only many months after Margaret Thatcher had forcibly removed Geoffrey Howe from the job he loved at the Foreign Office that a minister felt free to tell me the gory details of how she returned from the quarrelsome Madrid summit of European leaders, determined to have him out of that key post. I could find no outlet for this information then, long after both principal characters had left government. But now I hope it will add some flavour to the world's — perhaps even to Lord Howe's — knowledge of how the final drama of the Thatcher era began.

A word about sources and confidentiality. In most periods covered by this book, so many politicians have already published diaries or autobiographies that any illusion of the Cabinet Room as a Masonic temple has been dispelled. That is as it should be. If open government is to mean anything, freedom of information laws and a loosening of the Whitehall bureaucracy are less important than a transformation of attitudes among public men and women, an acknowledgement of the public's right to know what the issues in a debate within government are, rather than just the conclusions.

In their memoirs, politicians are now helping that process, though retrospectively. The task of the political journalist is to accelerate this process of change. That is what I, like many others in both newspapers and broadcasting, have tried to do throughout my working life: to roll back the frontiers of public knowledge a little further, year by year. I hope this book is another small step in that campaign. By disclosing the main lines of argument which went on *within* governments and political parties, as well as *between* them, I attempt to lead readers further into a world in which there are still too many net curtains.

I have some inhibitions in this process. My conversations with politicians down the years have been conducted on the understanding that, while I might use what they told me in my journalism and broadcasting, I ought not deliberately to expose to embarrassment those who had helped me with information. There is a narrow line to be trodden here. Any information given to a journalist, other than through an officially sponsored departmental press statement or news conference, may easily offend against either the Privy Councillor's Oath, which Cabinet ministers take, or the Official Secrets Act.

When I joined the BBC, I was required to sign a document acknowledging the existence of the Official Secrets Act. This seemed as bizarre as signing for the road traffic acts or the larceny laws, before the police could charge you with speeding or theft. I told the BBC 'suit' who administered this procedure that I understood my job would entail persuading ministers and other public servants to tell me as much of the truth as they could be persuaded to divulge. Otherwise, political journalism becomes pointless.

In this book, I have tried to follow the rules I applied when I was active on the political beat, either as a newspaperman or a broadcaster. The principal one may be tersely expressed: 'Never deliberately put in difficulties a person who has helped you with information.' This cannot mean, of course, that the journalist does not criticise an informant. There is nothing worse than reporters who are the prisoners of their contacts. From time to time, we all err in this respect. But the general principle that a journalist must maintain an independence of his sources is a good one.

The passage of time and politicians' own diaries and memoirs have further loosened the restraints. I have used my notes of conversations to get as near as I can, not only to the truth of what happened, but to the flavour of the discussions within Downing Street, Whitehall or party headquarters. Sometimes I have felt free to quote, or to come near to quoting remarks, in a way I would not have thought right at the time when they were made, ten, twenty or thirty years ago. Especially in conversations which took place more recently, I have taken care to consider whether what I have written will embarrass or damage the source. If in any case I inadvertently give pain, I am sorry.

Some readers may find confusing the uneven intensity with which different periods, people and parties are treated. Over these years, my view of what was going on in British politics was more or less closely focused, depending on which job I was doing. So, because in the late fifties and early sixties I was labour correspondent of the *Guardian*, my knowledge of that period spreads out from study of trade unions and the Labour Party to include those Conservative ministers, such as the Chancellor and the Minister of Labour, who dealt with the economy, and talked with the TUC about wages and strikes. But because I was not working at Westminster then, I had scant knowledge of the Tory back benches.

In the later sixties and seventies, when I did various editing jobs at the *Guardian* and the *Observer*, my spectrum of contacts widened to cover politicians concerned in all the subjects about which I was writing editorials and features: the overall political scene, the economy, the labour market, Europe, and Northern Ireland. By the time I went to Westminster full-time for the BBC, Margaret Thatcher was Prime Minister, so most of my work concerned the inner workings of the Conservative government and Party, though I also kept as close an eye as I could on the opposition, by then divided between Labour and the Alliance. My book, unapologetically because inevitably, varies in the attention it gives to different incidents and people.

Because I spent the last period of my full-time career as political editor of the BBC, some readers may expect me to be more concerned with what politicians say in front of a camera or a microphone than the point of view they put across in background conversation. I do not take this conventional broadcaster's attitude. I can best explain why by previewing one section of this book. It describes the astonishing events before the dismissal of Margaret Thatcher from her leadership of the Conservative Party and government:

Real broadcasting people – as distinct from late interlopers like myself – have, almost *ex-officio*, a reverential attitude to what politicians and others say 'on the record', even more so if they say it to *them*, in an interview, on *their* programme; or even, in the case of a news programme, if it provides the stunning quote in the headline sequence. For television presenters, unlike newspaper or broadcasting correspondents, an on-the-record comment is, after all, their bread and butter. They do not have the responsibility of reporting in the real world, where politicians' private thoughts are sometimes quite different from what they have to say in public.

The occasion of that choleric little outburst was a question I was asked, 'on air', on the day before Margaret Thatcher resigned. During the first-round ballot against Michael Heseltine, I had been going out on a limb to alert audiences to what I detected was really happening: this hitherto invulnerable Prime Minister appeared to be in terminal difficulties. Once she failed to win outright on that first ballot on 20 November 1990, I turned up the volume on my warnings.

But when she went across to the House the following afternoon, she had to say something to cameras and microphones assembled in Downing Street. So she uttered defiant words, agreed in advance with Sir Bernard Ingham: 'I fight on, I fight to win.' Difficult to see what other line a Prime Minister *could* have taken, until the moment when she announced her withdrawal.

But because of this remark, I was asked on the next news bulletin: 'John, the rumours ran strong that she would call it a day. What went wrong in the rumour factory?' Just before appearing, I had learned – unofficially, as ever – that Cabinet ministers were at that moment trooping, one by one, into Margaret Thatcher's room behind the Speaker's Chair, to give her their views about what she ought to do. This proved to be the crucial event of the whole affair. If the ministers were saying to her what many of them had said to me privately, her resignation was inevitable. As evening wore on, as I learned more, and as programme succeeded programme, I made firmer my predictions about the dangers then engulfing her premiership.

That is the difference between 'on the record' comments and what politicians are willing to say in background guidance. Just as in bad Western movies, 'a man's got to do what a man's got to do', so at turning points of political history, when speaking 'on the record', a political leader sometimes has to say what he or she 'has to say'. It may be, in the words of the legal oath, 'the truth and nothing but the truth', but it is not necessarily 'the whole truth', which I have always regarded as a more onerous criterion. In this book, there are many examples of the tendency to speak only partial truth. I record these without cruel intent, for politics would often be impossible without public reticence. But if a reporter wants his audience to know what is going on, he must dig deeper than comments made 'on the record'.

Another illustration of the difference between 'on the record' reality and the real kind: during the later round of that same 1990 Conservative leadership election, I met John Major, Chancellor of the Exchequer, and front-runner in the contest with Michael Heseltine and Douglas Hurd, as he emerged from the committee room where he had just cast his own vote. We had a brief chat, and he hurried off to canvass a few doubtful supporters before the poll closed. Courteous as ever, John said he would be glad to have a longer talk with me when it was all over.

What I knew, but politicians rarely understand, was that if he did win, our next conversation would be on a new basis, and less useful to me than many in the past. In this, John Major would be no different from other Prime Ministers and party leaders I had known. For a journalist, it remains worthwhile to meet these elevated creatures, even when they no longer roam the commoner clearings in the political jungle. Such encounters can provide some impression of their mood and morale. But once they reach the top, their days of enlightening indiscretion are usually over. The Prime Minister's view, after all, is now the government's view. A minister with an independent stance has more reason to give a journalist a taste of the real debate going on within Whitehall.

My aim, as a political journalist and broadcaster, has been to provide what I think of as 'politics for grown-ups'. Nobody can hope to get everything right, either in daily or weekly journalism, or even in a book like this, which describes events months or years ago. Any policeman experienced in investigating traffic accidents will tell you how differently witnesses see something relatively simple. If they have axes to grind, the inconsistencies in his notebook grow worse.

I have set out what this book is, and what it is not. The title, *As It Seemed To Me*, is a comfort blanket. I have tried to come as near as possible to what actually happened. Sometimes this is given in what novelists call 'the God's eye view' of events, which may sound arrogant, but is often necessary to conceal the source of my information. The danger, which I admit, is that this may cloak in apparent certitude a single witness's version of what happened.

Inevitably, these recollections are eclectic. I believe them to be a true and fair account of some great events, and some interesting or amusing ones. But they are an account from my vantage point, seasoned by my own views; and I am happy to acknowledge that this is not the only vantage point or the only set of views. My judgements have altered down the years, thank goodness. Friends from long ago will recognise the influence of what Wordsworth called 'emotion recollected in tranquillity'.

I

FROM BELFAST TO THE GUARDIAN

Unlike Philip Larkin, I do not assert that politics 'began in 1956', when I left Belfast to join the *Manchester Guardian*. Yet it was then that my own long love affair with what I prefer to think of as the art of the *impossible* took fire. With remarkable lack of prescience, I had decided that Ulster's politics were sterile (right); and that nothing would change (wrong). Stormont had preoccupied me for long enough, and I wanted to swim in the larger pool at Westminster.

But it was only after spending another quarter-century in national journalism that the House of Commons became my full-time work-place, when I was appointed political editor of the BBC in 1981. My arrival there was postponed, not by chronic shortage of taxis, but by a series of interesting diversions on the road, which immersed me for a time in the politics of Fleet Street, and specifically the struggle to preserve Britain's two great liberal newspapers, the *Guardian* and the *Observer*.

I do not regret any of my eleven years in Belfast journalism. Not only did I learn my trade there, including some skill in persuading people in public life to tell me more than they originally intended. It also provides me still with a reminder that politics is only important through the effect it has on the lives of ordinary people – a fact too easily forgotten in the Westminster isolation ward, where attention often focuses exclusively on the temperature charts of 651 MPs.

Even when working on the *Belfast Telegraph* I had occasional encounters with national politicians. Harold Macmillan came to Belfast as Chancellor, to address the Unionist Party's annual lunch – their alliance with the Conservatives was then close. I was impressed by his style, but somewhat startled when the typescript of his speech, distributed to reporters in advance, congratulated the Northern Ireland government on establishing an economic development council – a step which had been urged upon them by local Labour MPs, but which the government had until then steadfastly resisted.

I pointed out this error to my editor, who was a guest at the lunch, and pondered whether I ought to mention it to Macmillan before he put his foot in it publicly. The editor, Jack Sayers, was a Conservative, but he was above all a journalist: 'You do what you like, John, but my own view is that if they know as little as that about what's going on here, we ought to leave him to swim for it.'

It was good advice for a young journalist aspiring to write about politics: never confuse your own role with that of the politician; you can be friendly, but his job and yours are different. Years later, during the Callaghan government, a Cabinet minister, who was a helpful contact, had been asked by the Prime Minister to write a paper on the Labour Party's future direction. He wanted me to read the draft for him, and offer criticisms. I suspect he thought I was being stuffy when I demurred, saying I might later have to write an editorial on it for the *Observer*, and wanted to keep my hands free.

My most formative encounter with a national politician during my Belfast years was when I was a cub reporter, and Clement Attlee, then the Labour Prime Minister, visited Ulster on his way home from a holiday at Sligo, in the Irish Republic. He was to stay overnight with Lord Brooke-borough, the Northern Ireland Premier, at his home near the Fermanagh border. A senior reporter went there to cover the press conference Attlee was to give later, and I was dispatched to a little village called Belcoo, where the customs post was, and where we could get our first sight of the Prime Minister. The taxi-driver who took me out from Enniskillen pointed out a signpost to the romantically named village of Swanlinbar, which he proudly pronounced to be 'the smuggling capital of Ireland'.

Attlee came to Fermanagh on a Monday. The previous day's *Observer* had contained a lead story saying that he was going to discuss with Lord Brookeborough the ending of partition. If this had been true, it would have been the most important scoop locally for a quarter of a century. Before setting off to meet him, armed with a cutting of this report, I enquired from Jack Sayers, then the *Observer* stringer in Belfast, what lay behind it.

He rolled his eyes to heaven, and groaned: 'I spent the entire day on Saturday trying to convince those clever young men in London that they had got hold of a ringer, but it was no use.' Years later, I was to be the boss of a later generation of 'those clever young men in London', and I learned how difficult it was to convince them that they were occasionally given bum steers about Ireland.

When Clem Attlee arrived at the border, his wife was driving the car. There was no police escort. The biggest danger to the British Prime Minister was from his wife, who had a reputation as an eccentric driver, but the roads were blessedly empty. Smuggling being a major local industry, the customs officials in Belcoo, no respecters of rank, required Mrs Attlee to open the suitcases in her car boot, presumably to ensure that she and the Prime Minister were not making a killing out of imported nylon stockings, then in short supply.

Attlee took all this with his customary composure. A reporter from the local weekly paper and myself went to the passenger door, pencils poised. The Prime Minister swung his legs to the ground, stoked his pipe, and waited for questions. He agreed with my colleague that the grass in Ireland was greener than that in England, and that he had enjoyed his holiday. Then I produced the cutting from the *Observer*, which he had not seen. His eye ran up and down the two columns with well-practised speed. He took a suck at his pipe, and enquired in his usual staccato tone: 'Got y'notebook?'

He then proceeded to dictate a statement of about 400 words, without hesitation or amendment, contradicting the *Observer* story, point by point. His sentences fell naturally into paragraphs. I was able to go at once to the telephone and, composing a brief news introduction while I waited for the copy-taker, dictate it straight away. My story caught the last evening paper edition, and put us ahead of the main body of reporters, who were waiting for the press conference at Brookeborough's house. I was impressed by the Prime Minister's performance, and decided there might be more to journalism than reporting the agricultural estimates at Stormont for all eternity.

In 1956 I joined the then *Manchester Guardian* as a reporter in the Cross Street office in Manchester, where the ghost of its great editor, C.P. Scott, still looked over our shoulders, demanding moral earnestness and good writing. His journalistic *obiter dicta* were soon ringing in my ears: 'A newspaper's primary office is the gathering of news. At the peril of its soul it must see that the supply is not tainted. Comment is free, but facts are sacred ... The voice of opponents no less than that of friends has a right to be heard ... It is well to be frank; it is even better to be fair.'

A colleague in Belfast gave me, as a parting gift, his much-thumbed paperback copy of the autobiography of a great *Guardian* man, Neville Cardus, the self-educated assistant cricket professional at Shrewsbury School, who became both cricket correspondent and music critic. Being something of an auto-didact myself – an external graduate of London

University – I empathised with Cardus. Soon after I arrived on the *Guardian*, I was having a lunchtime sandwich at the pub near my digs in Didsbury, and discovered that pub was described in the book I was reading, *Fame is the Spur*, a political novel written by another *Guardian* reporter, Howard Spring. In this hive of journalistic and literary tradition, I was soon drunk by association.

Politics during my eighteen months in Manchester was dominated by two events: Britain's invasion of Suez, the humiliation of Anthony Eden's government by withdrawal of American support, and Eden's own resignation; and the first of many attempts I have witnessed, under the chancellorship, and subsequently the premiership of Harold Macmillan, to achieve 'growth without inflation', the holy grail of post-war British politics, to which, even now, ministers still unavailingly aspire.

My introduction to this world, after a period as a political cor-respondent at Stormont, was exciting, if oblique. I covered several by-elections dominated by the deep divisions in the nation over Suez. At one, in Chester, I heard Quintin Hogg (before he became Lord Hailsham for the first time) and Aneurin Bevan speak on successive nights. Both were orators in a class I had not heard before, and although I agreed with what Bevan was saying about Suez, I thought that Hogg, with his back to the wall, made the better speech.

I had a personal encounter with Quintin Hogg as well. He was Minister of Education at the time, and because I was writing an article about 'Flemingism' – an earlier scheme to give places in public schools to bright boys from working-class homes – I asked for an interview. To my surprise, he offered to come to the *Guardian* office when he was next in Manchester. The Reporters' Room retained an antique atmosphere: legend had it that an aged member of The Room had walked out when one of the new-fangled telephones first rang.

The tradition of The Room was a proud one. We all mentally pronounced it with capital 'T' and 'R'. Quintin Hogg clearly enjoyed these Dickensian surroundings, and we conducted an amusing con-versation, which had one bizarre moment. The minister was arguing the case for choice in education, and I was pointing out that most people did not have much choice. He then said:

Look, Mr Cole, I am an Anglican and a Conservative who believes in flogging. I therefore send my son [Douglas, later a minister at the Foreign Office] to Eton. You, being a Belfast Presbyterian, would not want your son to go to an Anglican school, and since you work for the *Manchester Guardian*, I assume you don't favour flogging. Very well! There is no pressure on you to send your son to Eton. If you want to spend the money on a fur coat for your wife, that is your choice.

At this time, I was being paid £16.50 per week, so fur coats did not loom large in our thoughts.

My first friend in England, Brian Redhead, in his own outrageous style, told me that even this modest wage had caused great consternation among my new colleagues, when Brian happened to find my letter of appointment in the office of the editor's secretary. As he bought me my first half-pint in the Bodega, behind the office, he summed up thus: 'We said to ourselves: "Bloody hell! Here we all are, with our firsts from Oxford and Cambridge, getting the National Union of Journalists' minimum of fifteen guineas, and they're paying this bastard from the Irish bogs fifteen bob more."' He looked to see my reaction.

I decided that if these were the local rules of conversation, I had better adopt them. Taking what I hoped was a self-confident swig at my beer, I replied: 'Ah, yes, well that would presumably be because I have these eleven years of rather wide experience in journalism, while you all arrived wet behind the ears.'

He laughed, and in the succeeding thirty-eight years our friendship never wavered, until his death in 1994.

Suez was an issue also at the Carmarthen by-election, where Megan Lloyd George, favourite child of my boyhood hero, was the Labour candidate. She had just switched from the Liberal Party, and summoned the young man from the *Manchester Guardian* to coffee at her hotel, so that he would entertain no doubt that, if her illustrious father had still been alive, he would have done what she had done.

She was very *grande dame*. While I was talking, or rather listening, to her, a man in a brown bowler hat and country suit arrived, swept off his hat, bowed deeply, and kissed her on the cheek. I had never seen a brown bowler before. (In Belfast, they wore them black, either to denote that they were shipyard foremen, and therefore needed protection from maliciously dropped rivets; were attending a funeral; or belonged to the Orange Order.) The two had a friendly conversation. He was Jeremy Thorpe, one of Jo Grimond's lieutenants.

Suez was a turning point in British history. Only sixteen years after we had been the essential rallying point for democratic resistance to Hitler, it cast doubt on our whole future place in the world. Eden's generation believed in the simple verities, of national interest, and the need to fight back against international illegality. For a time, the Labour leader, Hugh Gaitskell, seemed likely to take the same view. But gradually a great national debate began, of a bitterness unparalleled in modern times. At the Chester by-election, even the reporters almost came to blows. Being new to such exhibitions of English passion, I judged it prudent to keep my fists carefully unclenched.

To give some idea of the more primitive nature of political coverage then, I recall Anthony Eden's key broadcast to the nation – on radio, of course, not television. The *Guardian* was printed only in Manchester, so to get a report into our London edition, which went to press at 10 p.m., the news editor mobilised a not too highly skilled team of shorthand writers, including myself. I can still remember the chill of fear at my heart when, after a couple of minutes, our opening bat, in a strangled voice, whispered: 'Take over, I'm losing him.' I managed to hold on to Eden's pace, more or less, for four minutes, until I handed over to our third man. It later emerged that he, though renowned as one of The Room's finest writers, had won a cup for shorthand writing, which was held to be a most eccentric achievement.

Among my jobs in Belfast had been industrial correspondent. So when a rash of strikes broke out in the summer of 1956, principally in shipbuilding and motor manufacture, the *Guardian* sent me to cover them. I also reported many conferences of individual trade unions, gaining an encyclopedic knowledge of the less fashionable seaside resorts of Britain.

The subject which kept coming up at these union conferences was a theme of Harold Macmillan's: that Britain's economic progress depended on creating 'a plateau of wages and prices'. The Treasury has always been extremely fertile in coining phrases that imply a new beginning in policy. In my experience these usually refer to the same unchallengeable truth: that if expansion of the economy produces a rise in wages and prices, the end result is a sharp application of the brakes, with resultant recession and unemployment. But this was a post-war world, which had only recently emerged from long years of austerity and rationing. So a message of restraint was not one that industry found digestible. Unions and management alike were then innocent of the realities of 'boom and bust', and they gave a dusty answer.

When Macmillan succeeded Eden as Prime Minister, the accepted wisdom was that he would have the greatest difficulty in reuniting a Conservative Party still divided by Suez, and that his election defeat was probable. His opponent, Hugh Gaitskell, was a man of strong and unbending – perhaps too unbending – character, whose reputation with the public, and even the anti-Labour press, stood higher in the latter half of the fifties than that of any leader of the opposition in modern times.

In 1957 I moved to London as labour correspondent of the *Guardian* (as it was soon to become, having decided to drop 'Manchester' from its title). This was a job that combined coverage of industry, and especially labour relations, with that of Labour politics outside the House of Commons. The logic of this grew out of the nature of the Labour movement: the trade unions, then under right-wing leadership, were influential in Labour's National Executive Committee (NEC) and at the party conference. So for a journalist to understand how the unions worked and thought was halfway to understanding Labour politics.

C.P. Scott had appointed the socialist academic, G.D.H. Cole (no relation), to be his first, and part-time, labour correspondent. Scott wanted him and subsequent occupants of the post to explain to a largely middle-class readership the activities of the Labour Party and the unions, with which he had considerable sympathy, though he had himself, for a short time, been a Liberal MP. Scott knew his own limitations as a student of working-class life. His managers once induced him to present a *Manchester Guardian* Cup for greyhound racing in the city. Subsequently they had to make strenuous efforts to prevent their stern Nonconformist chief learning that working men actually placed wagers on these animals.

The *Guardian* of that period intended to be sympathetic to Labour, with or without a capital letter, not least because the balance of the serious press was so heavily pro-Conservative. But it was always tortured by respect for three, not easily reconcilable, parts of its tradition: Liberal roots; a quite Conservative readership in its own regional heartland, the north-west; and the modern reality: that the left or centre-left of British politics now lay in the Labour Party. C.P. Scott grasped that last fact as long ago as the twenties. Some of his successors have judged it less simple.

2

LIFE WITH GAITSKELL

I wrote my first article criticising the trade union block vote in 1957, previewing a debate that was not to become fashionable in Labour circles until the eighties and nineties. I argued that the Labour leadership could only create a proper democratic base for itself by winning support in the constituency parties, then mostly in the hands of Nye Bevan's left-wing supporters.

This article was one factor in my uneasy relationship with Hugh Gaitskell. Another was that he operated his press relations through the parliamentary journalists in the Lobby system. This was sensible enough, but it meant I did not have a chance to see him regularly. Gaitskell had won the leadership when Attlee retired, against the opposition of Bevan and of Herbert Morrison. His victory was helped by the support of the right-wing union leaders of the period. Although Labour leaders then were elected by MPs only, many of those sponsored by trade unions would not have dared to defy the wishes of their autocratic General Secretaries.

Judging by one item in my files, Gaitskell seems to have told the editor of the *Guardian*, Alastair Hetherington, that my article criticising the block vote was illiberal nonsense. I wrote to Hetherington:

> I think Gaitskell is too interested in the trade union leaders, and too aware of his need to woo them. Under the present set-up, this is undoubtedly necessary, and he, of course, saw the advantage of it personally some years ago. [Gaitskell was close to the editor, and this was a sly reference to the undemocratic background to his leadership victory over Morrison, who had been deserted by the union barons.]
>
> But I can't help feeling that this kind of patronage is completely unhealthy, if only because it causes an intelligent man like Gaitskell to mouth platitudes about the unions such as he used at Blackpool. I am not even sure whether

the union backing is going to be such a sure foundation in the next few years
... [This proved to be prescient, though a massive understatement.]

Gaitskell may find in the end that there is no alternative to the rather
painful and slow process of preaching the Facts of Life to the rank-and-file.
He certainly has a nerve calling anything we say 'illiberal' when he's preaching
the perpetuation of the block vote system in its present form. But they all
have a closed mind on this subject...

If my nostrils seem to quiver at these 'old, unhappy, far-off things, and
battles long ago', it is because I found Gaitskell difficult. One evening at
his party conference, a group of us labour and industrial correspondents
(the terms were interchangeable) had dinner with him. In conversation
later with a friend of mine, John Bourne, of the *Financial Times*, Gaitskell
said: 'I thought John Cole was in rather good form tonight. I'd always
assumed he was a Trotskyist.'

Bourne indignantly rebutted this bizarre suggestion. It may have arisen
from the fact that I found the Trotskyist politics of the time amusingly
newsworthy. They were conducted by a veteran Trot, Gerry Healy, and
a hilarious building worker, Brian Behan, who invited me to his 'coming-
out party' – his release from a week's prison sentence for some picketing
offence. Behan was every bit as iconoclastic as his brother Brendan, the
Irish playwright, whom I also encountered briefly.

I had gone to the Theatre Royal, Stratford East, to see one of his
plays, and while having a sandwich in the bar beforehand, met a sea-
going man from Tipperary. When the author arrived, uproariously
drunk, my Tipperary companion went to buy him another – unnecessary – drink. Behan eyed me blearily, as a circle of theatre-goers in duffle
coats (the left-wing mess kit of the period) observed him closely.

'D'ye see me?' he said challengingly. 'D'ye see me? If I stay any longer
in this bloody city, I'm buggered!' He paused to consider further, and
then added: 'I'm fucked!' In those pre-Chatterley days, it was a word
not often used in public. A dozen pairs of duffle-coated eyes swivelled
to see with what Wildeian *bon mot* his companion would respond.

The best I could manage was a nervous: 'Is that so?' I felt I had let
them all down.

The younger brother, Brian, was not so fond of his liquor. He had
been on the national executive of the Communist Party, but since he
defected to the Trotskyists, he and Gerry Healy had combined an
addiction to industrial mayhem, on the restricted front of the London
building industry, with some of the most Erewhon ideology ever known
to man. So I wrote about them from time to time, though I did

not think they were the most important element in British industrial relations.

But to the Gaitskellites, who were quite illiberal in their attitudes to the press – 'he who is not for me is against me' – to *report* something was to *support* it. On the same principle, Gaitskell's biographer was later to categorise me as 'a Crossmanite', though as will become clear in this book, I viewed Richard Crossman with some scepticism.

I judged it wise to tell my editor that the leader of the Labour Party had thought I was a Trotskyist. Hetherington smiled comfortingly, but said it was much worse than that: Gaitskell feared I was a Wilsonist, which was more serious than being a Trotskyist. Trotsky had died with an ice-axe in his head, Wilson was very much alive, and an immanent threat to Gaitskell.

This is an interesting example of how politicians fail to understand what makes journalists tick. With Harold Wilson in barely concealed opposition to Gaitskell, he was the man with whom any reporter who wanted to know what was going on in Labour's inner councils would keep in touch. Hence the journalistic maxim mentioned in my intro-duction: a party leader rarely has any reason for leaking; the rival does. When Wilson himself became leader on Gaitskell's death, I mentally wrote down the thought: There goes my best contact! He remained friendly, but of less use with inside stories of what was going on. By then, however, I had become news editor, and others had the job of following day-by-day manoeuvrings within the Labour Party.

Politicians often wonder whether a journalist is prejudiced either for or against them or their cause. They can be safe with one assumption: all reporters are prejudiced in favour of discovering news ahead of their rivals; and of being proved right. Our vice is usually vanity rather than partiality.

I had been appointed labour correspondent in the late summer of 1957. Alastair Hetherington, who was on a visit to London, telephoned me at home in Manchester. This call came on the day we were due to travel to Belfast, to display our newly born first son to his grandparents. Alastair told me what he wanted to talk about, and volunteered to come to the Liverpool–Belfast ferry to see me, since anything else would have thrown our carefully made arrangements into chaos. Since he was still a bachelor, I thought he simulated decent enthusiasm for the baby, as we walked him round the deck.

After our Belfast holiday, I travelled from Manchester to London to take up the post in late September – by way of a shipyard strike on the Clyde. It was the City editor, Richard Fry, who advised his inexperienced new colleague that Harold Wilson was the man in the Labour Party to cultivate: I should invite him to lunch. That began a series of lunches and other meetings with Wilson, usually at Kettner's in Soho (which, Terence O'Neill, the Ulster Prime Minister, told me when we met there, had in Edwardian times been a high-class bordello).

My period as labour correspondent from 1957 till 1963 was a marvellous time to cover the Labour Party. It fell into two natural periods. Up till the 1959 election, Hugh Gaitskell led a united effort to produce new policies. This was effectively the time when the wartime and post-war consensus first began to erode. Until the retirement of Churchill and Attlee in the mid fifties, party divisions had still been mitigated by memory of shared experiences in the wartime coalition. With Gaitskell taking over the Labour leadership, and first Eden, and then Macmillan as Conservative Prime Minister, a new era began. Normal party politics were resumed, though with nothing like the partisan virulence which appeared in the eighties.

With my job being to cover Labour politics outside the House of Commons, I suffered frustration. Westminster had been my original aim, and though labour correspondent was senior in the *Guardian* pecking order to number two at the House of Commons, that was the post I had originally coveted, ever since I had assisted the political correspondent, Francis Boyd, at the Liberal Assembly of 1956.

Labour's aim in its policy-making was to counter Macmillan's reliance on the post-war spurt of prosperity – 'you've never had it so good' – by reasserting its commitment to social justice, linked to a more consistent industrial performance. Harold Wilson was writing *Plan for Progress*, which was to form the basis of many later Labour economic policies. The patience and openness with which he took me through his ideas formed an important part of my education in political economy, for which I was always grateful.

Wilson revealed to me one other piece of tactical wisdom, which he used in politics, and I occasionally applied to newspapers. It was: 'Always try to arrange that you write the first draft. They may mess it around a lot later in committee, but if you have written the first draft, something of your ideas will survive.' Only occasionally are newspaper editorials written 'in committee', at some crucial moment like a general election. But the Wilson dictum became my guide for such occasions.

It was at those lunches with him that I first grasped a concept which was to dominate the economic thinking of a whole generation of both Labour and Conservative politicians: that the growth which would create ever-increasing prosperity could only be sustained if wage-bargainers considered the national interest. In an overheated economy, with what, from the perspective of the nineties, seems an astonishing level of full employment, the temptation was to let wages – and prices – rip. But that would lead to what later became the British mid-century vice – 'stop-go'.

I was fortunate in my tutors in these mysteries. The second of these was George Woodcock, one of the great General Secretaries of the TUC. Through Woodcock, I was given access to the spirit of John Maynard Keynes, whom he had worked with, and revered, in his youth. He told a good story about Keynes's wife, Lydia Lopokova, the ballerina. Woodcock was so fascinated by Keynes's thinking that he could scarcely tear himself away from a lunch at the great economist's home. Eventually Lopokova deposited the star-struck young union man on her Bloomsbury doorstep – with skills, he skittishly assumed, that she had developed under Diaghilev.

Harold Wilson had worked for the other great intellectual architect of post-war Britain, William Beveridge. He gave the offer from Beveridge to stay on at Oxford to help with his research as excuse for not accepting a job he was offered on the *Manchester Guardian*. Who knows, he might have become editor, instead of just Prime Minister. (I subscribe to the comparative values of the man who met Stanley Baldwin, then Prime Minister, on a train, and said: 'What have you been doing since you left Harrow, Baldwin?')

Early in our acquaintance, Wilson demonstrated to me his engaging penchant for self-mockery. At our first lunch, he explained that the unions would only attempt to deliver wage restraint if they were convinced the government was devoted to social justice. How, I asked, would they judge? He outlined Labour's plans for further development of the welfare state, for pensions and other social benefits. Then he said that I might think his next point trivial, but it was important to set an atmosphere for wage restraint. Harold Wilson, remember, learned his trade under the austere chancellorship of Stafford Cripps.

'Business entertaining,' he said merrily. 'Look around you here. Do you think they're all entertaining foreign buyers? That chap over there with the rather attractive redhead? Or the two jolly looking fellows at the window? My guess is that one director buys the other lunch today, and they reverse roles tomorrow. And the Chancellor pays! That's the sort of thing which convinces union leaders their poor members live in a different world. We've got to convince them otherwise.'

After arguing that our own lunch fell into a different category – as I think it did – he looked around the room, and said: 'I expect when a

Labour government gets to work, this place will have to close down.' Then he picked up his knife and fork, and said: 'Still, they do cook very well.' This was the kind of joke that gained him an unjust reputation for cynicism. Harold Wilson is a prime example of what I believe applies to most politicians: that they come into public life with a conviction they can improve the lot of their country and their fellow-citizens; that along the way they make compromises, inevitable in a democracy, and certainly within a party system; but that most retain a streak of their idealism and beliefs to the end. That was certainly true of Wilson. But his quick wit, and an irresistible desire to make people laugh, sometimes concealed his deep convictions.

Reporting industrial relations and wage negotiations brought me into touch with Conservative ministers as well. I began to understand how politicians of both main political parties, often originally hostile to becoming involved in the labour market, found themselves driven to consider incomes policies, either formal or informal. This is now an unfashionable doctrine, but I suspect Britain will eventually find its way back to a voluntary incomes policy. In this, government, employers and trade unions reach agreement about what level of increase in incomes will allow growth without inflation. My various jobs allowed me to watch a series of considerable politicians wrestle with this problem: Macmillan, Selwyn Lloyd, Reginald Maudling, Iain Macleod and Edward Heath on the Conservative side; Harold Wilson, George Brown, James Callaghan, Denis Healey and Barbara Castle for Labour.

When the 1959 election came, I was given the job of reporting Hugh Gaitskell during a large part of his election tour. In those days, party leaders left London for long periods, sleeping each night where they had held their last meeting. I followed Gaitskell from East Anglia, through Yorkshire and the north-east, to revivalist rallies in Edinburgh, where he enlisted the moral fervour of the Church of Scotland behind his exco-riating criticism of the government's record in colonial Africa; and in Glasgow, where he adopted the same tone in denouncing unemployment at levels then thought disgraceful: several hundreds of thousands!

Labour lost in 1959, by a disastrous margin. Its Bevanite split had been patched up, but the scar tissue remained in the public's memory; and advance shadows of internal divisions over nuclear disarmament revealed to voters a party that was still not at ease with itself. What certainly sank Labour's hopes of victory was confusion over its tax policy, the same confusion which has dogged the party right up to the present. As Conservative opponents argued that Gaitskell could not pay for his programme without an increase in income tax, he replied that this would not be necessary, because economic expansion would finance extra expenditure.

I was with him in Yorkshire when he gave this pledge. We in the accompanying press corps did not realise at once that the speech would have such monumental consequences – depriving him of what then seemed the certainty of becoming Prime Minister; as it turned out, for ever. After this statement on taxation, his programme seemed not quite credible.

There is a clash of evidence about Harold Wilson's role in the affair. Richard Crossman, not always the most reliable witness – and nursing a grievance, because the campaign committee at Labour Party head-quarters, over which he presided, had not been consulted – gave me his version of events. He maintained that Gaitskell had 'just phoned up poor little Harold Wilson at the Adelphi Hotel in Liverpool, and was told to go ahead'. Wilson – who was to discover as Prime Minister what an unpredictable ally Crossman could be – maintains that he advised Gait-skell against such a pledge, though he did it for what he later told me was the wrong reason: that it would lead to demands for pledges on *every other* tax. This problem is now familiar to John Major, who in the nineties has been severely criticised for what *he* promised on taxation during his 1992 election campaign.

This recollection of events in 1959 may help younger readers under-stand why, during the 1992 election, John Smith felt the need to be franker about income tax, however painful the subsequent Conservative attack on Labour; and why Kenneth Clarke, in reflective moments during George Bush's electoral agony, wondered whether governments of the right, in Britain as in America, would not one day have to face the voters with the truth that taxes sometimes have to go up, rather than down.

3

WILSON THE CHALLENGER

After 1959, Labour fell into one of those bouts of internecine quarrelling which seem, inevitably, to follow defeat. The party's chief press officer, Arthur Bax, told me about an article in the right-wing Labour magazine, *Forward*, in which Douglas Jay, a close ally of Gaitskell, was advocating a change in the party's name to 'Radical'.

This, said Bax, was only the tip of a dangerous iceberg. It turned out that immediately after the election, the Gaitskellites – Hugh Dalton, Roy Jenkins, Tony Crosland, Douglas Jay, Patrick Gordon Walker, among others – had met at Gaitskell's home in Hampstead, and decided to repeal Clause IV of the party constitution. This called for 'common ownership of the means of production, distribution and exchange', and was widely recognised to be an anachronism. The Attlee government had already nationalised the great public utilities – coal, electricity, gas and the railways – but there was no strong demand for the state to move into manufacturing.

But Gaitskell's initiative seemed to many Labour politicians, not all on the left, to be insensitive and unnecessary. That group included Harold Wilson. He said to me one day: 'I gather your editor sees a lot of Hugh. He'd be better informed about our party if he were to meet a few other people.' I duly conveyed this message to Alastair Hetherington, who arranged a dinner at the Athenaeum. The other guests were Francis Boyd, the political correspondent, and myself.

Harold Wilson went out of his way to amuse and charm, though his anecdotes about cricket and football were of more interest to Francis and myself than to Alastair, whose sport was hill-walking. Eventually, one of us challenged him to say how he would have handled the Clause IV issue. The reply was clear: if Gaitskell really believed he *had* to change it – and Wilson thought the proposal was a divisive irrelevance – then he needed to show sensitivity to

Labour traditions. So how ought he to have gone about it?

Wilson then gave a mock speech, which went roughly like this: 'Comrades, in our deliberations on what this great party of ours must do next, let us never forget one undeniable fact: the Tories are a bunch of bastards. But as we consider the future of public ownership, let us not leave ourselves open to the slanders and lies our opponents will throw at us. For never forget, comrades, that the Tories are a bunch of bastards. But do we really want the state to take over every corner sweet-shop or petrol station? Of course we don't, but that's what the Tories will say about us, because the Tories are a bunch of bastards . . .'

He claimed that in this way the party could have been weaned away from an obsession with nationalisation, without dividing traditionalists from reformers. It was methods in politics, rather than any great difference in beliefs, which divided Hugh Gaitskell and Harold Wilson. Before he became Labour leader, as afterwards, Wilson did not believe in confrontation. He gave high priority to party unity, as the only way to achieve and use power in a democracy. This belief, and the inevitable inconsistencies it produced, was to prove the most controversial aspect of his leadership.

Gaitskell and Wilson had never been friends, but it was at this time that the rivalry between them, and more particularly between their supporters, became bitter. It is difficult to be fair in apportioning blame. To Wilson's friends there was a snobbery about the way in which he was excluded from the political discussions which the Gaitskellites conducted on social occasions. Yet Harold Wilson did not enjoy that kind of social life.

If he had a class chip on his shoulder, they helped to put it there. Perhaps it was because Gaitskell and his friends made disparaging remarks about his competence as an economist that he used to say to me, rather naïvely for a senior politician talking to a young journalist, that he had the only starred double first in economics at Oxford between the wars. Nobody meeting Harold Wilson in his prime would have doubted that he possessed a formidable and fertile mind.

I once had a remarkable conversation with Tony Crosland, a man whom I later came to admire – though, unlike his closer journalistic friends, more than 'a little this side idolatry', for he had an arrogance which he tempered with charm only when he had accepted you as an intelligent interlocutor. At one encounter, he was criticising Wilson: political stances, lifestyle, personality. I tried to put the opposite case, but Crosland would have none of it, and finally exploded: 'But the bloody man plays golf!'

I replied that I had better confess, if sport was to be a hanging offence, that I played tennis myself.

He capped that: 'But *you* don't hang around talking to the people afterwards.'

I heard later that Tony Crosland and Roy Jenkins, in those days before the grievous subject of Europe distanced them from each other, used to play tennis together near their homes in Kensington, thus presumably avoiding the tedium of club bores – an attitude which, as I grew older, I learned to appreciate.

Hugh Gaitskell's Clause IV initiative ended in a face-saving 'clarification' clause added to Labour's constitutional garbage, and was soon forgotten. By the 1960 conference he was in much deeper trouble, because of the growing strength of the Campaign for Nuclear Disarmament. I believe he was right to oppose unilateral abandonment of Britain's nuclear capacity. The uncertainty created then in the public mind about Labour's defence posture haunted it until the eighties, and was one factor which kept the party out of office for so long.

But I also felt vindicated in the warning I had given a year or so before about Gaitskell's reliance on the block vote. I had foreseen the left-wing influence of Frank Cousins, who had become General Secretary of the largest union, the transport workers. Since Ernest Bevin founded the union in the early twenties, this post had always been held by the right. Now Gaitskell had lost assured control of his party conference. His courageous speech at Scarborough, in which he promised to 'fight and fight and fight again to save the party that we love', could not convert this and other block votes, and he lost.

It was one of the most emotionally charged Labour conferences I have attended, and the crisis over defence soon turned into mutterings about Hugh Gaitskell's leadership. One evening I heard a rumour that Harold Wilson was to stand against him in November. When I put this to him, he asked: 'Do you think that would be a smart thing for me to do?' I gave my opinion that he would be heavily defeated, and he agreed. As Michael Heseltine understood thirty years later, a plan to challenge a sitting party leader is more attractive to plotters than to the individual who has to raise the rebel standard. The thesis that whoever wields the dagger rarely wins the crown is not universally true, but it guides most politicians most of the time.

Hugh Gaitskell was sitting only thirty feet away in the hotel lounge, surrounded by journalists. Wilson took the pipe from his mouth: 'Take it from me, John, when the dagger is shoved between the shoulders of that chap over there, there will be six policemen, none below the rank of sergeant, standing around J.H. Wilson.'

I have no doubt this represented his intention at the time. But the left was determined that Gaitskell should be challenged, so they put up Anthony Greenwood as what was later to be called a stalking-horse. In this case, they were using Greenwood to force the hand of the heir-apparent. Wilson stood, and lost as heavily as we both believed he would. He did well enough, however, to satisfy that other great cliché of leadership elections: he 'put down a marker', which helped him to win the leadership when Gaitskell died two years later.

The incident led to one of those embarrassments into which my garrulous Irish nature occasionally leads me. I told a number of friends about Wilson's witticism: the fact that his police witnesses as to alibi were all to be sergeants, or above, tickled my sense of humour. Others, too, must have thought it was funny, for the story did the rounds. The BBC was just launching *That Was the Week That Was*, its first excursion into satire – not a genre, at least in its current nihilist manner, which I admire. A researcher telephoned me, and gave a not wholly inaccurate version of the Wilson conversation.

I quickly decided that my duty to my contact overruled that to frankness. No cloud of Wilsonian tobacco smoke could have obscured the story better than the mixture of bluster and bluff which I emitted. Subsequently, I called in a debt from a BBC executive, who promised to 'do what I can'. The story never appeared – until now, when it hurts nobody.

If I had made it available to the BBC at the time, David Frost and his script-writers on *TW3* – people whose knowledge of, even interest in, the political process I rated very lowly – would have used it to ridicule Harold Wilson, and illustrate their thesis that everyone in public life is a knave or fool. *TW3*, unlike satire in earlier ages, did not grow out of deep political convictions, but had a flavour of Shakespeare's Thersites.

At risk of labouring the point, I explain for non-journalists why I acted as I did. I had accepted Wilson's confidence on the understanding that I might use the answer he gave to my question – that he did not then intend to challenge Hugh Gaitskell – on my own authority, not by quoting him. The same applied to the witticism which, if published later, when events had changed his mind, could have made him look foolish. Indeed, that was *TW3*'s only purpose in taking interest in a trivial incident. My purpose was more serious: to find out what was going on in politics, and report it.

★   ★   ★

It is difficult to convey to modern readers, or even to younger journalists, the secrecy which enshrouded such bodies as Labour's National Executive Committee in the fifties and early sixties. Party officials held no press conferences or formal briefings. We pursued our friends and contacts by telephone or in the pubs they used. There were right-wing pubs and left-wing pubs for most important venues in the Labour movement. My predecessor as labour correspondent, Mark Arnold-Forster, took me on an acclimatisation drive round central London to instruct me in the topography of the more significant licensed houses.

I cannot now remember the name of the East End pub which was vital in dock strikes, but I do recall a notebook with the entry 'barmaid called Rose – will take messages'. What Rose could not protect me from was ordering the wrong drink. When I entered her pub for the first time, I wanted to remain inconspicuous until I had established myself with the dockers, who did not regard the Fourth Estate as their natural friends. I ordered a half-pint of bitter. Only when she placed it in front of me did I notice that everyone else was drinking pints. I felt like a character in those cynosure-of-every-eye cartoons by Pont: 'the man who ordered a half-pint in a dockers' pub'.

The atmosphere of the age was secretive. Even now, we have not achieved 'open government', but at least political parties do not regard all their meetings as gatherings of a Masonic Lodge. In the early sixties, I heard of a meeting, to be held in a Bloomsbury hotel one Sunday. The purpose was to hammer out Labour's economic policy. I knew the venue, but not even who was attending. So I telephoned the hotel as the members were gathering and asked for Jim Callaghan, then shadow Chancellor, who was sure to be present.

Callaghan came to the phone, and enquired how I knew about their meeting. When I dodged this question, he laughed, and said: 'Well, your phone call caused the Irish porter to come into our room, and announce ceremoniously: "Mr John Cole, of Granada Television, for Mr James Callaghan." The others were all shocked that you knew we were meeting, though rather amused. Anyhow, my colleagues know I'm talking to you, so I can't help you, even if I wanted to.' (I was doing some freelance work for Granada at the time: television had blown even a print journalist's cover!)

I said gloomily that I supposed I would have to come up and stand on the doorstep to find out who was present, and would that not be embarrassing for all concerned?

The future Prime Minister, who recognised a well-directed blackmail, took a stern, but politically realistic stance: 'I've a jolly good mind to tell you just to do that, and to miss church and the delicious roast beef I've no doubt your wife is cooking. However, I'll tell you who's here, but absolutely nothing else.'

I thanked him, and spent that evening telephoning those participants whose lips were not sealed by the friendly zeal of Irish hotel porters.

Sometimes the obsession with secrecy took a nasty turn. One legal action by the Labour Party became something of a *cause célèbre*. 'The Morgan Phillips case' produced one of the fattest files in the *Guardian*'s history. Morgan Phillips was General Secretary of the Labour Party, and had written a paper for the NEC after the 1959 defeat, proposing changes in party structure. In retrospect, as I looked at my rapidly yellowing cutting, with 'shades of the prison-house' engulfing me, it was a boring document. The one distinctive proposal I can remember was a suggestion that Labour needed the equivalent of the Tory Party chairman, a figure other than the leader who could take a high political profile during elections. 'A Labour Lord Hailsham' was my phrase for this proposal, for Hailsham had enjoyed a barnstorming success as Macmillan's galloper, ringing a bell at the party conference to rouse the faithful, and taking early morning dips in the October sea to seduce newspaper snappers.

At the next Executive meeting, the roof fell in. A writ arrived at the *Guardian*, with a large number of counts, including defamation, breach of copyright, conversion, and heaven knows what else. The allegation was that we had 'converted' to our own use a document which was the property of Morgan Phillips, the plaintiff; that we had breached either his or the Labour Party's copyright; and that by publishing it we had libelled him, by implying that he had given it to us himself.

At that time the *Guardian* did not have in-house lawyers, so I was sent to see the legally conservative, but shrewd firm of Fleet Street solicitors we used. The senior partner airily dismissed most of the counts as frivolous, though he conceded that, because I had put a few words of the turgid prose in quotation marks, we might be liable for several pence in damages for breach of copyright. He confirmed what I knew: that the real purpose was to uncover my source.

These events occurred long before the issue of journalistic sources became a matter of public debate. So much so that our solicitor said I must give the name. I said I could not do so. Apart from the journalist's code against revealing sources, the individual concerned would probably lose his job. (He was a trade union official, long since dead.) The solicitor said kindly that I need not tell him there and then, but that when the judge asked I must do so, or I would go to prison for contempt, and stay there till I had complied.

I reported back to Alastair Hetherington on this conversation, and he took the point immediately. Within a few days, I had a letter from him agreeing that I could not reveal the source, and another from the *Guardian* chairman, Laurence Scott, supporting that. It seemed that the two most senior men on the paper and myself were to be in adjoining cells.

The action dragged on for six years, without ever reaching court, and at times seemed like a comic opera. The NEC appointed a distinguished leaks committee: Aneurin Bevan, Sam Watson, a veteran Durham miner and close friend of Gaitskell's, and Morgan Phillips himself. I did not know Bevan well, but he himself had been a formidable leaker in his time, and I had the impression he did not take the enquiry too seriously. His contribution was to accompany his two colleagues to the Marquis of Granby, the pub near Labour headquarters, presumably to see if any examples of rape and pillage by journalists were visible to the naked eye.

While I was still anxious about prison, Morgan Phillips sent me a Christmas card, with a touching quotation from Robert Burns: 'There's nothin' worth the wear of winnin', but laughter and the love o' friends.' Eventually, concerned about what my reporting zeal might be costing the paper in legal fees, I suggested to Hetherington that we should make sure that our various acquaintances in the Labour leadership knew that the action was still dragging on. The editor spoke to Hugh Gaitskell and Richard Crossman, and did not get the impression that they knew much about it.

I mentioned the case to Harold Wilson. He clearly was not *au courant* either, but added that, though he thought I was innocent of vile intent, he did resent the way in which an NEC colleague was leaking their internal documents. What's more, he was pretty sure he knew the name. I steered him away from that perilous line of thought. There then followed one of those discussions which usefully remind a journalist how far his own attitudes are divided from even the closest of political friends.

Here was a man who had taught me much about politics, discussed freely what was happening in the Labour Party, how its policies were developing. At a personal level, he had been extremely sympathetic when I was unwell. He had even offered to lend me his bungalow in the Isles of Scilly, though since he would not accept rent, arguing that most of it would go to the Chancellor in tax, I did not accept. Yet when it came to straight leaks of NEC documents, a huge gulf of understanding separated us.

I expressed surprise that he took such a dim view of the series of leaks – not all from the same source, incidentally – which had irritated the NEC. I added that he himself had been kind enough from time to time to – adapting the police phrase – 'help me with my enquiries'. Wilson was equally surprised: our minds did not touch at any point. He said that he himself had never leaked without a political purpose in mind, whereas this fellow seemed to do it incontinently. He ended the conversation with the words, 'See you in court', uttered quite without malice.

The Morgan Phillips case was eventually settled, with each side bearing its own costs. I think the Labour Party received the couple of hundred pounds the *Guardian* had paid into court, to cover the possibility that we had breached copyright, and that the jury might take a more elevated view of the literary merit of Morgan Phillips's prose than our solicitors had done.

Fifteen or sixteen years later, there was an illuminating sequel. Lord Goodman had been the Labour Party's solicitor, and was presumably responsible for advising continuance of the case. Soon after I joined the *Observer* in 1975, I encountered him at a meeting to discuss a supposed threat to press freedom, where he was in the chair. I was less convinced than some of the participants about the wickedness of the legislation, and said so. When Arnold Goodman and I were introduced later, I mentioned that our paths had crossed before, during the Morgan Phillips case.

'Ah, yes!' he replied. 'We never did find out who your source was, did we?'

I nodded, and said tartly that was the occasion when I felt obliged to make my stand for press freedom, implying that he had been on the other side of the barricades.

The only moral of the story is that lawyers and politicians do not think like journalists.

4

'SUPERMAC' AND THE UNIONS

As a journalist covering the industrial relations beat, my contact with Conservatives was principally with occupants of the old Ministry of Labour. The most prominent of these in my time was Iain Macleod, whose early death left him as the lost leader to a whole generation of liberal Tories. It is from Macleod's period at the ministry in the late fifties that I would date a steady toughening of Conservative attitudes to the trade unions.

If Winston Churchill had a favourite among his Labour colleagues in the wartime coalition, it was Ernest Bevin, the illegitimate Bristol boy who founded the Transport and General Workers' Union, organised manpower for the war effort as Minister of Labour, and later became Attlee's Foreign Secretary. It was admiration for Bevin which convinced Churchill that the Conservatives and the unions must never again descend into the state of mutual hostility which existed in the two decades before and after the General Strike of 1926.

When he returned to office in 1951, he appointed as Minister of Labour the emollient lawyer, Sir Walter Monckton, who had been close to him in support of Edward VIII during the abdication crisis. Monckton's brief was to avoid any renewal of conflict with the unions. He used to say to union leaders that he was not really a Conservative, but that 'Winston had asked me to do this'. This irritated some of them, but his policy was one which subsequent Tory Prime Ministers, Anthony Eden, Harold Macmillan and Alec Douglas-Home, broadly followed.

It remains a sadness to me that I missed the chance to know Macmillan personally, for he was a seminal figure of mid-century politics. He was the last instinctive pragmatist to lead the Tories. Indeed, it was reaction to his pragmatism which caused both Ted Heath and Margaret Thatcher to adopt a more ideological stance, though Heath was later converted to what seems to me the wiser way.

In political style, Macmillan's heir was Harold Wilson rather than anyone from his own party. Wilson nursed a more than sneaking admiration for him, and especially for his methods. It was not the Labour Harold, after all, who devised the idea of solving industrial disputes by Downing Street intervention. Long before he was in a position to serve his first beer and sandwiches there, I was given a graphic account of how the Conservative Harold behaved in similar circumstances.

During much of his premiership Number 10 Downing Street, which was suffering the ravages of old age, not to mention eighteenth-century jerry building, was under repair. Macmillan lived and worked at Admiralty House, further up Whitehall. In the hope of averting one threatened railway strike, he invited the unions to meet him there. Since the Prime Minister's Press Office was excessively discreet in its dealings with industrial correspondents, I arranged to meet one of the union leaders, Ray Gunter, who was also a member of Labour's National Executive, after he left Admiralty House.

When Ray arrived at the Charing Cross Hotel, just across Trafalgar Square, he was almost speechless at the performance of the Prime Minister (aka the Great Actor-Manager). Macmillan, he said, had begun by showing them the pictures in his temporary headquarters, not a subject on which the union leaders felt they had any expertise. Then he invited them to present their case.

This was done by Sidney Greene, General Secretary of the National Union of Railwaymen, the largest of the three. Greene had not got far into his presentation when he complained that the wage offer made to them by British Rail, under heavy government influence, was not fair.

This spurred Macmillan to a dramatic intervention: 'Not fair, Mr Greene! Not fair!' He paused, and his deep-set eyes watered reminiscently. 'Let me tell you a story. As a young man, I was at Passchendaele. The cream of my generation was cut down in that and other battles during the Great War. I often think that it was the less worthy among us who survived. That was not fair. Life, Mr Greene, life is rarely fair.'

The Prime Minister's style of industrial negotiation made the task of down-to-earth union leaders more difficult. But later they sorted out a compromise.

As economic difficulties forced policies of 'stop-go' on the government, relations with the unions deteriorated. In 1958 Frank Cousins, now settled in as the transport workers' leader, called a strike against London Transport. It was about bus wages, but was also a dispute of wider political significance, because Iain Macleod was determined to enforce government wage restraint. To give way in a nationalised concern would send bad signals to the rest of industry.

Industrial correspondents competed to detect the first sign of any improvement in the London Transport wage offer. I began to receive phone calls from a man with a Cockney accent, who turned out to be the editor of an unofficial busmen's paper called the *Platform*. For very modest payments, he enabled myself and, as it turned out, the veteran labour correspondent of *The Times*, Eric Wigham, to predict accurately what was 'on the table'. His taste in newspapers was obviously elevated, though he also gave the information to the *Daily Worker*, I suspect free of charge.

These useful leaks had a ludicrous consequence. I did not mind much when the chairman of London Transport invited me in – as he separately invited Wigham – with the intention of ticking me off for making his task of reaching a settlement more difficult. I explained that he misunderstood our respective roles. As a traveller, I would be happier if the buses were running normally. But as a reporter, my job was simply to tell people everything I could find out about what was going on, especially behind closed doors. It was his task to sort out his labour relations.

What did irritate me, however, was an item in the *Economist*, written very much *de haut en bas*. This explained, in world-weary fashion, that London Transport was behaving in the classical style of a nationalised industry: leaking its latest offer to 'the posh papers', in order to soften the public up for yet another surrender. Fresh from resisting an attempt by that organisation's chairman to kick my backside for my journalistic enterprise, I immediately lost faith in the *Economist*'s methods of reporting. If this writer invented theories, and printed them as fact, on a subject I knew about, what was I to make of their reports from, say, South America, where I had no personal knowledge? I have never subscribed to the *Economist* since, though I see it from time to time. Comment is free, but facts are sacred.

There was another, internal *Guardian* handicap to reporting this politically significant strike. The paper's London edition, then printed in Manchester, had to go to press at 10 p.m., so I was competing with colleagues who had several hours' advantage over me. I made great efforts to rush news of late-night negotiations to catch this edition, but was frequently frustrated by apparent lethargy in Manchester.

When I protested, and tried to explain the significance of the dispute, the night editor, later a good friend of mine, brushed this aside. He said wearily: 'I know it must be very inconvenient for you all in London that the buses aren't running, but they're still going in Manchester – and I imagine in Leeds, Bristol, Glasgow and Edinburgh as well.' A year or so later, the same man, a highly intelligent journalist, came to London to establish our new southern printing. Within months, he was asking whether we ought not to be writing more about a work-to-rule on the Central Line of the Underground. A useful maxim in any newspaper is that the hub of the universe is where the night editor eats his breakfast.

One of the most significant offices in the industrial relations field during this period was that of Chief Industrial Commissioner: a predecessor, though within the Ministry of Labour itself, of ACAS, the conciliation body. During Iain Macleod's time as minister, the incumbent was Sir Wilfred Neden, a legendary peace-maker. At a crucial point in the bus strike, it became known that Neden had brokered a settlement which satisfied both London Transport and Frank Cousins. But Iain Macleod vetoed it.

Neden must have been cruelly disappointed, but his briefing for industrial correspondents was a model of urbane even-handedness. In this dispute, he said, the minister was a man with two hats. As Sir Wilfred's boss, he had responsibility for averting or settling strikes. As a member of the Cabinet, he had an obligation to sustain the collective policy on incomes. The second duty had prevailed. The strike was settled eventually, but more on Macleod's terms than Frank Cousins'. This was the first of many turning points in relations between Conservative government and the unions.

When Selwyn Lloyd was Chancellor under Macmillan, he established the National Economic Development Council, Neddy, a tripartite body where ministers and industrial and union leaders discussed 'obstacles to growth', a current *bête noir* of Britain's political economy. Neddy was what would now be stigmatised as 'corporatism', but in those days of ideological innocence, many people, of different political outlooks, thought it a good idea. Harold Macmillan, the arch-pragmatist, had no doubt, ever since his days as Chancellor, that some form of incomes policy was essential.

Two principal groups of journalists reported Neddy's monthly council meetings. Industrial or labour correspondents like myself were principally concerned with the Chancellor's efforts to secure support from industry and the unions for 'growth without inflation', which effectively meant voluntary incomes policy. But we soon realised that another group of journalists had different preoccupations. They kept asking questions about something called 'indicative planning on the French model', a fashionable economic nostrum of the period. The most knowledgeable among these were Samuel Brittan, then of the *Observer*, before his more prominent years as a columnist on the *Financial Times*; and Nigel Lawson, then City editor of the newly founded *Sunday Telegraph*, before *his* more prominent years as Chancellor of the Exchequer. *O tempora, O mores!*

Those early days of Neddy had another echo in the Thatcher era. On the council's twenty-fifth anniversary, Downing Street offered interviews with the Prime Minister, at very short notice. Her press secretary, Bernard Ingham, had dug out a yellowing cutting of mine, reporting the first Neddy debate on incomes policy. Before we began, the Prime Minister asked the cameraman whether he would be able to show the cutting when she waved it at me, to emphasise that there would be no incomes policy under *her* government. Unfortunately, the cameraman was almost deaf, so I had to interpret her wishes. This did not improve my temper, for I scented a minor, but shameless piece of news management, so I gave her a tough grilling on current inflation.

In the sixties, the decisive period in the debate about how to achieve growth without inflation came during the chancellorship of Reginald Maudling, from July 1962 until the Conservatives lost office under Macmillan's successor, Alec Douglas-Home, in October 1964. Maudling's incisive mind, which seemed as oblivious of ideological as of party considerations, grasped that he needed the help of the unions. He had the good fortune to have as General Secretary of the TUC George Woodcock.

Reggie Maudling had first interested me when I met him in Moscow. In those darkest days of the Cold War, the *Guardian* was having great difficulty obtaining visas for anyone to visit Russia. When a British trade fair was arranged, they managed to get one for me, though only on a ridiculously expensive basis: a 'businessman's package', which provided me with a chauffeur-driven car and interpreter for so many hours a week – though only if I could foresee my activities a day in advance, which is a tall order for a journalist. Maudling was then President of the Board of Trade. As a father of a young family myself, I was impressed to hear that he and his wife, Beryl, were travelling on separate airline flights, so that if one crashed their family would not be left orphans.

Moscow was a drab place at that time, so isolated for journalists that, when the Reuters man heard I was in town, he was able to assemble nearly every British and American correspondent for a get-together. They were a sad and lonely bunch, with few Russian contacts, and in some cases squashed into hotel bedrooms with wife and children, because the Foreign Ministry refused to rent them a flat. But the receptions in the Kremlin in connection with the trade fair were lavish.

At one, I caught my first glimpse of Robert Maxwell. The magnificent reception hall was divided into two sections, a VIP area behind a gilded rope, and the larger part for the rest of us. Suddenly, I saw a very large man step over the rope, and proceed to engage Nikita Khrushchev, First Secretary of the Communist Party, in conversation. Within a minute, two even larger Russian men put their hands on his shoulders, and he was wafted back among the common people.

I remarked to my companion, a British civil servant, that this seemed eccentric behaviour, and from what I had observed of Russian obsession with security, he was lucky not to be hurried off to the Lubianka. 'Ah,' he replied, 'I see you haven't yet come across Captain Robert Maxwell. You will, you will.' And he proceeded to give me a highly prejudicial account of Maxwell's business history and methods. Back in London, I read that Captain Maxwell of Pergamon Press had personally negotiated a copyright agreement with Khrushchev. I could only conclude that the 'negotiations' took place during that minute, but with rather a lot of details filled in later at the Ministry of Foreign Trade.

The highlight of the evening for me was an encounter with the head of that ministry, Anastas Mikoyan, who was effectively Khrushchev's number two. I had heard much about him from Harold Wilson, who had often negotiated with him, both in his Board of Trade days and when he worked for Montague Meyer, the timber importer. Suddenly, Mikoyan became available to the press, together with interpreter, in a corner of the reception. He was answering questions from British reporters about the trade fair. Yes, it was truly splendid, he said, the goods on display were magnificent. He dearly wished to see a vast increase in Anglo-Soviet trade. Sadly, unless the British government showed more flexibility in the trade negotiations then taking place, and specifically unless they took more Russian oil, his country would not have enough hard currency to buy those splendid goods, and all these British businessmen, who had worked so hard, would go home sadly disappointed. It was a bravura performance.

A few minutes later, I met Reggie Maudling, and read him out the contents of my notebook. Many politicians, in the middle of difficult negotiations, would have stalled. Maudling's instincts were different. He growled: 'I hope you're not going to fall for that. You know what he's at, don't you? He's hoping to put the pressure on me through you and all these poor hopeful British businessmen. We're not going to take his oil. Bloody oil's coming out our ears.' (This was well before the series of oil crises.) Thus the President of the Board of Trade ensured that

HMG's attitude was explained in the British papers, beside that of Moscow's most artful dodger.

At the trade fair, I tried to interview Khrushchev himself about oil, but his KGB men diverted me as nimbly as they had Robert Maxwell.

My other foreign trip of that period played an interesting, if minor part in attempts to cure Britain's economic malaise. In 1961 the Swedish employers' association and trade union federation invited four industrial correspondents to study their labour market system, of which they were rightly proud, for it had greatly reduced the number of strikes in a once turbulent industrial relations system, and enabled Sweden to become one of the richest countries in Europe. The Swedes are an earnest people, and they worked us hard. Each day there was a minister for us to talk with at breakfast-time, an employer or union group at coffee, other ministers at lunch, meetings during the afternoon, and a dinner.

Soon afterwards, George Woodcock told me that he had decided, as a result of what we wrote, to take the TUC Economic Committee to Stockholm. This was to be a key part of his attempt to persuade them that there must be a better way of running the economy than successive governments in Britain had been condemned to by, among other factors, trade union conservatism. The visit to Sweden had considerable influence on the attitude of a whole TUC generation to cooperation with employers and government.

Woodcock recognised in Reginald Maudling a man with whom he might have been able to do business. Labour relations was then a major political story, so I was appearing often on television, principally for independent companies. After one interview with Woodcock, he gave me a lift home. We settled down in our living-room to discuss the political situation. By 4 a.m., we had made some progress, both with that and with a bottle of whisky. I had a meeting the following afternoon with Reginald Maudling. The Conservative government, by now under the leadership of Douglas-Home, badly needed a deal which would allow economic growth before it faced the voters, and he was interested in what Woodcock had to say.

And there was the rub. Woodcock himself was a keen Labour supporter. His wife, Laura, was the first Labour Mayor of Epsom, where they lived. But he took a puritanical view of the TUC's political role. When he was Deputy General Secretary he had been outraged by an invitation to Hugh Gaitskell to speak to the annual Congress, as part of his campaign to win back control of the Labour Party in the nuclear weapons controversy. Woodcock once told me that Gaitskell, who only met him casually, said: 'You ought not to take the unions out of the Labour Party without talking to me first.'

It was not within the power of the TUC General Secretary to do that, nor would such a committed Labour man as Woodcock have wanted to do so. But Gaitskell had caught something of his attitude: that the TUC had to work with governments of both political parties, and while individual union leaders might have a significant role in the Labour Party, they ought to forget this when pursuing their members' interests in negotiation with governments. Anyhow, he once told me, Labour's biggest electoral handicap was the charge of kowtowing to the unions: if Gaitskell had said after his election defeat in 1959 that he would treat the unions just as he would treat any other section of the community, Woodcock would have given him support.

But that was George Woodcock speaking. For most union leaders, the election was too close to contemplate doing a deal on wages which would help a Tory government. Reggie Maudling ran the economy at an annual growth rate of six per cent in his final six months. At any other time the TUC, which has a vested interest in industrial expansion, might have been tempted to a deal. But politics made the chance pass.

Yet only a couple of years previously, Labour leaders' doubts about their prospect of winning power had been graphically illustrated in a remarkable appointment which, incidentally, gave me the best scoop of my career.

Alf Robens, who had been Minister of Labour at the end of the Attlee government, was a leading right-wing member of the opposition front bench. He was often mentioned as a possible successor to Hugh Gaitskell. In 1961, a friend in the Coal Board asked me if I had heard a rumour that Robens was to become their chairman. We both thought it would be astonishing if Harold Macmillan appointed a political opponent to such a job.

I made enquiries from two likely sources. Alan Birch was not only General Secretary of Alf Robens' union, the shopworkers, but also a part-time member of the Coal Board. He said scathingly that such an appointment could scarcely be in the wind without news of it reaching him. Harold Wilson, who had a long-standing interest in the coal industry, was equally sceptical that a man who sat with him in the shadow Cabinet could be contemplating such a move.

I had practically abandoned the story, until one Sunday, in the *Guardian*'s old Fleet Street office, a pile of Press Association copy landed on my desk, reporting the weekend speeches. One, by Will Paynter, the communist General Secretary of the miners, commented in delphic terms on the government's attitude to his industry. The Tories, he said, need not think they could force unacceptable closures on the miners by appointing so-called friends of Labour to influential positions.

It was obvious that he knew something I had been in the process of dismissing as a mere rumour. So I shattered his Sunday calm by telephoning with this question: 'What would you say if I told you I am going to write that Alf Robens will become chairman of the Coal Board?'

His reply was stunned: 'Heavens, be careful!'

I replied: 'Thanks for the confirmation, Will,' and went off to write a story which won me a *What the Papers Say* 'Scoop of the Year' award.

In those competitive days, when the supposedly antediluvian hot metal printing methods allowed many edition changes, the *Guardian* held the story out of its first editions, in order to maintain its exclusiveness throughout the night. The *Daily Herald* Manchester office phoned the Robens home at 2.30, when they saw our second edition, but understandably were not given a warm reception. By 10.30, Downing Street had confirmed the story.

Michael Frayn, with his fame as novelist and playwright still far in the future, wrote his column in the room we shared. In a gap in the congratulatory phone calls I was receiving, he came shyly over to murmur: 'Well done! I haven't read anything but the *Guardian* this morning, and the way your story was written made me assume it was an official announcement.' One of the happinesses of working for the old *Guardian* was that individuals could pursue their own enthusiasms in companionable isolation.

Only two years later, Labour people had become confident that the Conservatives' thirteen years in power were near an end. Hugh Gaitskell's death in January 1963 had been a shattering blow. It left his large following on the right feeling rudderless and bereft. Politically, it came at a time when he was at the zenith of his reputation with the public, having overcome internal difficulties over defence. George Brown, Labour's often brilliant, but unpredictable deputy leader, was heir-not-quite-apparent. Most Gaitskellites supported him to succeed, but with a heavy heart. This derived not simply from their personal grief, but from a fear that he did not have the gravitas, the bottom, to lead Labour to victory in an election, and to run a government.

Harold Wilson was the obvious candidate of the left. He was more centrist than left-wing himself, but because he had stood, unwillingly, against Gaitskell in 1960, and willingly against Brown for the deputy leadership in 1962, he had gathered a following. This came both from those who were impressed by his ability, as shown in the Commons, and from others with increasing doubts whether Labour could be led exclusively from the right.

Some Gaitskellites, notably Anthony Crosland and Douglas Jay, were unhappy at the prospect of George Brown as leader. They persuaded Jim Callaghan to stand. Years later, Crosland told me his refusal to support Brown in 1973 began his distancing from Roy Jenkins and other old friends who were more fervently pro-European than himself. Crosland later came to take a more charitable view of Harold Wilson's character and achievements, but he found it impossible to vote for him so soon after Gaitskell's death.

The Callaghan candidature produced an interesting debate at the *Guardian*. The editor, Alastair Hetherington, asked the political correspondent, Francis Boyd, and myself as labour correspondent, for our opinions. We both favoured Wilson. No doubt he consulted others as well. He eventually decided that the paper would come out for Jim Callaghan. I met Callaghan in the cloisters of the House of Commons. He grinned broadly, and said: 'It's awfully nice of Alastair to support me, but I hope he does realise that I have no chance, that I'm only a candidate because Tony Crosland and others can't bring themselves to vote for either George or Harold, so they persuaded me to stand.'

Wilson's time had come. He was within eight votes of victory on the first ballot, and when Callaghan, in third place, was eliminated, he defeated Brown in the second round by 144 to 103.

In victory, Harold Wilson proved both shrewd and generous to old enemies. He knew it would take time to win over most of the leading figures, who had been bitterly opposed to him in the past. But politicians are realists, and as Hugh Gaitskell's friends slowly adjusted to his death, they saw their duty, after twelve years in opposition. They must not allow personal dislike to stand in the way of possible Labour victory.

As a journalist, I have often been impressed – occasionally *depressed* – by the fact that, whenever you talk to two or more participants in a private meeting, their accounts often vary so much that they might have been in different rooms. Soon after Harold Wilson became leader, I had the comfort of experiencing an opposite phenomenon. One of Gaitskell's closest friends and supporters had been John Harris, Labour's press director. When I met Harris (now Lord Harris of Greenwich), he described emotionally his first conversation with Wilson since Gaitskell's death. Harris shared the animosity of all the old Gaitskellites towards the new leader. He said he had told him he could offer his loyalty, though not his affection.

I confess that I had some doubt as to whether these were the precise words he used, for we are all capable of self-dramatisation at times of personal stress. But my doubts were soon proved false. The following week Harold Wilson invited me to dine with him at the House. He mentioned that John Harris would be handling his press relations. Naturally, I did not repeat what John had told me. But his leader related it, in precisely the same terms: 'He told me he could give me his loyalty, but not his affection.' Suck of pipe. 'I am entitled to his loyalty, and I don't want his bloody affection.' Subsequently, the two worked well together: John Harris has a highly developed sense of fun, and life with Harold Wilson was rarely short of laughter.

The leader of the opposition's purpose in asking me to dinner showed how the right v Bevanite feud in the Labour Party, perpetuated in the Gaitskellites' hostility to Harold Wilson, had affected his trade union contacts. He had always been proud of his close links with the National Union of Mineworkers, of whom he had seen a lot as a wartime civil servant. After coming into politics, he had also helped them with research.

But Wilson admitted that he had few close friends in the unions now, and he was not willing to expose himself to slanted advice. How should he approach the delicate business of deciding which major union conferences he wanted to address in his first year as leader? I suggested that since, conveniently, both the transport workers and the railwaymen were meeting in Scarborough during the same week – one led from the left, the other from the right – he might avoid appearing to play favourites. His speeches at both were well received.

5

FEET UNDER THE DESK

Life never works out quite as we would plan it. In 1963 I was happy as labour correspondent of the *Guardian*. British politics was approaching one of its post-war turning points. After twelve years in office, the Conservatives showed signs of fatigue. Harold Wilson, as a new leader of the opposition, had made a great impression on public opinion. The press treated seriously his series of speeches on Labour policy: the broadsheet papers reported each one fully, before analysing and criticising it in the leader columns. In those days the media approached their role as servants of democracy with more self-effacement. They were less determined to set the agenda than is the case thirty years later; more willing to let elected politicians have their say.

I had enjoyed reporting labour relations under a Conservative government, as well as the activities of the Labour Party outside the House of Commons. But clearly my job would be more interesting if there was a Labour government. I now had the contacts which would help me to find out what was going on inside that government. I knew well the thinking of key figures such as Harold Wilson, Jim Callaghan, Ray Gunter and Frank Cousins, and I also had the inside track at the TUC, principally through my friendship with George Woodcock.

But back at the *Guardian*, times were troubled. In 1961 we began to print in London as well as Manchester, using a system called tele-typesetting. This saved money by avoiding what other national news-papers did, typesetting their complete papers in both cities (in some cases, in Glasgow as well). But our system, though ingenious, hit teething troubles, and however many dentists we employed, these never went away.

Alastair Hetherington, the editor, still based in Manchester, was car-rying an immense burden. Our finances were overstretched by the new venture, and nobody had recognised the scale of the editorial changes which would be needed to turn us into a national newspaper. Because the *Guardian* had been highly praised, right back to C.P. Scott's day, as a provincial paper with an international reputation, those planning the changes had missed a significant fact: that once we went national, readers would apply quite different criteria of judgement. Up till then, our single-centre printing had excused the characteristically cruel jibe of Cecil King, of the *Mirror*: 'What the *Telegraph* reports today, the *Guardian* comments on tomorrow.' Once we called ourselves a national paper, this was a barb directed at the heart.

Not knowing the depth of Hetherington's problems, I may have been a pain in his neck at this time, though to his credit he never showed this. What worried me was that the new production arrangements had given a primacy to sub-editors which they had never enjoyed before. Form was prevailing over content for the first time in *Guardian* history. More subs were employed, and they interfered more with copy. The *Guardian*, and especially the old *Manchester Guardian*, had been famous for picking good reporters and giving them their head. The specialist cor-respondents, most of them based in London, felt this tradition was slipping away. I acted as Chief Whip in a revolt among them, we had a meeting with the editor, and he took our criticisms aboard.

Whether what followed was cause and effect I have never cared to ask. The thunderbolt struck in October. I was looking forward to the Labour Party conference. It was Harold Wilson's first as leader, the election was coming soon, and the Scarborough air was crackling with excitement. The editor usually came to each party's conference for a day or two, but on this occasion he warned me to set aside time for a proper talk with him.

Alastair took me for a walk along the Scarborough cliffs. Both his superior fitness and what he had to say took my breath away. He had concluded that he could no longer effectively edit the paper from Manchester. He was coming to live in London, and he wanted me to take over as news editor there, with responsibility not only for general reporters, but also for the specialist correspondents who – myself included – had until then been a law unto themselves.

This anarchic system produced good journalism, because it left responsibility to the individual, and we nearly all overworked ourselves. But it did not ensure that the *Guardian* had full coverage of the day's news, for sometimes two correspondents would write about the same subject, and sometimes nobody would. The news service needed to be reorganised, and he wanted me to do it. I was pleased, but anguished at having to give up as labour correspondent at such an exciting time.

The announcement of my new job had to be postponed for a time, to coincide with other changes, so I went through the remainder of a busy week in Scarborough nursing my secret. But when I was asked to reply to the vote of thanks to the press on the final morning of that 1963 conference, I knew it was my swansong. Afterwards, Harold Wilson gave a drinks party for the industrial correspondents, and revealed that while my jokes – some of them at his expense – had made the delegates laugh, he and others on the platform had been frustrated when they could not hear every punch-line. It was some years before I had to learn how to keep my head close to a microphone.

He himself made a more significant speech that week. It has been much jeered at since, as all speeches with a key phrase – Wilson's 'white heat of the technological revolution', John Major's 'back to basics', and so on – are fated to be, especially if their results do not fulfil expectations. But Britain's subsequent economic failures, in Harold Wilson's period and beyond, cannot alter the fact that this speech caught a mood in Britain at the time. Alastair Hetherington assured me later that I avoided being swept off my feet, as many reporters were. If this is so, my reservations must have been expressed in conversation with him, by way of advice for his editorials. For my report does not suggest any great doubt that Wilson had hit an electoral jackpot:

> The annual conference has not previously been a happy hunting ground for Mr Wilson, who prefers the intimacy of the Commons for his subtler shafts of wit. But the alchemy of leadership and a shrewd choice of subject today combined to produce a 50-minute speech which won him a long standing ovation. It also probably did as much as long months of work at Westminster to establish him in the public mind as the kind of man who would make a Prime Minister.

Then, the cautionary sentence: 'But, for the certainty of that we must await a sharper verdict than the cheers of the committed.'

This speech was his attempt to equate scientific advance with socialist planning. It produced a passion that had previously eluded him:

> Mr Wilson's theme was a redefinition of socialism in terms of the scientific revolution, and it drew him on to a fervent denunciation of privilege, poverty and inefficiency at home, and of underprivilege and poverty abroad. This was a speech on a scale which, for the first time, gave a clear public answer to the question sceptics have asked so often: What makes Mr Wilson tick? The answer is what it has always been. Labour's new leader showed that he is no more a 'desiccated calculating machine' than was Mr Gaitskell, and the hard political shell covers a sincere and reforming spirit.

6

THE PRAGMATIC SIDE OF 50

For me, the Labour government of 1964–70, on whose prolonged birth pangs I had spilt so much printer's ink, was a tale of two economic crises. One was the recurrent troubles of the government itself. The other was a crisis at the *Guardian*, which at one time threatened its existence. As the paper's newly appointed news editor, I organised our coverage of the 1964 and 1966 elections. The first produced a Labour majority of only three; the latter gave Harold Wilson a mandate for a full parliament, but a life full of troubles.

I found it was the crisis closer to home, at the *Guardian*, which dominated my life, and I had much less to do with the new Prime Minister and other old political friends in the early years of that government. It was only when the *Guardian* emerged from the worst of its financial troubles, towards the end of the sixties, and I became deputy editor, that politics again took first place in my thoughts.

The Labour government of 1964 took office in a wave of hope, and its proclaimed programme went well enough. By December 1964 Harold Wilson's deputy, George Brown, had agreed a Declaration of Intent with employers and unions. This aimed to keep money incomes in line with increases in national output and to get rid of restrictive practices, in return for which workers were to expect greater security in employment. The following year, Brown's National Plan set out a programme of expansion. From the moment Labour achieved power, however, pressure on the pound began. International bankers are inherently suspicious of governments of the left; and Labour inherited a worse deficit than predicted.

I had one long discussion with the Prime Minister in that early period. Just before the 1966 election, I wrote an article on the occasion of his fiftieth birthday, based on a meeting in his room at the House. The aim was to explore his philosophy of politics, a venture which produced the first recorded use of 'pragmatic' in connection with Harold Wilson. The headline on my article was 'The pragmatic side of 50'.

What made the encounter extraordinary was that the Prime Minister was simultaneously engaged in a complex manoeuvre to score an electioneering point against his rival, Ted Heath. This concerned some obscure aspect of party election broadcasts, which were then of even less interest to me than they subsequently became. But it kept intruding into our philosophy seminar.

Just because Wilson was by temperament a problem-solver rather than an ideologue, he was reluctant to concentrate on the longer term, rather than on his immediate political concerns. With the scale of his problems, this was scarcely surprising. Later, when the Heath government was running into its own troubles, Wilson once told me, with some feeling, that at least Heath didn't have the Friday morning nightmare of awakening to find that sterling was draining away. He himself did, from the first sterling crisis only six weeks after he took office.

But no sooner had the Prime Minister put his mind to expounding his long-term ideas to me than his political secretary, Marcia Williams, entered with the latest news on the saga of the party election broadcasts. She could not reach the Liberal leader, Jo Grimond, on the telephone, because he was travelling between the islands in his Orkneys and Shetlands constituency, so should she try his deputy, Jeremy Thorpe?

After several interruptions, Wilson explained what this was all about, and added: 'It would be a good story for the *Guardian*, John. I'll ask Marcia to get your office on the phone.' I murmured reluctant assent, but pressed on with my philosophical quest. Just as we seemed to be making progress, the telephone rang. He indicated it was for me. There were two phones on the small table between our armchairs. I thought the red one was ringing, and reached to pick it up. The Prime Minister acted very rapidly to direct me to the green phone. I speculated afterwards whether I had come close to launching the British nuclear deterrent.

The night news editor of the *Guardian* was called Ken Dodd (no relation). When I explained my call, he was incredulous: 'Heavens, John, I thought you were doing an LPA [leader page article] on Harold Wilson's philosophy of politics. We know all about this party election broadcast story already, and a right bunch of old scrap it is too, in my opinion.'

I replied: 'Yes, Ken, very interesting, but so long as you have it in hand ...' Since then, I have always been doubtful about the merits of videophones.

Once this distraction had been dealt with, Harold Wilson con-

centrated. He said he was pragmatic, because all government was pragmatic. For example, he thought equality of opportunity mattered more
than equality. The difficulty was that everybody was different. The idea
of a proletariat was nonsense. Marx did not understand people. (Wilson
parenthetically confessed that, because the footnote on an early page of
his copy of *Das Kapital* was longer than the text, he had proceeded no
further.) He himself was interested in people as individuals rather than
in the mass. He was interested in the family, because most happiness was
family happiness. He was interested in 'Saturdays and Sundays and Bank
Holidays'.

This was a preliminary to what was a most radical thought at that time
from a man who had emerged from the left of the Labour Party. He
recalled that the Labour movement – trade unions as well as the political
party – had been born out of the solidarity of labour, the miseries of
work. That was a thing of the past. Labour was not now marked by
solidarity in any real sense. If there was a bus strike, would the engineers
come out in support? No, they would complain about not being able to
get a bus.

He added: 'I don't like theory. I got an alpha–plus in economic theory,
but I never understood it. I think my examiner must have been very
kind. Or perhaps he didn't understand it either.' One of Harold Wilson's
endearing characteristics has always been his gift for self-mockery.

He thought the public trusted him for his good management, rather
than as a theoretician. Nor was he a social butterfly: he 'didn't go in for
dinners with Lady Pamela Berry', preferring to concentrate on knowing
everything that was worth knowing of what was going on in government
and politics. His ministers realised he expected to be told about all
decisions of importance, and he sometimes sent for files – for example,
that week one from Tony Crosland's office, on universities – to remind
them of his interest.

He scoffed at ideological debate. If he had been leader earlier, there
would have been no rows about Clause IV of Labour's constitution
(public ownership) or about unilateral nuclear disarmament. He had
stood against Gaitskell in 1960 not because he himself supported the
Campaign for Nuclear Disarmament, which he did not, but because
Gaitskell's leadership was essentially divisive. He himself led the party on
a loose rein, as over Vietnam, about which he was having endless trouble.

I detected in him a Peter Pan reluctance to accept even such a
modest milestone as a fiftieth birthday. Crowing with the same disarming
effervescence as Barrie's most famous character, he reminded me that
he was the youngest Prime Minister since Rosebery, and speculated on

the possibility that the rivalry between Ted Heath and himself might go on longer than any since Gladstone and Disraeli. I expressed some doubt whether, under modern media exposure, such long political careers were likely, but he persisted. With a puff of his pipe and a grin, he said: 'If you don't fancy the prospect, John, you'd better emigrate.' Within ten years, they had both gone, Harold Wilson voluntarily, Ted Heath after Margaret Thatcher's successful challenge.

With a majority of only three, he needed a fresh mandate, which he was to win in the general election of March 1966. But three months before that, the death of a Labour MP caused a by-election in a highly marginal seat, Hull North. The *Guardian* had a more intimate interest in this than was comfortable. Feeling against American involvement in Vietnam ran strongly among many on the staff. It was an office joke that one Conservative-inclined correspondent, not professionally concerned with foreign affairs, had been observed high-stepping his six-foot-three-inch frame down Whitehall, in the middle of a line of demonstrators, their arms linked, chanting 'Ho, Ho, Ho Chi Minh.'

But one of the leader-writers, Richard Gott, decided to go further, and stood as an anti-war candidate in Hull North. He was later to make news on two other occasions: once when he discovered the body of an icon of the international left, Ché Guevara; and years later, when he resigned from the *Guardian* after admitting he had taken money from the KGB. Some in the office thought he would win, and foolish hints of this possibility were published. In the event, there was a significant swing from Conservative to Labour, and Richard Gott received only 253 votes.

Even before Labour's success in Hull, Harold Wilson had told the Queen he would require a dissolution soon. I was kept busy that spring organising the *Guardian*'s election coverage. We sent reporters all over the country to write constituency surveys, intended not only to provide interesting reading, but to give some idea of how opinion in various parts of Britain was moving.

I had to overrule a reporter who came back from Ted Heath's constituency convinced that he was going to lose his own seat. I explained patiently that party leaders whose seats were vulnerable received advance warning, and found a new and safer one. He was not convinced: he had been there, I had not, and local opinion was moving against Heath. There was a strong tradition in the *Guardian* of printing what the reporter wrote, but I decided in this case to go against it: we had endured enough electoral embarrassments over Hull. I would not publish his forecast, but I offered him a generous bet: a pound to a penny that Heath would survive. That was an old penny, so the odds were 240 to 1. I did not have to pay up.

That 1966 general election was a temporary swansong for me. Up till then, I had never been to America. There was a suggestion I should go to a seminar at Harvard, conducted by Professor Henry Kissinger, whose call to Washington still lay some years ahead. Instead I was given an Eisenhower Exchange Fellowship, a generous travelling award, which enabled me to see much of the United States, rather than just the eastern seaboard. So I was away from Britain between April and September.

In the early months of my absence, the seamen's strike and the gathering economic storm at home still obsessed me. The strike had begun before I left, but although it had serious implications for the economy, and therefore for the government's political health, it was impossible to make out what was going on, even from the serious American press. When Americans describe the *New York Times* as 'the good grey Times', implying high seriousness, I always recall my frustrated perusal of it that spring. Whereas I wanted to know what ministers and leaders of the major British unions were saying about the strike, I could only discover the views of an early pipsqueak sound-biter, who assured the *NYT* reporter that this was the biggest showdown since the Battle of Hastings. This is the kind of historical context which even comparatively sophisticated Americans apparently expect in stories about the island from which their nation grew.

The strike was not the only one of Harold Wilson's troubles to reach climax in July 1966. He had brought Frank Cousins, General Secretary of the Transport and General Workers' Union, into his 1964 Cabinet, in the hope that this would help relations with the unions. This was probably a misjudgement, on several scores. Cousins was an able union leader, but he had a craggy personality, took offence easily, and for months the Prime Minister knew that his resignation was near.

I had known Cousins well when I was labour correspondent. He had been one of Hugh Gaitskell's main adversaries during the nuclear arms dispute in 1959 and 1960. His prominence owed more to the size of his block vote than to his powers of persuasion. He was a forceful speaker, and believed passionately in the rightness of his own views. But his thoughts were more urgent than his syntax could control. Those of us who had to report his speeches developed a technique for recording their meaning as accurately as we could. When he sat down, seven or eight reporters would gather in a group. Those with shorthand would read out as much of his machine-gun oratory as we had been able to write down. Those without shorthand were deputed to attend to the meaning, rather than the words. We would then agree a version of what he had said.

At the TGWU conference during the nuclear dispute with Hugh Gaitskell, Frank Cousins' speech was almost upstaged by events on the fringes. Randolph Churchill, son of Winston, frustrated in his efforts to win a parliamentary seat, was then writing a column for the London *Evening Standard*. He rode around Douglas, where the conference was being held, in the Isle of Man's most dignified, but ancient, chauffeur-driven car. He was less like a journalist than a Governor-General, with only the plumed hat missing.

Apparently unconvinced by Frank Cousins' views on the bomb, Randolph wrote a column whose metaphorical exuberance derived from the most striking feature of the Douglas waterfront. Why, he asked his readers rhetorically, should a great international statesman like Mr Gaitskell take advice on this cataclysmic issue from such as 'the horse-tram drivers of the Isle of Man'? This snobbish remark gave the greatest offence, particularly as these drivers probably did not belong to the union. By the time this column appeared, Randolph was back in London, prudently.

Frank Cousins did not enjoy his time in parliament. He found the procedure frustrating, the point-scoring puerile. He wanted to make frequent factory visits, but Labour whips complained that he asked for 'a pair' too often. They told him that to see senior ministers in late-night divisions would encourage the backbenchers. He tartly reminded them that he arrived at his office shortly after seven o'clock every morning, in order to get work done before the civil service arrived – a practice he had brought over from his union job. Wouldn't it be nice, he said with withering sarcasm, if some Labour backbenchers encouraged *him* by turning up then to cheer him in?

By July 1966, Frank Cousins found his colleagues' resort to statutory backing on wages – under pressure from international creditors – too much for him to swallow, and he resigned and went back to his union. Harold Wilson's troubles that month came in battalions. He had begun soundings about possible British entry into the European Common Market. When French briefings indicated that Britain was not a suitable partner for the original six unless it devalued, pressure came on sterling, more July measures of retrenchment became necessary, and George Brown, a keen European, began to move over to the pro-devaluation side of the Cabinet.

The seamen's strike, which was not settled until the final days of June, made the balance of payments look dreadful, and added to pressure on the pound. Harold Wilson, who was already in trouble with Labour MPs because of American bombing of Hanoi, increased his political difficulties by denouncing some of the leading figures in the seamen's union as 'this tightly knit group of politically motivated men'. He was undoubtedly right that the Communist Party was fishing, as it did whenever possible, in troubled industrial waters. But what interested me more was this first example of his tendency to be over-impressed by reports he received from MI5.

This willingness overcame his normally cautious political instincts. On another occasion, I assume on the same authority, he described a more significant union figure to me as a communist. When I asked why he thought that, he replied that 'think' was not the correct word. He *knew*. Because Harold Wilson, in his early days at Downing Street, was so inclined to accept the security services at their own inflated valuation, I could never take seriously the allegations of treachery which their more corrupt members later peddled against him. This was done with the willing cooperation of parts of the press, notably that great defender of human liberty, *Private Eye*. If I were a Chancellor or Chief Secretary looking for reductions in public expenditure, I would at least know where to begin.

The Eisenhower Fellowship invited Madge and myself to the United States for up to eight months, and gave us both a chance to study subjects we had chosen: in my case, American labour relations, to give me a comparison with the British scene; and foreign policy (in which I had little experience) through American eyes; in Madge's, the Head Start programme which President Lyndon Johnson had started for pre-school children in deprived areas.

Because we then had three children under ten, she decided that six weeks was the maximum period she could be away from home. So it was arranged that I would travel immediately after the British general election in April, and that she would join me in June, allowing us to drive right across the country together. We started in New England, drove down the east coast, and on to New Orleans; west through Texas, and via the Grand Canyon to Los Angeles and San Francisco. On the way, we discussed trade unionism, foreign affairs and pre-school teaching with a splendidly mixed bunch of Americans.

Early preoccupation with the seamen's strike apart, this was a unique chance for me to detach myself from British politics, the only time I have done so completely in almost forty years. Occasionally I was given home thoughts while abroad. Harold Wilson was an old friend of the Vice-President, Hubert Humphrey, and with his help I arranged a meeting. The long talk we had, about both Britain and America, was to prove useful when I covered part of the Humphrey campaign for the presidency in 1968. Vietnam was still a burning issue then, and I was sitting beside the Vice-President on his campaign plane when, out of the blue, he told us he was detaching himself from Lyndon Johnson on the subject.

Vietnam also provided the most vibrant political encounter of my 1966 fellowship. This was with the Secretary of State, Dean Rusk. I had gone to a 4.30 p.m. meeting with his deputy, George Ball, who, when I was about to leave, invited me to see Rusk. I telephoned a friend at the AFL-CIO (the American TUC), at whose home I was due to have dinner, asking to be excused for arriving late. He was violently against Dean Rusk's policy on Vietnam, and replied: 'You can be as late as you like provided you tell the bastard he's wrong.'

I could not give that undertaking, for although I was as horrified as anybody else in those early stages of what became a terrible war, I was less sure than others that when the Americans withdrew, a benevolent regime would emerge. Dean Rusk was a generous host, plying me, and himself, with whisky at the somewhat early hour of 5.30. But soon he produced a folder of *Guardian* leading articles. This was not my field, but he was not about to miss the opportunity of telling any representative of the *Guardian* how mistaken we were. Since I felt an obligation, almost inbred in a journalist, to challenge his arguments, especially when a sort of collective loyalty to colleagues impelled me, we had a combative, but enjoyable hour together.

My absence in America during the middle part of 1966 was a personal oasis in the two crises with which I was concerned. The crisis at the *Guardian* did not affect me till the end of my fellowship, when I was summoned back a month early, because the paper's finances had gone badly wrong. There was a personal irony when I received this message. I had formed a strong friendship with the director of the Eisenhower Fellowship, Hampton Barnes – on the walls of whose house I saw discreetly displayed a letter from a young man called Abraham Lincoln, asking one of his ancestors for a job. Hampton was an Anglophile, so I suppose it was natural that he should choose the British Fellow to speak at what amounted to a fund-raising lunch. The targets were his trustees, mostly chief executives of some of the largest companies in America. Hampton told myself and the Brazilian Fellow – fortuitously called Harry Cole – that these were busy men, and we must each speak for precisely seven minutes. If we got the tone right, we would be raising money for his fellowship at the rate of $100,000 a minute (1966 prices).

I faced this challenge by twitting these mostly Republican businessmen about the American obsession with private enterprise as an ideology, rather than as a practical matter: the theme of this book, it will be clear, has not come into my mind overnight. Despite such *lèse majesté*, the speech seemed to go down well enough, and apparently served Hampton's purpose. But when I heard of the *Guardian*'s financial difficulties, I wished it were possible to raise money for that good cause at a comparable pace.

7

WOODCOCK THE LAST BEST HOPE

In my final weeks in New York, I met an eminent American labour relations lawyer, to whom Harold Wilson had also given me an introduction. We had a stimulating talk, but he found it impossible to believe my assertion that the United States lost much more time *pro rata* through strikes than Britain did. Eventually I challenged him to send his secretary to check the figures with the local office of the International Labour Organisation, and she confirmed that I was right.

Britain had an unenviable reputation for industrial anarchy, which made it harder to convince international institutions that the pound was a currency worth backing. Annual deflationary packages in 1965, 1966 and 1967 were a symbol of this uncertainty. Statistically, the press stereotype of Britain as perpetually strike-bound was wrong. What was true, however, was that the country suffered from a perpetual rash of small, usually unofficial stoppages. Even worse, managers became reluctant to make improvements in production methods which might provoke such strikes, and often surrendered to unreasonable wage claims.

The man whose judgement I trusted most on the twin problems of labour relations and incomes policies was George Woodcock, General Secretary of the TUC from 1960 till 1969. He offered the last best hope for British trade unionism to avoid its later unpopularity and decline. His achievement in the sixties was to explain to the public what trade unions were about, what they could do, and what he believed to be beyond their capacity. Despite the unions' frequent follies, they enjoyed a remarkably favourable image then. This image was largely created by the reasonableness Woodcock managed to convey on television, his bushy eyebrows lowered, his face contorted with thought, as he answered questions with an honesty which has gone quite out of fashion, since politicians were taught to 'use the medium', to their supposed advantage.

George Woodcock tried to teach union leaders that they must coop-

erate with governments of all political colours to tackle the great unresolved problem of advanced democracies: how to combine free trade
unions with industrial efficiency and reasonable freedom from inflation.
I regard his as the most unremittingly honest intellect I have encountered
in politics. He had a mind of great clarity, illuminated by a powerful
imagination and human sympathy. As he took me into his confidence,
he provided insights into how politicians and trade unionists interacted.

Woodcock was one of the last leaders of either the industrial or
political wings of the Labour movement to come from a harsh industrial
background. He had started work as a part-timer in Lancashire cotton
mills when he was twelve, won a trade union scholarship to Oxford,
where he got a first in PPE, and had a TUC career which stretched
from the eras of Keynes, Bevin and Cripps to those of Macmillan and
Wilson. As a young head of research at the TUC, he worked closely
with Keynes on the 1944 White Paper on employment policy. That
White Paper was the charter of Britain's post-war economic consensus.
Margaret Thatcher later carried it in her handbag for a time, though not
with unalloyed reverence.

There was one sentence which Woodcock cherished, and he thought
his career would have been worthwhile for this alone: 'The government
accept as one of their primary aims and responsibilities the maintenance
of a high and stable level of employment after the war.' He understood
the heavy burden this cast on union leaders. Once they abrogated
responsibility, all the disasters that have befallen them since became
inevitable. Woodcock often warned the TUC General Council of the
risks they took in the sixties and seventies. In retirement, he gave a
lecture to the British Association in 1975. In this he stated prophetically
the price to be paid if the unions did not manage to work out a deal
with governments:

> The most likely alternative to cooperation is that governments will have to
> modify or abandon their commitment to maintain a high level of employ-
> ment, and their consequential responsibilities for economic growth, stable
> prices and good industrial relations. If this country were to return to the
> industrial instability and the heavy unemployment of pre-war days, that
> would certainly not improve the ability of the trade unions collectively to
> secure greater social justice and fairness for their members.

Within three years of his death in 1979, cooperation between government
and unions was an historic relic, and 3 million people were unemployed.

What he realised was that the commitment of successive governments
in the post-war era to full employment had shifted the balance of power

in industry, so that unions were in some respects more powerful than employers. They derived this power from full employment, so it was in their interests that governments should stick to that objective. He regarded threats of legislation either on labour relations or incomes restraint as short-sighted. The unions must be persuaded to act responsibly.

He was obsessed by politicians' need for action within the two or three effective years of a single parliament. By contrast, he cited the case of an industrialist having to decide whether to undertake investment which might only bear fruit in three or four years' time. How could he have the confidence to invest if governments were blown on and off course, and adopted stop-go policies? Similarly, he was confident that he could move the trade unions in the right direction, but this would take time. Many politicians found Woodcock a distressingly Hamlet like figure, operating under the aspect of eternity, whereas they had to operate under the aspect of glowering currency markets.

When the Labour government was formed in 1964, George Woodcock told George Brown, first head of the new Department of Economic Affairs, that if he demanded from the TUC acquiescence in a wage freeze lasting six months, he would make Woodcock's own life much more tolerable, but it would be the wrong policy. What Brown ought to ask for was a sustained voluntary policy of relating the national wage bill to the growth in production. This would give the leader of the TUC a terrible and permanent headache, but might offer hope of a lasting improvement in Britain's economy.

That was what Brown did ask for, and the Declaration of Intent in November 1965 was the first step in what would have been a long process. Woodcock managed to persuade the TUC General Council to set up a vetting committee, a remarkable surrender of the jealously guarded independence of their individual unions. But in the July crisis of 1966, the government had to convince American and other creditors that it was serious in the fight against inflation. Against its better judgement, it gave statutory backing to the Prices and Incomes Board. The chances of voluntary agreement on something permanent gradually disappeared.

George Woodcock was primarily a great educator, of both unions and politicians. He would tell ministers that unions were reactive organisations, and could act only if governments put them under pressure to undertake difficult tasks. Simultaneously, he would tell those union leaders who, especially during Conservative governments, saw themselves as a protest movement, that they had now moved from Trafalgar

Square demonstrations to the corridors of Whitehall: they needed benign government policies to make their members' prosperity secure.

Just as Churchill complained that the heaviest cross he had to bear in wartime was the Cross of Lorraine (symbol of the truculent de Gaulle), so Harold Wilson might have claimed that his was the Cross of Belper, George Brown's constituency. Brown was a volatile figure, his ministerial career a long succession of threatened resignations, and one real one. When the government had been in office for only nine months, the Minister of Labour, Ray Gunter, a friend of Brown's, who tried unavailingly to save him from himself, told me how worried he was about him. At every moment of tension, the bitterness against Wilson, born of their rivalry for the leadership, came out. Gunter, no mean drinker himself, said that Brown sometimes drank whisky at nine in the morning.

Those who knew him better than I did credited George Brown with a vibrant personality, combined with incredible energy. It was one of the frustrations of my divided life that I missed a close view of this comet who flashed so briefly across the Whitehall sky. In the early years, he drove through policies aimed at economic expansion; but soon an unstable currency frustrated his efforts, and enticed the government into the very traps of short-termism that George Woodcock had warned him against. The Prime Minister went the second mile to keep George Brown in the government, when a man with a shorter fuse might have accepted an earlier resignation.

In his account of that government, Harold Wilson pays a characteristically kind tribute to a man who rarely said a kind word about him in return. George Brown, he wrote, commanded 'more respect in the wider Labour movement than any of us. His strengths far exceeded his weaknesses, but it was his weaknesses which ended his ministerial career.'

8

A TALE OF TWO CRISES

The *Guardian*'s economic difficulties in 1966–7 mirrored those of the country. As hire purchase controls, higher interest rates, a wage freeze and a stiff dose of inflation hit Britain, rising costs and falling advertising revenue afflicted the paper.

The *Guardian* and its sister-paper the *Manchester Evening News* were owned by the Scott Trust, with one of C.P. Scott's grandsons, Richard, the *Guardian*'s Washington correspondent, as its current chairman. His cousin, Laurence Scott, a newspaper manager, was chairman of the group. After the *Guardian* began printing in London in 1961, the group became seriously overstretched. What alarmed me was a proposal to merge *The Times* and the *Guardian*.

The proposal was eventually killed by strong opposition from the editorial staff. Alastair Hetherington, the editor, and Richard Scott bore the heat and burden of that battle. The trust's responsibility was to maintain the *Guardian* as a newspaper in the same tradition as that left by C.P. Scott, its great editor. The merger was not consistent with that. The intentions of Laurence Scott, who conceived it, were honourable. He and others saw this as the only way to maintain two great British newspapers: *The Times* was also in financial trouble before Roy Thomson took it over.

But there was a fallacy at the heart of the scheme. My own interest was in maintaining the *Guardian* as Britain's only serious newspaper of radical reform. I argued that a merged *Times/Guardian* could only logically be run in the tradition of *The Times*, since any of its readers who were unhappy with the merged paper could easily switch to the *Telegraph* or *Financial Times*, whereas *Guardian* readers would have nowhere else to go. This view was confirmed by the assumption of those promoting the merger that Alastair Hetherington, a fine editor in the Scott tradition, would not be acceptable for the new paper. I took the view that even if they changed their mind about the editorship, the merger would not be acceptable to the staff, and told Alastair so.

There was a price to be paid for maintaining the *Guardian*'s independence. Staff and other costs had to be heavily reduced, and we ran the paper on what was euphemistically called a 'belt-tightened' basis: in other words, the sizes were cut to levels that made it more difficult to compete with a *Times* revived by the Thomson fortune. It was an anxious time, and it was touch and go whether we would survive.

Fleet Street has an unlovely carrion tradition, and during that period other papers tried to poach the best of our staff. My successor as labour correspondent, Peter Jenkins, received an attractive offer from the *Sunday Times*. Alastair Hetherington countered by offering him a political column, the foundation of his later splendid career in journalism. Peter was doubtful which offer to accept, fearing the *Guardian* might be unsaveable. As an old and candid friend, he suggested I ought to be worrying about myself, since being news editor kept me out of the public eye, and might make it difficult to find a new job if the ship sank. However, in an evening of long debate, over many glasses of beer, I persuaded him we would survive, and he agreed to stay, an immense bulwark to staff morale.

The *Guardian* did survive, and later – much later – prospered. But the crisis gave me less time for Westminster. The politics of Fleet Street, like those of the BBC, hold great and permanent fascination for many journalists and broadcasters. But ever since 1967 I have known that I prefer the wider scene, if only as an observer. Perhaps *especially* as an observer.

While the *Guardian* and I fought our way out of these preoccupations, the nation's economic crisis had profound effects on the Labour government, leading in November 1967 to devaluation. This broke up the triumvirate at its head: Harold Wilson, George Brown and Jim Callaghan. First, Callaghan left the Treasury, and took Roy Jenkins' place as Home Secretary, in a straight swop of jobs. But devaluation soon provoked strains on the dollar, and in the gold crisis of the following spring, George Brown finally carried out his long-standing threat to resign.

Suppressed disagreement about sterling was debilitating throughout the first Wilson government. Devaluation became like a tenet of religious belief, and the battle was fought with the ferocity of the Wars of Religion. To my knowledge, nobody on either side has ever confessed to error on the basic question of whether or not the devaluation ought to have been voluntarily undertaken in 1964, rather than forced in 1967.

The parity was then $2.80, and because Labour retained a damaging reputation, since Sir Stafford Cripps's period as Chancellor in the late forties, of being 'the Party of Devaluation', the Wilson-Brown-Callaghan triumvirate determined from the beginning to stick to that value. This has sometimes been presented as misplaced jingoism, but it was more practical than that. Many have argued too glibly that Harold Wilson ought to have devalued immediately on taking office in October 1964 and that he could have blamed this on the profligacy of the outgoing Conservatives.

From a party point of view, that sounds attractive, but it misses a central economic truth: that the price rises which inevitably follow devaluation would quickly have generated increases in wages and other incomes, giving another twist to the inflationary screw. The unions were certainly not ready to swallow in 1964 what was forced on them in an atmosphere of crisis three and four years later.

We all argue from our own experience. The Whitehall machine, and notably the Treasury, have always seemed to me too far removed for their own good from the world of production, work and wages. In a highly unionised labour market – which Britain, like Australia or Sweden, but in sharp contrast with the United States, is – the intended benefits of devaluation are likely to be nugatory, because union wage-bargainers quickly recoup the damage to their members' living standards by winning more (devalued) pounds in their wage packets. True, one worker's wage increase may be another's loss of employment, but our society has not yet reached the stage of sophistication at which that sobering fact strikes home.

Roy Jenkins, the new Chancellor, had favoured devaluation, because he felt $2.80 left Britain permanently vulnerable to currency crises. Those who agreed with him included an odd mixture of right and left: Tony Crosland, Dick Crossman, Barbara Castle, Peter Shore and Tony Benn, among others. After devaluation, as meeting after meeting of ministers gloomily pored through the Treasury's demands for cuts in public spending and reductions in living standards, the price of the government's enforced retreat painfully emerged. Three years of battle between pro- and anti-devaluation forces had conditioned Labour ministers, who had entered government with high ideals about what they might achieve, to accept second best. At one Saturday meeting, when social and other budgets were being heavily pruned, Jim Callaghan and his former Treasury junior, Jack Diamond, exchanged wry smiles from opposite ends of the table, as they saw how ministers accepted cuts which would have been unthinkable two or three years before. Prescription charges, housing and roads programmes, defence, even the school leaving age all suffered.

Callaghan was able to view the issue with greater detachment from the comparative calm of the Home Office, where he had issues such as crime and the Northern Ireland crisis to handle. In January 1970, six months before Labour lost office, he was in reflective mood one day, and began to talk about devaluation. He declared: 'I am absolutely sure ...' then grinned and said he wasn't sure, but he believed that if Labour *had* devalued shortly after coming to office, they would have been facing a second devaluation about that time. Only the crisis after the 1966 election had conditioned the country and the party to the sacrifices it entailed.

Harold Wilson took a similar view. Soon after he left Downing Street, he drew my attention to a National Economic Development Office report on devaluation as a trigger of inflation. He believed those who had thought this was an easy option had been shown wrong in 1968. In Roy Jenkins' first budget then, he was forced to introduce swingeing increases in indirect taxes, which had raised prices.

On returning to the political scene after the *Guardian* crisis, I was struck by the strains imposed on what had been reasonably good personal relations. When Jim Callaghan and I talked in April 1968, I recorded that his mood was one of 'all passion spent'. Callaghan wears his heart more on his sleeve than many politicians. Over the years I have occasionally seen him downcast, and then have been astonished by the way his appetite for political activity lifts his spirits.

Now, as Home Secretary, he felt left out from the central conduct of the government. Callaghan was hurt by his perception that since moving from the Treasury, he was no longer in the Prime Minister's confidence. He had been pleased at the way in which Wilson, Brown and himself, the three men at the top of the government, had worked intimately together for the first three years. Callaghan felt he was being consulted about everything, and that relations with Wilson, after bumpy years in opposition, were good.

What I suspect happened was that the Prime Minister was preoccupied in helping his new Chancellor to force through Cabinet the slashing cuts in public expenditure which devaluation made necessary. He had no time for ministers, however senior, who were not engaged in that task. But Jim Callaghan's sudden isolation from the political core of the government underlined for him how much damage he had suffered through a devaluation which had, after all, gone against the Prime Minister's deepest instincts also.

The other downside of devaluation was that it led to ever more frenzied attempts by the government to restrain wages through statutory means. This is always a short-term expedient, both because it is inflexible, and because men and women who have only their labour to sell see it as inherently unjust. Ministers who came originally from the left of the Labour Party, such as Barbara Castle, accepted statutory wage-fixing with greater equanimity, since they saw it as part of a more widely controlled economy. A later General Secretary of the TUC, Len Murray, sardonically described this attitude as 'all power to the Soviets'. Frank Cousins had warned the former Conservative government: 'If it's a free-for-all, then we [the trade unions] are part of the "all".' The Labour government might purport to be planning for all, but in a turbulent financial world, that plan never looked like becoming effective.

9

HAROLD'S TROUBLE AND STRIFE

The strains towards the end of the first Wilson government seemed to be about the consequences of devaluation and proposals for trade union legislation. But these cloaked uneasy personal relationships among the new big three in the Cabinet: Harold Wilson, Roy Jenkins and Jim Callaghan. From July 1966 onwards, there were quarrels about whether either one or other of the two senior lieutenants was plotting to remove Wilson from the leadership.

Because I was in America when these stories first erupted, and then was heavily engaged in the *Guardian*'s own crisis, I still find it hard to judge how serious the plots were. In political journalism, absence at a key moment is a great disadvantage. Yet distance from Westminster can also provide valuable perspective, for it is a frightful echoing chamber for gossip, as I was to discover during the Thatcher years; and even more forcibly during John Major's various crises in 1993 and 1994, when I was no longer attending the Commons every day.

Harold Wilson's peace of mind was afflicted by two groups within his Cabinet. One were the critic-enemies, the other conspirator-friends. It is difficult to say which caused him more trouble. From the moment he became leader, George Brown was the most constantly niggling of the first group. He could not be classed with Roy Jenkins and Tony Crosland. These were men whose loyalty to Hugh Gaitskell made Wilson's accession to the leadership initially intolerable to them – a feeling which time and proximity healed in Crosland's case, and largely so for Jenkins.

Wilson's leadership was also intolerable to Brown, but this was because Labour MPs had rejected him for the leadership, in favour of a man he despised. By all accounts, even from hostile witnesses, Harold Wilson tried to win George Brown over in every way he could. From early on, it was clear that his deputy was not a threat to him. As early as the summer of 1965, Ray Gunter realised that his old ally was damaging his own cause. His judgement was that even if Labour lost the second election, which was expected either that year or the next, Wilson would hold on as leader, but he was not at all confident that Brown could continue as deputy. If anything did happen to Wilson, Brown would certainly not get the leadership. Like many deputies before and since, his time had passed.

One of the livelier paragraphs in Wilson's austerely proper book about his first government describes the mood during his absence in Moscow in July 1966, when he believed the first plot against him took place: 'Seminars were taking place all over the Palace of Westminster; Dick Crossman in the tea-room was instructing the young, and George Brown, whose voice tended to get a little loud when analysing the intricacies of monetary economics, was also involved, principally with junior ministers.'

Crossman was one of Harold Wilson's few Cabinet intimates, together with Barbara Castle, and later Peter Shore. He could be exciting and amusing company, though when we had our first meal together, I could not conceal my discomfort when he gave a waiter who was barely able to speak English a hard time over an unripe avocado. I found him something of an intellectual bully. Yet George Woodcock assured me that when Dick taught him as a mature student at Oxford, he was both brilliant and thoughtful, and a dazzling host.

To Lobby correspondents of this period, he was an invigorating contact, willing to explain in detail the thinking behind government decisions, and certainly his own views about them. His period as leader of the House, when he briefed the Lobby each Thursday, was regarded by many who worked there as a golden age. I was not in the Lobby then, so saw less of him, but when our paths did cross, I often wondered whether he had been permanently marked by the work he did in wartime as a black propagandist. He was more sure that he was right, in whichever cause he was arguing at a given time, than almost anybody else I have ever met.

It was a misfortune for the history of this period that the first of the diaries about the Wilson government was that of Dick Crossman. Because Harold Evans and the *Sunday Times* became embroiled in a legal tussle with Whitehall over the right to serialise these diaries, they achieved a somewhat spurious authority as Holy Writ. Crossman had a brilliant mind, was a great polemicist, and a subtle – though sometimes self-defeating – political operator. But if you were Detective Constable Plod seeking a reliable witness, he would not have been your first choice. I sometimes wondered if he knew how to distinguish what he said to the Prime Minister from what the Prime Minister said to him.

Others were perplexed by his mixture of corruscating intellect and uncertain political judgement. Ray Gunter described to me a meeting of a sub-committee of the NEC, dealing with some staffing matter at Labour headquarters. It consisted of Dick Crossman and four trade unionists. At the start, all the trade unionists were on one side, with Dick on the other.

'But one by one [as Gunter explained it in his lilting Welsh accent] Dick won us over by the sheer brilliance of his argument, until the last of my colleagues said: "All right, Dick boy, you've convinced me – I'll go along with the rest." At that moment Dick suddenly struck his forehead with his palm, and said: "One moment, comrades! I've forgotten about Factor X, which undermines the whole of my argument. I'm now of the mind that you all were originally." '

This, according to Ray Gunter, was too much for simple-minded trade unionists: 'We just said: "That's one too many for us, Dick", and we voted him down.'

While I was working in the *Guardian* office one Sunday afternoon at the end of June 1968, I received a telephone call from Ray Gunter. This signalled the next stage of what was to turn into a leadership drama – or not, according to your interpretation of a bewildering series of events. When the government was formed in 1964, Gunter had gleefully announced to waiting reporters: 'I've got the bed of nails.' He had been shadowing the Minister of Labour in opposition, and believed he was more suited to the job than anybody else on the front bench, because he had recent practical experience of industrial relations, as president of his union, the Transport Salaried Staffs Association.

In the spring of 1968, he was offended when the Prime Minister moved him to the Ministry of Power. His replacement was Harold Wilson's old ally, Barbara Castle, who was also given George Brown's former title of First Secretary. She did not like the name 'Ministry of Labour', so this was changed to the Department of Employment and Productivity. Its role was also changed, never to be restored. The ministry had long been regarded, like many other Whitehall departments, as an embassy to an interest group: in this case the trade unions and employers' associations.

The wartime legend of Ernest Bevin's ability as Minister of Labour to make industry work with Whitehall had lived on, through Tory and Labour governments. Now a new direction was contemplated. It was three months later that I received my Sunday afternoon phone call from Ray Gunter, alerting me to his intention to leave the government.

The only former union leader now remaining in the cabinet was Jim Callaghan, who had been Assistant General Secretary of the Inland Revenue Staff Federation many years before. His was to prove a significant, if exposed, position within a government which now had fewer members from a traditional Labour background than any before it.

The action which the government then took launched Britain into a long period of continuing strife between the trade union movement and successive governments, which has lasted till near the end of the century. It leaves me with an uncomfortable sense of a country which is stranded on Matthew Arnold's 'darkling plain ... where ignorant armies clash by night'.

The first task of Barbara Castle's renamed department was to handle the report of a Royal Commission on Trade Unions and Employers' Associations, which Ray Gunter had set up in 1965, under Lord Donovan's chairmanship. This contained representatives from both sides of industry including, significantly, George Woodcock. By then, George was near to despair at the inertia of his TUC General Council, not to speak of the matching employers' bodies. So he decided to use the Royal Commission to provoke some fresh thinking.

The commission rejected calls for legislative action, and suggested a patient programme of step-by-step improvement, very much in the Woodcock tradition of 'the art of the possible'. But the politicians, who are supposed to be the original exponents of 'the art of the possible', had a different view of what that phrase meant. They had decided that the rash of short and sudden strikes, which gave British industry such a bad name internationally, was *impossible*, and central to the problems of the government and of its currency.

So when Barbara Castle published her White Paper in January 1969, this contained compulsory powers for her. Its title, *In Place of Strife*, became a joke, for nothing the Labour government did caused more internal strife. Among these powers was a compulsory 'cooling-off period', which went in the opposite direction from that suggested by the Royal Commission.

I happened to have had recent experience of the 'cooling-off period', which Barbara Castle had imported from the American statute box. When I was in the United States in 1966, President Johnson called a cooling-off period in a threatened airline strike. It turned into a hotting-up period. By the time it expired, the employees concerned were ready for an extremely long and bitter strike. I was in San Francisco when this began, and so had to travel right across America by rail.

By then, long-distance railways were little used by passengers, and breakdowns occurred. Once, the locomotive failed deep in a torrid Minnesota countryside, leaving me stranded for several hours, fortunately in the pleasant company of a professor of Greek. Failure of the air-conditioning, and then of the beer supply followed soon afterwards. An earlier, and longer journey, from California to Nebraska, lasted thirty-five hours, and I sat opposite a friendly black woman, whose husband was an undertaker. I had a unique opportunity to learn more about the mortician's trade than I have ever wanted to know.

So I felt qualified, both from personal experience, and from my talks with industrial relations practitioners in the United States, to believe that legislative ideas borrowed from there were a two-edged sword. The line I argued in the *Guardian*'s editorial columns throughout the dispute was not universally popular within the office. It says much for the paper's tradition of relying on the judgement of the person who has done the work on a subject that I was allowed to oppose Barbara Castle so persistently.

At that time Fleet Street was obsessed by its own appalling industrial relations, caused by a mixture of anachronistic unions and management which was by turns weak and petulant. I suspect that Alastair Hetherington was not at all certain I was right. But he allowed me to keep the *Guardian* as the one national paper (apart from the communist *Morning Star*) which opposed the government.

Eventually a lunch was arranged with Barbara Castle. She was accompanied by our former colleague and her then press secretary, Bernard Ingham. Although several other *Guardian* people were present, she selected me as her sole target, and a full and frank exchange of views followed, with nobody except the two of us getting many words in. I felt embarrassed by my own performance, which met hector with hector. Bernard Ingham looked disapproving that anyone should speak to his Secretary of State in the way she spoke to them.

The *Guardian*'s latest historian, Geoffrey Taylor, in a general assessment of my character, wrote: 'He loved argument, and could make an opponent feel personally to blame for the heat-death of the universe.' I judged that Barbara Castle was a tough enough specimen not to leave our lunch with any such feelings of guilt, even if her subject was marginally less important than the heat-death of the universe. But I was uneasy enough to enquire of Alastair, as we walked back to the office, whether he thought I had been impolite, beyond the call of duty, to his guest. He considered for a moment, and replied judicially: 'I think it was about even pegging.'

It was in the troubled political and economic environment after the

1967 devaluation that personal relations in the Cabinet first began to deteriorate. The fact that a Labour government was now trying to introduce legislation to control the trade unions soured the atmosphere further. But the first indication I had of a change in mood came earlier than that, in the spring of 1968. Just because Jim Callaghan believed his chances of ever leading the Labour Party had been blighted by devaluation, he regarded his ambitions as being 'past the burning stage'. He still had reservations about ways in which Harold Wilson operated, but in my experience that is true of almost every minister and every Prime Minister. By 1968, Callaghan maintained, Wilson could have had him as a political friend and adviser, without any strings. But he felt the Prime Minister was no longer consulting him.

Others suspected that Jim Callaghan's ambitions had not yet run their course. They believed he wanted Harold Wilson to remain leader so that the change would not come at the worst possible moment for himself. Callaghan was in low political water after devaluation, and before his sure-footed performance in the Ulster troubles restored his reputation, and even his relations with the Prime Minister. In early 1968 he was anxious lest an alternative heir-apparent might emerge.

The obvious alternative leader at that time was Roy Jenkins, who had taken over from him as Chancellor. Jenkins was in an unusually strong position, because his views on devaluation had ultimately prevailed over those of the Prime Minister and the former Chancellor. Callaghan acknowledged that if Harold Wilson was removed, Roy Jenkins would be the successor.

His opposition to a Jenkins leadership was fired by more than personal ambition, though that was a factor. The two men's temperaments were so different that their political postures were poles apart. Callaghan saw in Jenkins the reincarnation of Hugh Gaitskell. He blamed Gaitskell for splitting the Labour movement through his inability to compromise. Callaghan himself had come from the centre-right of his party, and was not averse to an occasional showdown with the left. But he believed that Jenkins was simply contemptuous of the left, and would undoubtedly provoke division.

The personal and political chemistry of Labour's three leading men, Wilson, Callaghan and Jenkins, was decisive in what happened next. Between 1966 and 1974, Wilson often regarded Callaghan as a possible threat to his leadership, so their relationship was always watchful. But beneath this personal tension, they were men of similar character, who saw their party, warts and all, as the only available vehicle for their kind of reform politics.

Roy Jenkins showed greater fastidiousness about party politics. Long before his break with Labour in the eighties, he had reservations about 'party' as the be-all-and-end-all of democratic politics. As early as the eve of the 1974 election, he speculated that the Liberals would win at least eighteen and possibly sixty seats. This proved badly out. But the significant fact was that one of the Labour triumvirate already suspected that the ice on the present party structure was thin.

Although the differences between Roy Jenkins and Harold Wilson were both political and temperamental, in the three years when Jenkins was his Chancellor they formed a remarkably good relationship. Jenkins said that Wilson's great strength was that he was genuinely unflappable in a crisis, especially of the kind encountered at the Treasury. He never lost his head when things were going badly, and never recriminated or blamed the Chancellor for having taken a wrong decision earlier.

But Jenkins found that their preferred methods of doing business, even of conducting a conversation, were miles apart. By 1970, Labour's hope of re-election depended entirely on these two's ability to convince voters the country was recovering from devaluation. They used to meet once every week or so. Roy worried because the Prime Minister never seemed to eat properly in the evenings, unless he had to go to an official function. Throughout Jenkins' writings, he never conceals his own need for 'a proper dinner'.

So he regarded his chief's eating and drinking habits as eccentric, especially as they affected himself: he was either offered nothing, or had half a tumbler of whisky poured for him. As a result, he found himself emerging from Number 10 at nine o'clock, instead of eating dinner at a proper time, and if he was not careful, no decisions had been taken, for he found Harold inclined to discuss tactics rather than substance. So Jenkins developed a habit of having firmly in his mind half-a-dozen points he wanted to raise, and of slipping one in when there was a gap in the Prime Minister's conversation. He praised Wilson for giving quick answers on policy issues, but worried that he believed increasingly he could finesse his way out of any problem.

If the Prime Minister's relations with his new Chancellor were close, though guarded, those with his former Chancellor were now dangerously distant. When the dispute about *In Place of Strife* erupted in 1969, Jim Callaghan began to express his doubts. An old Labour Party issue soon arose: how much freedom at NEC discussions is available to a Cabinet minister, bound by the principle of collective responsibility?

The Prime Minister and those close to him were deeply suspicious of Callaghan, and after he attacked *In Place of Strife*, he was excluded from the inner Cabinet. He attributed this to the influence on the Prime Minister of Castle and Crossman, and later recorded Crossman as saying Jim would be dropped from the Cabinet altogether. This proved to be a massive misjudgement. The Prime Minister was more interested in keeping his government and party together than he was in vendettas.

From the autumn of 1969 onward, when Harold Wilson and Barbara Castle had to give way on their industrial relations legislation, it was the Prime Minister himself who began to argue that the Home Secretary must be brought back into the inner Cabinet. When I met Jim Callaghan soon afterwards, he was in more cheerful mood than he had been for a long time, and the reason for this quickly emerged. For some time, Downing Street had been sending out smoke signals, and recently, when he had gone to see Wilson about a Home Office issue, he had been invited to stay to tea. (According to Crossman, his expulsion from the inner Cabinet had been decided, in his absence, over brandy.)

A general political discussion followed, and both Wilson and Callaghan acknowledged that mistakes had been made in the row over the trade union legislation. Callaghan said he had no wish to widen the breach, and Wilson replied that he felt the same. It was agreed they must work together well from then until the general election. Despite all the excitement, when Labour lost in 1970 no challenger to Harold Wilson's leadership appeared.

It was the Home Secretary's performance over Ulster which convinced the Prime Minister it was essential to bring him back into the heart of the government. Jim was pleased to find he was again getting all the papers for the Economic Strategy Committee of the Cabinet, and that even when he attended simply to present a Home Office item, Harold invited him to take a full part in all discussions.

Real or imagined conspiracy inside, it is a measure of Harold Wilson's political professionalism that, as the general election approached, he suppressed personal animosities. When I saw him in May, I had read that Roy Jenkins would be given the second largest exposure in Labour's election campaign. The Prime Minister quickly corrected me: '*And* Jim. And of course George Brown [still deputy leader, though now outside the government] will be doing the stomp which he does very well.' When I suggested that the Home Secretary would be there to combat the Conservative attack on law and order, he went out of his way to make clear his role was more than that: Jim was such a great speaker, and so confident. He had been superb about the South African cricket tour on television the previous night, and his whole behaviour over Ulster, the cricket tour and other matters had been outstanding. When I asked how relations were, he replied that they were very good. Jim and he settled the line on all these delicate issues, and were often on the phone to each other.

Clearly, the Labour leadership was closing ranks. Naturally, since I believe Callaghan was right to oppose *In Place of Strife*, I take a more charitable view of his motives than others, including Harold Wilson, did. The general press reaction, being fervently in favour of any conceivable curbs on the unions, assumed his only possible motivation must be personal ambition.

This was the same kind of judgement which was to be made many years later, when Michael Portillo, the most convinced Euro-sceptic in John Major's Cabinet, began to throw his weight about. Again, I regarded it as simplistic to believe his only thoughts were of his party's future leadership. The politician who reaches senior office and does not have some ambition to lead his party is probably not up even to the job he is doing. The politician who thinks of nothing else but the leadership is a fool, since only one person in most political generations of each party can have it.

Jim Callaghan was lucky in this respect. As long ago as Hugh Gaitskell's time, Harold Wilson told me that he was 'being asked to make way for older men': that is, to let Callaghan have his turn as shadow Chancellor. In 1976, it suited Wilson again to make way for an older man, and Callaghan unexpectedly had his turn in Number 10. The title of his autobiography, *Time and Chance* − a quotation from Ecclesiastes − was well chosen.

10

LABOUR'S LOST SOULS

By the time of the 1970 election, I was deputy editor of the *Guardian*. Moving from the news editorship was a wrench. Although that had been a back-breaking job, it was stimulating, and I had at my fingertips most of what was going on in the paper. But the attraction of the new post was that I would have more time to talk with political leaders, and much more time to write.

Although being news editor mainly means organising the work of other journalists, I had taken care to find opportunities to keep writing myself. That, after all, was why I had become a journalist when I was seventeen. I managed brief visits to the United States in most of the presidential election years from 1968 onward, until I moved to the BBC in 1981.

I was in Chicago in 1968, but not at the time of the Democratic Convention riots. I was there earlier, covering the Illinois primary, always a controversial affair, since Mayor Richard Daley's Democratic machine was unscrupulous in its electoral methods. I once had the pleasure of accompanying a US marshal – a legendary title to anybody who watched Westerns as a boy – to deliver a court order instructing Daley's election officer to desist from some malpractice. Although I was there as a reporter, the police at City Hall were so hostile that I tried to look as much like the marshal's sidekick as possible (though I kept my hand cautiously away from any putative shoulder-holster). When the election officer appeared, he scanned the court order, smiled, and addressed my companion: 'So the judge says I can't! Well, I already have. Thanks for calling by, Marshal.'

Mayor Daley seemed a suitable subject for a *Guardian* profile. His office must have suspected hostility, for he refused to see me. I interviewed enough other witnesses, pro and con, to ensure I got a rounded picture of this Mid-Western equivalent of Tammany politics. My only worry was that, although Chicago was a heavily black city, I had not discussed the regime with many blacks. So I had myself invited to a Sunday service and lunch at a huge black church in south Chicago.

The church was highly evangelical, with two large robed choirs, one in green, the other in purple, and constant interruption of the prayers by shouts of 'Hallelujah!', 'Praise the Lord!' or 'Tell it like it is, Reverend!' The Reverend, an elderly and gentle man, invited me to sit in the pulpit with him. When I demurred, another visitor, about six feet six inches tall, who turned out to be a psychiatrist from California, reproved me for having hang-ups about being white, so I gave in.

When we went into the church, I saw this was not a 'pulpit' in the ordinary sense, but a platform on which sat the two choirs, all the deacons, and a large number of visitors. I felt less conspicuous than I feared. Until, that is, the Reverend came over, without warning, raised my hand, and announced that Mr Cole would now give his message. A congregation of 2,000 waited expectantly, and I found that, apart from my Daley profile, which seemed unsuitable to a sacred occasion, I had not a single thought in my mind.

I stumbled through about three minutes of 'Thank you for having me', as my mother had taught me I always should; and as I warmed, slightly, to the task, noted that their Christian tradition was somewhat different from the sober – and, though I did not mention this, severely intellectual – tradition of Irish Presbyterianism, in which I had grown up; or indeed from the English Nonconformity to which I now belonged. I sat down to tumultuous applause.

This, I fear, had less to do with my eloquence than my unique pigmentation – certainly in that church, and so far as I could see, in south Chicago. I had found the Reverend's Southern drawl difficult to follow, and had not taken in his announcement that he was feeling unwell that morning, so had decided to make his guests 'sing for their lunch'. When I had finished, so briefly, the Californian psychiatrist filled the breach with a twenty-five-minute discussion of the drugs problem on the west coast.

My other overseas journey in 1968 was to Zambia, where President Kaunda was launching a new economic programme. One of my few regrets about my career in journalism is that I have not done more reporting overseas. There is nothing more fascinating than to descend on a country which is new to you, and study its problems with a fresh mind. Whether this is also so enlightening for the audience is another matter. A more worldly wise colleague has written that 'the purpose of journalism is travel'. In retrospect, my puritan nature blinded me to that aphoristic, if cynical, truth, and kept me too close to subjects I might know something about.

When I visited Zambia, the Rhodesian rebellion was still going on to the south. Alastair Hetherington suggested I should see if I could gain entry for a weekend which I had free at the end of the Zambian visit. The *Guardian* was not popular with Ian Smith's regime. In those days, air travel from Lusaka to Salisbury was forbidden. I finished my Zambian meetings in Livingstone, and crossed by bus to Victoria Falls.

The form I had to fill in before being allowed on to the aircraft to Salisbury asked the name of my company. I wrote '*Manchester Guardian*' as illegibly as possible – which I find easy; and in clear, round hand '*and Evening News Limited*', which from a Rhodesian point of view I hoped would be the respectable end of our partnership. The young official in white shorts was not deceived, underlining '*Guardian*' in heavy red pencil. But he did permit himself a wintry smile at my other prevarication. The form demanded to know not only my nationality, but my race. I answered 'British' to the first, and 'Irish' to the second, which would have satisfied neither Ian Smith nor Gerry Adams. But the official let me in.

When I plunged back into Westminster in the early months of 1970, I detected a sharp change in mood. The 1967 devaluation, so long resisted by Harold Wilson and Jim Callaghan, had proved to be what industrial reporters like myself, arguing against the fashionable consensus, always suspected it would be: a trigger of inflation. The statutory incomes policy had broken down, and the government had nothing to put in its place. After the trauma of *In Place of Strife*, any formal understanding with the unions to restrain their demands was out of the question.

I had two interesting discussions with Harold Wilson in Downing Street that spring. The first was in February, just five months before he was defeated by Ted Heath. He denied that the pattern of wage increases then emerging was serious enough to damage economic recovery, and took comfort from the fact that other countries' inflation was still worse than Britain's: the Italians twenty-four per cent, the Germans thirteen, the American deteriorating. As illustration, he told a story about the Whit Walks – which, from my Manchester days, I remembered as an important part of Sunday School life and recruiting in the north. At one of these great events, Wilson said, the Baptist minister prayed as follows: 'Oh Lord, we did not have a very good attendance today, but we thank thee for giving us more than the Methodists.'

He had been through the fire in the previous few years. These conversations in 1970 brought me up sharply against a difference in our attitudes, which was *ex officio*. He had taught me most of what I knew about the importance of incomes policies as a means of achieving growth without inflation. I had been disappointed that his government had been pushed off the voluntary principle by – as I saw it – ignorance of the labour market among international bankers and our own Treasury.

But Wilson now had other preoccupations. He clearly had no realistic hope of achieving a return to a voluntary incomes policy at the tag end of a government which had provoked a bitter dispute with the unions. I recorded this impression of our conversation: 'He kept skipping off to the electoral implications, and said that people were now *feeling* the extra money in their pockets, and that this should soon begin to show in the polls. I got the distinct impression that, realistically as well as electorally, he was not bothering much about incomes policy now. I didn't even attempt to discuss social justice or redistribution.'

Looking back on that comment now, I find it naïve. Democratic party leaders have to concentrate on winning elections. I realise that I was thinking as a leader-writer, who would have liked government to be conducted under the aspect of eternity, rather than in accordance with a democratic timetable which lasts, at most, five years. I certainly was not thinking like a politician. That was not my chosen career.

On the same theme, that cheerful advocate of *Realpolitik*, Jim Callaghan, laughingly acknowledged what most politicians know: that in election year, politics forces you to be more concerned with votes than policies; as someone has put it, 'to be immoral one year in five'. He offered me a quotation from Jimmy Maxton, the Clydeside Labour leader, that nobody should come into politics without realising that he could only be as good as he was allowed to be.

Harold Wilson certainly never forgot that his primary task was to get his party re-elected. He was to suffer his one failure later that year, but he won four elections out of five, in less propitious circumstances than those in which Margaret Thatcher won three in succession, so his is a remarkable record. That spring he adumbrated a theory of opposition electoral tactics. It is one which politicians still argue about at every election.

He believed the Conservative opposition was talking too much about its own policies, and thus giving Labour a chance to attack them, instead of having to defend the Labour government's record. He was finding it hard to keep going with his own 'Labour's achievement' speeches – from boredom, rather than lack of conviction. But he was encouraged by the targets provided by the Conservative opposition during their policy re-think at Selsdon Park, a hotel in Surrey. Wilson said that after 'Ted had been on television every few minutes', he himself had been able to prepare 'ten questions on Tory policy', which he would put into his speeches. He believed the Selsdon policies were a watershed in British politics. So they were, though this proved a false start down a more ideological Conservative path. They retreated after 1972, and did not resume the journey until Margaret Thatcher became leader in 1975.

Harold Wilson was a natural optimist, who loved politics and elections. Roy Hattersley's most embarrassing moment came during that 1970 election, when he was accompanying the Prime Minister to an Irish club in Birmingham. The junior minister was flattered to find himself marching, side by side with his chief, down the centre aisle of a huge meeting, while pipers lifted the emotional temperature. Labour's ethnic card was being played for all it was worth. Even the police were saluting, and claiming to be Irish, and Harold was just promising – or threatening – to tell how many more Irish Catholics there were in his Liverpool constituency than in most Irish towns. Suddenly a drunk man marched from the crowd and cut the feet from under the Prime Minister, leaving him on his back. According to Roy, he took it remarkably well, and gave no hint of rebuke for having been led into such a ludicrous event.

The electoral razzmatazz was not matched by any great policy content in Labour's campaign. A week before polling, I wrote a deeply disillusioned article. If Labour won, I argued, a party of reform in Britain would never have been elected on such a negative vote, or after such a Baldwinesque campaign. Confession being good for the soul, I had better tell readers of this book, who will be confronted often enough with my aversion to ideology, that even I worried about its absence in 1970:

> This is not an article I would have written at the end of the fifties, a period during which ... I watched a Labour party obsessively concerned with its own soul, and apparently oblivious of the damage this caused to the body politic. The struggles over nationalisation shopping-lists, Clause IV of the party constitution, and nuclear disarmament were the antithesis of today's non-ideological sleep, and equally undesirable.

This, my one negatively kind word about ideology, was provoked by a suspicion that Labour had abandoned all talk of greater equality, which Gaitskell and Crosland had substituted for public ownership as the party's guiding beacon. Now no beacon was visible at all. Instead, they were concentrating on a Tweedledum versus Tweedledee competition with the Conservatives, about which were the more efficient economic managers. Since there was no honest answer to that question, I believed voters deserved a better choice.

What motivated me to write an article adequately reflecting the headline, 'Labour's lost souls', was a sense that Harold Wilson and his Chancellor, Roy Jenkins, had abandoned the most important task of democratic leaders, to educate their own followers. Labour's support, which had once been from the poor and dispossessed, now came from all income and occupational groups, as Jenkins boasted. But both the new middle-class voters and the manual workers who had moved into the income tax-paying brackets did not — surprise, surprise! — like high taxation when it applied to them, rather than to some abstraction called 'the rich'.

I thought Labour ought to be telling its better-off supporters they would have to pay more tax, that pensioners and the low-paid had borne the brunt of post-devaluation price rises at home, and that Britain had also deprived Third World countries of the level of aid we ought to be giving them. If ministers did not present themselves as a party of conscience and reform, willing to tax the better-paid, even among their own supporters, in order to help the less fortunate, they would not have the moral authority to ask for less selfish attitudes.

From the devaluation of 1967 onward, the Labour government of 1964–70 was probably doomed, though in 1970 only Ted Heath was convinced, despite unfavourable opinion polls, that the Conservatives would win. Roy Hattersley told me later that he had suffered an attack of nerves late on the evening of polling day, but John Harris had telephoned a friendly journalist, who assured him that Labour was practically past the post. Most people thought the same.

When the votes were counted, the Tories had an overall majority of thirty-one. Somewhere in my possessions, I have the proof of an editorial I wrote before the results were known. It urged Harold Wilson to make Tony Crosland Chancellor. The article was not required, and his opportunity never came.

11

HEATH THE PROBLEM SOLVER

At the time 1970 seemed like the beginning of a new political era, the Heath years. In the event, this proved to be only an entr'acte, followed by the return to office, less than four years later, of Harold Wilson, whom the electors had so unexpectedly dismissed.

Yet it was a significant turning point in Conservative history, and therefore in British politics. For the Tories went sharply right with Ted Heath; then moved back to the centre, under pressure of economic misfortune; and so became even more determinedly right-wing when Margaret Thatcher led a reaction against all that had gone before.

Despite later disillusion among Conservatives about Heath's unrelenting hostility to Thatcher, there is a generation to whom he remains the lost leader. Many Tories made their peace with the new leadership, and criticised Ted for his stubbornness, yet still felt the tragedy of a lost talent. Jim Prior, a Cabinet minister under both Heath and Thatcher, once said sadly that a man who could be Prime Minister, win the Sydney to Hobart yacht race, and was also a considerable musician was worth a place in history.

Yet he lost his leadership when he was only fifty-eight, after Harold Wilson had defeated him in both 1974 elections. These defeats would probably have made his fate inevitable, whatever he had done, for the Tories are ruthless in punishing failure. He did not help his own cause by his growing remoteness from his backbenchers. As Douglas Hurd, then Heath's political secretary, observed, he was 'not very good at being interested in uninteresting people'.

Heath himself once told me the moment when he decided that he could not serve under Margaret Thatcher. On a flight from Geneva to Paris, he read an interview with her in which she said there would be no room in her government for people who disagreed with the central thrust of policy. He believed that was not the way to run a Cabinet. So he occupied himself with international interests, including the Brandt Commission on North–South relations. Willy Brandt, the former socialist Chancellor of Germany, recognised in him 'a real internationalist', a description that would satisfy him.

But the former Prime Minister occasionally offered the House of Commons a witty and often acerbic commentary on his Conservative successor's policies. Roy Jenkins, an old political opponent and Balliol contemporary, paid a just tribute to his domestic performance, which I included in a radio profile: Ted's value as a backbencher, in the years after his premiership, was as a great lighthouse, casting the beams of his 'curmudgeonly integrity' across the waters of Westminster.

While in Downing Street, Heath's overwhelming preoccupation, and the achievement which will always be associated with his name, was to take Britain into Europe. That seminal act, and also the turbulence it later provoked in both major political parties, will be described in later chapters.

The domestic scene was less cheerful. Every Prime Minister would like to begin with a clean sheet. Few are privileged to do so. Just as Harold Wilson in 1964 believed he was undermined at once by a dreadful inheritance from the Conservatives, so Ted Heath quickly discovered that nothing was so cut and dried as it had appeared when he and his shadow Cabinet assembled at Selsdon Park to make their election plans.

The dominant fact about the early Heath years, and certainly about the Prime Minister himself, was his determination to make a fresh start. When elected Tory leader in 1965, he had been the youngest since Disraeli. His policy and style of government were a conscious reaction against what had gone before: not just what he criticised as Harold Wilson's 'meaningless posturing', but also the tendency of his old chief, Harold Macmillan, to drift along, dealing with issues as they arose. It sounded like ideology versus pragmatism, with Heath in the former camp; but this proved a premature judgement.

Although Ted Heath had briefly been Minister of Labour, I had not known him well during my industrial relations period. When he was Prime Minister, I saw him principally at meetings with editors, never the most satisfactory way to plumb a politician's innermost thoughts. In retrospect, it is possible to cast him as a tragic hero, though in the early years of his premiership he appeared as a dogmatic and unyielding man.

My best contact in the government was Reginald Maudling, then Home Secretary, and responsible among other things for Ulster. I had known Maudling well when he was Chancellor in the early sixties, and we spent much of our time together during the first couple of years of the Heath government glooming over its economic policy. Heath's revulsion against what had gone before led him to believe that he must take Britain's economy by the scruff of the neck and shake it. He wanted industry to stand on its own two feet, he aimed to tame union excesses through legislation (again), and he promised cuts in direct taxes and more selective social benefits. The government was resolutely opposed to any form of incomes policy.

Maudling sometimes sounded even more unhappy about this course of events than I was. He was sceptical about the Selsdon ideology, and a group which included the Minister of Labour, Robert Carr, and Heath's former Chief Whip, now leader of the Commons, Willie Whitelaw, soon shared at least some of these doubts. Yet Maudling loyally urged me to understand how governments got themselves into such dogmatic postures. The Tories, he explained, had been elected in a reaction against 'Wilson and compromise and consensus and all that'. Most of these, apart from Harold Wilson, were things that he approved of.

Indeed, he confessed that he enjoyed Wilson's company, but criticised him for 'politicking over everything'. In private, when he said something outrageous, Maudling would expostulate: 'That's a lot of tosh, Harold, and you know it!' He always felt that Wilson took this quite well. Ted Heath and Harold Wilson did not get on well together. Maudling once told me that when they were having meetings 'on Privy Councillor terms' (of confidentiality), Heath froze as soon as Wilson came into the room. I gathered separately from both Wilson and Maudling that these two *did* enjoy good personal relations. Maudling described Wilson as 'quite a nice human being', which is a judgement I think most who knew them would have made about either man. Politics do not always overwhelm personal feelings.

Because I had been a labour correspondent, part of my commentary on the Heath government's early years came from contacts I had made then. As early as November 1970, George Woodcock told me he had been appalled by the Prime Minister's ideological determination that governments must not intervene in the workings of the market-place. He described Heath's government as the most dogmatic since the war. Woodcock was horrified at the prospect of constantly rising unemployment and the possibility of further devaluation. He divided blame between the government and the unions. It would be politically impossible, he argued, for ministers to sustain the level of unemployment which would slow down wage claims. He put this at six or seven per cent – horrifying in those days, but one which, in the recessions of the eighties and nineties, came to seem comparatively modest. Norman Tebbit, who was a backbencher until Thatcher took over, said later that Heath's mistake, after his U-turn, had been to judge post-war attitudes by pre-war criteria.

Unemployment is the key to any comparison between Ted Heath and Margaret Thatcher. Jim Prior observed that when unemployment rose above 1 million in Heath's period, the House of Commons had to be suspended, because of disorder; but the total went above 3 million in the Thatcher years, without comparable trouble. Here was the difference between the generation of Tories who had served in the war, and remembered the pre-war depression, and those who were ten years younger.

Ted Heath knew about the pre-war suffering, and in the army had commanded men who had been affected. Having worked at Tory Central Office after the 1945 election defeat, he understood public revulsion against the apparent indifference of pre-war Conservative governments to unemployment. When he saw history apparently repeating itself, he decided he could not put his political judgement into commission to any particular economic dogma.

John Biffen, who also had to wait for his promotion until Margaret Thatcher was leader, disagreed with Heath both on Europe and on his retreat from Selsdon ideas. Yet he gives him credit for being a man of principle, though certainly no ideologue. His politics were those of a businessman, a problem-solver: he tried something, and if that did not work, he tried something else. Biffen maintained to me that Ted Heath had moved from a classical free enterprise policy to 'modified collectivism'. Norman Tebbit saw him as a man who tried radicalism, turned away from it, but opened the way for Thatcherism.

Ted Heath began with a real problem in retaining public confidence. There was never any chance that he could deliver his decisive election promise: to reduce the rise in prices 'at a stroke'. After only five months in office, the Organisation for Economic Co-operation and Development was warning him that inflation was becoming dangerous. Wage increases were running ten per cent ahead of productivity. Britain was in its all-too-familiar state of crisis.

The government's inherited difficulty was that, although some Labour people blamed Roy Jenkins for losing the election by introducing a 'responsible' budget, this puritanical stance did not extend, in Labour's dying months, to wages. So Ted Heath came to office with wage inflation accelerating. Iain Macleod, his first Chancellor, and a street-wise politician, died less than five weeks after the Conservatives won the election. Anthony Barber succeeded him. In opposition, the Tories had largely turned their backs on any kind of incomes policy, so Heath and Barber were slow to look in that direction.

There was an added difficulty. The government was committed to bring in an Industrial Relations Bill, to control the unions. In this, it had much support from a public which was fed up with wildcat strikes. But this legislation forced the TUC, fresh from its victory against Harold Wilson and Barbara Castle over *In Place of Strife*, into opposition to Ted Heath. It was therefore unwilling even to consider the voluntary wage restraint which was so obviously needed. George Woodcock, who in 1969 had been appointed by the Labour government to head a new Commission on Industrial Relations, regarded the Heath bill as a massive irrelevance. In the end, because of the new law, he found it impossible to carry on his work of conciliation and reform through that body. Thus British public life lost one of its wisest servants.

During 1970, the row over the bill became irretrievably mixed up with that about who was to blame for inflation. Heath confirmed his determination to have nothing to do with the various incomes policies which Labour had tried. But some ministers soon concluded that, unless there was restraint, the economy would spin out of control, with both high inflation and unemployment at a level with no precedent since before the war.

Reginald Maudling later revealed to me that he had tackled all these issues in a dissenting memorandum on economic policy, which he wrote in the spring of 1971. But he had been dissuaded – I believe by Number 10 – from circulating this to Cabinet colleagues, on the ground that a leak would be damaging to the coherence of a government which was already running into squally weather. He said he had discussed the memorandum with individual ministers at that time, though it was only in October 1972 that he published it in *The Times*, as a justification of the government's change of course.

Maudling watched in frustration as the economic events of 1970 and 1971 developed. Although he enjoyed being Home Secretary, he longed to be back in charge of economic policy. Harold Wilson had heard a rumour that Maudling wanted to be Foreign Secretary, but when I asked him about this, he dismissed it, saying the Foreign Office was a dreadful department. So what would he have liked, apart from Downing Street? That, he said sadly, was the problem: the only department worth having was the Treasury, and nobody could go back there.

My contacts on the opposition side, recently removed from office, watched with fascination as the new government struggled with the same problems which had faced them. They always saw the sceptical group of ministers, with Maudling as its outstanding member, as the ones who could tackle the gathering economic crisis more effectively. Jim Callaghan, who had taken over from Maudling at the Treasury in 1964, told me late in 1970 that this group could not be effective unless Maudling came out in the open. Callaghan, who was close to him, also knew he would like to have become Chancellor again, but said that this would not happen, partly because of Maudling's personal money troubles, partly because the City would not have him. Harold Wilson noted that Maudling had written an article in the *Spectator* which was enthusiastic about incomes policy, and not all that distant from Wilson's own views.

Callaghan volunteered his belief that (Lord) Rowley Cromer, former Governor of the Bank of England, hated Maudling so much that he had practically loved Callaghan himself when he succeeded to the chancellorship. He had reason to believe that the then Governor had helped to thwart Maudling's ambitions during the Tory leadership election in 1965. Cromer was very close to the *Daily Mail*, and that was where the Heath bandwagon had really begun to roll. Callaghan said he had eventually got rid of Cromer, because if he would knife one Chancellor he would knife another. Personally, he liked Etonians, but they were quicker with the dagger than most.

What lay behind Callaghan's poor opinion of Cromer was that he had inserted that dagger in Labour during the 1970 election campaign, making the damaging statement that Heath's economic inheritance in 1970 would be tougher than Wilson's in 1964. Such things are a matter of judgement and of perspective. Callaghan recalls that in 1964 he was glooming over the statistics in his new study at Number 11, on his first day in office. Suddenly Reggie Maudling, carrying a number of suits over his arm, put his head round the door and said: 'Good luck, old cock. Sorry to leave things in such a mess.' Callaghan did not take this 'mess' to mean the state of his new residence.

There is often a freemasonry among Chancellors of different parties. Jim Callaghan offered Tony Barber two pieces of worldly wise advice, when he took over after Iain Macleod's death. One was to learn to use the jargon of macro-economics. This might not mean much, but if you did not use it, economic journalists refused to take you seriously. (Kenneth Clarke has shown a refreshing tendency to ignore that risk.) The second piece of advice was not to stay more than two years at the Treasury, and to try to leave on an upswing. Good advice, but not easy to take.

As early as the summer of 1971 the government began a slow change of direction. Anthony Barber took fright at the fall in investment and when unemployment passed 1 million for the first time since before the war. About this time, I asked Willie Whitelaw whether he did not think, with what was then an unbelievable number of people out of work, the government might already have lost its chance of being re-elected in three years' time. Whitelaw looked suitably worried.

Reggie Maudling was having none of my economic determinism. When I asked him the same question, he said voters did not take stark decisions to punish governments for economic failure. They had a general view that a government was making a mess of things and deserved to be replaced; or, alternatively, that it was making somewhat less of a mess of things, and that 'the opposition were a bunch of carping bastards, always running the country down.'

In this conversation I had a preview of one many years later, with another tough-minded Conservative Chancellor, Nigel Lawson. I was foolhardy enough to quote a Labour frontbencher who said the electorate had concluded a Faustian bargain with Margaret Thatcher: she delivered prosperity, in return for which they submerged their concern about social issues like the National Health Service and poverty. Lawson immediately denounced Faustian analogies as 'a bit Pseuds Cornerish'; the economy had always been the overwhelming determinant of elections.

In 1971 the economy was not prospering, and both Prime Minister and Chancellor realised that current investment and unemployment trends were a poor basis for Britain's entry into the Common Market. So in July Barber brought in a mini-budget aimed at expanding the economy by between 4 and 4.5 per cent. There was more spending on infrastructure, cuts in purchase tax, abolition of hire purchase controls, and tax incentives for investment.

A year later, when the Chancellor had gone further down the same revisionist course, Reggie Maudling was delighted at a 180-degree turn. As the U-turn began, he scrupulously avoided any premature crowing. Tony Barber, fortified by a CBI initiative to restrain prices, began to make tentative approaches to the TUC to take 'parallel action'. Incomes policy was back on the agenda.

Ted Heath later placed great emphasis on this CBI voluntary initiative. He believed the TUC would like to have done the same about wages, but simply could not deliver. This was why he legislated, though in ever closer consultation with the unions. The two decisive figures at the TUC, in addition to Len Murray, were Jack Jones and Hugh Scanlon, both men of the left. Both learned much about bargaining with government from Ted Heath, who achieved a good working relationship with them. During the miners' strike which preceded the fall of Heath's government, Jack Jones told me he regarded the Conservative Prime Minister as an honourable man with whom he could do business, though he feared that he was receiving bad advice. He had even greater respect for Whitelaw, who took over as Employment Secretary towards the end of that government.

Heath's defence against the charge that he chickened out on the new Conservatism worked out at Selsdon Park was an angry one. Years later, he told me that those who said a government should not adapt to changing world circumstances – in his case, the frightening inflation which was ignited by a world oil shortage – were 'stupid'. He was scathing about a Conservative government, under Margaret Thatcher, which took the simple view that if it stuck to monetarist theory, everybody would be successful and happy. Life was not like that, he said, and true Conservatives realised it.

When the Heath government did consult the social partners about prices and wages, this was music to Reggie Maudling's ears. His own simple doctrine was 'cooperation rather than mutual destruction'. He said it was 'just bloody nonsense' to talk of having no incomes policy. Every government had one whether it liked it or not. It just did not work to use the levers of monetary policy and interest rates to control incomes. You had to have some form of direct influence on them. This view of the limitations of monetarism was well before its time. Later, when Nigel Lawson was Chancellor in the late eighties, it was Ted Heath who accused him of being a one-club golfer – that is, relying entirely on interest rates.

It would be wrong, however, because of their disagreement in the first couple of years of the 1970 government, to present Heath and Maudling as the classic contrapoint between ideologue and pragmatist. Ted Heath later proved himself, under pressure of events – that Macmillan word again! – as supple a pragmatist as might be imagined. But early on in the life of the Heath government, this contrast was what struck me forcibly whenever I went to see Reggie Maudling at the Home Office.

I have often thought that the difference between pragmatist and ideologue may be largely a function of temperament. Reginald Maudling was the perfect pragmatist: sceptical, self-doubting, with an instinctive aversion to enthusiasm. At that time Ted Heath, by contrast, was gripped by a revolutionary desire to change things. Yet Maudling came to admire Heath, even though, so far as I understood from two sources, they rarely saw each other alone. He told me they had never had a meal together in all their years as leader and deputy leader of the Conservative Party.

But the Home Secretary praised the Prime Minister, whose victory had deprived him of the Tory leadership, as a man of immense mental energy and intellectual resilience. With unemployment, inflation, Rhodesia and Ulster all crowding in on him, Reggie believed he thrived on crises, and 'would be happier without any ministers at all'. By halfway through the government's life, he generously concluded that 'Ted is turning into rather a good leader for the Tories'. He was not as inflexible as people said, and when he became convinced of something, he worked hard at it.

Whenever I met Reginald Maudling, either to discuss the economy when he was Chancellor, or to talk about Northern Ireland when he had responsibility as Home Secretary for my native province, his style was wonderful to behold. Let me confess – if it has not already become obvious – that I admired him more than any other Conservative politician I have encountered. Warts and all. While I was writing this book, some Tories whose views about their party I normally find persuasive told me that they had not supported Reggie Maudling for the leadership, and had never detected the outstanding intellectual brilliance I was praising. One said Maudling 'was just too lazy to be leader'.

At one level the charge of laziness was just. He was a large man, ostentatiously unfit, who seemed to find most physical exertion painful. I remember, when the Home Office was still in Whitehall, his imposing presence in the large and gloomy Home Secretary's office. We would be sitting on easy chairs near his desk – if he had his way, drinking whisky at five o'clock in the afternoon – and the conversation would turn to something in the newspapers. These were spread out on a table in the bow window at the other end of the room.

Maudling would rise, with almost palpable reluctance, and waddle – no other word adequately describes his walk – to the alcove to check his recollection. It would not have been easy to imagine him skippering a yacht in the Fastnet Race, as Ted Heath did. But his mind was razor-sharp, one of the best I have encountered, and it remained so through all the mistakes and misfortunes of his business life.

There you have the two views on Reginald Maudling. This book is called *As It Seemed To Me*. Speak as you find. Doubtless I am influenced in my judgement by the fact that he was one of the most open and friendly among the senior politicians I have met. For once he decided to take a journalist into his confidence, he did not prevaricate. He would review the options as he saw them, and doubtless as they had been presented in numerous civil service briefs. He would give his judgement on each, ask courteously if I could see a hole in the reasoning, and invite other suggestions. He would treat any I made in the same open-minded way, sometimes taking notice when they were about Ireland, where he felt I had access to people he did not know; and even on the economy, where I found his views more congenial than those of any other Tory.

Edward Heath had a less self-questioning nature. He was a driven man, and remained so until some years after the end of his premiership, when the blessed mellowing of old age sometimes worked its magic on his personality. His supporters claimed that he was 'a man who gets things done', and his success in taking Britain into Europe justified that claim.

Douglas Hurd, from his perspective as Ted Heath's political secretary at Number 10, had valuable insight into what motivated his boss in the early days of his premiership. Heath believed that Macmillan had tended to drift, taking decisions only when they became inevitable, and without any strategy of government. He felt this even more strongly about his Labour predecessor, Harold Wilson. He used angrily to say that Wilson combined Macmillan's 'drift' style of government with an excess of public relations techniques. Heath may not have accepted it, but Macmillan was like Wilson in many ways. He was no slouch at public relations, either: it was he, after all, who first turned the *Visit to Moscow*, complete with fur hat, into an electoral art form, later to be adapted by Harold Wilson and Margaret Thatcher.

Heath determined to be different. Hurd described his method of government as: 'Here is a problem. This is the solution. How do we get from here to there?' I responded that this sounded too much like a certain kind of editorial-writing of which I disapproved: the assumption that every problem had a solution, when the truth often was that the best you could hope for was sensible amelioration or containment.

The difference in approach to economic policy between Heath and Maudling was quite fundamental, and I have no doubt that events proved Maudling right. The reason that Maudling, as Chancellor, had risked the 'dash for growth' was that he belonged to a school of political economy which sought to reconcile the 'dismal science' of economics with politics, 'the art of the possible'. It is when politicians attempt to treat their art as a science that things go awry, for they leave out the human factor.

Ted Heath was often criticised for being a loner. Douglas Hurd was firm in saying that he did have close private relations with some ministers: Alec Douglas-Home, Peter Carrington, Tony Barber and Willie White-law. The Prime Minister liked to start his day slowly, looking at the newspapers between nine and ten, having a bath, and ringing up people.

It was an unusual day when he did not ring one or other of those four, or indeed invite them in, specifically to talk about some departmental problem, but also for a more general political chat.

Mention of the newspapers reminded Hurd to make another contrast between Harold Wilson and Ted Heath, to his own boss's advantage. Wilson was shocked if a paper was unjust to him; whereas Heath was confirmed in his prejudice that the press would never give him a fair deal. For me, a journalist who enjoyed his morning diet of newsprint, this conjured up a frightful picture of what breakfast-time must be like for these rival Prime Ministers.

12

EUROPE SPLITS THE PARTIES

Europe has been a complicating factor in British domestic politics for three decades. In that time, the fundamental shift in the nation's constitution which it is gradually bringing about has shattered the unity of both main political parties. It is an unfinished – perhaps an unfinishable – story.

My account of this fascinating political drama, here and in later chapters, takes its colour from the jobs I was doing at various times. When Harold Macmillan sought entry to the then Common Market in the early sixties, I was labour correspondent of the *Guardian*, so knew less about de Gaulle's veto of this first Conservative application than about the earliest convulsions which Europe caused in the Labour opposition.

In the later sixties, when Harold Wilson, now Prime Minister, renewed Britain's attempt to gain membership, I was heavily engaged as news editor, so did not cover the second French veto. The shape of the Labour split to come was already visible, with Euro-doubters in the Cabinet deciding not to resign, because de Gaulle would do their work for them. But what would happen when the French eventually unlatched the door?

That happened in the early seventies, when Edward Heath achieved his long-standing ambition of taking Britain into Europe. The Conservative rebellion then was fierce, but containable. It was the Labour opposition which began to tear itself apart. The decisive vote on Europe came on 28 October 1971, when sixty-eight Labour MPs joined Roy Jenkins in the government lobby, with twenty others abstaining. Thirty-nine Conservatives rebelled and two abstained. Ted Heath had a majority of 112.

The seeds of Labour's worst schism for half a century were sown at that time, and came to harvest in the eighties. In the act of this long-running drama which took place in the seventies, I was close to the principal actors, Harold Wilson, Jim Callaghan and Roy Jenkins. The turbulence continued for several years, until Wilson, back in Downing Street in 1974, achieved a remarkable political catharsis. I shall describe that in Chapter 16. But even then the drama was not over.

As the curtain fell on what turned out to be the most profound period of Labour division, the Conservatives picked up the baton of discord. By the time Margaret Thatcher and John Major led the Tories through their European anguish, I had moved to the BBC and to the Press Gallery at Westminster. There I had a close view of what Chris Patten, later to become Tory chairman, considered the most dangerous schism for Conservatism since the Corn Laws a century and a half before.

In any account of how politicians have handled the European issue, the reader is entitled to know where the writer comes from, what baggage of opinion or prejudice he brings to the subject. I had better declare myself a Euro-enthusiast, though not, I think, a fanatic. For example, at one of Margaret Thatcher's early summits in Dublin, I annoyed *Observer* colleagues by supporting her case against excessive British budget contributions; whereas they shuddered at what our partners would see as another outburst from the 'Nation of Shopkeepers'.

But although I concede the right of Britain, like every other country, to fight its corner on the details of European politics, I have been convinced for at least the past twenty years that a tide in history is running. This has brought reconciliation among the ancient nations of our continent, ending the centuries of warfare which reached their nadir in the slaughter of the Somme, Arnhem and − most shamefully − the concentration camps.

Personally, I feel happier travelling in Europe than in the United States, Canada or Australia. Our common tradition as the cradle of Western history, literature, art and music far outweigh any practical difficulties of language. I am an indifferent, but enthusiastic amateur of the French and German languages, with a smattering of Italian. I understand why people who share the heritage of Michelangelo, Shakespeare, Beethoven, Goethe, and Monet think proudly of '*notre Europe*' or '*unser Europa*'. I wish we British could throw off our national disease, parochialism, and bring ourselves to think of 'our Europe'.

The economic arguments also seem compelling. British trade is now predominantly with Europe, and will increasingly be so. The sooner we cease to half-insist on the nostalgic self-indulgence of behaving like an offshore island, the better. As one forced by birth to bear a little of the burden of parochialism in John Bull's Other Island, I write with feeling.

If one Atlantic island cannot afford to refight for ever the battles of 1690 or 1916, neither can its neighbour indulge for ever in nostalgia for Crécy and Waterloo.

The tragedy of Britain's post-war isolation from Western Europe began with Churchill. Nobody can challenge his titanic qualities, but by the time European unity became an issue, he was too old and tired to give an inspiring lead. He was also, doubtless, conditioned by his wartime experience. I heard from a colleague at the *Observer* an amusing, but bizarre illustration of this. A friend of his, an army officer, was sent to discuss with Churchill, in his extreme old age, the arrangements for his funeral. These had been set out in what Whitehall calls 'a war book', a detailed plan for any major event which can be anticipated – and none is more predictable than death.

The officer expected that Churchill would simply leaf through the plans, and confirm them. But to his surprise the old man said he wished to change the arrangements for the cortège after it left St Paul's: instead of going by gun-carriage to Paddington Station, en route to his ancestral home at Blenheim, he wanted his coffin to be taken the short distance upriver by Admiral's Barge, and to leave from Waterloo. The officer pointed out that Paddington, on British Rail's Western Region, not Waterloo, on Southern Region, was the terminus for Blenheim. But Churchill, remarkably alert for a man of his age, recalled that there was a connection between Southern and Western Regions at Reading.

Seeing that the young officer was perplexed by his proposed change to the plan, the old man twinkled, and said: 'Look, if de Gaulle dies before me, we can stick to present arrangements. But if he's to be at the funeral, I want it to pass through Waterloo.'

Europe only became a live political issue in the sixties, when Macmillan sought British entry. I had no part in covering those negotiations, which were skilfully conducted by Ted Heath, until de Gaulle's veto ended them. But in my last couple of years as labour correspondent, the subject preoccupied the Labour opposition also.

The traumatic year was 1962. It was Harold Wilson's turn to be party chairman. Both he and Jim Callaghan were at that year's TUC in Blackpool, Wilson as Labour's fraternal delegate, Callaghan as shadow Chancellor. One lunchtime, Jim Callaghan invited me to join him and his old union, the Inland Revenue Staff Federation, who were gathered in Yates's Wine Lodge. There I was promised what that ancient institution – founded originally to wean the northern working classes away from gin — called 'champagne on draught'. The party actually consisted of a steady succession of *bottles* of champagne, but the effect of continuous process was achieved, and I felt distinctly weary when we emerged. Jim, who had a sailor's hollow legs, showed no effects, and suggested we go on the beach to eat whelks, mussels, or other seafood delights.

Remembering my duty to write the *Guardian*'s main report on the TUC, I insisted that it would be wiser to return to the Imperial Hotel for soup and roast beef. When we got there, most lunchers had finished, and Harold Wilson was eating on his own. We had an entertaining lunch together, because although the two men's relationship had its ups and downs over the years, like that of any two ambitious politicians of the same party, they enjoyed each other's company. When we were returning to the conference hall, Geoffrey Goodman, industrial editor of the *Daily Mirror,* joined us in the walk along the promenade. He and Callaghan were in front, Wilson and I behind. I was taking the opportunity to find out where all the leading Labour figures stood on Europe. The subject had not arisen during my social encounter with Callaghan, so I asked Wilson where he stood. The answer was a tease.

'I thought you journalists were supposed to be hawk-eyed observers of the scene. Have a look at the seat of Jim's trousers. Can't you see the mark of the fence?'

There were to be many fence-marks on many pairs of trousers before the European issue was settled. The general mood among Labour leaders, including Harold Wilson himself, was one of scepticism. He was a Commonwealth enthusiast, and feared membership of the Common Market would draw Britain in another direction, as indeed it inevitably did.

A month later, at the Labour Party conference, I had breakfast with Hugh Gaitskell in his hotel room. We continued our talk on the walk down to the conference hall, where he was to make his big speech. I gained no impression of what a hand-grenade he was about to toss into Labour politics. His friends, most of whom were pro-European, had been working hard to persuade him to support British entry.

What they heard instead was a powerful speech in which he denounced any thought that our entry into Europe could be decided on purely economic grounds, and declared that the end of 'a thousand years of history' was no trivial matter. Most delegates were delighted with the speech, for their leader, who had quarrelled with many of them over Clause IV and nuclear weapons, was at last articulating their own half-formed antagonism to the Common Market. Some feared British entry would mean abandonment of old friends in the Commonwealth. Others saw Europe, more simply, as a capitalist ramp.

But Gaitskell's pro-European friends were horrified. I walked back from the conference with Ray Gunter, then of the Transport Salaried Staffs Association, a Gaitskell loyalist. He was almost speechless with fury, just repeating over and over again: 'The bastard, the bastard.' Europe had produced a division on Labour's right which was not wholly healed by the time Gaitskell died three months later.

My personal insight into this story now moves on, past both de Gaulle's first veto of the Macmillan application, and the Labour government's conversion to the need for Britain to join. Among some of its members, this was a highly qualified conversion. But Harold Wilson and George Brown undertook a fact-finding tour of European capitals early in 1967, and on 2 May the Cabinet decided to make an application. Despite de Gaulle's opposition, the government pursued this for the remainder of its term, without success.

Britain's entry into Europe in 1973 will always be Ted Heath's political memorial. After all the vicissitudes since European unity began without Britain in the fifties, Heath pursued his convictions with that single-minded stubbornness which is the virtue of his faults.

Roy Jenkins, later President of the European Commission, who helped him to get British membership through parliament, said afterwards that Ted Heath would be a major figure in British political history for this alone; he set the country on a new political course. After the rebuff he had suffered as Macmillan's negotiator in the sixties, entry into Europe was a sweet triumph for him. He was determined that de Gaulle's veto must not be repeated by his successor, President Pompidou. Douglas Hurd, then his political secretary, believes the crucial event in the process was the Prime Minister's visit to Paris in 1971, when he convinced the French that Britain was now ready for entry.

Jim Prior, who as leader of the House was responsible for getting the legislation through, is equally sure about Ted's unique contribution. Nobody but him, with his powerful, driving conviction that this was where Britain's destiny lay, could have overcome difficulties at home, in the Commonwealth, and with what seemed then like an anti-European rump in the Tory Party. For Prior, everything else about the Heath premiership, except its brevity, which he thought tragic, pales into insignificance.

Reginald Maudling, who had never been a great enthusiast, worried about federalism, which he thought was the logical conclusion of entry. I thought that was the logic also, but this did not alarm me. If we were to have a European Union, I wanted it to be as democratically controlled as the member countries. Maudling said wearily that Geoffrey Rippon, the government's Common Market negotiator, maintained that federalism was all twenty years in the future, and not to worry about it now. Those twenty years have passed, and we still await effective democratic control of not only the Commission, but the Council of Ministers.

The story of Harold Wilson's European path after 1970 is less single-minded, or glorious, than Ted Heath's, though in the end it led to the same destination. When the cement of office is removed, and the power of patronage has gone, party unity is more fragile. Yet such unity has always been an obsession with Harold Wilson, a reaction against what he called Hugh Gaitskell's cavalier willingness to divide the left from the mainstream. He argued to me that the public was less excited by Europe than the politicians and the newspapers. His aim above all else was to prevent Europe doing any more damage to the Labour Party than was inevitable. There must be no bloodshed, since they would all have to work together when the debate was over.

Simultaneously, however, he kept in mind his wider political objective: for Britain to be in the Common Market. When Labour's row was blowing up into a gale in 1971, he assured anxious European socialist leaders that, if Heath did get Britain in this time, he would not allow Labour to be impaled on a commitment to come out. It was a long haul, and his reputation for deviousness was magnified during those years, but he eventually preserved both British membership and Labour unity.

How was this done, and, anyhow, why did Europe become such a divisive problem for a Labour leadership which had itself sought entry? After defeat in 1970, the party swung sharply to the left. Opposition to the Common Market was one symptom. Barbara Castle's justification for the failure of anti-European ministers like herself to resign in 1967 is the fissiparous tendency of governments of the left. George Brown, she argued, had been a great politician and an immense power in the Cabinet, but he was a Euro-fanatic. So why thwart George (not to speak of Roy Jenkins and his supporters), when de Gaulle might helpfully veto Labour's reconnaissance? Once in opposition, Barbara Castle was determined to oppose British entry, and during the referendum of 1975, when back in power, she took a leading part in the anti campaign.

Europe inevitably dominated the 1970 parliament, and almost destroyed the Labour Party. It drew Harold Wilson, Roy Jenkins and Jim Callaghan into a complex political gavotte, in which the party leadership, as well as party policy, was again at stake. Once Wilson left Downing Street, he began to write his book about the first term in government. He assured me he was also making more speeches than ever before, but he certainly approached the book with great energy.

He and Jim Callaghan met in the division lobby one night, and Callaghan confessed that, because of the interruptions inseparable from political life, he was making slow progress on his own book on Ulster. As they waited to vote, Harold described his day: a full programme at Westminster, a *Panorama* broadcast in the evening, back for the first vote in the House at ten, home to do a couple of hours on the book – 'mostly encomium for Jim Callaghan in Ulster' – and then back to the House for more votes. Callaghan was deeply envious of his leader's unstoppability.

Wilson had bad luck with the timing of the book, which though inevitably self-justifying, was better than many reviews suggested. By the time it appeared in July, however, Labour's rows over Europe had erupted, and that section of the book received almost all the attention. After my own review appeared in the *Guardian*, he thanked me for the second half (on general policy), which he found 'kind and understanding', but said it was a pity I had not resisted the temptation to do the European bit at the beginning. A literary editor would have agreed with him; a news editor could not.

As a meticulous historian of his government, Harold Wilson provided the materials to criticise his inconsistency over Europe. He reproduced the text not only of his own government's application for entry, but also that of Macmillan's. My review described the Macmillan document as 'Circumlocution Street', and noted that, if Wilson had chosen to use it, this would have provided a perfect text to allow for later retreat, if necessary. He had patently not intended that. His text was a model of precision, and left no doubt that this was not a probing operation, but that the Labour government was applying to join, no more, no less. These two texts, read together, effectively cut off his own retreat routes.

But Harold Wilson faced appalling problems in opposition. The way in which he handled these illustrates as well as any incident in this book the pressures which divide a political leader both from most of his followers, and from those, like myself, who comment on his activities. On the one hand, he had a group of enthusiastic pro-Europeans, led by Roy Jenkins. On the other, he had anti-European ex-ministers such as Barbara Castle, Tony Benn and Peter Shore, who were using the freedom of opposition to criticise the proposed British entry.

Roy Jenkins was by now deputy leader, having replaced George Brown, who lost his seat at the election. As he himself judges it, between his appointment as Chancellor at the end of 1967 and his resignation as deputy leader in the middle of 1972, he was by far Harold Wilson's most likely successor. And because many of his closest supporters despised Wilson, the thought of a Jenkins challenge for the leadership was always a possibility.

Yet the underlying reality was different, as Jenkins later acknowledged to me. Among MPs, who then elected the Labour leader, his position was weaker in opposition than it had been in government. Some blamed his too austere budgets for election defeat. Others feared that he adopted what Wilson had accused Heath of, 'a theological position' on Europe. This was where Wilson's other possible rival, Jim Callaghan, came in, for he was a man who relied on political feel, rather than ideology.

Callaghan used to scoff at the belief – of which he called me an adherent – that Europe was a great transcending issue, which must be above party politics. He was not willing to pull any chestnuts out of the fire for a now unpopular Conservative government. For him, the advantages and disadvantages of entry were quite evenly balanced. Europe was Labour's best chance of forcing the Conservatives out before the end of their term, and if he could find ways of doing that, he would.

Experiences with the French during his chancellorship had put the iron into Jim Callaghan's soul. In all those negotiations about sterling, the aloof arrogance of Giscard d'Estaing, then a senior functionary, had offended him as deeply as it later did Margaret Thatcher. In one of our many arguments about Europe, he expressed astonishment at my naïve assumption that European politics might be fun: 'What! Haggling with the French? The French are awful.' (My memory bowdlerises, for this was the only occasion I can recall when Callaghan resorted to the language he picked up in the navy during the war.)

He recalled his experiences in the OECD and other gatherings. He knew it sounded bad, but he feared the French would run rings around the British in the Common Market. He had not enjoyed his hours spent in the *couloirs*, while French politicians or diplomats blew cigar smoke over him. Then, when you believed you had agreed on something during the lunch-break, you got back into the meeting to find the French had changed their minds, and though the Germans, Italians and Dutch might talk behind their hands, they would all go along with the French in the end. At that stage in his career, Jim Callaghan's view of 'the partners' was not a cheerful one.

He and Harold Wilson saw Labour's dilemma in remarkably similar terms. Yet the Prime Minister, whose immediate differences were with Roy Jenkins, was still doubtful, at one stage, about what Jim Callaghan might be up to. He still thought Jim was 'a bit all over the shop' on Europe. Remarkably, in view of subsequent events, he felt that while he and Roy Jenkins were very close to each other personally, Callaghan was 'doing a bit here and there' – that is, stirring the political pot. It was amazing how, over the years, his attitude to his two possible successors oscillated, as did theirs to him.

Jim Callaghan was not preoccupied with thoughts of leadership at this time. When I saw him soon after I heard of Wilson's anxieties, he was feeling unwell, looked flushed, and complained that bad indigestion in the night was leaving him tired and without energy. He had suffered few health worries while in government, had not seen his doctor for ten years, and laughingly wondered whether opposition did not agree with him. Later, after a prostate operation, he was restored to good health, and his 'Sunny Jim' view of life.

Even when unwell, he displayed gallows humour. He expressed surprise that, unlike most journalists, I hadn't asked about his leadership ambitions. He said such matters could not interest a man with two peptic ulcers and throat cancer (which he had decided he was suffering from when he became hoarse before a recent speech). As he showed me out, he said; 'See you soon. No, I won't. But do try to come to the funeral, if it's a dry day.' I invited him to join an organisation I would form called Hypochondriacs Anonymous. In return, he counselled me against playing football for a new *Guardian* team now that I had reached my mid forties. We both noted each other's advice, and ignored it.

Callaghan, who has always had more self-awareness than he is given credit for, acknowledged that his enemies would say he was simply using the European issue to advance his own interests: finding where Labour Party opinion had reached, and putting himself at the head of it. That, he noted philosophically, was what enemies were for. But he knew his own weaknesses, and had examined himself about this. He was happy to know that his present attitude went back as far as 1962. His secretary had recently pulled out of her files a speech he had made then, and it read remarkably well in the light of his present attitude.

In Jim Callaghan's European tactics then, there was an indication of the shape of things to come over the next quarter century. During the entry negotiations, he wanted Labour to criticise Ted Heath for displaying excessive European zeal, rather than acting as a Prime Minister who safeguarded British interests. This was just the first occasion on which the 'easy touch' taunt was to be used. In the nineties, there was a remarkable exchange of roles between the two major parties. Labour's attitude to Ted Heath offered an accurate preview of what *Conservative* ministers in John Major's government in the nineties would say about *Labour* under John Smith and Tony Blair.

Jim Callaghan has always been a mature politician. He used to discuss Roy Jenkins' dilemma in surprisingly affectionate terms. When I asked whether he thought Jenkins would resign as deputy leader if Labour came out against entry, he wondered if it might be a good idea for him to go into the wilderness, so that in five years he might be regarded as the man of conviction the Labour Party would want as leader. But even if he were able to talk frankly to Jenkins, that might not be the wisest advice. He would need to do a head-shrinking job on his younger rival, discover how deep his feelings really were, and how badly he wanted to be leader of the Labour Party, and whether he was prepared to get down into the dirt for it. He would have liked to talk to Roy about this, and offer advice, or at least an opinion. But he realised that, coming from him, this would sound patronising. So far as I know, no conversation ever took place.

Among those who abstained in the European vote in 1971 was Tony Crosland. Like Harold Wilson, his principal concern was with party unity. At a lunch with Alastair Hetherington and myself in 1972, we asked whether Wilson was still keen on the job. There had been rumours he was wearied by constant criticism. His reply was enlightening. He reckoned Wilson enjoyed the most remarkable health for a politician. He had missed only one Cabinet meeting throughout his government, and he had not missed any shadow Cabinets at all, which was true of scarcely any other senior member. He believed Wilson would want to fight the next election, because his one abiding concern was to see himself going through the front door of Downing Street, as Ted Heath and his piano went out through the back. Harold Wilson had the appetite for winning elections of an instinctive politician.

Crosland was at his most extravagant that day in his criticism of the press. He declared he was going to waste no more time talking to Lobby correspondents, each of whom knew only about ten MPs, most of them encountered while at Oxford or Cambridge. Half of these were on the extreme left, and half of them Jenkins supporters. The Lobby were only just beginning to realise that there was a significant centre section of the Labour Party. He praised the *Guardian*'s political correspondent, Francis Boyd, for understanding this.

Tony went on to accuse the newspapers of being grossly unfair to Harold Wilson, over Europe, and more generally over his leadership. They demanded of him a standard of consistency they did not expect of Ted Heath. They did not recognise that a Labour leader's primary responsibility was to hold the party together over such difficult issues. He went on to argue eloquently that it was a misreading of history to think that political leaders were tremendously consistent. From Abraham Lincoln through Roosevelt, Lloyd George and others, a pattern of inconsistency ran. It was a spirited performance, and pleased as well as amused me, because Tony Crosland and I had many happy meetings at which we boxed and coxed over our opinions of Harold Wilson.

Both Crosland's pro-Wilson outburst, and Jim Callaghan's questioning of whether Jenkins was prepared to get down into the dirt and fight for the leadership, had echoes of a complaint Harold Wilson himself made later. He told colleagues that, during the long-drawn-out European debate, while others in the party leadership had been free to take stands on high principle, he himself had 'had to wade through shit' to maintain unity. Roy Jenkins, the most obvious target of this shaft, was later generous enough to acknowledge what Harold Wilson, by his own circuitous methods, achieved on Europe.

13

ROY JENKINS' DILEMMA

The latter half of Ted Heath's term in Downing Street was a turbulent period for his government, for Britain, for the opposition, and for me personally. On the opposition side, the key figure was Roy Jenkins, for his dilemma symbolised that of many in his party, and also foreshadowed the more cataclysmic Labour divisions of the following decade.

When Jim Callaghan was at odds with Harold Wilson in the late sixties, Jenkins had emerged as heir-apparent. By his leadership of Labour's European rebels in the seventies, he sacrificed his chance of leading Labour to his European principles. Harold Wilson says this division introduced 'a miserably unhappy period'. The wounds created then were not to be healed for years. Indeed, arguably they have never completely healed, and sowed the seeds which produced the Social Democrats' breach with Labour in the eighties.

Unlike Callaghan, Jenkins did regard Europe as a transcending issue. Without the votes of the dissident Labour MPs whom he led, Heath would not have won parliamentary approval for British entry into Europe. But after the exhilaration of the vote on 28 October 1971, Jenkins was oppressed by the compromises he had to make during the later stages of the legislation, so he resigned as deputy leader.

Europe was only one of the issues of the time, and not the one which caused trouble for me at the *Guardian*, for I was in accord with, sometimes ahead of, the paper's European enthusiasm. At home, the Heath government found halfway through its term that its economic policies were not producing results. His subsequent U-turn attempted to tackle the same complex of problems – inflation, incomes policy and relations with the trade unions – which had concerned me for almost twenty years.

The *Zeitgeist* was turning against the unions, as George Woodcock had warned them years before. Within the newspaper, I felt I was being cast as apologist for the unions, whereas I believed I had been among their more knowledgeable, though sympathetic critics. But the *Guardian* board of directors, on which I had been serving since 1969, was having endless trouble with its own print unions. Their follies washed off on the paper's attitudes to trade unionism as a whole, and also to the Labour Party, to which Alastair Hetherington had previously given broad support. When the February 1974 election came round, that affected my relations with him.

By the autumn of 1973, Roy Jenkins realised his resignation had left him with a huge personal dilemma. Ted Heath was facing conflict with the miners, and an election looked likely to come sooner rather than later. So Jenkins had to decide whether to stand again for election to the shadow Cabinet. At the Labour conference in October, he and his wife Jennifer invited me to have lunch with them.

He was bemused by his experience at Blackpool. Labour's is the most unpredictable of all the party conferences, perhaps because a collectivist political philosophy has never inhibited the most individualistic behaviour among the delegates. Roy had been uncertain about his current standing in a party whose grassroots shared popular doubts about his European stance. He had made a speech on the Tuesday morning when we met, and confessed that he had fully expected to be greeted with cheering, counter-cheering and perhaps a good deal of booing. So he had armed himself with an opening sentence: 'Well, that was a controversial reception, so let me make a controversial speech.' He had been non-plussed, though pleased, when there was no booing at the beginning and a surprising amount of applause at the end.

I discovered that the lunch was part of a wide trawl of opinions. He had already ruled out the possibility of running for the leadership against Harold Wilson. Right through that summer he had seriously considered such a challenge, though he knew he could not win. The argument in favour, as he explained it, was that it would be the most honest thing to do, to mark his disagreement with the direction in which Labour was going, and not only over Europe. He might also build up support for a future leadership election, as Wilson had done in 1960. But the damage to party unity was overwhelmingly against such a challenge.

The problem he saw about re-entering the shadow Cabinet was that he might find Labour's programme in the general election unconvincing to him. At that time, as well as Europe, a great controversy was raging about taking into public ownership Britain's largest companies. There were other disagreements over planning agreements, participation in industrial decision-making, and worker-directors. Most of these had arisen from grassroots disillusionment with the previous Labour government, and a feeling on the left – indeed, almost a chronic condition, which has had periodical resurgences ever since Ramsay MacDonald's betrayal in 1931 – that the party must tie down its leadership to specific policies.

Jenkins was more disillusioned with Wilson than I had ever heard him, and certainly less inclined to be tolerant about him than he was later. But these were strained times for Jenkins. He had a difficult decision to take. Paradoxically, the unspoken advice which his old rival, Jim Callaghan, had discussed with me had echoes in his own mind. The wilderness had attractions for him. But he knew he would not be forgiven if he did not play his part in driving the Tories from office. So he floated an idea: what if he were to serve on the front bench in opposition, but not to take office if Labour were elected?

I apologised in advance for replying so brutally to this. My judgements on politicians' actions is normally given, not to their faces, but in the happy never-never land of media commentary, which is my natural habitat. But I asked whether his proposal would not be tantamount to saying to the public: 'I recommend a Labour government to you. It is a Labour government which is good enough to govern you, but not good enough for me to serve in.' His eyes lit up at this, and he said it roughly represented his dilemma. But could I realise how uncongenial it was for a person who had been Home Secretary and Chancellor of the Exchequer in his forties to accept office in a government whose policies he would not be happy with?

My suggestion was that the only course open to him was to go into the government, but continue to fight for the policies in which he believed. That has always seemed to be the inevitable course for a party politician, until he feels the strains so intolerable that he decides to change parties or leave politics. Jenkins' experience was that fighting successfully inside a Cabinet was easier said than done, and he wondered how real such a fight would be. Jennifer Jenkins was clear in her view that he must first attempt to return to the shadow Cabinet that autumn, and leave the decision whether to join the government until after the election. Roy Jenkins thought the election of Labour was much less certain than Tory unpopularity made it appear on the surface. But he reminded me that when a government was being formed, he would have only forty-eight hours to make up his mind.

His memoirs later recorded that all his followers among Labour MPs wanted him to stand for the shadow Cabinet, as did a group of moderate union leaders with whom he dined a few days after our lunch. The following week, Willy Brandt gave the same advice. So the Labour movement at home and abroad was in favour of his return to the front line. David Steel, not yet Liberal leader, but a friend, understandably urged him to stay off the Labour front bench. Another old friend, Sir Nicholas Henderson, British Ambassador in Bonn – who was later to show how little his diplomatic role inhibited him in expressing political opinions critical of the Labour government he was then serving – gave similar advice: he 'thought it much more sensible for me to keep my distance from Wilson'.

In the event, he did return to the shadow Cabinet that November. I might, with the benefit of hindsight, have detected hints of more significant things to come. Behind Roy Jenkins' difficulty in deciding his own future was a belief that the Liberals would do well, and that no politician could know how thin the ice on the present party structure might be. If I had only had the wit to understand, the seeds were there of his decision in the early eighties to 'break the mould' of British politics. But they were only in embryo. It took two difficult years of serving in another Labour government, his final loss of the premiership to Jim Callaghan, and four years of detachment and reflection as President of the European Commission in Brussels, before the discontents I detected in Blackpool in 1973 produced their explosive result.

There could scarcely have been a greater contrast in political natures than that between Roy Jenkins and Harold Wilson. An incident involving Roy Hattersley, by now in the shadow Cabinet and acting as education spokesman, brought home to me the extent to which Wilson, while Prime Minister, had developed further the pragmatic attitudes which divide him from the other protean character in this book, Margaret Thatcher.

Before reaching the shadow Cabinet, the ambitious Hattersley had toiled away at politically difficult briefs: employment, defence, and foreign affairs. He was pleased to be handling education, where his own natural radicalism had an outlet. He made some rumbustious pronouncements on public schools and on educational deprivation, but was at once amused and slightly worried to hear that Harold Wilson had told intimates: 'The difficulty about Hattersley since he took over education is that he has "got religion".'

Hattersley recognised the description: for the first time in his decade in parliament, during which he had watched other people carrying banners, full of certitude about nuclear weapons, he himself was carrying a banner – i.e. 'getting religion' – on behalf of the educationally deprived.

He gloomily suspected that when Labour returned to power he would be given another difficult department, or else would become a spending minister, only to be thwarted by a Labour Chancellor bent on economies. But in the meantime, he and his wife Molly, a comprehensive school head, were idyllically happy.

By then, Harold Wilson was distrustful of enthusiasm, almost as distrustful as a traditional Tory such as Ian Gilmour worrying about Margaret Thatcher's ideological excesses. His description of a young politician 'getting religion' will strike those who pride themselves on political ideology as cynical. But there is a real lesson here about the deep divide between those who lead parties and even their most senior colleagues.

The leaders are set apart by the unique duty imposed on them by the democratic process and the party system. This is to ensure that their party is elected to government, because they believed in its essential merits. By the early 1970s, after the shock of his only election defeat, Harold Wilson had become profoundly cautious about any radical initiative which might conceivably thwart that objective. Nobody could argue that his anxiety about his party's prospects was unjustified. Labour was not favourite to win the 1974 election. The damage done to its popular standing by devaluation proved lasting – as it was to do, many years later, for John Major's government.

Those who find the whole party political process distasteful, and yearn for politicians who have 'principles' of policy to which they stick, will have no doubt that the attitudes I have ascribed to Harold Wilson and Jim Callaghan on the Labour side, and such Tory pragmatists as Willie Whitelaw or Peter Walker, are mistaken ones. I would set against this the Burkeian principle that an MP 'owes you not his industry only, but his judgement'.

Burke is usually called in aid of MPs whose constituency parties are trying to bully them into conformity, and properly so. But his principle can be more widely applied. Politicians offer their 'judgement' to the public by standing unashamedly as 'party men'. This allows voters to choose among parties, not simplistically according to their manifestos, but also according to each party's long-standing traditions and attitudes, which will guide individual judgements made by their leaders. Such traditions are widely, if not precisely, understood by voters. This method should elect whichever party accords with the prevailing public mood, and turn it out when that mood changes.

There are politicians who believe a political party can only renew its powers, and purge itself of wrong ideas, in the pure waters of opposition.

Woodrow Wyatt argued that about Labour. In the nineties, some right-wing Conservatives, disillusioned by the change between the Thatcher and Major leaderships, have used the same argument. It is a luxury in which those who lead parties cannot afford to indulge themselves. For in politics, as in life, 'the moving finger writes, and having writ moves on . . .' And chances to govern are rare.

By 1973, with a general election looking ever more likely, doubts about Harold Wilson's leadership began to evaporate. For all the criticisms of his inconsistency, he was seen to have guided Labour through that stage of its European crisis in a way that nobody else could have equalled. By then, Labour MPs wanted to win a general election.

Although Europe and the leadership preoccupied many of the Labour people I talked to during the later Heath years, the more difficult issue, the one to which no politician seemed to have a convincing answer, was how to deal with the central economic problem: high inflation and unruly industrial relations. If the Labour government's plans for trade union reform had never been tried, at least in their original legislative form, Ted Heath's Industrial Relations Act had been tested and had failed, with the Official Solicitor hastily called in to end a dock strike by conjuring dockers out of jail.

In the early days in opposition, Harold Wilson told me he hoped the TUC, after the shock of tough treatment by the Conservatives, might be more willing to do a deal on incomes policy with Labour. In a speech in New York in May 1971, he set out more clearly than ever before the ideas in which he believed. A voluntary compact between government and both sides of industry would allow ministers to introduce economic policies aimed at increasing production and national wealth, without fear of inflation. So long as government could rely on industrial cooperation and restraint, the sacrifices required of workers would be related to a guarantee of full employment and greater social justice.

This was an exposition of what I believed – and still believe – to be realistic economics. It was Harold Wilson who had convinced me of this many years previously. What was new was his expectation that such a policy would probably emerge from some kind of national crisis. In the account of this lecture in his book, *Final Term*, he reproduces the leading article I wrote in the *Guardian*. This speculated about whether this crisis would be unemployment, unacceptable inflation, and/or a balance of payments crisis.

At that time, unemployment under Ted Heath's government had reached the then staggering level of 800,000, without obvious impact on wage settlements. My editorial railed at the hypocrisy of union leaders who wanted Heath to do something about this unemployment, but did not think they themselves had any responsibility. It was another year before he faced them with this problem. Ted Heath made a valiant, and for a time successful attempt to restrain wages, by statutory methods, but with union support. Yet before he faced the voters, the chances of any permanent policy seemed as distant as ever.

14

A STORMY WEEKEND IN 1974

The year 1974 was when my career began the turn which led me, some years later, and almost by accident, into broadcasting. This personal move was intricately connected with national politics, so the two stories are best told together.

From 1972 onward, Ted Heath's government adopted more pragmatic policies than those on which it had fought the 1970 election, the Selsdon programme. It had been educated by events: by the damage which would be done if the government allowed great industrial firms to collapse, throwing thousands of workers on to the dole; by the dangers of leaving wage settlements entirely to the vagaries of the labour market.

After the government had lost office in 1974, Keith Joseph and Margaret Thatcher decided that this U-turn into industrial intervention and incomes policies was a profound mistake, although it had been taken by a Cabinet of which they were both members. The decisive turning point in post war politics came in 1975, when Thatcher challenged and replaced Heath as Tory leader, and led her party in a more ideological direction than ever before.

These events were the background to our own debate about public policy at the *Guardian*. As it turned out, by the time Margaret Thatcher was well settled into her new job as leader of the opposition, I had been around the world in twenty-one days, and had left the *Guardian* to take up *my* new job on the *Observer*. This ridiculously Jules Verne-like journey, to three developing countries, Kenya, Sri Lanka and the Philippines, and to the World Bank in Washington, had to be squeezed in between obligations to the two newspapers, and was in preparation for writing a quick book about Third World unemployment and poverty. But that is a story for later.

Accounts of what seemed to us on the *Guardian* a significant debate about the direction the paper should take have been given in its official history for that period (*Changing Faces* by Geoffrey Taylor, formerly foreign and northern editor) and in the memoirs of the then editor, *Guardian Years* by Alastair Hetherington. This briefer account is what my title implies, 'as it seemed to me'. What happened may seem of no great importance to many non-journalists, but it mattered to myself and others, at the time and since, so I am setting down briefly my view of these events, for the first – and I expect the last – time.

What gave this internal newspaper debate about national politics its spice was that it became enmeshed with the selection of an editor to succeed Alastair Hetherington, when he moved to be Controller of BBC Scotland in 1975. None of us knew during the turbulent political years, 1973 and 1974, that he intended to leave the paper. He had been its editor for nineteen years, during most of which its commercial future was in constant doubt. Only a man of immense strength and dedication could have borne the burden for so long.

My relationship with him was a good one, and despite political and journalistic disagreements at the end, we remain friends. We were both workaholics, fascinated by what we were doing. He wanted a strong-minded deputy, and he got one, perhaps to excess. Over Ulster, after long cooperation, we disagreed, and I will mention that in a separate chapter on the Irish crisis. But the decisive disagreement was over British domestic politics.

Alastair concludes a kind and generous comment on my contribution to the *Guardian*: 'Our differences over the 1974 elections were not painful.' They were painful to me. The paper's historian, Geoffrey Taylor, clearly regards them as a significant factor in why I failed, apparently by six votes to four, to win the editorship, which I wanted more than any other job before or since.

With the benefit of hindsight, there are other reasons why I believe Peter Preston was a wiser choice than myself. By age, temperament and interests, he has been able to keep the *Guardian* in tune with the rapidly changing, and to me exotic, culture of this *fin de siècle*, in a way which would not have engaged my more narrowly focused mind. So it all turned out for the best, for Peter, the paper and me. While politics may have played a decisive part in the choice of editor, it is not necessarily politics which sells even serious newspapers; though a serious journalist ought to take his paper's politics seriously, and we all did.

In Hugh Gaitskell's time, Alastair had not known Harold Wilson well. As I mention earlier, at the then shadow Chancellor's request I promoted a meeting. After Wilson became leader, the two men met often. Any Labour leader was likely to try to woo the editor of the *Guardian*, as both Gaitskell and Wilson did. In that period it was the only broadsheet paper from which Labour could expect anything other than unrelenting opposition. Just before the 1974 election, Jim Callaghan, apparently with Harold Wilson's knowledge and approval, made a last desperate attempt to persuade Alastair to support Labour. Alastair resented this, and it was probably counter-productive.

Many leading Labour figures felt that the *Guardian* was 'their paper': it was what they read first in the mornings; they would enquire with genuine anxiety from Alastair and myself when the company's finances were in crisis; and would complain bitterly when they felt unfairly treated in its columns. Harold Wilson once said that the *Miscellany* column was as inaccurate as *Private Eye*; but added philosophically that at least it was better written; and waspishly, that you knew the printing errors were genuine, rather than jokes. When the *Guardian* harshly disapproved of Jim Callaghan's position on an immigration issue, his wife, Audrey, cancelled their home order.

Despite Labour people's feelings of intellectual intimacy, none of us on the paper accepted that it ought ever to go closer to that party than as a normally friendly, but sometimes acerbic critic. I had no doubt myself about the *Guardian*'s natural place in the political – and therefore also in the commercial – market-place. It was as an independent left-of-centre paper. How independent? In my belief, quite unwilling to toe any party line, as the disillusioned article I wrote about Labour before the previous election in 1970 illustrates.

Just before the first 1974 election, Roy Hattersley and I had a brief exchange which catches the differing postures of politician and journalist. The occasion was a major speech he had made on education. He had with difficulty dissuaded his working party from writing angry letters to the paper, complaining that the *Guardian* had been less generous in its editorial comment than the *Times Educational Supplement* and others. I said that I was sure he did not expect us to be 'a left-wing *Daily Telegraph*', because our readers were not the kind of people who could be marched up and down by a Grand Old Duke of York, disguised as an editor. After recent divisions in his party over Europe, I argued, he must, as a pro-European, realise this.

Roy sadly accepted the argument, 'as a rational being'. But he added that, since he regarded the attitudes of other newspapers to his party as being corrupt, he had this irrational wish that the *Guardian* could be comparably corrupt/loyal on the other side. He was not actually advocating such an editorial course, but said it was just natural for party politicians to wish they had some dependable support. He reported

Gaitskell as having once said to Woodrow Wyatt, then a Labour MP, and a close friend: 'You support me when I'm right. What I need is people who support me when I'm wrong.' Gaitskell had borrowed this paradox from Melbourne. In any event, it was not a course available to the heirs of C.P. Scott.

By the later years of the Heath government, Alastair had fallen out of love with Labour. More specifically, he and others were fed up with the trade unions. This was an area where the conduct of the business and the editorial policy of the newspaper overlapped. At one of our board meetings, a comparatively trivial incident blew up into a storm. The engineering unions were proposing a one-day strike, which Newspaper Publishers' Association lawyers believed was in breach of Ted Heath's Industrial Relations Act. Our chairman, Peter Gibbings, himself a lawyer by training, brought this news from an NPA meeting, and commended their advice: that to accept an advertisement from the union, urging its members to support the strike, would leave us open to claims for damages from any engineering company which could quantify its losses.

To me, this financial risk seemed nugatory; the NPA and its lawyers were playing politics. I argued that to reject this advertisement would introduce a dangerous principle of censorship, and urged the practical case against giving our own print unions a future excuse for interfering with the contents of the paper. Others were against such pragmatism, arguing that this was a matter of principle, or perhaps of financial risk.

I forced a vote, for the first time in the history of the *Guardian* board. Peter Gibbings' recommendation was carried by five votes to three. The production director, Harvey Thomas, who had to deal with the print unions, voted with me, as did the editor. I assume Alastair saw some merit in my argument about censorship, but he thought I had been maladroit in forcing him and myself into a minority position on the board. It was one of only two occasions during a long friendship when we had a shouting-match.

The other was during the weekend of the general election of 28 February 1974. After the dispute with the miners which had caused Ted Heath to put industry on a three-day week, he had called this election on the issue of 'who governs?' The result was indecisive: the Conservatives were down 26 seats to 296, Labour up 14 to 301. Some combination of smaller parties held the balance of power: the Liberals had 14, Scottish Nationalists 7, Plaid Cymru 2, and there were 11 Unionists and 2 Nationalists from Ulster.

At this crucial period in British politics, the *Guardian* was in serious danger of having its production stopped by a strike of its journalists over pay. So I spent one of the most fascinating weekends of recent political history locked in the boardroom, together with the managing director, Gerry Taylor, and others, in sustained negotiations. These were with my own union, the National Union of Journalists (of which I am now an honorary Life Member). Because of our good relations at the *Guardian* then, nobody thought it anomalous that an NUJ member should also be one of the board's negotiators.

My principal preoccupations were to avoid a strike, which in such a significant political period would gravely damage the paper; but to avoid a pay increase on anything like the scale the NUJ was seeking, which was financially insupportable for what remained a perilously poised business. My industrial relations experience until then had been as a reporter or commentator, but I tried out skills I had observed in others.

One was to persuade Gerry Taylor that the best way to reach a settlement was to keep the negotiations in almost permanent session. As a result, we sat on Friday from mid afternoon until two o'clock on Saturday morning; we reassembled at eleven a.m., and stayed until midnight; and we continued from Sunday before lunchtime until six o'clock on Monday morning, without a break. On one occasion, I suffered blurring of my vision, and assumed this was a result of tiredness. But one of the union negotiators pointed out that I had picked up his spectacles by mistake. Many feeble jokes were made about 'seeing this through our eyes'. In the course of these marathon talks, we reached a pay settlement of a size that was manageable.

I was frustrated that almost everything I was interested in – the paper's coverage of the election aftermath, and particularly of the negotiations between Ted Heath and Jeremy Thorpe – was being conducted in the editorial department, at the other end of the corridor, while I haggled over ha'pence in the boardroom. So I was irritated, when I was reporting to Alastair that we had averted a strike without incurring a crippling pay settlement, to be tackled on a minor concession Gerry Taylor and I had agreed to: paternity leave. This was a few days off work for new fathers, more common now than it was then.

Alastair thought this innovation, though unlikely to torpedo the company's finances, was unnecessary. He reminded me that he and I had fathered four children each without benefit of such leave. I was feeling deprived of both sleep and politics, so enquired testily whether he would have preferred a strike, which this *pourboire* had helped to avert.

The incident was of no importance, except as a hint of a less easy relationship than we had enjoyed before. It was certainly minor compared with our disagreements over the *Guardian*'s policy during the election period. In the previous year the editor had held a series of discussions with senior staff, during which it became clear that most of them, including myself, thought a change of government was needed. We shared some of Alastair's doubts about the state of the Labour Party, but Harold Wilson, in his own pragmatic way, was winning his internal battles: to avoid a commitment to come out of Europe or to nationalise everything in sight. We believed he had more chance of bringing industrial peace and social justice than the Conservatives.

By this stage, Alastair had lost faith in pragmatism, and was looking for a solution to Britain's long malaise. He was seriously worried that the country was becoming 'ungovernable', and saw the solution either in continuation of Heath's government, or in some form of coalition, which would avoid sharp changes of direction in policy. This latter was the view of some businessmen in the sixties, when there was muddled talk about 'a businessmen's government'. In its new form, under the initial prompting of the Liberal leader, Jeremy Thorpe, it had become 'a government of national unity' – GNU, for short, meaning a coalition of Conservatives, Labour and Liberals.

At various times, before and after the two elections of 1974, the *Guardian* was to advocate Lab-Lib-Nat, Con-Lib-Lab, and GNU admin-istrations. The leading article with which I disagreed most was on 4 March, just after the first election. This said: 'Logically the situation points to a Grand Coalition of all three parties, possibly with Mr Thorpe at its head. Although it is unlikely to come about, it would represent the nearest approach to what the public appears to want.' The logic of the last sentence, in particular, eluded me. The Conservative and Labour parties had each gained almost 12 million votes; the Liberals had received a little over half of this. Fewer than twenty per cent of the votes cast did not seem like a copper-bottomed democratic claim for Jeremy Thorpe to have the keys of Downing Street.

For me, the disagreement had two elements. The first was an honest difference between Alastair and myself about the purpose of newspaper leading articles. I believe them to be exercises in the art of the possible, an attempt to seek serious solutions which might feasibly be applied. I feared any drift into wish-fulfilment. I believed my approach fell well within the tradition of C.P. Scott, who argued that the task of the *Guardian* was 'to play on the minds and consciences of men'.

I disliked editorials which advised readers to vote Liberal where there was a strong candidate, Labour where their man or woman was not a mad left-winger, and Conservative where their candidate had a specially honourable record. This was not the real world: readers were capable of

making up their own minds about how to vote in their own constituencies. All they required from us was a clear statement about which
party the *Guardian* believed would provide the best government at that
time.

The second factor concerned the state of the British national press as
a whole, which by then was overwhelmingly hostile to Labour. This
anxiety, again, had roots deep in the *Guardian*'s history, from a time
when the paper had once before supported coalition. In 1931, when
Ramsay MacDonald split Labour by forming a National Government,
the senior staff was bitterly divided. The social issue was profound: the
cutting of unemployment benefit for working people already devastated
by the great depression. Ted Scott, who had recently succeeded his
father, the great C.P., as editor, was on holiday. The man left in charge,
W.P. Crozier, came out for the coalitionists. Scott, on his return, switched
the editorial line, and opposed the coalition.

The *Guardian* historian of that period, David Ayerst, encapsulated the
significance of this incident, and pointed up a contrast I saw between
the decision taken then, and what happened in 1974 and later. Ayerst
took Scott's reversal of the pro-coalition policy as a turning point in the
paper's history. He wrote: 'Thus in two months Ted Scott had taken the
paper from a position where a continued drift to the Right might have
been expected, to the empty place on the Left where it was needed.'

In the seventies and eighties, it seemed to me, the right half of
British politics enjoyed properly critical support from most broadsheet
newspapers, and unquestioning support from most tabloids. Only the
Daily Mirror consistently supported the left. As I had explained to Roy
Hattersley, the *Guardian* certainly must not be a mouthpiece for the
Labour Party. But there was little doubt about 'the empty place ... where
it was needed.'

Even before the drama of 1931, C.P. Scott, though himself a Liberal
MP for a time, had seen the significance of the replacement of his own
party by Labour, in the first half of the century, and had given the new
party fair wind. It was to understand the Labour Party, after all, that he
appointed my namesake as the first labour correspondent. Now, I
thought, we were in danger of ignoring the dramatic changes in British
political history which had taken place, particularly since 1945, and were
hankering after an unobtainable Liberal past. In retrospect, the difference
between us was a forerunner of those which took place in 1981, across
the left-of-centre political spectrum, and led to the Social Democratic
schism.

Alastair and I conducted a running debate on these matters, as did other senior members of the staff. But it was in one of the comfort breaks from the negotiations with the NUJ, in the crucial first weekend of March 1974, that I realised my arguments had outstayed their welcome. Alastair, Jean Stead, the news editor, and myself were standing outside his room, as I asked to be brought up to date with the news I had missed while locked in the negotiations, and offered my views about what ought to happen.

I do not remember the argument as being particularly fierce, though admittedly my idea of the threshold of fierceness may be higher than that of others. Suddenly, Alastair said angrily that I was not going to be able to bully him on this occasion, turned on his heel, and headed off in the direction of the gents' lavatory. Jean and I looked at each other in astonishment. She asked me what this was about, and I said I didn't know.

I did not know either that a contest for succession to the editorship was to come a year later. If I had, this would have been the moment to conclude that I would not have the important support of the outgoing editor.

15

WILSON'S FINAL TERM

Harold Wilson's final term as Prime Minister, from February 1974 until March 1976, coincided with two of the most important turning points in British politics since the war: the replacement of Ted Heath as Conservative leader by Margaret Thatcher in February 1975; and the beginning of Tony Benn's campaign to set Labour on an irreversible road towards socialism. It was also a turning point in my own career, for in the spring of 1975, staff at the *Guardian* enjoyed their own little 'leadership campaign', leaving only the two leading candidates to be editor, Peter Preston and myself, feeling that politics was not nearly as enjoyable a participant sport as our colleagues thought.

Three days after Peter became editor, the *Observer* asked me to join them. So the climax of the second Wilson government came in a disjointed period for me. I had already been contracted by the International Labour Organisation, the oldest of the United Nations agencies, to write a popularising book in advance of a conference on Third World employment, to take place in Geneva in 1976. I remained at the *Guardian*, writing the leading articles on the European referendum in June 1975, then went round the world for the rather frenzied research for this book, and turned up at the *Observer* in August, to take on the domestic political editorials.

The actual writing of the short book (*The Poor of the Earth*) was equally arduous. Knowing I was returning to London to start a new job, I used to get my typewriter out on long journeys across Indian, Pacific or Atlantic Oceans. Sometimes I met the same friendly cabin crew members I had encountered on earlier legs of the journey: their rest periods in delightful places like the Seychelles seemed to take about as long as my working visits to Nairobi, Colombo or Manila. They would find me three seats together in the back row, where I could spread out my papers or, *in extremis*, myself.

When I got home there was a heatwave, so I wrote the rest of the book sitting in my shorts each evening after a day's work at the *Observer*. As I wrote, I had to peruse the economists' reports on which the conference was to be based. The hot weather may have been a factor, but I concluded that development economists do not always produce pellucid prose. I do not recommend mine as the ideal method of authorship.

Between times, I observed the new Labour government. Harold Wilson, restored to office, thought not to his former vigour, had to cope with a party which was always teetering on the edge of rebellion. In opposition, he had been simultaneously seasoned and made weary by the herculean task of preventing Labour flying assunder. In February 1974 he gained no overall majority, and had a margin of only four over the Conservatives. Even after a second election in October, his majority over the combined opposition was only four, fatally vulnerable to by-election losses.

He faced three connected policy problems: Europe, inflation and unemployment. Labour had been elected almost by default, because the Heath government ran into the sands of conflict with the miners, and the three-day week. Loose talk that Britain was becoming 'ungovernable' found some echoes even in the sober corridors of the *Guardian*. Profound suspicion of trade unions was the flavour of the times. Another worry was Trotskyist infiltration of the Labour Party. That boil was to fester for another decade before Neil Kinnock finally lanced it.

Harold Wilson had too many balls in the air for comfort: the decline in manufacturing, inflation, unemployment, public doubts about both trade unions and left-wing plans for public ownership, and Labour's internal troubles. Yet he could not afford a great row with his left wing before the European referendum was safely over.

For his most immediate battle was to resist attempts to take Britain out of Europe. By converting Tony Benn's proposal for a referendum to his own, quite different purposes, he achieved what he knew was right: to keep Britain inside Europe. He did this, without destroying his party, through a skill that came close to political genius. History is already beginning to judge Harold Wilson's efforts more generously than did his contemporaries. The way in which he handled the European issue is an intriguing story, on which I hope to cast fresh light in a later chapter.

The economic inheritance in March 1974 was not a happy one. Wilson himself said, four months after taking over, that the outlook was just as dark as suggested in the many gloomy articles we were publishing in the *Guardian*. A second election was inevitable, but when Alastair

Hetherington suggested to him that, with world and British economic conditions as bad as they were, nobody in his right mind would want to be re-elected, he replied that if you assumed you could handle such a crisis better than others, you wanted to retain office. That is ultimate political reality.

Harold Wilson always thought it was worthwhile to be in government, not simply for reasons of ambition, but for what he could achieve. I believe that to be true of most political leaders, of all parties. Towards the end of this second period in office, Harold gave me a modest assessment of what he hoped would be permanent improvements in the condition of the people. It was practical, rather than grandiose: increases in the basic pension, and a new earnings-related superannuation scheme, which Barbara Castle had agreed with the Conservatives, in the hope that it would survive from governments of one party to the other. (In the event, the Thatcher government drastically revised it.) He added these to achievements in his first term: the Open University, which he had created over much criticism; and a separate Overseas Development Department, which reflected his own long-standing interest in the Third World.

Wilson's sober opinion of the economic outlook was commonly held: the whole of the Western world was in deep recession, after a quadrupling of oil prices at the end of 1973. Britain's inflation was already fifteen per cent, and the new government also faced the dangerous detritus of Ted Heath's incomes policy – just as Ted had been forced to pick up what Labour left behind in 1970. The Conservatives' threshold agreements meant that rising prices would automatically trigger wage increases.

People began to murmur about 'Latin American inflation'; often the same people, astonishingly, who during the Heath era had hared off after the latest fashion, inflation accounting. Some even advocated a system of indexing most aspects of the economy, including wages. This had been conceived as a good idea under the military government in Brazil.

By coincidence, I was invited to visit Brazil for three weeks during 1974. Because this was a dictatorship, I went fearing I would meet a blank wall of non-communication, by people too frightened to talk freely. Instead, the governor of the central bank invited me to his home in Brasilia for a lunchtime swim, and spoke freely, not only about the deplorable human rights record of the government, but also about economic policy. On that visit, I confirmed a view that military governments had little to commend them; and also concluded that indexation was not the panacea some people thought. Brazil's inflation record ever since has been disastrous.

By contrast, four months after Labour took office, the new General Secretary of the TUC, Len Murray, persuaded me that Britain was not facing some new, hyper-inflationary phenomenon, but more of the same that we had sadly experienced before. He predicted that price inflation would rise to a peak of twenty-five per cent, and then come down, under the influence of a series of voluntary incomes policies negotiated by industry, the unions and government. Twenty-five per cent sounded frightening enough at the time – and made a considerable hole in the twenty years of (un-indexed) pension contributions I left behind at the *Guardian* in 1975 – but Murray's forecast proved to be right, to within a couple of percentage points.

Harold Wilson left negotiations with the TUC to Denis Healey and Michael Foot. Healey, like Roy Jenkins, favoured 'a proper dinner', so instead of beer and sandwiches at Number 10, there was more substantial fare at Number 11. They agreed in 1975 to a £6 a week limit on pay increases. At the TUC Congress that September, I had a revealing discussion with Jack Jones and half a dozen of his union's regional and trade group officials. Jones said gloomily that unemployment was all too likely to be their real incomes policy in the following year. His colleagues told me that there was no great push on wages from their members. Many of these, in unskilled or semi-skilled jobs, probably did better under the flat-rate policy.

As well as inflation, Harold Wilson had inherited rising un-employment. I was told he was 'worried sick' about the economic blizzard he knew was coming. Britain might be heading back to the thirties. In our last talk in Downing Street, towards the end of 1975, he told me one of the reasons he had decided not to join the *Guardian* when he graduated in 1937 was that Beveridge had asked him to work on unemployment. His father, whom I used to meet at Labour conferences, had two long spells out of work in the thirties. Harold had a strong sense of family, and remained close to his parents until their deaths, so he had no doubt this was what he ought to do.

He reminded me that he had always been an industrial economist, and added, with the touch of flattery he rarely resisted, 'like you'. I felt obliged to remind him I had never studied economics, having merely picked up what I could, from people like himself, while pounding my various journalistic beats. He said he meant that we had both always been primarily concerned in our economic thinking or writing about industry and jobs, rather than just money.

This was why, although he had vetoed the left's attempt to commit his government to nationalise Britain's largest companies, he was keen on the National Enterprise Board. Its aim was to channel government money into manufacturing industry. By 1974, the decline of British manufacturing, which has since afflicted successive governments with permanent anxiety over the balance of payments, was under way with a vengeance. Wilson saw the NEB as a non-doctrinaire activity to help industries with investment capital. This was a modern alternative to the old Keynesian public works cliché of the thirties: having to pay the unemployed 'to dig holes and then fill them in'.

Despite the documents which poured out from Labour's left-controlled National Executive, I had neither expectation nor fear that there would be any rash extension of public ownership into manufacturing. My attitude was largely based on conversations with Harold Wilson during the opposition years, when he was notably cooler on the subject of public ownership, as a pragmatic instrument of industrial policy, than even the *Guardian*, at least for a time, was.

In the sixties, the paper had been concerned about regional unemployment: Alastair Hetherington's origins were in Scotland, mine in Belfast, and those of Bernard Ingham, another increasingly urgent political voice in the office, in the north of England. The less ideological Tory governments of the fifties and early sixties had tried to help the depressed areas with grants to new industry, and by guiding investment there through the negative weapon of refusing Industrial Development Certificates in the crowded south and Midlands. Reginald Maudling had taken a brave, if much criticised stand on IDCs for the motor industry, and achieved success in Scotland and on Merseyside. Quintin Hailsham was active in the north east.

When these methods did not cure chronic unemployment in some regions, selective public investment to create new enterprises seemed not unthinkable, certainly a logical extension of Conservative government methods which Labour might reasonably try. But it soon became clear to me that so long as Harold Wilson was in charge, the 'risk' for the taxpayers' risk capital would be strictly monitored.

But it was trade union abuses, as much as fright about public ownership, which drew press criticism. Just before Harold Wilson retired in March 1976, Shirley Williams retailed to me the renewed rumour that he was about to do so. She then said sweetly, in premature political obituary, that at least Harold had dispersed all that talk about the country being ungovernable. Shirley attributed press hostility towards even sensible trade unionism to an assumption that the poisonous industrial relations of Fleet Street mirrored what was happening in British industry as a whole. She said sadly that too many people no longer acknowledged the need for trade unions even to exist.

Parenthetically, this failure by newspapers, in the dark days of the seventies and later, to distinguish between good and bad trade unions, and to realise that responsible trade unions are a bulwark of the pluralist society, is a sobering example of British parochialism. At a time when a Polish shipyard trade unionist, Lech Walesa, was beginning the long struggle which ultimately demolished communist dictatorship in Eastern Europe, the British press saw the iniquities of London compositors and machine-room staff as evidence that Britain was becoming ungovernable, and that trade unionism was to blame.

16

EUROPE: KEEPING BRITAIN IN

The two dominant political figures in the period covered by this book are Harold Wilson and Margaret Thatcher. Had they been strict contemporaries, instead of merely overlapping briefly, they would have shared few attitudes. But they did share one problem which caused each of them endless grief: the ambivalent attitude of their own parties, indeed of the British public, to Europe. He survived it. Her loss of office can be ascribed to this issue, almost above all others. Nothing illustrates more clearly the difference in their styles of leadership.

Yet no issue did more immediate damage to Harold Wilson's reputation in the predominantly pro-European media. His manoeuvres to maintain Labour unity, both in opposition and in government, were inevitably contrasted with the principled stand taken by Roy Jenkins, his main pro-European rival for the Labour leadership. Wilson went doggedly on to achieve the two objectives he had set himself: to maintain British membership of the European Common Market; and to keep his party in existence as a coherent political force. But he did it his way, and this earned criticism from pro-European critics within the Labour Party, from Ted Heath and the Tory opposition, and from the majority of the press.

For many, Europe was just a symbol of Harold Wilson's apparently infinite flexibility. The most serious charge made against him retrospectively, even by a moderate critic like Roy Hattersley, was that he ought not to have turned so sharply against Europe in the summer of 1971, and ought not to have stayed in that position for his two further years in opposition. The damaging effect was that constituency Labour parties during that period had taken their lead from him, and many had chosen anti-European MPs. In government, that tide was difficult to reverse. When the Cabinet recommended parliament to accept the terms gained in renegotiation, fewer than half the Parliamentary Labour Party supported that decision in the lobbies. Hattersley, one of the front-bench speakers in that debate, observed how downcast his chief had been to have to survive on opposition votes.

Harold Wilson's immediate problem was how to prevent the Labour Party flying apart. He laid great emphasis, privately as well as publicly, on the terms of entry, which his new Foreign Secretary, Jim Callaghan, immediately began to renegotiate. There has been great and continuing scepticism about this renegotiation, as indeed there later was about Margaret Thatcher's. On both occasions – 1974 under Wilson, 1980 under Thatcher – I found myself more sympathetic to each of the Prime Ministers than were colleagues, first at the *Guardian*, then at the *Observer*. Their understandable anxiety was that Britain, having dithered from the fifties onward in attitudes to closer European unity, was once more showing itself to lack enthusiasm, and displaying an unattractive face as, yet again, 'a nation of shopkeepers', aware of the price of everything and the value of nothing. Only long after Margaret Thatcher had waved her handbag at Giscard d'Estaing in Dublin did the press generally accept that an idealised Community had developed into a bargaining room.

Harold Wilson's careful handling of the European issue extended to all the appointments which had a bearing on the renegotiation and the subsequent referendum. The key one was that of Jim Callaghan as Foreign Secretary. By this stage, the Prime Minister had accepted that the long, usually undeclared war between them was over. Callaghan, at sixty-two, was four years older than him, and would not challenge him for the leadership. They shared a proper obsession with the need, especially during a government with a majority of four, to hold the Labour Party together.

The Prime Minister made a shrewd choice of deputy to Jim Callaghan in the European talks. This was Roy Hattersley, who was himself strongly pro-European, but with an equal commitment to maintaining Labour unity. The appointment began with a chapter of accidents. Hattersley, who has a penchant for self-mockery, felt that his appointment to this government, like all major incidents in his life, turned into farce.

He and I had an early morning meeting when we discussed the possibility, if he was not offered an acceptable post, that he might write a column for the *Guardian*. Like many others, he was still waiting to hear from Number 10. While doing so, he received a telephone call at the House of Commons from a Foreign Office official, who said: 'The meeting has been assembled, and is awaiting your arrival.' Hattersley asked which meeting this was, and the official replied: 'The meeting on Common Market policy.' When Hattersley expressed complete ignorance of this, the FO man suddenly registered alarm, and said, in pompous officialese: 'In that event, I must terminate this conversation immediately.'

This patent jumping of the gun confirmed for me yet again that civil servants often know more of what is about to happen in a reshuffle than those directly concerned. This reveals nothing more sinister than the human instinct, when anyone is in possession of a piece of news, to tell other people. As a journalist, I say 'thank heaven for the instinct!'

Still mystified, Roy Hattersley went off for what might have been a condolence lunch with James Margach, the *Sunday Times*'s veteran political correspondent – as our breed was, more accurately, called in those days before everyone became an 'editor'. While they were having a pre-lunch drink, Downing Street came on the telephone: the Prime Minister wanted to see Hattersley at once. He murmured that his host was waiting for him, but the Prime Minister's office would brook no delay: if he was missing his lunch, so must even the most enthusiastic of lunchers. Roy Hattersley had to borrow a pound from Jimmy Margach for the taxi to Number 10.

He was not to be in the Cabinet, which was a disappointment, as he had been elected to the shadow Cabinet in opposition. But Wilson left Hattersley with the impression that for him to become Minister of State at the Foreign Office, helping Jim Callaghan with the European negotiations, was not only the most important job in the government, but almost the only way of saving Western civilisation. For Harold Wilson, holding the Labour Party together amounted almost to that, for he had devoted his life to it, and he expected people like Hattersley to do the same.

Hattersley's exuberant personality was not totally immersed in Common Market negotiations. His other FO duties included visits to Covent Garden with visiting dignitaries. He invited Madge and myself to one such occasion, but we had another engagement. Later, he told me what fun we had missed. He had been briefed to expect the guest of honour, the Romanian Foreign Minister, to pay back £10 million of the £50 million his country had owed Britain since the nationalisation of Shell in 1946. When Roy Hattersley said: 'Well, Foreign Minister, I understand you have a figure to mention to me', his guest replied bluntly: 'No, I haven't.' He added that further technical discussions were needed before any repayment could be considered.

When the accompanying FO officials pointed out that technical discussions had now been going on for more than a quarter of a century, the Romanian said yes, and didn't that just show how complicated an issue it was? Hattersley cited the incident as symbolic of the strains of diplomacy, and said he felt like tearing up the tickets for the opera in a rage. The future essayist contributed a nugget of non-political information: from the royal box he had an excellent view of singers doing breathing exercises before they came on, but he could not see them when they were actually singing.

Jim Callaghan's renegotiation was handled subtly. Some Cabinet ministers taking part – notably Peter Shore at Trade, Tony Benn at Industry, and in the early days, Fred Peart at Agriculture – were deeply suspicious of most things European. Sometimes the pro-European Hattersley was left on his own with a Cabinet member who outranked him, but who was a Euro-sceptic. His brief was to exercise extreme tact in dealings with his senior colleagues, but with the implicit right to say, if their interpretation was different from Callaghan's: 'I am satisfied that the Secretary of State for Foreign Affairs will not accept what you say, and I must now telephone him.' Callaghan's own conducting of the orchestra was masterly: he might pretend to favour one or the other course being advocated by colleagues, but he usually finished up with the solution he himself wanted. No football manager was more ruthless in achieving his results, regardless of the damage done to the *amour propre* of individual players.

One of the factors which changed his attitude to Europe was happier experiences as negotiator in 1974 and 1975. By then, the principal European leaders wanted to keep Britain a member. At first he may have been treated coldly, but he put up a spirited performance, and other foreign ministers put him at his ease. Politically, Callaghan decided that Europe was not developing at an alarming speed; and economically, he began to see that Britain had little alternative.

What also improved Jim Callaghan's attitude was the replacement of Willy Brandt as German Chancellor by the more pragmatic Helmut Schmidt, who was to become one of his closest international friends. Schmidt won golden opinions when he was invited to Labour's post-election conference. Harold Wilson was nervous about the kind of speech he might make: Britain's negotiations were at a crucial stage, the essential deal with Germany on the budget had still to be done, and the Labour NEC remained strongly anti-European. Roy Hattersley was dispatched to the airport to meet Schmidt, and quickly decided that his fellow-social democrat had the sensitivity needed to do Wilson a favour. He even took the chance to check up how to pronounce the surnames of Ernest Bevin and Aneurin Bevan, and wanted to know if there were any other past Labour statesmen he ought to pay tribute to.

To some, Helmut Schmidt emerged as the real hero of Britain's renegotiation. For when he was driving to Chequers with the Prime Minister, he spoke bluntly: 'I am prepared to work to get you the proper terms, provided I know you wish to stay in. Do you?'

Harold Wilson, according to my informant, replied unequivocally: 'Yes.'

Schmidt pressed on: 'Will you say that to the President of France?'

Again Wilson answered: 'Yes.'

As soon as they reached Chequers, Schmidt telephoned Giscard d'Estaing, and suggested he should invite the British Prime Minister for dinner the following week, before the first of the European summits, which he was to host in Paris a month later.

Pro-Europeans in the government believed their cause took a giant step forward when Jim Callaghan declared at Cabinet meetings in April and June that the government was not asking for any alteration in the Treaty of Rome. Their view, supported by attitudes in other European capitals, was that if Britain *had* wanted the treaty changed, it would inevitably have found itself outside the Common Market again. What surprised them, and also the Foreign Office, was that those opposed to British membership, especially ministers such as Tony Benn and Peter Shore who followed the detail closely, did not challenge Callaghan.

Before Wilson's success was assured, he faced the promised referendum, in June 1975. The Prime Minister had still to settle the issue of collective responsibility within his government. Wilson and Jim Callaghan put their heads together about this. When the Foreign Secretary and his Minister of State, Roy Hattersley, were having supper together, Hattersley expressed doubt about the wisdom of Labour members, inside the Cabinet or out, enjoying freedom to go their own way. Teasingly, Callaghan said: 'I noticed in the *New Statesman* that you want to be leader of the Labour Party. Well, suppose you were leader now, what would you do?'

Hattersley replied that he would apply Cabinet responsibility, not because he feared damage to Britain's position in Europe if they did otherwise, but because he feared the damage to Labour. He could imagine a situation in which, on one night Roy Jenkins and he were addressing a pro-Europe rally in Birmingham town hall, and the following night Michael Foot and Tony Benn were on the same platform denouncing it. This would make their party look ridiculous.

Callaghan listened patiently to this, smiled, and said: 'Well, you're not leader of the Labour Party, and the fellow who is is going to allow people to go their own way.' But Roy Hattersley now had no remaining doubt that Harold Wilson's own support would be for remaining in Europe.

I saw the Prime Minister on the day before he made his announcement on what came to be called 'the agreement to differ'. He was scornful of the idea that the Cabinet as an entity should remain neutral in the referendum. Less than three months later, he led his Cabinet, by a margin of two to one, in support of Britain's continued membership.

Judgements on Harold Wilson's performance at the time depended entirely on the perspective of the person making them. The anti-Europeans were disappointed, but reconciled to the fact that he was never likely to come out on their side. The pro-Europeans, with Roy Jenkins as president of the cross-party campaign, complained that they were left to bear the burden of the campaign.

A more temperate view from the pro-European side came from Harold Lever. He thought his leader ought to have fought earlier within the party, and he believed he could have won. But in his view, Wilson's redeeming action was that, once he became convinced that an exit from the Common Market would split Labour, he then fought to stay in. Perhaps, he added enigmatically, the Wilson strategy was to realise that, in the current state of Britain, it was not possible to have a strategy.

The most generous assessment of Harold Wilson's achievement came from his old adversary of the Gaitskell era, Tony Crosland. He believed the Prime Minister's place in the history books was now secure, because in Labour's long struggle about British membership of the Common Market, he had achieved what historically had defeated other statesmen: to hold his party together over a great and divisive issue. Harold Wilson had done over Europe what Peel had failed to do over the Corn Laws, and Gladstone over Irish Home Rule. (Tony Crosland was not alive when Margaret Thatcher and John Major struggled, with much less conspicuous success, against similar internal party divisions over Europe.)

By the time I discussed the referendum result with Harold Wilson himself in September, the controversy had faded with astonishing speed. A 'yes' margin of more than two to one in the referendum caused the anti-Europeans to accept, at least for a time, that they could not challenge the will of the people. The Prime Minister was in his all-passion-spent mood. He had known the period before the referendum would be bruising, but thought the issue would have disappeared within a month.

With a puff of his pipe, he added: 'I was wrong; it had disappeared within a week.' He believed the crucial decision had been the 'agreement to differ' within the Cabinet. Without such an arrangement, he would not have been able to keep together a credible Labour government. He knew it would cause a row, but also thought it would work. The following weekend the Cabinet had coalesced quickly, and he had made his ministerial changes. These included the swopping of Tony Benn and Eric Varley, which gave Varley, a Wilson favourite, though an anti-Marketeer, the more influential Industry Department.

I put to Harold Wilson the most serious charge laid against him on Europe: that he had created his own difficulties in 1971 by coming out so firmly against. He replied that he realised the media, which were pro-Market, did not think the terms were of any significance, but he did not agree. He also felt the absence of full-hearted consent to entry by the British people was a strong point, which he was entitled to exploit.

His wry acceptance that he would not be given credit for his achievement is best caught in his book, *Final Term*. Noting press criticism of his style of government, he wrote:

> To bridge a deep political chasm without splitting a party or provoking dramatic ministerial resignations is sometimes regarded as something approaching political chicanery ... The highest aim of leadership is to secure policies adequate to deal with any situation ... without major confrontations, splits and resignations. It may be bad for the headlines and news placards, but it has been sought and achieved by our greatest leaders, Conservative as well as Liberal or Labour. Baldwin, Macmillan, Churchill ... always sought consensus. It is sometimes galling to be criticised for achieving it.

During the referendum I was able to argue, in my final editorials for the *Guardian*, the case for continued British membership. I was enthusiastic about Europe, first on the then conventional view that it might give a much needed stimulus to British industry; and also in the – perhaps chauvinistic, and certainly misplaced – hope that Britain would help to create a more democratic Europe. I believed this must replace the profoundly anti-democratic, top-down Council of Ministers system which still effectively controls – or fails to control – the European Union.

17

ULSTER'S TRAGEDY BEGINS

Soon after Labour returned to office in March 1974, Northern Ireland was overwhelmed by one of its periodic tragedies. Not in this case a tragedy of human death, but the death of what I saw – and still see – as the best hope of a just peace in my native land.

The tragedy was the overthrow, in a strike organised and supported by Protestant paramilitaries, of a power-sharing executive in which, for the first time, Unionist and Nationalist politicians had served amicably together for five months. It was a political project in which I can claim part-parentage. Even twenty years later, its untimely demise still fills me with despair.

When I settled down to plan this book, I bridled at the prospect of writing anything worthwhile about Ulster within the constraints of space available. Too much nonsense has been written and broadcast over the past quarter-century to give me any appetite for adding to the torrent of words. I suspect that this logorrhoea leaves most non-Irish readers bewildered or bored, while augmenting the inaccurate myth which creeps into even reputable histories and biographies.

So this is not a brief history of Ireland, beginning either with Brian Boru or the Battle of the Boyne. Rather, like the rest of my book, it is a brief account of the Northern Ireland crisis 'as it seemed to me'. I have observed events there in greater or less detail, depending on which job I was doing. The fact that the years since 1974, and especially since 1981, are dealt with more briefly in a later chapter is partly because my job at the BBC kept my nose to the Westminster grindstone, and left time only for social visits to Belfast. But I had better confess that political developments in the past two decades, including those of the 'peace process' in the nineties, have never seemed to me to contain the *logical* hope of a just peace which flourished so briefly in 1974.

The disturbances which began in Ulster in 1968 seemed at first to be concerned only with civil rights, and had parallels in France, America and elsewhere. Instead, the Ulster disturbances, unlike the others, turned out to be a preview of the frightening outbreak of nationalism which engulfed Europe after the dissolution of the Communist empire. Perhaps if Yugoslavia and the Caucusus had erupted first, the world would have understood better how deep-seated the Northern Ireland problem was: not some bizarre re-enactment of seventeenth-century religious wars, as it was presented in a thousand glib articles and programmes; rather a dispute over the far from negligible issue of which country people wanted to be part of.

I observed these events from London, though in my newspaper years I went to Belfast three or four times a year. This produced in me a frustrated sense that the ignorant armies that clashed by night included not only the two factions in Ulster, indeed in Ireland as a whole, but also the British. As long ago as the Great War, Churchill had blamed the Irish for preserving the integrity of their parochial quarrel through Europe's first Armageddon. Now a weary sense that it was all breaking out again produced in London, on the political left as much as the right, certainly in the civil service and the Foreign Office, and above all – so far as my own interest was concerned – in journalism, a nasty bout of neo-imperialism. Kipling's reservation about 'lesser breeds without the law' was implicit in much that was written and spoken.

A failure in historic memory has undermined much of the commentary on Ulster. By this I do not mean memories of 1690, 1798 or 1916: those largely irrelevant events have been raked over all too often. But when John Major and Albert Reynolds issued their 'Downing Street Declaration' in 1993, nobody seemed to see the ironic comparison with the earlier 'Downing Street Declaration' issued by Harold Wilson in 1969 (even assuming anybody in Whitehall remembered it). This not only contained the often repeated constitutional guarantee that 'in no event will Northern Ireland or any part thereof cease to be part of the United Kingdom without the consent of the Parliament [and elsewhere "of the people"] of Northern Ireland.'

That Declaration then ended with the most unequivocal words Harold Wilson could find to demonstrate to Ulster Unionists that the troubles which had engulfed them were only about civil rights, and did not question the partition of Ireland almost fifty years earlier. The words – 'The Border is not an issue' – were honestly meant at the time; but within two years, in opposition, Wilson was advocating steps leading to Irish unity over a period; though with the Republic, ludicrously, being asked to come back into the Commonwealth and accept the Queen as its head. By the time the 1993 Downing Street Declaration was framed, after fifteen years of Conservative government, nobody could claim that 'the Border is not an issue', since the IRA had made it one, and Irish Nationalist politicians were determined to keep it so.

Those of us who have always hoped for the creation of a modern political structure in Ulster, with attention centered on the economic and social condition of its people, have observed with sadness that the Border is a recurring issue, because it is a card that can be played from either the Green or the Orange side of politics, according to convenience. Lord Brookeborough, in what was called 'the Union Jack election' of 1949, memorably invoked fears about Dublin's anti-partition campaigning. By doing so, he defeated not the Nationalists – whose support could be accurately and immutably gauged by the electoral rolls kept in each Catholic parish – but the non-sectarian Northern Ireland Labour party, which had made too much progress in the immediate post-war period for the comfort of Brookeborough's Unionist party.

It is worth looking briefly at why the Border was created. Its architect, Lloyd George, is my greatest political hero. (The reader may have concluded by now that I have an addiction to flawed heroes: not an irrational position for a Nonconformist Christian who does not believe in human perfection.) The Irish settlement he brokered in 1920, after many earlier mistakes, has attracted retrospective criticism. Yet it was a necessary mixture of sound democratic principle and practicality.

After the 1916 Easter Rising and the executions which followed it, Nationalist Ireland was determined to win freedom from Britain, and was fighting for it, so Lloyd George conceded that independence. But after Ulster's anti-Home Rule campaign under Edward Carson in 1912–13, and particularly after the British citizenship enshrined in the Ulster Covenant had been sealed in the blood shed by the Ulster Division on the Somme and in Flanders, the Northern Protestants were clearly not to be forced out of the United Kingdom without a fight. So Lloyd George acknowledged their right to remain British.

Both these decisions preserved the democratic principle of the self-determination of free peoples. Practicality pointed in the same direction. London would not have been able to impose a settlement on either Irish Nationalists and Republicans or Ulster Unionists. Imperial *instincts* might live on into the second half of the century, but the imperial *will* to impose solutions had disappeared much earlier.

During the present crisis, failure to recognise these truths has diverted public debate in Britain from two areas where it was badly needed. One was long-standing neglect of Ulster's chronic unemployment and poverty, which exacerbated relations between the two communities. There was similar or worse deprivation in the rest of Ireland, often mitigated only by massive immigration to, of all places, England. But economic hardship in the South was not complicated by the poison of sectarian dispute, for the Protestant population there, never large, diminished steadily after independence.

The other failure was to recognise why the political system in Northern Ireland did not provide equal rights to Protestants and Catholics. This was not due to Original Sin, but to an impossible political conundrum. Because the national issue dominated politics, and because Unionists were in a permanent majority in the population, the Unionist party was permanently in government. Nationalists disputed the right of the Northern Ireland state to exist, so they were ambiguous about participating in its politics. But they also saw little point in this, since mathematically they could have no hope of power. The swing of the pendulum, that essential ingredient of democracy, was missing. This was why I concluded in 1969 that power-sharing between Unionist and Nationalist politicians, with the Border issue left to periodic votes, was the only solution in such a divided community.

For much of my Protestant childhood in Belfast in the thirties and forties, the national issue was quiescent, a matter of folk memories. My mother told us how, in the twenties, she had cradled in her arms a dying man who had been shot outside the shop where she worked. In the mid-thirties, when the London newspapers briefly grew excited about an outbreak of rioting in Belfast, fellow-guests in our holiday boarding-house in Blackpool offered to raise funds for my father, so that he could keep his family away from danger for another week, but he assured them there was no real cause for anxiety.

I went to a state primary school, which Catholic families did not attend, preferring their own church schools. Fortunately, a couple of mixed marriages among the parents of my friends gave me access to a group of boys from both communities who played together. I can recall only one occasion when politics arose. It was when France surrendered in 1940. During our evening meal, my father was telling my mother how serious this was. I intervened with a thought I had picked up, but not understood, from one of my Catholic playmates. He had the Irish name of Donal, but most of us thought he was called Donald, and he cheerfully accepted his nickname, 'Duck'.

Into our gloomy family conference on the war, I interjected my twelve-year-old wisdom: 'Still, as Duck says, England's difficulty is Ireland's opportunity.' My father laid down his knife and fork.

'What did you say?' I repeated my quotation, my self-confidence draining away, for I realised from his frown that the sentiment I had parroted – as probably Duck had parroted it to me – was not totally acceptable to an ex-soldier of the Great War, now heavily engaged as an ageing training officer in the Home Guard. He gave me a brief lesson in politics, in which I then had no interest, and then enquired of my mother: 'Who the hell is Duck?' Explanations followed, and my father shook his head sadly. But it never occurred to him to suggest I should change my friends. He himself ran a small electrical firm, in which his right-hand man and half the electricians were Catholics, and he did not regard the bigotry of segregation as an option.

The only other occasion when I remember Orange-and-Green sentiment impingeing on my boyhood was when the football team I supported, Distillery – whose non-sectarian credentials were affirmed by its supporters' scarves, white silk ones, normally the badge of privileged young men with dinner jackets – were playing Belfast Celtic. Celtic, a Catholic team, were the best in the Irish League during the war, and decisive home victory over Distillery was no surprise. Their supporters greeted each of a depressing number of Celtic goals with the Nazi salute. Yet like us, they suffered from savage German air-raids.

My first sight of Westminster politicians taking any detailed interest in Ulster came soon after the defeat of the Attlee government. In 1952, a Labour party delegation, consisting of Alf Robens and Arthur Bottomley, both former ministers, and Jim Callaghan, who had held junior office, came as guests of the Northern Ireland Labour Party. At the end of their visit, they endorsed a report on economic development prepared by Sam Napier, the local party secretary. Copies of this for other reporters and myself were slow in appearing, for Sam's secretary, though undeniably beautiful, was at an early stage in her typist's training. So I speeded up the process by typing the hand-outs. They contained elaborate proposals for tackling unemployment.

Years later, Jim Callaghan told me that when he was visiting Derry as Home Secretary during the 1969 riots, a man in the crowd waved a yellowing newspaper cutting at him. When they came closer, he recognised a photograph of his youthful self on the 1952 visit, and said – with a politician's bonhomie, as he self-mockingly put it: 'We were all a lot younger in those days.' This did not satisfy the Derryman.

'Yes', he said, 'but I didn't have a job then, and I still don't have one now, and what have you done about it?'

What Callaghan would like to have done about it was to seduce Ulster away from Unionist-Nationalist politics and towards Conservative-

Labour ones, with candidates from the mainstream British parties, as in other areas of the United Kingdom. In the late sixties and early seventies, he promoted discussions with trade union and Labour people in Belfast, and hoped he was making progress. But others at Westminster had Labour's traditional preference for a policy of Irish unity. The National Executive eventually took that line, and the party's attempt to build up non-sectarian politics eroded.

My first articles about Northern Ireland for the *Guardian*, in 1956, dealt with unemployment, and gave a gloomy economic prognosis. With its three basic industries – agriculture, shipbuilding and linen – in decline, Stormont's efforts to provide new jobs had been a case of running hard to stay in the same place. So far as Whitehall was concerned, in the half-century between 1921 and the outbreak of the troubles, out-of-sight, in a devolutionary parliament, was out-of-mind. If many Ulster families had not suffered unemployment for two or three generations, the civil rights grievances of the late sixties might have been remedied without rioting and terrorism. In the vicious spiral which violence created, Ulster sentenced itself to a lingering death by economic suicide.

Less than a year after leaving Belfast, I was sent back to cover the outbreak of an earlier IRA campaign. This began in December 1956, and dragged on for six years, but with a tiny death-toll compared to that of the past quarter-century. Madge was newly pregnant with our first son, and we were making a slow start to our day when we heard on the radio about the first IRA raids. The news editor came on the phone soon afterwards, and told me to get to Belfast as quickly as possible. The morning plane from Manchester had already left, so I made an unavailing effort to catch one from Liverpool, but the minicab driver, who had never been to Speke airport before, could not make it.

I spent the day in heavy telephoning to old colleagues in Belfast, drafted a report in the departure lounge at Manchester airport, as I waited for the evening plane, and dictated it as soon as we touched down in Belfast. When working in my old *Belfast Telegraph* office the next day, I was flattered to see that the Press Association had quoted at length what the 'Special Correspondent of the *Manchester Guardian*' had written, with a Belfast dateline. They made it sound as if I had been there for months, in deep study of the political background. This was not so misleading as it may seem, for I was trading on knowledge built up over eleven years in Ulster journalism.

In the weeks that followed, when Madge and I were living with her parents, I relied on colleagues in the main Belfast hotel to warn me of late-night incidents. When a police station in Fermanagh was attacked by a large IRA contingent, reporters from *The Times* and *Glasgow Herald* arrived at about midnight to pick me up, and fortified by Madge's bacon sandwiches, we were hurtled through the night to the border. It all seemed like a great adventure, nobody was hurt, and nobody thought the IRA were getting anywhere. Later, the army took me out in an armoured car patrolling the Fermanagh border, but the principal danger lay in the driver's propensity to reverse at forty miles per hour.

By 1968 I was news editor of the *Guardian*, and became deputy editor the following year. In our early editorials, we urged Terence O'Neill, the modernising Unionist who had taken over from Brookeborough as Prime Minister, to speed up his reforms. He was in permanent conflict with hard-liners in his own party. Under pressure from Westminster, the local government franchise was reformed, the RUC reorganised, the B Specials disbanded and discrimination in housing ended. But the pace of reform did not satisfy civil rights activists.

Successive British Home Secretaries, Jim Callaghan and Reginald Maudling, grew frustrated when they saw that the righting of these grievances did not produce peace on the streets. Understandably, they had accepted the assurances of the civil rights leaders that they were seeking reform, not political revolution. But the rioting and petrol bombing continued, because many of the demonstrators had concluded that the Border was always an issue. Early successes in the civil rights campaign had depended on concentrating on Catholic grievances, rather than on partition, so the British press was slow to accept that militant Republicanism was having a resurgence. I was criticised within the *Guardian* for saying so in an editorial, but soon even reporters who had laughed when O'Neill's successor, James Chichester-Clark, suggested the IRA was involved in the disturbances had to acknowledge this tragic development.

My dominant editorial argument in those early years of the IRA campaign was that there could be no purely military, or security, solution. A political *modus vivendi* between the two communities must be found, and from August 1969 I was arguing that this should be through power-sharing at Stormont between Protestant and Catholic politicians, setting aside their differences on the Border to concentrate on providing jobs, improving social conditions, and guaranteeing fairness between the two communities.

It was only after the power-sharing executive had been destroyed by Protestant paramilitaries in 1974 that I acknowledged an addendum to this dictum: if there could be no purely security solution, there could be no purely political one either: democratic politics could only work if communities were freed from the terror of gun, bomb, beating and intimidation.

One of the least reported aspects of the Ulster crisis is the conspiracy of fear. I recall an evening I spent in the home of a Catholic family in the Upper Falls. The father was an accountant, his son a solicitor. They were strongly anti-IRA. But late in the evening the son confessed that when he went into the local pub on a Saturday evening, and the hat was passed round for what was euphemistically called 'prisoners' families', but which he assumed was for buying arms for the IRA, he threw a pound in like everybody else, because he did not want a beating on his way home. The same coercion applied to electoral politics. When Gerry Adams defeated Gerry Fitt in West Belfast, SDLP supporters feared IRA violence against them.

My preferred political solution, power-sharing, first derived from a pamphlet by the Northern Ireland Labour party. That party's efforts to replace sectarian politics by a division between right and left having been frustrated, it suggested that the alternative was some form of government which would involve both communities. In 1969, as the civil rights demonstrations were followed by riots, with militant Republicanism standing in the wings, I picked up this idea.

The decisive editorial appeared on 16 August:

> Somehow Catholics have to be brought into positions of influence and decision in Ulster. For fifty years, they have been on the outside, partly because they have been excluded, partly by their own wish to ignore a state they do not accept. Only when ordinary Catholics feel that their own leaders are part of the decision-making process will they have faith in its fairness . . .
>
> Is a crisis coalition feasible? It would have to consist of, say, five or six Unionists, dedicated to the maintenance of the British connection, and with twelve general elections proving that they have overwhelming support for that view; and three Catholics, equally dedicated to the unity of Ireland and a break with Britain, and secure in the support of their own constituencies on this issue.

We had run this flag up the pole, but nobody saluted immediately, either inside the office or in the wider world. A lot more blood had to be shed before a British government – Conservative, as it happened – was ready to suspend Stormont, and before some Ulster politicians were willing to make the necessary compromises.

In 1970, the deaths increased. As well as paying regular visits to Belfast, for discussions with politicians of all parties, and army and police chiefs, I was seeing a lot of the new Home Secretary, Reginald Maudling. He was heavily criticised, then and later, for a detached attitude to Ulster. To anyone who knew him, and talked a lot about Ulster with him, that is a monstrous injustice. He once said to me that, unlike the economic problems he had handled as Chancellor, this was one nightmare which lived with him all the time.

What gave him an air of detachment is that Maudling was the ultimate rationalist, and could see better than most how dangerous the irrationalities in Ulster were. As early as 1970, he complained to me that the more intransigent Unionists 'couldn't see beyond the ends of their bloody noses'. A quarter of a century later, it would be difficult to fault that judgement.

As a Conservative Home Secretary, Reggie Maudling saw the value of retaining the support of the *Guardian* for his policies of reform, and he was franker about the dangers than any other minister. By February 1971, when another round of trouble broke out, he was telling me that both the Catholic hierarchy and ordinary Catholics were pleased with the reforms, and that within the Unionist party moderates were gaining strength; but that such improvements were precisely what the IRA didn't want, hence the renewed violence. He quoted Cardinal Conway as saying that the secret of securing a political settlement was for the government to take an initiative when the Catholics knew the IRA was beaten, but before the Protestants realised this. A shrewd comment, but sadly the IRA never seemed about to be defeated.

Maudling's acute mind saw the impossibilities which faced him. He summarised them to me thus: the IRA's use of arms led to house-to-house searches by the army in Republican areas, and people resented it when 'a lot of innocent floorboards' were torn up. Yet soldiers who had been shot at, stoned and attacked with petrol and nail bombs were probably not too delicate in the way they carried out this task. Those who criticise Maudling for indolence should know that he was often aroused at 5 a.m. to authorise an army search.

In private talks with the Home Secretary, as well as in the leader columns of the *Guardian*, I pressed the case for power-sharing, especially in 1971, when Whitehall was clearly in the market for options. Maudling's initial view was that no coalition could succeed with two parties which were so diametrically opposed to each other. He did not think the Unionists were ready for that. I put to him the view, which Jim Callaghan had also adopted before he left office, that the Unionist log-jam might be breaking up more quickly than anybody expected.

When I went to Ireland, North and South, Maudling would ask me to come and see him again when I got back, because he wanted to keep in touch 'with circles I don't have access to'. This was both dissident Unionists and the SDLP, who were boycotting the British government because of internment. Maudling was determined that he must not use power-sharing to entice the SDLP back to the conference table, otherwise a useful option would be lost. Instead, he must draw them back first, and then hope to negotiate some form of coalition.

At first I did not think this large, shambolic, apparently lazy man could be taking much notice of ideas I floated about a situation he clearly thought almost hopeless. But like many others, I under-rated him. Slowly he grew interested in the possibility that power-sharing might get off the ground. I detected his seriousness one afternoon when, a few hours after I had seen the Home Secretary alone in his room, his private secretary telephoned me. By then, this official possessed detailed knowledge of everything I had said, and was briefed to keep in touch with my views of how far Brian Faulkner might be able to take his Unionist Cabinet in accepting Catholic participation.

The answer turned out to be 'a long way'. But that was only confirmed publicly after Ted Heath and Reggie Maudling had suspended Stormont, and when Willie Whitelaw, as the first Secretary of State for Northern Ireland, negotiated with the local politicians.

Before Maudling had been able to turn his mind to political developments, however, he had to deal with an ever more virulent terrorist campaign. At our meeting in February 1971, he raised the issue which caused more trouble, at the *Guardian* as elsewhere, than any other in the Ulster crisis. Maudling said the paper had been very sturdy in its leader comment so far, but what would its attitude be if the British Cabinet had to agree to internment? I said we would be fairly unhappy about it, for obvious civil liberties reasons. He replied that he would be unhappy also, but the authorities were worried about the impossibility of getting convictions in courts where jurors and witnesses were subject to threats.

He was scathing about the Republic's courts, and said the whole attitude to the IRA in Dublin was ludicrous: the Chief of Staff of an illegal organisation was appearing on television and virtually being asked: 'What are your murder squads doing today, Mr Goulding?' He cited a notorious IRA man who had been released on bail in the South, although the authorities in the North believed he took part in a particularly savage murder of three young Scottish soldiers. Maudling argued that the Taoiseach, Jack Lynch, ought to be clearing up the IRA training camps in the Republic. When I asked if he was sure these existed, he said he had a list of the camps, even the names of their commanders. The long, usually submerged dispute between London and Dublin over how serious is the Republic's fight against terrorism began a long time ago, and has rumbled down the years.

Internment was introduced in August 1971. I was in Brittany on a family holiday at the time, but Reginald Maudling saw the editor, Alastair Hetherington, and the *Guardian* supported its introduction. The evidence of what happened behind the scenes before internment began is contradictory. Maudling told Hetherington that Faulkner and the then army commander, General Sir Harry Tuzo, came to Downing Street a few evenings before, and convinced the Prime Minister and other ministers that it must be introduced.

Many commentators, including some with military connections, maintain that the army was against the policy. There is no subject on which politicians and others have adjusted their attitudes retrospectively, and with more suppleness. I know of one opposition politician who urged Brian Faulkner to intern Provisional IRA men six months before he did so, but denounced him when it happened.

British politicians were equally ambiguous. Before the Ulster death-toll reached double figures, Bernadette Devlin asked Harold Wilson to repeal the Special Powers Act, under which previous internments had taken place. Although there was no proposal at that time to reintroduce internment, Wilson replied that no government facing a situation like that then existing in Ulster could think of divesting itself of such powers. He was right, yet more than twenty years later London and Dublin are still debating the same question.

Yet in opposition, when the situation had become far worse, it was on this subject that he and I had the only quarrel of a long friendship. He said, with some innuendo, that they all recognised that the *Guardian* was taking a different line than it might have done if it hadn't had 'such a statesmanlike deputy editor'. I did not take this as a compliment, so replied sharply that I had not been the only person on the paper to support internment, and did it not occur to him that reasonable men might have examined the facts and come to the conclusion that its introduction was inevitable? I added my suspicion that if he had been across the road in Downing Street, he would have approved it.

He avoided answering this question, so I told him the other question not answered in an emergency debate on Ulster was Maudling's: would Wilson turn interned gunmen on to the streets? He replied that he would not do this. Whether internment was right or wrong originally, he would not end it in this way. Maudling later argued to me that it was all right for Labour to demand the release of some innocent men who had been interned, but pointed out that they had studiously avoided calling for the release of hard-core IRA men who had shot soldiers in the back, and would do so again.

Three months later I asked Maudling what was the truth about General Tuzo. He said that Tuzo had declared there was no military necessity for internment. He could continue his campaign, and in the end, he could win, but he could not win quickly. Internment would speed up the army's ability to defeat terrorism. Faulkner later told me Tuzo had put on paper to him a recommendation not to end internment.

By January 1972 Alastair Hetherington was determined to change the *Guardian*'s line, especially on internment, which was unpopular within the office, as elsewhere. I disagreed with him, believing that any easing of pressure on the IRA would lead to more death and destruction. But I dutifully put to Maudling an idea which Alastair was arguing to me: for a timetable in which political talks and release of internees – one-third of the total at a time – would move in step.

Maudling said this was like releasing prisoners-of-war when the war had not ended. He feared the IRA would simply say 'silly old British!' gratefully use a ceasefire period for a rest, and be even more glad to get its interned leaders back. They would start again when they were ready. He was remarkably prescient about what subsequently happened. Looking back on the arguments two decades later, I am struck by how little the issues – ceasefire in return for prisoners – have changed in the intervening period, though now the prisoners are convicted terrorists, not internees.

But shortly after this talk with the Home Secretary, and while the debate between Alastair and myself was still going on, Bloody Sunday changed everything. On 30 January, during disturbances in Londonderry, the Parachute Regiment killed thirteen civilians. The next morning Alastair ran his timetable proposal in the leader columns. Maudling immediately invited him in, to ask whether it represented hard infor-mation from within the Republican movement that releases would produce a ceasefire. Alastair told him it did not, that the idea came from within the *Guardian*, and that he could not guarantee anything. The leader also contained a variety of proposals, including 'hot pursuit' – along Israeli lines – of terrorists who escaped into the Republic. No more was heard of this.

In the years which followed, not only the *Guardian*, but successive ministers, with proper regard for civil liberties, kept seeking ways to phase out internment. The political imperative for something to break the log-jam clashed with the realities of security and a legal system which was under the cosh of terrorism. Whenever politicians established committees to look in detail at the facts, rather than theories, they received truthful, but unhelpful answers.

Willie Whitelaw established the Diplock Committee, which is principally remembered for proposing non-jury courts. But this committee, which included George Woodcock, lately of the TUC, and Sir Kenneth Younger, a former Labour minister, also looked at how the 'godfathers' – those who organised, but did not themselves carry out terrorist acts – might be convicted. They concluded that the state simply could not guarantee the safety of witnesses, having been impressed by the story of a man who was murdered in his home, in front of his infant child, the day before he was due to give evidence.

Then came a classic statement of the dilemma, which has never been refuted, though it was soon ignored. As long as the godfathers remained at liberty, it would not be possible to find witnesses against them, apart from soldiers and policemen, who could be protected. They could not be convicted in a court of law:

> The dilemma is complete. The only hope of restoring the ability of the criminal courts of law in Northern Ireland to deal with terrorist crimes is by using an extra-judicial process to deprive of their ability to operate in Northern Ireland those terrorists whose activities result in the intimidation of witnesses. With an easily penetrable border to the south and west, the only way of doing this is to put them in detention by an executive act, and to keep them confined until they can be released without danger to the public safety and to the administration of criminal justice.

Whitelaw's Labour successor, Merlyn Rees, also resorted to a committee, chaired by Lord Gardiner, the former Labour Lord Chancellor, which reported in January 1975. After stating the libertarian position, Gardiner concluded:

> We would like to be able to recommend that the time has come to abolish detention [the new name for internment], but the present levels of violence, the risks of increased violence, and the difficulty of predicting events even a few months ahead make it impossible for us to put forward a precise recommendation on the timing. We think that this grave decision can only be made by the Government. Only they can decide the time, taking into account a wide range of political, social and economic factors, as well as the security situation.

The ball was back in the politicians' court, with a clear recognition that security and politics could not be divorced. Much later, long after internment had been abolished, but the killing continued, the ball came back into the politicians' court in even more deadly form. In his time in Ulster, General Sir Harry Tuzo had a better grasp of both its politics and security than any other outsider I encountered, whether politician, civil servant or soldier. He had a suitably balanced position between the two communities, but had no doubt of his duty to defeat terrorism, and believed it was possible to do so.

In this, he contrasted with senior army figures who served in Northern Ireland after him. In my judgement, the greatest single contribution to the persistence of the IRA campaign, and the consequent growth of Protestant paramilitaries, was the writing, and then the leaking, of an army intelligence report saying terrorism could not be defeated, and that only a political solution could work. This was an act of deepest treachery to those – soldiers, policemen or civilians – who have died.

The truth is that democratic politics cannot operate when the veto of violence is so freely exercised as it has been in Northern Ireland. Once the IRA were told they could not be defeated, they had no incentive to stop. Once the Protestant paramilitaries discovered they could destroy the power-sharing executive, set up with the support of what were grandiloquently called 'the two sovereign governments', but which proved unable to exercise sovereign power, another Rubicon was crossed. The destruction of that brave experiment confirmed the existence of the veto of violence, on either side. Like all cases of lost innocence, this is probably irredeemable.

18

FIRST AMONG CROWN PRINCES

By the time he returned to office in 1974, Harold Wilson found the continuous search for new ideas an impossible burden. He sadly told his last private secretary at Number 10 that, while in the 1960s he had come down in the morning with about twenty ideas of what he wanted done, or at least investigated, now he had few fresh ideas. When people seek some mysterious explanation of why he resigned in 1976, aged sixty, an age at which Churchill had not yet become Prime Minister for the first time, I reflect that he had simply worked himself out.

Tony Crosland, who was one of Wilson's most perceptive – if latterly more friendly – critics, observed that in this second period, Harold concentrated on what he did best: a commonsensical and ameliorative approach to Britain's fundamental problems, which most people acknowledged could not be solved overnight, if at all. When I raised the charge that the Prime Minister lacked a longer-term political objective, he enquired what I meant. Well, didn't Harold often boast that he had the only starred double first in economics at Oxford between the wars, so ought he not to be providing a solution to Britain's economic difficulties?

Crosland fixed me with one of the most sardonic eyes in politics, and replied: 'Ah, well, if *you* have got a structural solution to the problems of the British economy, for goodness' sake tell us about it in this Sunday's *Observer*.' Harold, he said, had no such solution. As an applied economist, he had an incredibly detailed knowledge of railway development in the nineteenth century. But if he had stayed in academic life, he would have written the definitive work on something like the Eurodollar market, rather than turning into a new Keynes.

Crosland found this second period of government more relaxed than the first, and speculated to me that one reason might be that they were all more experienced, older, and perhaps more tired. He confessed that he found himself thinking a lot about his next holiday; he had just returned from France, where he had had a marvellous time, but already he was contemplating the Christmas break. A year after that conversation, Tony Crosland had died, tragically young.

Others had greater doubts about Harold Wilson's style. In the opposition years, Roy Jenkins thought the Prime Minister believed he must just finesse his way out of Labour's problems. In government, he said with a sigh, Wilson would not change now. He would deal with such crises as came up, but would not confront people in the Labour Party who were going in the wrong direction. He had built a most successful career on holding the party together and winning elections, but he had no strategy at all.

Yet despite such reservations, Jenkins acknowledged that Wilson now ran the government in a much less frantic way. A full day's meeting at Chequers to discuss devolution had been precisely what was needed: calm consideration of a major issue. In the old days, he twinkled, the US President, Lyndon Johnson, would have been on the telephone several times, and crisis sub-committees would have been set up, interrupting the main business. Now Wilson either recognised Britain's diminished role in the world, or else they were all just ten years older.

Another Jenkinsite pro-European, Harold Lever, who had grown fond of Wilson while he worked as his guru in the world of finance, regarded him as the ultimate in political realists. Wilson had come to the conclusion that his was the only way to win power in Britain at that time. Economics, Lever observed, was the principal subject of political debate, but it was harder to explain to the public than, say, free trade or Home Rule. Harold Wilson therefore behaved like a shaman. Eh?

Harold Lever, who had suffered a stroke, entertained lunch guests he knew well in his dressing-gown. He picked up his stick, and walked slowly across to the bookshelves for a dictionary. A shaman, he declaimed, was 'a medicine man among North American Indians'. He explained: Wilson had realised that his own 1964 government and Heath's in 1970 had failed to solve Britain's economic difficulties. He saw himself as the captain of a ship who steered it in the same direction as the current. He had two aims: to remain captain, and not to have a collision in which people would be hurt. He was a decent man, who shied away from hurting people, so he wanted society to change, but not too quickly.

The battle between right and left within the government dominated political commentary. Trotskyist groups were gaining influence in constituency Labour parties, and making MPs look over their shoulders.

The Jenkinsites thought Wilson ought to have acted against this. Other centre-right Labour men such as Tony Crosland and Roy Hattersley believed MPs' futures lay in their own hands. Hattersley argued that an MP's duties included political education within his own back yard. Crosland thought Labour MPs ought to maintain solid support locally for their own ideas. That meant spending much time in the constituency.

He himself enjoyed Grimsby, and he revealed to me once that he made sure to buy the small cigars he smoked in half a dozen different tobacconists, so that he was seen by as many constituents as possible. He added tartly that those who could not be bothered with such activities had made an error in career choice: they ought to have gone into the civil service. Deselection of some Labour MPs did not worry him. He thought one who was in the dining-room in which we talked drank too much, and did not attend the House; while another was 'a hanger and flogger, and in many ways a fascist'.

The other worry for the party leadership was that Tony Benn and the left on the NEC were zealous in their determination not to let this Labour government stray from their own path of socialist rectitude, as they believed those of the sixties had done. After joining the *Observer* in the summer of 1975, I had a long conversation with Benn. It consisted mainly of his criticism of the liberal press.

His accusation was that the newspapers were not preparing the public for the profound debate about the nature of British society, which he thought the new unemployment of the seventies would provoke. He criticised especially papers like the two I worked for, because they pretended to be on the reform side of politics, but were not prepared to present seriously the views of what he acknowledged to be a minority within the Labour Party. He hoped – though I gathered with little expectation – that the press would not assume all good ideas lay within a spectrum running from the moderate wing of the Labour Party to the moderate wing of the Tories. After all, he argued, these two groups had governed continuously since 1945, and Britain had not been conspicuously successful.

From an opposite perspective, Tony Crosland later told me the newspapers were getting the state of Labour politics all wrong. He acknowledged that the activities of Trotskyist infiltrators needed to be watched, but claimed that by September 1975, with the European referendum won, 'Bennery' within the Cabinet was dead. I responded that Benn himself believed this debate was so important than it would continue even if he fell under a bus. Crosland said this only meant the left–right divide was a permanent one in the Labour Party, and observed with a sigh that he had been reading on holiday a book about Keir Hardie, and this had given him a sad sense of *déjà vu*.

Among other right-wingers, dissatisfaction with the direction of the Labour Party produced the first of the cracks which eventually led to creation of the SDP. Between the two 1974 elections, John Harris, one of Roy Jenkins' closest political friends, predicted that if Labour lost in the autumn, the party would split between right and left, within twelve months. That was why he refused to rule out realignment.

Roy Jenkins' experiences as leader of the pro-Europe campaign during the referendum later left him with mixed feelings about the people he had been working with. But mainly those feelings were warm, and aroused his interest in alliances across party lines. Yet Jenkins, who dearly loves a metaphor, noted suspicions between Tories and Liberals, and observed that the banks of politics were like a delta: it was true that the waters were particularly turbulent at the moment, but the banks were high. It was to be another six years before he decided they might be scaled, or breached.

Tony Crosland became disillusioned with Jenkinsite thinking. He felt his old friend's political judgement had deteriorated; and was especially suspicious of late-night sessions among close cronies, which led to excitable decisions, based on the view that one group in the Labour Party had all the right on its side.

On 16 March 1976, Harold Wilson announced to the Cabinet that he intended to retire. He remained Prime Minister while the Parliamentary Labour Party conducted the election of his successor, and formally resigned on 5 April.

Jim Callaghan was his inevitable successor. These two old adversaries within the Labour leadership had been drawn together by the need to avoid disastrous schism. They were both party men, and they discovered their affinity in adversity before the leadership election of 1976.

Oddly, I do not ever seem to have followed up a claim made to me by the secretary of the Parliamentary Labour Party, Frank Barlow, that when counting the votes he would be able to tell how Harold Wilson had voted. It turned out that Harold used green ink, and no other Labour MP did. I used to meet Frank on the train to Waterloo, and he would offer reminiscences of his party's idiosyncrasies. For example, as an office boy in the thirties he had once delivered a summons for a special meeting of the National Executive Committee to Sir Stafford Cripps, then a left-winger. Cripps read the note, looked at Frank and said solemnly: 'The message you have just delivered, my boy, will cost me £1,000.' Cripps was a leading silk, and at the time £1,000 was a large briefing fee.

Even without Frank Barlow's inside information, I had no doubt that Wilson's vote went to Callaghan. They had remarkably similar political attitudes, dictated by events. They were not exactly David and Jonathan, but in life they were no longer divided. For by then there was no realistic rivalry between them. Harold Wilson's leadership was invulnerable, until he chose to go, or until he was defeated in a general election. Jim Callaghan was effectively his inner Cabinet and Deputy Prime Minister rolled into one, even though it was Ted Short, the Leader of the House, who took PM's questions when Wilson was abroad.

The candidates in the leadership election set off by Harold Wilson's resignation were Jim Callaghan, Michael Foot, Roy Jenkins, Tony Benn, Denis Healey and Tony Crosland. The Prime Minister had told me a few months earlier that he had six crown princes, which was always more comfortable than one. Foot and Benn were competing for the left-wing votes. Benn, after a respectable showing of 37 on the first ballot, withdrew and supported Foot, who had been top, with 90, six votes ahead of Callaghan. But in the final ballot, Callaghan received 176 votes to Foot's 133. As the runner-up, Michael Foot was his effective deputy in the government.

When the leadership election began, one question was whether Roy Jenkins could recover from the eclipse in his position during the opposition years, and defeat Jim Callaghan. This was a contest for which both had been preparing through a long series of ups and downs in their respective fortunes. Many of Jenkins' supporters suspected that his time had passed. As far back as 1973, one of his closest friends outside the Labour Party, Jo Grimond, had criticised him for not handling with sufficient vigour his difficult role on the backbenches. Grimond felt that even while Jenkins was quarrelling with his party over Europe – perhaps *especially* because he was doing so – he ought to show its backbenchers some sport by scoring points off Tory ministers on other subjects. He compared him to a master of foxhounds who kept his pack in immaculate condition, but never chased foxes. And though the Westminster tearoom was a cliché, Grimond said, he ought to spend more time there, and less in the Smoking Room, which was a haunt of Tories and Labour's intellectual left.

That was in 1973. By 1976, Roy Jenkins had become what Bernard Ingham was later to call John Biffen: a semi-detached member of the government, unhappy at much of its political direction, and increasingly isolated at the Home Office. After Jim Callaghan became leader, Roy Jenkins was in elegiac mood, willing to contemplate, in his usual rational way, the steps which had stolen from him the destiny that his friends once firmly believed was his: heir at one remove to his hero, Hugh Gaitskell.

I asked him whether he attributed his failure to win the leadership to errors of judgement in the past, or simply that the vacancy occurred at the wrong time for him. He acknowledged that some of his friends thought his resignation from the deputy leadership in 1972 had been a serious mistake, from which his prospects had never recovered. He himself believed that if he had remained as deputy leader, he might have succeeded almost automatically, but he seemed to have few regrets, since he held it would have been impossible for him to remain in the job during Labour's European anguish.

Roy Jenkins saw the decline in his prospects going further back than that, to Labour's defeat in 1970. As Chancellor, he was criticised by Labour MPs for being too 'responsible' in his pre-election budgets, and giving Ted Heath the chance for an unexpected victory. In retrospect, Jenkins recalled that he had not been too despondent after that defeat, which earlier in the campaign he had half expected. But by 1976 he could see that it had made all the difference to his chances of becoming Labour leader. For it had turned him from a powerful post-devaluation Chancellor of the Exchequer, and effectively number two in the government, to a rebellious, and eventually resigning pro-European in a party which became, temporarily, anti-European. Once Roy Jenkins realised that the new Prime Minister intended to make Tony Crosland Foreign Secretary, rather than himself, he accepted the presidency of the European Commission.

If the former Chancellor had been unfortunate with his long-term timetable, the short-term timing of the current Chancellor, Denis Healey, was a disaster. It was during Harold Wilson's sixtieth birthday party that he revealed to Jim Callaghan his intention to retire. They were returning to Westminster to vote. During that division, Denis Healey, oblivious of the coming leadership election, was exchanging verbal abuse with a group of left-wingers who voted against the government. Wilson's resignation came a week later.

Donald Trelford, editor of the *Observer*, and I saw Denis Healey two days afterwards. He was hesitant about standing for the leadership, and it became obvious to me that his campaign team consisted principally of his loyal band of Treasury ministers. Healey has an interesting explanation of why he has never accumulated in parliament a band of personal supporters, comparable to the Jenkins or Callaghan coteries.

This went back to his days as an official at Transport House. He put it in his usual scabrous manner. Looking up at the great men of the

Labour Party from his humbler level, he had seen little but their dirty underwear, and became convinced that the Attlee government was destroyed by cliques. Many of its leading members spent too much time intriguing and conspiring. As a result, between 1952 and 1964 Labour had been wrecked.

So he himself had never encouraged a personal clientèle, though he admitted, with characteristic frankness, that his preference for a private life over a social life also played a part. Shirley Williams detected in him incurable optimism and deep inner exuberance. He tripped over more bricks than most politicians, but when he bloodied his nose, he just got up and carried on. This, she observed, was a quality politicians needed; Churchill supremely had it, because he kept detecting lights at the ends of tunnels. She also thought Healey a warm person, without being sensitive, so that although he enjoyed the company of others, he did not much mind whether or not they liked him in return.

Denis Healey was struggling to create for himself a new political *credo*. He had contempt for the class obsessions of British society, and was convinced these were a major cause of industrial inefficiency. He had always been influenced by his widespread international contacts, and noted how often American businessmen commented on class distinctions in Britain. His overall aim was to create a more efficient and dynamic economy, without destroying the humanities which distinguished us from elements of American and German society.

The problem which he said was exercising the minds both of himself and his rival in the same generation of Labour leaders, Tony Crosland, was that greater equality was only feasible if Britain could achieve a higher gross national product. It was central to Labour's approach to use transfer payments from the better-off to the worse-off. Yet because we had been unsuccessful in generating growth, taxation was now 'a felt burden', particularly among ordinary working people.

Denis Healey feared that simply to persist in higher taxes to create better public services and greater equality would not achieve consent, unless there was faster growth. He thought the government could easily destroy the bedrock of any labour movement, indeed suspected this was already happening to some extent. Ordinary working people were becoming angry because they did not think they were getting the material prosperity they were entitled to, and that all the money was being devoted to people called Pat with sixteen children, who had colour television (then thought of as a luxury) and took their holidays in Majorca.

One of the qualities of Denis Healey as a politician is that he is prepared to face up to the unpopular aspects of his own side's case. He himself was a great believer in social benefits, and when discussing the achievements of the 1974 government, gave precedence to that policy: what it had done for pensioners was better than 'a slap across the face with a wet fish'; and it had increased family allowances for the first time since 1968, and had extended child benefits to the first child. But he knew that the redistributive case would not carry public support unless Labour successfully tackled industrial inefficiency.

He confessed to being a natural optimist, clearly revelling in his belief that politics required more energy than any other job. But he would reel off frightening statistics about investment in British manufacturing: between 1955 and 1973, British firms had invested only two-thirds as much as German ones, half as much as the French, and less than one-quarter as much as the Japanese. In that time, French employment in manufacturing had risen by 11 per cent, German by 31, Japanese by 155, while British employment had fallen by 13 per cent. This was a trend that those who believed the future lay in services found easy to accept. I never did.

The other lost leader of Labour politics in the seventies was Tony Crosland. His early death has inevitably cast around him a penumbra of 'what might have been', like that which envelops the memory of Iain Macleod among a generation of Tories. In each case, death caused huge loss to the causes they served. Each generation in politics produces too few leaders of the highest qualities in mind and character that we can accept phlegmatically their disappearance from the scene.

Harold Wilson's delight in his wealth of crown princes was partly caused by caution about the safety of his own leadership, which he retained long after it was necessary. In part, it was a genuine feeling that he had done what all political leaders I have known, down to Margaret Thatcher, professed to want to do: provide their party with a dazzling choice of successors.

A few months before he retired, Harold told me his views of the criteria for party leadership, though not of the candidates. He still felt it important to be on the National Executive Committee, and added – with a smile which assumed we both knew he was misleading me about probabilities – that Barbara Castle and Shirley Williams both had that qualification. He observed that it was becoming more difficult for a moderate to be elected in the constituency section, which was the best power-base, since it measured popularity at the grassroots.

He was reluctant to go into the merits or otherwise of those we both knew to be the real candidates. At that stage, I had not detected his preference for Jim Callaghan, but had heard a rumour that, among other possibles, he preferred Tony Crosland to Denis Healey. In the light of subsequent knowledge, I doubt whether this was accurate. The Croslands heard the rumour too, but Susan said sadly that if Wilson thought of her husband as a successor, he had not helped him in 1968 by passing him over as Chancellor in favour of Roy Jenkins.

Tony himself was permanently worried that none of the jobs he had held in government had allowed him access to the core of economic policy, and therefore to the trade unions and a wider base in the Labour movement. He also had failed narrowly in 1970 to satisfy Harold Wilson's other criterion for a successful leadership bid: to be elected in the constituency section of the NEC. In that year, he was runner-up, in eighth place, but subsequently slipped to between ninth and twelfth.

Shortly before Wilson resigned, Crosland believed he was in the Prime Minister's good books. This was partly because he was known not to be plotting, partly because Wilson believed him to be a good minister. But their personal relations remained distant, perhaps because Wilson felt that Crosland, who could give the appearance of unbelievable arrogance, had high-hatted him too often during the Gaitskell period. In politics, as in other areas of life, the events of our early years often have excessive influence on the later ones; though this political Freudianism regards 'early life' as beginning from entry to parliament, rather than the womb.

One who admired Tony Crosland was Roy Hattersley. He saw him as among the few Labour politicians of the time who believed clearly in something, and had a set of priorities. Hattersley, however, voted for Jim Callaghan. He was in Bulgaria when Wilson's resignation was announced. As he inspected a guard of honour at the airport, the British Ambassador informed him that, while he was in the air, the Prime Minister had resigned. Hattersley, assuming this meant the Bulgarian Prime Minister, asked out of the corner of his mouth whether this was a good or a bad thing. The Ambassador stiffened, and said: 'I think that's a matter for you, Minister, rather than for me.'

After this misunderstanding had been cleared up, and Hattersley had returned to London, he went to see Roy Jenkins and Tony Crosland to tell them he could not vote for them. He found their reactions were quite different. Jenkins listened courteously while Hattersley explained his reasons, but Crosland greeted his news with an expletive, and when Hattersley asked if he would like to know the reasons, replied testily: 'Certainly not.'

The Minister of State at the Foreign Office, abashed, made his way down in the Environment Department lifts, only to be stopped by the doorman, and asked to return. Crosland said wearily: 'All right, you had better tell me why.' Soon afterwards, Roy and Molly Hattersley received a phone call from Susan Crosland, inviting them to lunch on Sunday. So while downstairs the small Crosland election team beavered away to gather the seventeen votes which eliminated him on the first ballot, upstairs their candidate was entertaining a Callaghan voter and his wife.

19

I WAS MARCIA'S GHOST

I have acted as a ghost-writer just twice, in very different circumstances. The first, when I was a junior reporter in Belfast, was for an ex-boxer, Pat McAllister, who had been, I believe, European welterweight champion. My first editor, Bertie Sayers, called me in, and revealed his problem.

Mr McAllister, he said, in the presence of that friendly pugilist, was a bit hurt that, while our weekly sporting paper, *Ireland's Saturday Night*, had recently carried the serialised life story of a local wrestler, one Buck Alick, it had failed to recognise his own more distinguished career in the Noble Art of Self-Defence. Mr McAllister, he added, had himself written an autobiographical article; and he pointed a fastidious finger at a small pile of crumpled school-jotter paper, covered in pencilled writing. They would both be happy, he said, with a menacing courtesy to which his minions were not accustomed, if I took it away and made whatever adjustments might be needed before publication.

Now both the editor and myself knew that Buck Alick's interest to our readership had lain not just in his wrestling, but because he was a colourful local character. For example, he kept a lion in the back yard of his small back-to-back house in a crowded area of Belfast. Nevertheless, the editor had decreed that Pat McAllister should also be immortalised, so I must do my best.

Pat spelled as he spoke. The contest in which he won his European title had been in Paris. I picked up his version of 'Champs Elysées' quite quickly, but was stumped for a moment by the dialogue with another Belfastman he encountered on that avenue. According to the manuscript, this man greeted him with the words: 'Aha low pat.' Eventually, I transcribed this as: 'Agh, hello, Pat!' He was pleased with my efforts, and apart from the £2 I received from the paper, Pat kindly gave me a table cigarette lighter with a hunting-scene. I neither smoked nor hunted, so

I gave it to my mother, reckoning it was the thought that counted.

The second time I ghost-wrote was for the *Observer*. On that occasion, I was amanuensis for Marcia Williams (Lady Falkender), who was struck down with a slipped disc at an unfortunate time. Joe Haines, with whom she had worked closely when he was Harold Wilson's press secretary at Number 10, published a book that was bitterly critical of her. Serialisation of this in the *Daily Mirror* caused a brief sensation, for it said that she had written out Wilson's controversial resignation honours list on 'lavender-coloured notepaper'. This struck me as among the less interesting parts of the internal disputes at Downing Street, but even the posh end of Fleet Street was obsessed with honours – not surprising, perhaps, when in the following decade it became clear how many editors were prepared to compromise their independence by accepting these from politicians.

I had known Marcia Williams from shortly after my arrival in London, when she became Harold's secretary in his period as shadow Chancellor. From early on, I discovered that she had a sharp political brain, and after he became Prime Minister, she was often helpful to me – as I have no doubt she was, more importantly, to him – in giving a well-balanced judgement of how the Labour Party would react to some policy. Although nominally an adviser, she was among the shrewdest Labour politicians of her period – a view confirmed by critics of Harold Wilson's, such as John Harris, who thought her the most sensible member of the Wilson kitchen cabinet.

It is some measure of the changes in British society in the past quarter-century that Marcia Williams' influence at Number 10 was discussed almost exclusively in terms of her gender. Sexual innuendo was a commonplace of criticism of Harold Wilson, and not exclusively from his political opponents. Privately, both he and Lady Falkender convincingly rebutted this innuendo, and she was understandably indignant that it interfered with a proper assessment of her political work. In her *Observer* articles, she sadly noted that Douglas Hurd did a similar job for Ted Heath, but attracted neither as much publicity nor criticism as she did.

She and her family were close to the Wilson family as a whole, as I saw at first-hand when I was working at her house, and they came visiting. Marcia Williams was notably warm about Mary Wilson, saying that, like Anthony Eden's wife, she 'did not want the Suez Canal flowing through her drawing-room'. She did her job as wife of the Prime Minister conscientiously and well, but she was a mature and understanding woman with her own interests, and she was no more obsessed by politics than, she imagined, the wife of the managing director at ICI was obsessed by man-made fibres.

In her articles, she noted that there had not been a woman in the private office at Number 10 since Neville Chamberlain's day, and added plaintively: 'Perhaps 20 years from now, as women are more widely accepted, there will be two women, one black and one white, in that office. Perhaps the political office will contain equal numbers of men and women advisers, black and white without discrimination. And no one will get excited.'

Work with Marcia on the articles took me a fortnight. Sometimes the *Observer* printers were kept waiting longer than they would have liked, since my drafts had to be edited not only by her, but by the former Prime Minister: she took the punctilious view that, since she was a personal assistant of his, he was entitled to oversee her journalism – and mine. But it was one of the more hilarious periods in my career. For although she was quite depressed by the attack Joe had made on her, she has a gutsy sense of fun, and could not avoid seeing the amusing side of her life and times.

We worked long days, Marcia remaining as still on her painful back as her animated conversational style allowed, me struggling to operate an unfamiliar tape-recorder (for in those days, most journalists of my generation normally used shorthand). I think somebody must have told her that Irishmen grow troublesome if they are not adequately fed and watered, for every few hours a Filipino maid led me downstairs to an appetising light meal, accompanied by Guinness. While in England, I don't normally drink Guinness, which is said, rightly or wrongly, to be much better in its Irish than its London manifestation. But it probably sustained the necessary mood for my work.

The articles contained useful insights into the way Harold Wilson's political life was organised. I think the shrewdest piece of advice Marcia Williams ever gave him was after the indecisive election in February 1974. Labour MPs were indignant because they feared Ted Heath was going to do a deal with Jeremy Thorpe to keep him in office, and there was pressure on Wilson to issue an angry statement. Marcia, who prided herself on her historical and constitutional knowledge, argued to him that Heath was entitled to attempt a deal with the Liberals, however dangerous this might be for Labour. She and Jim Callaghan both thought Wilson would look better if he simply went off to the house he had acquired in Buckinghamshire, near Chequers, for a rest with his wife and family, and waited for the talks to fail. Wilson himself told me he had concentrated on playing football with his dog Paddy.

Marcia was also an intense election campaigner. Just before the 1964 election, she was leafing through *Radio Times* to check if anything appearing on television on the evening of polling day might reduce the turn-out of voters. To her horror, she discovered that *Steptoe and Son*, one of the most popular programmes of the period, was scheduled an hour before the polls closed, the time when the largest number of Labour supporters traditionally came out.

She told Harold Wilson, who telephoned Sir Hugh Greene, then BBC Director-General, to argue that this temptation might reduce the turn-out, of Conservative as well as Labour voters. Sir Hugh accepted the point, but wryly asked what programme Wilson was suggesting as an alternative. The reply was: 'Greek drama, preferably in the original.' The BBC did not think that suitable for peak viewing, but they did move Steptoe. The incident caused Wilson to say that but for Marcia Williams he would not have been Prime Minister; the Labour majority was only four seats, so every vote had counted.

In 1974 Harold Wilson recommended Marcia Williams for a peerage, telling the Queen he wished to raise two fingers to the press, which had been critical of his political secretary over land deals involving her family. But he was often tempted by an almost boyish wish to manipulate the newspapers. During the Loyalist workers' strike, which eventually led to the collapse of the Northern Ireland power-sharing executive, a singularly fruitless discussion took place at Downing Street one evening. It was attended by ministers, civil servants, senior officers and the ambassador to Dublin.

Nobody had any fruitful suggestions. The Chief of the General Staff had arrived wearing battledress, and the Prime Minister, with a touch of gallows humour, said: 'Perhaps that's the answer: martial law.'

The CGS rather maladroitly replied: 'No, no, I can assure you there will never be martial law in Great Britain.'

Harold answered that he hadn't been talking about Great Britain.

The discussion got nowhere. The army said they could not run the power stations. The ambassador reported that Garret FitzGerald, the Irish Foreign Minister – whose government's insistence on an 'Irish dimension' had scuppered this last, best hope of a peaceful settlement in Ulster – now said Dublin would go along with anything London did.

The Prime Minister declared his intention of summoning the leaders of the parties in the executive to a meeting in London the following day. He made clear that this was primarily a public relations initiative, to show that something was being done: better that a couple of press officers should lose their evenings off than that soldiers should lose their lives. Nobody had alternative proposals.

Roy Jenkins, who was smoking a cigar described to me as 'of Marx

Brothers proportions', walked back to the Home Office afterwards, accompanied by Roy Hattersley, who had been standing in at the meeting for Jim Callaghan. When Hattersley expressed doubts about the value of the proposed conference with the Ulster party leaders, Jenkins urbanely told him that everyone at the meeting except him knew the PM was announcing Marcia's peerage the next day, and wanted the Ulster story to occupy the main headlines.

My ghost-writing partnership with Marcia must have been considered a success, for the publisher, George Weidenfeld, later suggested I might perform the same service on a book she was contemplating. I was tempted, for this would have given me a fascinating insight into the Wilson years. But Adam Raphael, the *Observer*'s political correspondent, sensibly advised me that, as deputy editor of the paper, I would need to concentrate on the Callaghan years; and perhaps soon the Thatcher years. In politics, the caravan continually moves on.

When Harold Wilson resigned in March 1976, I had assessed his premiership in the *Observer*, and tried to give the pros and cons:

> When people judge Harold Wilson, they are really judging the style he imposed on his era. He has never been ashamed of his belief in politics as the art of the possible; but his critics say he has made the famous pragmatism into an art form, and a decadent art form at that, where style totally dominates content.
>
> For this man in this period, events suggest that the style was the best. His most conspicuous failures – the British technologically fuelled miracle which did not happen; statutory trade union reform, which was aborted under his first government, and failed dismally when tried by the Conservatives (under Ted Heath); and his blurred vision of Ireland – have come when he deviated from his normal modest view of the limitations of political leadership, and succumbed to enthusiasm.
>
> His successes – voluntary incomes policy, Europe, modest social reform, party unity, the explosion of the frightened and dangerous myth that Britain is, in some unique sense, ungovernable – have been the work of a master in his own art, that of political management ... Wilson's deepest instinct is to conciliate, rather than to confront. It was the underlying theme, personal ambitions aside, of the long quarrel with Gaitskell.

It was Harold's practical common sense which commended him to me as a political leader, just as it was his instinct for personal kindness which commended him to me as a human being. By the end of his career, some critics believed he had lost all ideals. I believed he had lost only the more dangerous illusions that political flesh is heir to, notably omniscience.

As ever, I was interested in his contribution to industrial and incomes policies, and wrote, in an *Observer* editorial:

> It is easy to scoff at these essentially ameliorative measures to channel the conflict of human greed into less destructive ways. Yet it is wise to fear the Greeks bearing panaceas. The British genius has been a non-ideological, practical one. There are no absolute answers, no fair answers to such problems as relative rewards for endeavour, the rules of industrial warfare, the balance between individual rights and the communal interest.
>
> There is, however, an underlying common-sense which needs to be more actively asserted. Untidiness and conflict are the price we pay for the liberty we claim. Free collective bargaining – whether by doctors, dockers, teachers or tanker drivers – can be economically disastrous, socially disruptive and, if pushed to the limit, will destroy our liberal society. It is still better than the work permit of a Communist or fascist state. Our only safeguard is constantly to assert the common interest, which often conflicts with the individual interest.

After Harold Wilson retired, the press, with its then fashionable *penchant* for conspiracy theories, sought ever more fanciful explanations for why a Prime Minister might leave the job voluntarily. Unbelievably, some officers of MI5, paid for by the taxpayer, seem to have rumour-mongered about the supposed treachery of a British Prime Minister with such sober journals as *Private Eye*. I believe the truth is more obvious: that he no longer believed there was a simple solution to Britain's problems, within the timescale available to a man of his age.

He also realised his powers were diminishing. Years later, I heard a story which confirmed this. He had asked his principal private secretary, Kenneth Stowe, whether he had been promoted to deputy secretary, the rank he would have held if he had returned to his own civil service department instead of remaining at Downing Street, at Wilson's request. Stowe replied that he was still an assistant secretary. Clearly, the Prime Minister intended to rectify what he saw as an injustice.

Some months later, he asked the same question, and was told there was no change in the private secretary's rank. Stowe suddenly noticed that Harold Wilson's eyes had filled with tears, because he had forgotten to do anything after their first conversation. The famous memory was beginning to fade.

20

DENIS AND THE BANKERS

I found the Callaghan government, between 1976 and 1979, one of the most interesting in the period covered by this book. First, it was the last fling of the old post-war consensus, before the Thatcher revolution began a new era in British politics. This also happened to be a period when, having settled to the measured pace of Sunday journalism, I found more time to dig deeper into politics. And the government contained a number of ministers, of varying ages, with whom I had grown up – or old – in politics. Three of these – Jim Callaghan, Denis Healey and Tony Crosland – came to dominate my thinking about the future direction of the Labour Party.

What engaged my immediate interest was that for both ministers and the nation the fight against inflation was now deadly serious. Long-term weaknesses in the British economy and industrial system had been my journalistic subject for many years. I had been discussing incomes policies with Jim Callaghan himself since the early sixties. During the seventies, under both Conservative and Labour governments, Britain had looked over the precipice of hyper-inflation, and took fright at what it saw. Throughout the Callaghan years, despite successive agreements with industry and the unions, this spectre was never far away, and culminated in the Winter of Discontent.

Since my period as a labour correspondent in the late fifties and early sixties, I had maintained my industrial contacts, so was able to hear the story of Jim Callaghan's battle to avoid the collapse of his policy and government from a variety of perspectives. The versions of Len Murray, General Secretary of the TUC, Jack Jones, the transport workers' leader, and David Basnett, of the municipal workers, provided a useful counter-point to what I learned from the Prime Minister and his principal economic ministers, Denis Healey, Michael Foot, Shirley Williams, and later Roy Hattersley.

Jim Callaghan used to quote to me a remark of Jimmy Maxton, one of Labour's 'Red Clydesiders' before the war: 'If you can't ride two horses, get out of the bloody circus.' He was now riding more than two political horses. Apart from Britain's endemic economic weaknesses, he was under pressure from Scottish and Welsh nationalism. He was committed to introducing devolution in those countries, but that was bitterly opposed by some in his own party. He also had to manage without a majority in parliament, which he did for a time through a Lib-Lab pact with David Steel. I will describe various aspects of his dilemma in the chapters which follow.

But economic weakness dominated the Callaghan government's life, and led to the International Monetary Fund crisis in the second half of 1976. The principal actor in that drama was the Chancellor, Denis Healey. He is one of the most interesting figures in modern British politics, an odd mixture of brilliant mind and reckless naïveté in behaviour, of personal insensitivity combined with warmth and kindness. His tactlessness is legendary.

One story illustrates this. Jim Callaghan, who has a natural eloquence in the English language, used occasionally to indulge himself in Cabinet with a Latin or French tag. This is a habit to which most of us auto-didacts succumb, and to which, incidentally, Denis himself was not immune, though in his case it might be in Italian or Polish. He would greet Jim's ventures into foreign tongues with a playful demand for translation 'for the benefit of us simple minded fellows'. The sensitive soul who told me this anecdote from the Cabinet Room could imagine nothing more maladroit for a Balliol Exhibitioner to say to an alumnus of Portsmouth Northern Secondary School. Yet the Prime Minister seemed to take it all in good part: he liked Healey, and knew from personal experience the burden he was carrying.

Denis Healey resented the time he spent in negotiations with the TUC about wages. He understood how vital those long, often indecisive dinners were, but his mind rebelled against the irrationality which human factors often impose on a logical nature. Once, at a meeting with three of us from the *Observer*, I must have cross-questioned him too exhaustively about the minutiae of these discussions. As we left, he asked, with ostentatious sympathy, whether I had ever considered consulting a psychiatrist about my obsession with incomes policy.

I detect a slight irritation in the note I made that evening, in *esprit d'escalier*: 'The answer is that each Chancellor since Selwyn Lloyd has taken roughly that attitude – saying that planning, or monetarism, or the budget, or God knows what else is more important than wages; and each of them has finished up in a smoke-filled room with the TUC, telling them his life depends on their every word.' From today's perspective, I would add to that list of quack cures for wage inflation the one which dare not speak its name: unemployment. No politician will say this out loud, but it is consistently high unemployment which has brought inflation down in the nineties. Draw from that what conclusion you will. Mine is that it creates more problems than it may appear to cure.

When Jim Callaghan became Prime Minister, inflation was still twenty-one per cent, for lower wage levels negotiated under Harold Wilson had not yet worked through to the Retail Price Index. Two months later, the TUC agreed to hold wage increases during 1976–7 to between £2.50 and £4, which should have pulled inflation down to seven per cent. Sadly, a weakening of the pound thwarted this.

The devaluation crisis of 1967 seemed at the time to have destroyed Callaghan's political career. During the Heath government, the Bretton Woods system of fixed exchange rates had ended, so formal devaluations were no longer the danger. But as the pound floated downward, and prices inflated, Britain suffered the same malign consequences of devaluation which made Wilson and Callaghan so reluctant to devalue in the sixties. With the pound at $1.87, the pressure on wages was hard to resist.

Yet Jim Callaghan remained sure the objectives he had inherited from Harold Wilson were right. He himself had come up through the trade union movement, but as far back as our talks in the early sixties he had accepted that unfettered collective bargaining could have a bad effect on the Labour Party's aim of greater social justice. His instincts, as a party man, convinced him that he, rather than Margaret Thatcher, had the best chance of achieving a sensible voluntary deal with the unions which would stick.

This was one reason why he clung to office so tenaciously. His politics were grounded more firmly in gut working-class attitudes and experience than any other senior Labour figure of that time. His father, a former chief petty officer in the Royal Navy, had died when he was a small boy. After they had been evicted from their tied coastguard cottage, only a ten shillings a week pension from the first Labour government in 1923 had enabled his mother to bring him up in reasonable decency. He believed he understood working-class people better than politicians from a more privileged background.

The Prime Minister could not have had a better ally in the fight against inflation than his Chancellor. Denis Healey made tax concessions in his budget conditional on a satisfactory deal on wages. There was some public mumbling that, in allowing the actions of wage-bargainers to influence the shape of his budget, Healey was allowing outsiders into this Treasury holy of holies. In the *Observer* we had been predicting, and advocating, that he would and should take this course, so I found the constitutionalists' expressions of outrage histrionic. It seemed to me that he was engaged in a legitimate exercise of public education in the facts of economic life, making not only the TUC, but also non-unionists understand what effect their own actions about pay might have on employment and living standards. This fitted in well with Jim Callaghan's view that the job of political leaders was to mobilise consent for their right to govern, and not just during general election campaigns. That is what plural democracy means.

In October 1976, as the price of a loan to support the pound, the IMF demanded reductions in public spending. The crisis negotiations with the Fund in the autumn and winter of Jim Callaghan's first year as Prime Minister were the bizarre turning point in his government. Bizarre, because subsequent statistics showed the whole bruising controversy within the Cabinet was conducted at several removes from reality.

Callaghan confessed his fear that the government could suffer death by a thousand cuts: keeping to a programme of unpleasant actions, yet still not influencing the foreign exchanges. It was all so irrational. He did not understand the psychology of the money markets, and was suspicious of anybody who claimed to do so. When the Treasury proposed public spending cuts, left-wing opposition within the Cabinet was led by Tony Benn and Peter Shore. Their proposal was that Britain should threaten the IMF with the left's alternative strategy, which included import controls.

A second group, in the centre and right of the Cabinet, also had doubts about the Chancellor's prospective deal with the IMF. They were free-traders, and certainly did not want the left's siege economy, and they knew Britain needed a loan from the IMF to avert a sterling crisis. Yet because public spending was as near to an Ark of the Covenant as Labour revisionists now had, they were determined to avoid the cutting of a single unnecessary penny. The leader of this second group was the archpriest of public spending, Tony Crosland, now Foreign Secretary, who became the Chancellor's most effective critic during the IMF crisis.

Crosland's most fervent supporter in the struggle against savage cuts was a new Cabinet minister, Roy Hattersley. Having backed Jim Callaghan in the leadership election, Hattersley had been predictably miffed to see his hopes of a Cabinet post once again deferred. The new Prime Minister was aware of this. At a party soon after his election, he took the ambitious young Foreign Office minister aside, remarked that he must be disappointed, but told him: 'I just want to say that your time will come.' Hattersley murmured his thanks, but Jim Callaghan continued, with open acknowledgement of how politicians' minds work: 'You're probably saying: "Yes, but when?"' Hattersley uttered an unconvincing 'no, no', and Callaghan repeated several times the phrase 'your time will come.'

Roy Hattersley confessed later that he staggered away to consider this conversation, and came to the conclusion that it would allow the Prime Minister either to promote him to the chancellorship the following morning, or on the other hand never to appoint him to anything. When I suggested that Callaghan, in recollection of the conversation, would find the second course embarrassing, Hattersley said grimly that he thought the Prime Minister was the kind of man who could live with such embarrassment.

It was at this time that I began to appreciate Roy Hattersley's gift for self-mockery, and his boyish tendency to play jokes. He once arrived at a dinner party, and quickly realised that he was in the wrong company, which in his case meant that all the other guests were too right-wing. About midnight, Jonathan Aitken arrived, wearing a white dinner-jacket. Aitken, then a Tory backbencher, later became a Cabinet minister with a high profile, in Paris and the Middle East, as well as in Whitehall.

Roy Hattersley adopted an old Crosland trick, by pretending he had identified him wrongly. When they were introduced, he said, in apparent flattery: 'Your pieces in the *Guardian* are the first thing I read each morning.'

All around him, guests were shouting: 'Not Ian [the *Guardian*'s political editor], *Jonathan!*'

Hattersley ignored them, and ploughed on. He confessed later that the incident had given him some pleasure on a bad evening.

The IMF crisis dragged on through summer and autumn. Cabinet doubters would have been happier to face the cuts in public spending if they have been convinced these would serve longer-term economic objectives. But eager as the government was to switch its efforts towards manufacturing industry, nobody believed that elderly school dinner ladies, displaced by cuts in public services, would find jobs in factories.

That is not how the labour market works, as I had discovered a dozen years earlier, when Harold Wilson justified cancellation of the TSR2 military aircraft partly on the ground that skilled engineers were required in civil manufacture. Six months later, I sent a *Guardian* reporter to Lancashire, and he uncovered the sad truth: most of the engineers had drifted into jobs as commercial travellers or in other service trades. Why not? A car on the firm, and less arduous work. But not necessarily in the national interest.

As the Chancellor's appalling load of work and anxiety continued through the autumn, he fought great waves of tiredness to maintain at least the appearance of his normal ebullient nature. He had now sadly concluded that not much progress would be made during his term of office in tackling the real British disease, industrial inefficiency and decline. Denis Healey, like others before and after him, was near to despair to discover how little influence a government could have on industrial revival. His tragedy and that of the Callaghan government was that they were forced to spend so much time on crisis management.

The Chancellor, who resented his lack of support in Cabinet, contrasted ministers' disloyalty with the behaviour of union leaders. Jack Jones and Hugh Scanlon, both from the left, had taken time to be convinced that the alternative to wage restraint was rising unemployment, but then they went on television to defend government policy, even though this put them in trouble with their own members. Their support for him sometimes brought Healey, the cold logician, close to tears.

Tony Crosland was sensitive to the Chancellor's feeling of hurt, and did not want to make compromise more difficult. So a meeting I had with the Foreign Secretary at the height of the crisis was conducted with a lack of our normal combative candour. Indeed, he had warned me in advance that he might be wasting my time. But during such a major news story, in which good information was hard to come by, and he was among the most significant players, I was prepared to take the risk.

Our talk is an illustration of how even apparently oblique exchanges of ideas with the right politician at the right time can help a journalist to understand what is going on. Because Crosland did not want to talk about his disagreements with the Chancellor, I decided to ask him about the durability of the government, and the possibility of a coalition. Since Jim Callaghan was in a Commons minority, newspapers were beginning again to write about this.

I suspected that, for Crosland, coalition talk would be a red rag to a bull, and might encourage him to open up, perhaps more than he intended. This proved to be so. He said the Labour government would survive, principally because Callaghan was in very calm mood, much less gloomy than during the devaluation crisis of 1967. Neither he nor anybody in the Parliamentary Labour Party wanted an election at this disastrous time. Crosland argued that the then Cabinet consisted of some tough and able politicians, and was younger than previous ones. Despite their troubles, he detected no signs of demoralisation, rather a great will to survive.

He grew indignant when he reflected on the origin of coalition rumours. These were again going the rounds among businessmen, and he declared bitterly that they were a result of political and economic illiteracy, which was doing great damage to Britain abroad. He said the only newspaper many American people of influence saw was *The Times*, and when they read some of its leading articles, they thought nothing was right about Britain. Crosland did not deny that the country faced a grim economic prospect, and that many people's living standards were going to suffer for a couple of years. But this was still a good country to live in, for many reasons which foreigners here acknowledged. (His wife, the journalist Susan Barnes, was American.)

Having warmed him up, I edged into the delicate subject of cuts, asking how his own attitudes were developing. He picked up a phrase of mine about 'ritual cuts', and said this was what he was against, 'making marks on the breast because this impressed international creditors'. Paradoxically, since returning to government in 1974, he had become more aware of waste in public spending, though he meant something different by this than many other people did. While Environment Secretary he had opposed heavy subsidising of commuter rail services. Too much public spending went to better-off people, he said, and this offended his own redistributive instincts.

Yet Crosland believed Britain must have the IMF loan. Jim Callaghan eventually told him, privately as well as in Cabinet, that he was backing his Chancellor, and that therefore the government's life depended on acceptance of Healey's proposals. Even in our elliptical conversation in October, before this awkward crunch had been reached, Tony Crosland hinted that he saw the logic of making just enough cuts to satisfy financial orthodoxy and get the loan. The phrase he eventually settled on was that he was against 'slashing cuts'. On the basis of unreliable Treasury forecasts, which all Chancellors complain of, cuts were eventually made. They proved largely unnecessary, except for the cosmetic reason: that they impressed the markets.

Sadly, Tony Crosland, the man whose attitudes attracted me more than anyone else in politics, died suddenly in February 1977, at a time when British public life desperately needed men of his contemplative temperament. He was a middle-class intellectual who wanted to do the right thing by working people. Beneath the veneer of Hampstead and Oxford was an old-fashioned Labour man, with a conscience about inequality and injustice. Tony Crosland's death provoked in me a frisson of anxiety that no analysis would now emerge from the Labour moderates. I might not like ideologies, but they must know in which direction they were going. Without this, voters would have no clear choice, in competition with the alternative strategy of the Labour left, and the persistently more ideological tone of Conservative thinking under Margaret Thatcher.

I explored this at Labour's 1977 conference, eight months after Crosland's death, by talking to eight or nine centre-right members of the Cabinet. I have only general notes of these conversations, but from the opinions I recorded at the time, I deduce they were with those I knew best in that group: Denis Healey, whose embattled chancellorship made him the government's most significant figure, next to the Prime Minister; the Home Secretary, Merlyn Rees, Jim Callaghan's most trusted friend; David Owen, who had taken over as Foreign Secretary; Shirley Williams, another admirer of Crosland's attitudes; Roy Hattersley, his dead hero's *alter ego* in an obsession with the British class system and the need for greater equality; Edmund Dell, a highly intelligent minister, who even then was becoming slightly *dégagé*, and who subsequently left parliament; Bill Rodgers, who continued to carry the Jenkinsite standard after Roy's departure to Brussels; Harold Lever, the jovial financial iconoclast.

I suspected that in the next election Jim Callaghan might be forced into stealing an old Conservative slogan: 'You *know* Labour government works – don't let the Tories spoil it.' When I put this to one of my witnesses, he replied blithely: 'Why not? Why should the Tories have all the best tunes?' Others were less complacent: 'You can run a government without a philosophy, but you can't enthuse a political movement without one.' Some ministers admitted this, but did not have time or intellectual energy to remedy it.

One said cheerfully: 'The left have always refused to change their old clothes, however unsuited they are to the actual climate. We, on the other hand, occasionally do get a bit naked, but we keep ourselves warm by running around vigorously.' In the second Wilson and Callaghan governments, ministers had been running around so vigorously, to deal with the crisis they had inherited and the further crises which engulfed them, that they found little time to recharge their mental batteries.

The certitude in the other two principal political camps made this vacuum more obvious. The left was committed to an alternative strategy which emphasised public ownership and state intervention, leading to import controls, and hence to anti-Europeanism. It was grounded on suspicion that the mixed economy was a confidence trick, really a market economy with sops for socialists. In the Conservative Party, despite a pragmatic rearguard action, Margaret Thatcher and her allies were determined their party was going to be more ideologically directed towards pure market economics than at any time since the thirties.

I defined the risk of the dominant group in the Callaghan government as being 'stuck on a pragmatic sandbank in a sea that is choppy with ideology'. This problem had been growing for a long time. In the fifties, Hugh Gaitskell and Tony Crosland had removed public ownership from its place of honour in Labour's pantheon, and had substituted equality. They appealed to voters' sense of fairness, with a Galbraithian rejection of private affluence and public squalor.

Harold Wilson or Jim Callaghan, neither of them ideologues, would have accepted as a definition of their purpose the phrase 'a more just society', which was not an ideology, but at least indicated the direction in which they wanted to go. At the 1977 conference, one Labour thinker – frustratingly, at this distance in time, I cannot discover which – confessed that he had come to the conclusion that a new philosophy was not available for the Labour revisionists. What distinguished Labour from the Conservatives he could best define as 'feeling', a difference in tone and attitude as important as ideology, which communicated itself to voters in years when they were in the right mood.

This frank admission of the bog of uncertainty into which the Crosland analysis had run derived from one cause: economic failure, under both Conservative and Labour governments. To achieve a new synthesis, it seemed to me, Labour must solve the following dilemma: if low growth made it impossible to gain public support for 'a more just society' through the tax system, how was redistribution, the central revisionist objective, to be achieved? And where did free collective bargaining, incentives and restrictive practices fit into the effort to achieve greater industrial efficiency, and therefore higher growth?

It is a dilemma with which the modern Labour Party is still wrestling, so far without obvious success.

21

LOST IN THE SCOTTISH MIST

What made the life of the Callaghan government constantly perilous was that it never had an overall majority. The defection of two Labour MPs to a new Scottish Labour Party, together with by-election losses, deprived Labour of control of the Commons. For a time, Callaghan and Michael Foot were able to sustain themselves in office through a remarkable deal with David Steel's Liberals, the first pact of its kind in the post-war period. This began a public debate about the possibility of realignments in British politics, a subject which will concern us more, though in a different way, during the following decade.

This mould-breaking parliamentary pact with the Liberals produced a period of both political excitement and steadier government. The strains were sharpened by electoral worries, especially those associated with an old Liberal subject, devolution. Scottish nationalism appeared to be on the march, and both Labour and Liberals had to watch their flanks. Scottish devolution was to be the occasion of Jim Callaghan's loss of office. In 1979, he suffered defeat in parliament on this subject. His was the first government to do so since 1924. Those who wanted devolution (Nationalists and Liberals) combined with those who did not (Margaret Thatcher's Conservatives) to bring him down.

The Callaghan government had another troublesome item on its agenda: direct elections to the European parliament. Both devolution and Europe had a smell of sulphur about them, for either was likely to produce a government defeat in the House, followed by a general election. So a journalist could not afford to neglect them, and personally I found them interesting enough. Yet in the lives of ordinary people, economic success or failure remained of far greater importance. Those of us whose melancholy duty it was to chart the minutiae of the battles over devolution and the European parliament knew that they rarely caused fights in pubs.

The British people had decisively affirmed in the 1975 referendum that we were staying in Europe, so I could find no respectable argument for not having a proper parliament there. Not just the European Commission but, more importantly, the Council of Ministers ought to be democratically controlled. Otherwise, a Europe which was garnering more power each year would be ruled not by democracy, but by diplomacy, which is not my favourite art form. As Robert Burns wrote: 'it's coming yet, for a' that . . .'

The legislation to provide for direct elections caused the minority Labour government endless anguish. The Cabinet contained ministers such as Tony Benn and Peter Shore who remained implacably opposed to greater power for the Community. Yet the Lib-Lab pact, created in March 1976 to keep the government in office, was soon to commit Jim Callaghan to push through the legislation. Shirley Williams, who during the 1974 elections had made clear that her European conviction was not to be traded away for political reasons, believed the left again felt there was a chance of getting Britain out of Europe, and said this was the one issue which could blow the Labour Party apart.

Shirley Williams also spoke prophetically about Margaret Thatcher's attitudes. Her argument was that the new Conservative leader still had to prove herself a good European. She claimed that Ted Heath was going round Europe, speaking more frankly about his successor's attitudes than people in Britain realised. Her own friends in Germany were reporting this to her, and she thought the message ought to get back to Margaret Thatcher that she was still extremely suspect in Europe. I was not sure who Shirley thought might convey this message, but I had no difficulty in deciding it would not be me. Life is full enough of trouble, without seeking it out.

If I was enthusiastic about Europe, I showed more scepticism over devolution, principally because of my experience of Stormont: Ulster had suffered economically because Westminster governments could shuffle off responsibility for unemployment to the devolved parliament. The political shove behind devolution for Scotland came from the election of eleven Nationalist MPs in October 1974, an increase of four on their already good showing in February. Many Westminster politicians began to fear that backsliding would lead to a tartan revolt, with charges from north of the border against 'perfidious Albion', and electoral support for the SNP's real policy, independence.

The campaign was fuelled by the huge earnings that were expected from North Sea oil – or, as the Nationalists preferred to call it – 'Scotland's oil'. A Scots friend ended an argument with me on this emotive issue with a conclusive dictum: 'Well, it may no' be precisely Scotland's oil, but I'm buggered if it's all going to be spent on another extension to the Jubilee Line of the London Underground.' This seemed to catch the reality of the argument: Scotland's complaints were of economic deprivation. For many decades, the Central Lowlands had suffered some of the worst endemic unemployment in Europe. Successive regional policies had achieved much, in establishing industries like electronics and motor manufacture, but more traditional engineering and shipbuilding were in apparently permanent decline, and Scotland often seemed to be running fast to stay in the same place. Westminster insouciance was a natural whipping-boy.

The United Kingdom had been accustomed to run its economy nationally, and according to the *needs* of the various parts. Coming from Belfast, I felt strongly about what experience taught. During Northern Ireland's fifty-one years of devolution, it theoretically possessed wider powers to tax and spend than those now being proposed for Scotland. But both Whitehall and Stormont soon concluded it would be politically intolerable to maintain common services in the two areas if the tax levels were not identical. So an Ulster government of conservative outlook introduced the full welfare state services of the Attlee years, and its people paid the same income tax rates. The policy was called 'step by step', and it seemed the only feasible one. So was devolution worthwhile?

Parliamentary alliances on these troublesome subjects were shifting ones. The Conservatives under Margaret Thatcher had now resiled from earlier support for Scottish devolution. The SNP saw it as a halfway house on the road to independence. The Liberals favoured a federal system, with wider tax-raising powers to be devolved to an assembly in Edinburgh. The Callaghan government settled on a system of financing devolution through a block grant to the assembly. It was this scheme which Jim Callaghan himself submitted for second reading in December 1976.

His problems lay in later parliamentary stages. Labour backbenchers, some in England, as well as Scotland and Wales, were opposed to devolution. In February 1977 this changed the face of Westminster politics, when twenty-two Labour MPs voted with the opposition against a guillotine motion on the legislation, and another twenty abstained. The government was defeated. A few weeks later, Jim Callaghan faced another prospective defeat on his public expenditure plans. The government seemed in danger of falling apart, for want of a majority in the Commons. Margaret Thatcher tabled a censure motion to be debated on 23 March.

In the days before that debate, I was in Luxembourg, learning about the (then unelected) European parliament. I arrived back at Westminster for the end of the censure debate, and heard the story of a remarkable few days from an excited group of Labour ministers and MPs, who gathered in Roy Hattersley's room after the government had won the ten o'clock division. They included Bill Rodgers, Denis Howell and Giles Radice.

Immediately after Margaret Thatcher moved her censure motion, Jim Callaghan had announced that his government was entering into a pact with the Liberals. This provided for regular consultations on forthcoming legislation, and on Liberal ideas for amending it; meetings on economic matters between Denis Healey and his equally abrasive Liberal shadow, John Pardoe; and promises that the government would press ahead with bills on devolution and direct elections to the European parliament, with free votes on sensitive issues such as a proportional representation voting system for these elections.

The Cabinet had divided 20 to 4 in favour of the pact. The group I met in Hattersley's room regarded Michael Foot as their hero of the hour, an unprecedented choice for most of these right-of-centre figures. They praised the remarkable relationship which Jim Callaghan and his deputy had built up since they fought each other for the premiership the previous year. In the perilous life of the minority Labour government, the two men's backgrounds complemented each other perfectly, for they appealed to different strands of opinion, within their own party and beyond.

For supporters of the Lib-Lab pact, the other hero of the hour was David Steel. His leadership of the Liberals had a practical streak, compared with those of his more flamboyant predecessors, Jo Grimond and Jeremy Thorpe. David used to amuse me with tales about what he called the exclusive brethren tendency among his own supporters. Once he received a letter from a Liberal suggesting they should vote against a Lords amendment which would have introduced the PR principle for Scottish Assembly elections. But was PR not a long-cherished Liberal aim, one which if adopted for Westminster elections might transform their electoral prospects? Ah, yes, said David's correspondent, but party policy was for PR on the single transferable vote system, and the method proposed in the Lords amendment was not acceptable.

David Steel had no time for arguments about how many angels could dance on the head of a needle. He explained to me that his interest in politics was in influencing events, in getting things done. As a young

MP he had piloted an abortion bill through parliament, with the help of Tory and Labour MPs.

During the Lib–Lab pact, Jim Callaghan developed an almost paternal affection for him, though both were political realists, and knew they could only go a certain distance in cooperation between separate parties with different aims. But when the pact had been in existence for a few months, Callaghan told me with satisfaction that his government now had an effective majority of thirty, with the help of the Liberals and what he called 'various sources' (a sly nod at the Unionist MPs from my native land, who since direct rule in 1972 were no longer so reliably pro-Conservative). He had acknowledged, to himself and to Steel, what the Liberals' objective must be: to create a wedge between the two major parties. He hoped that history would credit the Liberal leader with having changed thirteen men who fought only on their own charisma into a team which negotiated to get things done.

The Lib–Lab pact seemed a natural development of Steel's career (as did the Alliance which he and Roy Jenkins created in the following decade). I have enjoyed many fascinating discussions with him down the years about the nature of his politics. Scots and Ulstermen share much social and religious background, not least in the democratic structure which Presbyterianism inculcates, so I have always felt I understood politicians like David Steel and John Smith better than most.

When Steel's father, later to be Moderator of the General Assembly, served in a west of Scotland parish, his son noted that the area's politics borrowed much from Ireland: he remembered stoning, and being stoned by children in the local Catholic school – which was worse than ever happened to me in Belfast. The Steel family neatly bridged their nation's domestic and international concerns. His father usually voted Labour. Both father and son criticised the Church for not doing properly the job of social Christianity in the inner cities. With a slightly different Church of Scotland, David Steel might have become a minister. But he shared his Church's *Angst* about colonialism and racism. While his father was serving in Kenya, David was horrified by the racist attitudes there. His school companions met blacks only as servants, and when his father started a multiracial Boys' Brigade company at his church, it failed for lack of numbers.

His hope was that, if the parliament lasted its full term, and Liberal support revived, Labour would need another deal after the next election. He had a recurrent nightmare that the Conservatives would come out of that election as the largest party, yet requiring Liberal support to form a government. Jim Callaghan took to pulling his leg about the dangers of 'getting into bed with Margaret Thatcher'. David Steel realised he would not have the luxury of choice. The mathematical logic of the Liberals' position was that they must do a deal with whichever party could govern with their support.

His personal relations with Margaret Thatcher were almost non-existent, partly because she was angry that he was sustaining a minority Labour government she had hoped to defeat. The only time when the two talked was on state occasions, and even when they sat together at Selwyn Lloyd's memorial service, she did not address a word to him. Judy Steel had a story to cap her husband's. She and the wife of Donald Stewart, the SNP leader, were sitting with Mrs Thatcher at a social event, when she astonished them by saying: 'You both have so much more time to get your hair right than us working women.' Mrs Steel thought that, with four young children to look after in Scotland, while David spent most of his time at Westminster, she might claim to be a 'working woman' herself.

When the Lib–Lab pact was launched, opinion in business, industry, the City and the press was strongly against an election – ironic, in view of their later enthusiasm for Thatcherism. One reason was doubts about Margaret Thatcher's evident rigidity. Another was that, despite Tony Benn and others on the left, they believed Labour had become more pragmatic. For all its turbulent history in the early eighties, that remained the long-term direction in which it moved. The lesson of adversity was that ideology was not enough, though it took a long time to learn.

The Liberals were not the only minor party the government had been pursuing. Roy Hattersley and I had a telephone conversation on the Sunday evening before the censure debate, when I was assessing the prospects. I expressed the opinion that the Ulster Unionists were not likely to do a deal with Labour. Hattersley immediately reported this to Jim Callaghan, to which his street-wise Prime Minister deflatingly replied: 'Oh, that comes from John Cole.' Jim followed up talks which Merlyn Rees and Roy Mason, successive Northern Ireland Secretaries, had been having, but the best that James Molyneaux and Enoch Powell could deliver among the eleven Unionist MPs was three abstentions.

Despite this, Callaghan fulfilled his promise to look at fairer Ulster representation at Westminster: seventeen MPs instead of twelve, to make the constituencies comparable in size with those elsewhere now that Stormont no longer existed as a devolved parliament. This was a subject on which, some years before, Harold Wilson had sent me a cheerfully aggressive message through Alastair Hetherington. He said to 'tell John he can write leaders until he's blue in the face, but I won't give him the extra seats.'

Nobody was quite sure at the time how significant the Lib-Lab deal would turn out to be. Roy Hattersley thought that although it would not produce a long-term Lib-Lab pact, in future it would not be thought wicked for minority governments to accept the support of the Liberals, or another smaller group. Inevitably, that meant a move away from 'manifesto politics', which at that time were becoming a bugbear to Labour moderates.

Bill Rodgers, who argued that the logic of the centre in politics was that Labour would have some overlap in policy with other parties, nevertheless made clear that at this time his view differed from Roy Jenkins': he had no doubt they must operate through the Labour Party, rather than after any realignment. A year later, when the Lib-Lab pact was drawing towards its close, another future member of the SDP's Gang of Four revealed a surprising attitude to cross-party alliances.

David Owen, discussing the German coalition, said it was a ridiculous situation that a party which got only five per cent of the vote (the Free Democrats) could dictate, or at least veto the policy of the government (led by the Christian Democrats). I drew the obvious British parallel with the Liberals, and Owen replied that this was why he was against PR; he favoured it for Europe and for Scotland (as I did), but not for Westminster, where voters were choosing a government.

Adam Raphael, an enthusiast for PR, suggested there should be a referendum, but Owen's position then was that if the next parliament was also a hung one, and if there were signs that our present system was breaking down, it would be better to refer the issue to a Speaker's Conference. In the event, the scale of Margaret Thatcher's victory in 1979 removed the need for any such inter-party negotiations, and PR remained an enthusiasm principally of Liberals, and later of the Alliance; though in 1992 it returned to haunt Labour.

Michael Foot, as Leader of the House, was in charge of devolution. He himself devolved day-by-day handling to a man who began to establish himself as a rising star of the Labour Party, John Smith, a proud, independent Scot. Many years later, some of us who attended the funeral in his parish church in Edinburgh realised clearly for the first time how significant his Scottishness was: the voice of his deputy, Margaret Beckett, reading a lesson, was the only non-Scot we heard that day.

The first time I had a long talk with John Smith he gave me a flavour of his robust politics. He had come from a meeting of the Parliamentary Labour Party, and was enthused by the Prime Minister's speech there.

Faced by more grumbling about the Lib–Lab pact, Jim Callaghan had laid on the line the future of his government, saying that if the party didn't want to carry on, MPs should let their whips know within the course of the next few days. The Prime Minister made clear that he also had his terms. The reason John Smith was anxious to make the pact work was the same as Jim Callaghan's: he still hoped Labour could win the next election, and believed Britain now faced the most favourable economic circumstances since the war, because of North Sea oil.

But he also shared his Prime Minister's view – which Callaghan had expressed to me as long ago as 1962 – that there was not much point being in opposition. John Smith told me in June 1977, before he had even reached the Cabinet, that he would not stay long in politics for a seat on the opposition front bench. Yet when he died, seventeen years later, he had served almost all of that time in opposition. He finished up as a leader of his party who looked to have a better chance of taking it back to power than his predecessors. The bug of politics is hard to get out of the system, and John Smith, as a successful Scots lawyer, made more financial sacrifices for what he believed in than most.

22

MILLIONAIRES' MISTRESSES

Two processes which took place in the spring of 1977 at first sight appear unconnected. Jim Callaghan and David Steel concluded the Lib-Lab pact, which was to help preserve the life of the minority Labour government for another two years. But simultaneously, in seaside resorts around Britain, trade union conferences were already sowing the seeds of a growth in wage claims which would destroy that government's *raison d'être*, the fight against inflation. This deterioration began in 1977, but reached crescendo in the Winter of Discontent, 1978–9. By then, the Lib-Lab pact had ended, and a general election was imminent.

Why do I put such emphasis on this last attempt to fight inflation through incomes policies? Have not the Thatcher years bid a final and unfond farewell to a theory of the labour market which has preoccupied politicians of all parties since the fifties? Not farewell, I believe, more *au revoir*! It is true that since 1979 a combination of high unemployment and trade union laws have reduced the impact of wage inflation – though we have learned new ways to debase our currency. But at the first sign of economic revival, with recurrence of skill shortages, the old problem recurs in altered form. Britain still does not know how to achieve economic expansion without inflation. All the methods which have been tried, partly succeeded, and finally failed are surely worth looking at again. The mere fact that incomes policies are unfashionable, among the Labour leadership as much as with the Conservatives, has never seemed to me a good reason for ignoring what I think important. Quite the contrary.

Notoriously, the longer incomes policies last, the more difficult they are to maintain. In 1977 and 1978 there was an added difficulty. The trade unions were facing a change of generational guard, which was significant. Apart from Len Murray, the General Secretary of the TUC, the two key figures in negotiations with the Heath, Wilson and Callaghan governments were Jack Jones, of the transport workers, and Hugh Scanlon of the engineers. Both were soon to retire. Although they were tough bargainers, both Conservative and Labour ministers had developed a wary appreciation of what they could deliver. Their successors were less predictable.

In April 1977 I had a sobering talk with Jack Jones. He reported that when he went round factories, workers knew what was happening to prices and dividends, and simply shouted at him; though he added that their shop stewards read the *Financial Times*, and it was possible to argue issues out with them. The backlash against incomes policy among ordinary union members was gathering momentum. The next day I saw Denis Healey, who offered a different, but equally bleak perspective. He declared that he was engaged in a multi-dimensional chess game. A weak pound had aggravated price rises during a period of tight pay restraint, so the fall in living standards in the previous six months had been 'savage'. People had not seen anything like this since the war, and they blamed the government. The Chancellor had been left in no doubt about this when he toured four clubs in his Leeds constituency.

But at a dinner with TUC negotiators, Jim Callaghan warned them, prophetically, that the collapse of the pay policy would mean the end of his government. Its task became more difficult because the fiscal policies it was now following did not appeal to the unions. Jack Jones regarded the budget as a disaster, and claimed that Denis Healey now knew this, and was chastened. I detected no sign of this the following day, when the Chancellor defended to me his tax changes to help middle managers. Half of Denis Healey's strength as a politician is that he never looks chastened. Jack Jones complained that the budget had failed to deal with the poverty trap, and had used some of the money which ought to have been devoted to this to help better-off people.

Amid the gathering gloom, ministers found occasional diversion from such intractable issues. In the autumn of 1977, Prince Charles provided one of these. He had asked the Prime Minister for opportunities to educate himself in what was called, in rather po-faced fashion, 'statecraft'. Note, not politics: the Prince's exaggerated view of what influence the heir to a constitutional monarchy ought to exercise in Whitehall may derive from this distinction without a difference. Jim Callaghan arranged a Chequers dinner with a group of ministers.

The Prince clearly had a briefing from his staff on each, for when Denis Healey was presented, he asked whether his youthful membership of the Communist Party had reduced his effectiveness as Chancellor. This maladroit remark irritated Healey. He gave an explanation of his generation's anxiety about fascism in the thirties, but this probably did not reach his particular audience. The Chancellor's opportunity for gentle retaliation came later. The Prince told a highly rehearsed story about a Qantas stewardess asking him whether being Prince of Wales meant he would later be King. When he confirmed this, she said: 'Gee! That's pretty scarey, isn't it?'

The young Prince said solemnly: 'When you think of it, it *is* pretty scarey.'

Denis Healey leant across the table, and in an Eric Morecambe gesture patted both royal cheeks, saying: 'Well, you shouldn't have joined.'

Later in the evening, when the Prince enquired why some of the diners had disappeared, Healey said ruminatively that one had gone off because he needed the lavatory, but didn't want the rest to know; another needed a drink, but didn't want the rest to know; and Michael Foot needed to read a book, but didn't want the rest to know. My informant said the Prince was so detached from their world, and Cabinet ministers so rarely got a chance to meet each other without an agenda, that they talked a lot among themselves, rather than to the young man who was to be King. It was suspected that the Prime Minister was not totally pleased with his colleagues. The Prince later attended at least one Cabinet committee, which was why Tony Benn was asked not to bring his camera that morning.

Meanwhile, back in the real world, the economic debate rumbled on. Two months after his budget, Denis Healey understood how angry the union leaders had become. I forebore to say I had told him so at our last meeting. The theory that all union discontent and militancy derives from left-wing leaders at the top does not bear much examination. The budget had put backs up. David Basnett, of the municipal workers, wondered what the Labour Party was for if it was not 'to inject a moral element into the market economy'. He believed ministers' first priority should be unemployment, and that the budget should stimulate public spending, to provide jobs. If there were to be tax reductions, cuts in indirect taxes provided more jobs than did those in income tax.

I have always found it difficult to accept the argument that reductions in income tax give substantial help to those on average pay or below. Paying *any* tax may irritate those at the bottom of the heap, but because they pay little, reductions are no great help to them. For example, in May 1978, a penny off income tax would give someone on average earnings just 27p per week, not much of an incentive.

By July, when I saw the Prime Minister, I decided an aggressive question on this might produce an interesting answer. I asked him what distinguished the Labour Party from the Conservatives, now that the incomes policy was in such difficulties, the government was committed to tight money supply, and he and Denis Healey were trying to move from direct to indirect taxation. He urged me not to make the issue between different kinds of taxation a philosophical one. When he had started in the Inland Revenue office in Maidstone as a young man, there had been only twelve officers, all engaged on middle-class incomes. Manual workers were dealt with by one man, who delved into this subject only once every six months. (This was before pay-as-you-earn, and employees then received retrospective bills for income tax.)

His guess was that there would now be sixty or seventy people in that office, and their work would be largely on manual workers' tax. That was bound to make direct taxation unpopular among people who voted Labour. Anyhow, there had been a long-term Labour view in favour of indirect taxes. He recalled Hugh Dalton, Attlee's first Chancellor, talking in his booming voice about the need to tax 'millionaires' mistresses' fur coats'. I said there were not enough millionaires' mistresses to finance the level of spending his government needed.

Jim made clear that his aim after an election would be to increase public spending again. Complaints that the health service was under-funded worried him. By then ministers knew that the IMF cuts exercise in 1976 had been based on wobbly statistics, and the Prime Minister went out of his way to assure me that so far as public expenditure was concerned, it was a case of *reculer pour mieux sauter*. But everything depended on the success of anti-inflation and wealth-creation policies.

The initial phase of Labour's incomes policy had halved inflation. In the second phase, even a slump in real earnings had not offset the disastrous slump in sterling, so price levels rose. But without wage restraint it would have been worse, and Britain might have plunged back into price rises of twenty per cent and above. In the lifetime of the Wilson and Callaghan governments, inflation was reduced from twenty-six to eight per cent. This was a worthwhile achievement, though the Winter of Discontent in the first six weeks of 1979 confirmed that this is a battle which is never finally won.

The government's 1977 talks with the TUC moved to an unhelpful climax. When Denis Healey and other economic ministers saw the union negotiators, each side was keeping its cards so close to the chest that the encounter began like a Quaker meeting, with nobody speaking. The next day, after the full TUC economic committee declared there could be no agreement, however informal, Jim Callaghan called them in for a meeting.

A minister who was not an uncritical admirer eulogised his performance: 'Jim was magnificent. He neither bullied nor wheedled. How do you avoid that, while telling them that the government's fate is in their hands, that the alternative is Mrs Thatcher, and that she would give them a hell of a time? Well, Jim did it.'

If he was being required to govern in confrontation with the unions, he would go to the country – and doubtless, thereafter, to his Sussex farm, with regret. The message was that unfettered wage bargaining meant inflation, unemployment, an election, and Margaret Thatcher.

Denis Healey was working with frenetic energy, but the stress showed. He became more openly sceptical about the value of the forecasts which the law required him to publish. Since the IMF affair, he regarded these as less lapidary than the Mosaic Law. The message got round the Treasury. His private secretary, picking up the boss's joke, used to announce the arrival of officials responsible for the forecasts with the words: 'Your soothsayers to see you, Chancellor.' Unfortunately, the markets took seriously the soothsayers' predictions.

Denis Healey's method of conducting a conversation is, by turns, deadly earnest and self-mockingly exuberant. As he led me to the door of his office at one of his blackest moments, he made the boxer's pass with which he often punched home his points, and said: 'This job is a bugger. Would you like a swop? *I've* had to do it without being an economist too.' This was a reference to an earlier encounter, at which he showed how little he was impressed by economists' expertise. I had confessed that his exposition of some point of monetary policy was taking me out of my depth. He roared his disapproval: I must not say this; there was nothing in economics that could not be understood by the layman, if he applied his mind; if he didn't, the experts would run rings around him.

During his years at the Treasury, Denis Healey did have his blacker moments. But he retained something of the Balliol man's 'effortless superiority', and much of the classicist's belief that '*humani nil a me alienum puto.*' His own memoirs of the period conclude with a remarkable passage: 'My first years at the Treasury were over. I had already accomplished most of the Labours of Hercules. The Augean Stables I had inherited from Tony Barber were cleansed. The Golden Apples of the Hesperides were now stored at the IMF. [He was repaying the loan.] I hoped I might still be able to take the Girdle of Hippolyta. Instead I was to find myself wearing the Shirt of Nessus.'

In the last two sentences, I found myself far out of my classical depth, and was tempted to adopt the cheeky demand Healey used to address to Jim Callaghan in Cabinet: a translation 'for the benefit of us simple-minded fellows'.

The winter of 1977–8 was difficult for the government, though nothing like as disastrous as the one which followed. There were many awkward wage claims: the police, local authorities, hospital auxiliaries, even the BBC, which the government felt had surrendered too easily the previous year. Later that winter, a hawkish minister complained to me that some colleagues wanted to surrender to militancy in the BBC, because they thought voters would punish the government if their screens were black over Christmas. He added grimly that this might be the first government to fall over yet another repeat of *The Sound of Music*.

23

CALLAGHAN'S LAST STAND

By 1978, after a rocky, though not disastrous winter, a pattern of gloom settled on the government. This was partly because of bad opinion polls and by-elections. But at a lunch with Michael Foot, I realised he had no hope the Lib-Lab pact would continue beyond that autumn, since the Liberals, themselves in low electoral water, must prepare to face the voters. Foot had become Labour's bulwark of the pact. David Steel found him a man who could get things done, whereas he thought Denis Healey rude and too inclined to lose his temper. But then the Chancellor had to deal with John Pardoe, and even David Steel did not always find that easy.

Healey had the faults of his virtues. His tactlessness grows out of his nature. It requires a refreshing irreverence, after all, to be an intellectually robust, overweight, workaholic, long-serving Chancellor of the Exchequer, survivor of the 1976 IMF crisis, midwife of fourteen budgetary packages in four years, with a gusto for music, the visual arts and photography, and yet retain a self-image of the cheeky chappie who can't resist making sharp remarks.

An election could not be long delayed. In the light of later controversy about whether Jim Callaghan would have been wiser to call it in the autumn of 1978, I should record that, as early as July 1977, I gained the strong impression from his conversation that he favoured carrying on till the spring of 1979. He joked that, unlike Harold Wilson, he did not have the dates of Yom Kippur or the Lancashire Wakes Weeks constantly in his memory.

Because the government was living such a Perils-of-Pauline existence in the Commons, some commentators thought the sooner we had a general election the better. Journalists crave excitement, and this mood certainly appeared at the *Observer*. I took the view that if the Prime Minister went to the country in the autumn of 1978, at such a difficult stage in his battle against inflation, voters would be entitled to assume he was seeking a quick victory before the wages storm burst, and that he could not risk facing the winter in office. Political honesty suggested he should carry on.

The signs that autumn were not auspicious. More and more unions were committed to a return to free collective bargaining. Jim Callaghan decided that if he was going to achieve the low level of inflation which British competitiveness required, he must commit himself to a wage norm of five per cent. It was a fateful decision. I had an interesting session that autumn with Len Murray.

When I arrived in his handsome panelled office at Congress House in Bloomsbury, he had a bottle of hock on ice. The building is a memorial to trade unionists who died in the Second World War, and contains not only a superb Epstein statue, which dominates the atrium, but also a puzzling one near the front door. This shows one figure apparently helping a fallen creature to his feet. In our long waits outside the TUC when I was a labour correspondent, we used to speculate irreverently on which union leader was depicted stamping on another's fingers.

Len Murray clearly felt like letting his hair down that day. He was well settled into his general secretaryship, no longer under the shadow of his predecessors, and now more senior than most leaders of individual unions. He felt that Jim Callaghan, for the first time since becoming Prime Minister, had reverted that summer to a bad habit from his Treasury days: he was too impressed by the Treasury's econometric models, and too little prepared to rely on his own very sensitive political instincts.

He said everybody knew politics was what Jim Callaghan was good at. His decision to postpone the election was an example. Murray himself had been in favour of autumn 1978, but he now realised Labour would inevitably have lost then, and that Callaghan had known this in advance. But on pay the Prime Minister had decided to plant his flag on five per cent, because that was what Treasury models indicated, when he ought to have known the TUC could not hold unions to that figure.

In November 1978, just as the wage round was beginning to turn nasty, the government suffered a bizarre rebuff from the unions. After weeks of negotiation, Denis Healey had agreed with the TUC economic committee a statement which restored the position of helpful neutrality it had taken in the previous year. This was not perfect, but it was the best ministers could hope for. At lunchtime, he telephoned Roy Hattersley, who had been involved in the talks, to say he thought the press conference announcing this agreement could go ahead in the afternoon. A meeting of the TUC committee that morning had an uncounted majority of about 11 to 4, so when the full General Council met later, the agreement would need only a handful of extra votes.

In the event, the General Council produced a tied vote, and the chairman, though personally in favour of the agreement, was obliged by convention to use his casting vote against. Other supporters went the wrong way for strange reasons. Moss Evans, who had helped to draft the statement, was abroad, so the other two members from his union voted on opposite sides. Sid Weighell of the railwaymen had gone to Birmingham to broadcast in favour of incomes policy, and therefore was not present to vote for it. Bill Sirs of the steelworkers supported in principle, but was not prepared to let the TUC commit his union.

With industrial strife spreading, ministers began to worry about their stance during a general election. Denis Healey told the Prime Minister that where previously they could have faced Margaret Thatcher on inflation with the argument that they were matching something against nothing, now they would risk offering nothing against nothing. He observed that Jim Callaghan felt hurt, because he believed he understood labour relations, and that the trade union movement, from which he had come to the very top of British politics, had let him down.

When the Prime Minister returned from an international summit in the West Indies early in January, groups of workers as unlikely as hospital nurses, ambulance men and airline pilots seemed determined to look after themselves by militancy. More conventional industrial groups, like lorry drivers, tanker drivers, Ford workers, local council manual workers – from dustmen to gravediggers – were moving into dispute with their employers. An air of disarray gradually invaded the Cabinet Room. The remarks of a suntanned Jim Callaghan to reporters at the airport were interpreted in a headline as: 'Crisis? What crisis?'

When ministers debated whether to call a state of emergency, some feared that failure to use the army to maintain public services would look like obeisance to the unions. But Bill Rodgers suspected the civil service had decided Labour was on the way out, and did not want the services to become too closely involved. He also noted that generals liked to protect their soldiers from doing jobs such as gravedigging. Others remembered the services' declared inability to replace power workers during the political strike in Ulster in 1974. Yet one observed gloomily that the public appeared to believe the army could fill the denuded shelves of every supermarket with Mars Bars, if only the government would let them.

A gallows humour occasionally appeared in the Cabinet Room. One minister, discussing the need for the government to stand firm in the council workers' dispute, which was leaving the streets polluted by rubbish and some dead bodies unburied, dug into his recollections of the revolt of the slaves in ancient Rome. Spartacus and his colleagues, he recalled, had fastened their heels to the ground, so that they would not be tempted to flee. Denis Healey is a classicist who is never willingly capped. Yes, he said, but in 1871 the Prussians had the Spartacus precedent in mind when they handcuffed themselves to their machine-guns. The only result was that the French bayonetted them.

In the after-shock of that bleak January, and in the few months remaining to the Labour government, Jim Callaghan and his economic ministers actually achieved an understanding for the future with the TUC. This covered not only useful ideas on long-term incomes policies, but also made promises about such notorious aspects of the Winter of Discontent as violence on the picket lines, intimidation, the need for ballot votes before strikes, and the maintenance of essential services. I had a sad conversation with the Prime Minister after his press conference, for we both guessed this agreement came too late to save him.

Surprisingly, what provoked the general election was not industrial chaos, but the failure of the referenda on devolution. The Welsh voted so overwhelmingly against that there was no political problem. Scotland gave a majority for a devolved assembly, but not sufficient to meet the stiff criterion of forty per cent of the whole electorate in favour, which Labour rebels had fatally inserted into the statute. The importance of this result at Westminster was that the Scottish Nationalists no longer had any reason for sustaining the government. Devolution was dead for this parliament – and, as it turned out, for much longer than that.

When it became clear that an election was imminent, Conor Cruise O'Brien, then editor-in-chief of the *Observer*, and myself had dinner with Denis Healey and his political assistant, Derek Scott. Our aim was to quiz the man who would probably succeed Jim Callaghan about Labour's future policy. If you were a boxing promoter of the time, seeking to arrange a contest for the Intellectual Heavyweight Championship of the World, a Healey-Cruise O'Brien bout would not have been a bad preliminary. Each is a highly intelligent extrovert, equipped to handle himself on most subjects, in politics, philosophy, literature or the arts.

We dined at the Connaught, which had one of London's better restaurants. The conversation, like the wine, flowed freely, Healey and Cruise O'Brien enjoying themselves immensely, as they ranged over their many interests. One would speak Italian, the other Russian. Healey quoted Dylan Thomas and Yeats. Cruise O'Brien offered a few lines in

Irish, in whose verse his wife, Maire, is expert. Derek Scott and I, unable to compete in this uninhibited showing-off, occasionally pulled the talk back to politics. The dinner lasted till late, and voices rose from time to time.

When making the arrangement, I had carelessly forgotten to ask for a private room, so we were in the restaurant. The next morning, Derek Scott telephoned me to express his own and Healey's thanks, and said in a hushed voice of awe and anxiety: 'I think we must assume that most people in that restaurant last night now know the views of the Chancellor of the Exchequer.'

As the Callaghan government drew to its close, I had time to reflect on my journalism during it. For me, this was one of the most enjoyable periods, partly because work at the *Observer* gave more time for talking to politicians, partly because I knew most members of the Cabinet reasonably well. I was also intellectually engaged with the central issue on the political agenda, the attempt to find a remedy against inflation.

Half the enjoyment of political journalism is in the chase. Often you despair of finding out the information you need to make a story complete, or even viable, and then a breakthrough comes unheralded. Many editors believe the solution to the problem of finding out what goes on in government lies in freedom of information legislation. I have always been sceptical of the value of legislative action to produce more open government, believing that politicians have an inevitable propensity to conceal information which is embarrassing to them.

The public's only hope of enlightenment is for journalists to keep padding their beats, like assiduous bobbies, picking up all the information they can, from a variety of sources, and adding two and two together (preferably without concluding that the total is twenty-two). I am glad to see that many younger colleagues are carrying that belief in the importance of journalistic digging further than I was able to do, in the even more secretive periods during which I have operated.

In my experience, though the government machine from time to time makes heavy weather about leaks, setting up endless futile enquiries, self-confident politicians themselves often do not remember when they have told a journalist something. I once wrote a profile of Jim Callaghan in the *Observer*, and produced some interesting nugget dug out of a conversation from many months before. When we next met, he referred to the point, and said: 'Where on earth did you hear about that, John?'

I replied: 'You told me, Jim.'

He dissolved in laughter, and said: 'Did I really? How very indiscreet!'

Most of what Whitehall anguishes so much about scarcely matters at

all. A minister once began a meeting with me by saying solemnly: 'I've
been filling in a leaks form about you.' The enquiry concerned a story
written by the *Observer* labour correspondent, Robert Taylor, but the
investigators' net was cast wide. The minister was asked: 'Did you know
about the government's pay offer to the civil service unions before the
Observer report appeared?' Answer: Yes.

'Did you see any member of the *Observer* staff before the report
appeared?' Yes.

'Who, where and when?' John Cole at the Gay Hussar on Friday.

'Did you discuss civil service pay?' No.

I find it hard to believe that grown-ups behave in this way. Whichever
civil servant promotes such enquiries ought to be prosecuted for wasting
police time. And ministers' time. Why do they stand for it? The answer
is obvious to me: British society had a deeply secretive culture, which
makes it sharply different from American society, often taken as an easy
model by those who favour a legislative solution. All Americans seem to
carry a copy of the First Amendment to the Constitution next to their
hearts. British instincts are different, dedicated to the dictum: 'What
business is it of theirs?' I doubt if mere legislation will remove the net
curtains that are in our souls.

All governments end sadly. The end of the Callaghan administration
was caught for me in a cameo painted by a friend. The scene he witnessed
took place in the hall of Number 10, on the day after the government's
defeat, by a single vote, in the censure debate. The Prime Minister was
sitting there, alone, waiting for his car to take him to the palace. Soon
he would be out on the famous doorstep, giving the traditional big wave
to the crowd, for he would fight the election vigorously. But as he sat
inside, my friend said, he looked incredibly old and tired.

24

THE FIRST — AND IRON — LADY

When the Attlee government was in terminal decline in 1951, the editor of the *Manchester Guardian*, A.P. Wadsworth, wrote a leading article headed 'Time for a Change'. For me, that headline has always been a reminder of the most potent electoral fact: if a tide is running – as in 1906, 1945, or 1951 – what happens in the election campaign scarcely matters. The country feels in its bones that it is time for a change.

It was such a mood which determined the result of the 1979 general election. It is an irony that the most ideological government of the century was elected less on Margaret Thatcher's plans for fundamental changes in British society, than because voters decided Labour was ready for the wilderness of opposition. Yet in the years between her surprising succession to Ted Heath in 1975 and the 1979 election, I was learning, principally through conversations with her colleagues, what an astonishing political phenomenon she was.

Because she was the first woman to lead a British political party, and was therefore in constant danger of being patronised, both by her colleagues and in media comment, she made up her own rules for the political game as she went along. You had only to talk to her in the couple of years before the election, when the Labour government's popularity had gone, to savour her self-confidence. In part this was ideological: all over the world, she told me, the long night of collectivism was receding. 'Impoverishment' and 'socialism' went together in her conversation, with the hammer-beat of a doctrinaire non-doubter. With Margaret Thatcher, Keynesian orthodoxy had been abandoned. She came nearer to laissez-faire liberalism than any Tory leader in this century.

Yet even when she was discussing economics, her certitude was temperamental, and also very personal. While talking about inflation in her room at the House one day, I mentioned that the Labour government's incomes policies were at that time bringing it down. She fixed me with her china blue eyes. I had been reading *Paddington Bear* to my youngest son, and the frivolous phrase, 'Paddington gave him a hard stare', invaded my mind. The leader of the opposition had sterner thoughts in hers. The Chancellor, Denis Healey, had been boasting about lower inflation, but she was sure this would not help him: 'Take it from me: ordinary people don't make this distinction between prices rising and the inflation *rate* falling. They just notice that goods in the shops still keep getting dearer, and when they notice that, they'll turn to me, because they believe a woman *knows* about prices.' This revealed the tough populism which alarmed more sober Conservative leaders. For whatever housewives might think, since the thirties prices had not *fallen* – as distinct from the rate of inflation slowing down. And they were not to do so during the lifetime of her three administrations.

Yet Margaret Thatcher's shadow Cabinet colleagues, almost all of whom had voted for Ted Heath, were learning what a hard-working, driven politician she was. Willie Whitelaw, working most closely with her, told me that he had also been astonished by how clever she was. Another admirer assured me that most of the interesting ideas came from her, because she was much cleverer than all those around her. I noted myself that she was an instinctive intellectual, fascinated by the clash of ideas.

Margaret Thatcher was at once politically intense and personally affable. On the day of our inflation discussion, she was suffering from a dreadful cold, and apologised frequently for her voice. But she was delighted with the extended office she had secured for the leader of the opposition's staff, glad that her secretaries now had a kitchen of their own, and did not have to rush off to the nearest of Westminster's then rather sparse ladies' loos to wash the coffee cups. She had little personal vanity: I had never seen a senior politician so willing to hurry off to the photocopier. She combined this engaging personal style with a passion for political ideas.

Her populism showed through in her utterances about immigration. A year before the election, she demanded 'a clear end of immigration', because people feared that 'the fundamental British characteristics which have done so much for the world' would be 'rather swamped by people of a different culture'. That pronouncement horrified many in her own party, but produced an overnight leap in Conservative poll ratings. Some Midlands Conservatives were advising her that marginal seats were there for the taking if she would continue to 'speak out' on immigration. 'Speaking out' was one thing, but reducing the number of people with black or brown skins who lived in Britain, some of them by then for several generations, was out of the question. Just like Denis Healey with inflation, she might reduce the rate of increase in the immigrant population, but she would not substantially reverse the ethnic mix in Britain, which was what many people thought she was talking about.

Her more liberal colleagues, afraid of the damage to race relations, told me despairingly that in their private conversations with her they had heard several times about 'the two Granthams' worth' of immigrants arriving in Britain each year. This evocation of her home town and a happy childhood clearly conjured up for her an ideal England. But for them, her immigration broadcast was only one example of a tendency that made them shiver: to transfer to television her long-standing habit of sounding off in private about subjects which aroused her emotions, rather than engaging her intellect.

The explanation was her deep conviction that she had greater empathy with ordinary people than any previous Tory leader. When she shot from the hip on race, crime and punishment, or trade unions, she genuinely believed she was 'speaking for the people'. Many in her awed shadow Cabinet suspected she might be right. The most significant turning came on economic policy. This battle went on right from 1975 until, and beyond the election. The parliamentary party Margaret Thatcher inherited was different in outlook from that which evolved over her years in power. Most Tory MPs were not, as Peter Walker once explained, madly dogmatic about politics or economics, but they were relieved when Keith Joseph, whom they liked and regarded as clever, told them that money supply was the key to Britain's problems.

But as the Callaghan government's incomes policy agreements with the unions brought inflation down again, many in the undogmatic heart of the Conservative Party nursed doubts about where they were being led. Margaret Thatcher and Keith Joseph might consider incomes policies nonsensical and wrong, but Willie Whitelaw, Reginald Maudling, Jim Prior, Francis Pym, Peter Carrington, Peter Walker — probably the majority of the shadow Cabinet — favoured some form of that policy. The debate went on constantly in the shadow Cabinet and its sub-groups.

In pursuing the journalist's normal obsession with finding out what is likely to *happen* — as distinct from what politicians say — the key figure was Margaret Thatcher, who sometimes appeared as a convinced ideologue, at others as a cautious politician. Yet it was her dogmatic belief that market forces could handle inflation which first raised my doubts about where she might lead Britain. Three years into her leadership, I noted that she was 'as aggressive a lady as any of us is ever likely to meet'.

Jim Prior, who because he was the only liberal with an economic portfolio, was at the eye of most of these storms, realised earlier than most how serious Mrs Thatcher was about her ideology. She really was a believer in 'freedom', as expressed by Hayek: 'Don't make any mistake; this is a very right-wing lady.' She certainly did not revere Tennyson's 'honest doubt'. One of her former civil servants from the Education Department used to say the only phrase he had never heard from her lips was: 'I wonder whether...'

Others told me that in shadow Cabinet she was more acerbic than Heath, but that when tête-à-tête her skilful femininity helped her to get her own way with many of them. When she went into the Commons Tearoom, she might not listen to the political anxieties of backbenchers, but she had an unfailing memory for the personal (wives, children, exams, illnesses), and this left a trail of Tory admirers along the Westminster corridors.

In July 1976, when Ted Heath said in public what so many shadow ministers were saying to me in private, and endorsed the idea of discussions about pay with the social partners; when Lord Watkinson, another former Tory minister, and then president of the Confederation of British Industry, committed that body to incomes policy and industrial regeneration, I wrote in an *Observer* leader: 'Compromise is inevitable when the architectural purity of monetarist theory is brought into the world of democratic politics. That theory may seem opaque to lay readers, but in the labour market it means simply this: if a government were willing and able to let unemployment rise to levels where the unions were frightened, inflation might be eased. But any government which needs to be re-elected will not let unemployment rip...'

Several years, several general elections, and several millions more unemployed people later, I had occasion to revise my judgement about how far a Thatcher government might go.

I cannot claim I had not been warned. Six months before the election, one of Margaret Thatcher's advisers – a man John Nott warned me was 'a nut' – said 'the trade unions must be allowed to live in their own muck.' A Conservative government must tell them truthfully that it could not prevent them causing very high unemployment through excessive wage increases. A Tory MP advised me to think of Thatcher as Chairman Mao: she was determined to lead her party on a Long March, which she admitted would take at least ten years, and she expected industrial casualties along the way. My judgement was based instead on a belief that the Conservative Party's instincts were ultimately pragmatic, rather than ideological.

The difference between leaders like Margaret Thatcher and Willie Whitelaw is one which divides all politicians into two classes. At that time, the Conservative right, like the Labour left, found that events had the comfortable habit of fortifying their original political creeds, or prejudices. Others — including Churchill, Attlee, Macmillan, Gaitskell, Butler, Wilson, Macleod, Callaghan, Whitelaw himself — allowed their dogmas to be refined or modified by experience. It was a crucial difference.

What part Margaret Thatcher's gender, specifically her pioneering role as the first woman party leader, played in her political persona will always be disputed. By a year before the election, I believe gender as an issue was over, even if the sillier journalists still felt free to note that she had 'good legs' (while leaving readers mercifully ignorant of the bottom-end beauty of Jim Callaghan or Michael Heseltine). She herself had a matter-of-fact approach to being top woman in a man's world. When Norman St John-Stevas, one of Westminster's more fastidious dressers, excused himself for leaving shadow Cabinet early because he had to change for a public dinner, Mrs Thatcher, who was going to the same function, said understandingly: 'Yes, Norman, it'll take you longer than me.'

Even before the election, Stevas had adopted the mocking tone about his leader that ultimately was to annoy her enough to get him the sack. When he did not approve of something she did, he would refer to her as 'Heather' (in the then style of *Private Eye* about the Queen). When he did approve, he offered a pastiche of his (Catholic) Church's language, and called her 'the Blessed One'. He did not confine this style of humour to Margaret Thatcher, but used it for all in authority. He had even been known to call Cardinal Hume, whom he admired, 'Basil Brush'.

This habit must have been familiar to her since Ted Heath's government, when he served under her at the Education Department. A Conservative MP, Anthony Fell, asked him for an encouraging letter to a Catholic choir going abroad. Norman modestly suggested it would come better from the Secretary of State, Margaret Thatcher. When Fell wrote through Stevas to ask for such a letter, Norman merely saw what the note was about, and simply put a minute on it: 'Margaret: This seems worth a letter from you.' He never received a response, and the choir never had a letter. Subsequently her private office told him that Fell had referred to her throughout as 'Heather'.

25

A FAST FILLY AT THE POLLS

The 1979 election was fought under two shadows. For the Callaghan government, there was, fatally, the public's too fresh recollection of its trench warfare with the trade unions during the Winter of Discontent. For the whole nation, there was the shadow of Irish terrorism, brought to the heart of British democracy by the assassination of Airey Neave, the Conservative spokesman on Northern Ireland, and one of Margaret Thatcher's closest allies.

From the moment that the Labour government's Chief Whip, Michael Cox, his voice breaking with emotion, announced that a bomb had gone off in the House of Commons car park, the security arrangements for leading figures had to be tightened up. This erected a new barrier, psychological as much as physical, between politicians and people. Five years later, after the Brighton bomb and the erection of security gates at Downing Street, I could not help recalling that thirty years before there had not been a policeman in sight when I interviewed a British Prime Minister on the Irish border.

Security is an imperfect business, and is often exercised whimsically, as I learned from one small personal experience during the campaign. This was the only general election during which I worked for the *Observer*. It came as an uncovenanted bonus of Sunday newspaper journalism that, while we worked hard during the campaign, once the paper for the Sunday before polling day had been put to bed, there was nothing to be done about politics until we knew the election result on the Thursday night or Friday morning.

Politicians often urge political journalists to get out of London, arguing that they cannot understand politics without frequent refreshment at the grassroots. Roy Hattersley had long been asking me to visit his Birmingham constituency of Sparkbrook, an interesting mixture of original Brummie, a constituency committee where the accents of

Dublin and Cork predominated, and a growing Asian population, which has since become the most influential element in local Labour politics.

The 1979 election at the *Observer* provided the necessary busman's holiday, and having seen the paper printed on Saturday night, I set off for Birmingham early on Sunday. Roy had been a Cabinet minister for the final three years of the Callaghan government, and when he went outside the city to speak for other Labour candidates in Leicestershire, he was joined by plain-clothes policemen, who told me they were armed. But in Birmingham itself, he happily drove himself and me round without any escort or protection.

There was no obvious reason for the discrepancy, but it deprived a few Birmingham policemen of a new cultural experience. Once the member for Sparkbrook had bought me an introductory drink in his Labour Club, he asked whether Madge had sent me out for the weekend with a clean handkerchief and socks that were free of holes. I affirmed that this was so, but enquired why one of Her Majesty's ministers should concern himself with such personal detail.

We were going to a Sikh temple, he said, where shoes must be shed and heads covered, in our case with handkerchiefs knotted at the corner, in the style favoured on wet days by spectators behind the Sheffield Wednesday goal. We went on from there to lunchtime at an Irish Club in the Catholic Church, and then to interrupt the showing of the main film at two Asian cinemas, where Roy made yet more brief speeches. I told him if any politician during my youth had interrupted the film at the Lyceum, Belfast, I would have urged my parents to vote for an opponent. He acknowledged the danger, but said this was what his Asian supporters told him was expected. Sure enough, on the cinema steps, many Asian constituents clearly wanted to talk to their MP, and soon Roy Hattersley was taking down their housing and other problems in a little notebook. It confirmed my belief that there are strengths in the British system, which makes Cabinet ministers continue as constituency MPs.

By the time of my Midlands visit, the election was lost and won. The Conservative lead in the opinion polls never looked in serious danger. Only Jim Callaghan's continued personal popularity left Labour with sneaking hopes of retaining power. Conservative tax and spending plans provided most controversy. Labour posed the classical question to opposition leaders seeking power: 'But how would you pay for it?' In this case, the 'it' was the lower taxes Margaret Thatcher was promising. Labour predicted she would have to double VAT to pay for cuts in income tax. She and Geoffrey Howe denied this, though he also used the classical defence of needing to 'see the books'. In his first budget, he combined VAT rates of 8 and 12.5 per cent into a new rate of 15 per cent.

But what really fascinated both politicians and reporters was how Margaret Thatcher would perform during the campaign. Her party chairman, Peter Thorneycroft, was so senior that he had resigned as Chancellor in Macmillan's government the year before she entered parliament – as it happened, over public expenditure which he thought excessive. He adopted a paternal attitude towards his inexperienced leader.

I had lunch with Lord Thorneycroft at the beginning of the election campaign. He gave his opinion that Margaret Thatcher was 'like a fast filly' (shaking his head in imitation of a racehorse). She didn't feel the need for reins or harness at all. It was true that she tended to make policy on her feet, and go off in her own direction. But when the reins were pulled, she did come back. He warned me against believing she was as bad a listener as some people said. If a colleague argued with her, she responded in a most aggressive way, and that put some people off. The trick was to keep going and, although she kept talking too, to realise she was taking in what was said. What she was very good at was coming out with an idea, but then if she discovered it was not viable, dropping it rather quickly.

Over that lunch, he had taken me back to my days as a labour correspondent, to discuss 'the state of Britain'. He recalled that as Chancellor he had set up a body known as the Three Wise Men, to which I had given evidence about the labour market. His current position about incomes policy in the private sector was rather sceptical; he thought the best idea was productivity bargaining to restore some enterprise. But he was quite frank in saying that the effects of either incomes policies or the Tories' proposed tax changes were likely to be at the margins. Experience has taught former Chancellors not to expect economic miracles, even if current Chancellors see these just around every corner.

Reporters observed with amusement Margaret Thatcher's performances at election press conferences. She was on a nervous high, obviously enjoying herself, feeling already like a Prime Minister. It was the first time her headmistress tendencies had appeared in public. After Geoffrey Howe had modestly declined to add anything to several of his leader's economic answers, she finally said: 'Geoffrey, you've got to speak *sometime*'; and because reporters were slow to tackle law and order, she said sharply: 'Perhaps someone will remember that Willie Whitelaw is here.' The media saw that this team would be dominated by its captain.

Her campaign, like the manifesto, was light in policy detail. The Callaghan government had gone through such a debilitating period since the IMF public spending crisis of 1976, and again during the Winter of Discontent, that she was dining out on a public mood. There were promises that she would alter the balance between capital and labour, but only modest proposals on how to do this. There were hints about immigration, hanging, law and order, and 'short, sharp shocks' for young offenders. To win votes, detail was neither needed nor offered. Margaret Thatcher knew she was going to win.

Although Jim Callaghan was on the defensive from the start, he did not give up. Labour's procedure for composing its manifesto is formal: 'the Clause V meeting', consisting of representatives from the front bench – in this case, the government – and the National Executive Committee. It was an exhausting process, lasting for twenty hours, until 3.15 a.m. True, the Prime Minister had recently gone on record as believing that all sensible people were in bed by 11 p.m., but he was also an old trade union negotiator, and knew the value of loss of sleep in achieving a compromise. The worst fears of the left were realised: Callaghan and Denis Healey dug in their heels and refused to accept, in anything like their original form, the most cherished notions of the left – abolition of the House of Lords and a pledge to forego the next generation of nuclear weapons.

Inevitably Labour had to fight on the government's record. When Harold Wilson took over from Ted Heath in 1974, after the Conservatives had declared a three-day week in industry, there had been loose talk that Britain was becoming 'ungovernable'. This had largely evaporated in the mid-seventies. But Jim Callaghan did not receive any reward for his efforts in those middle years in preventing Britain's price increases reaching South American levels. This seemed unjust, especially since that inflation had begun before Labour took over. The government had used its clout in negotiations with the unions to bring inflation down from the twenty-six per cent it once reached to eight per cent. But the public mood of greater calm had been dented by a feeling of despair over the Winter of Discontent. Wage settlements the previous winter had set the index off upwards again, though more slowly. It was to peak again at 21.9 per cent in 1980, under Mrs Thatcher. But it was the strikes and inflation of the previous winter that turned voters against the Labour government.

At the *Observer* there was fierce debate about the election, and what editorial line the paper should take. We had a complex proprietorship and editorial control. The paper was now owned by Atlantic Richfield, an American oil company, which had taken over when it was in financial difficulties in 1976. The new owners had a rather Erewhon view of what the *Observer* could become: a great international newspaper, influencing opinion worldwide. They seemed to believe that papers like the *New York Times* had such influence. Any newspaper has real influence only in its core circulation area. When it comes to owning newspapers, denizens of the market economy often astonished me by their ignorance of how our particular market works. Readers' interests usually begin close to where they eat their breakfasts, and read their papers. Atlantic Richfield hoped, through the *Observer* and through conferences it organised at Aspen, Colorado, to change the world, though in which direction was never clear to me.

It was in pursuit of this project that they had appointed Conor Cruise O'Brien editor-in-chief. I had known and liked Conor for many years. Of the people I have known well, he is as near to a Renaissance man as any. He began, briefly, as a school-teacher; indeed, I had narrowly missed being taught by him when he arrived in Belfast, straight from university in Dublin, and married my headmaster's daughter. After that he became, successfully, a diplomat in the Irish Republic's foreign service; a politician, and a Labour minister in a coalition government in Dublin; an academic, in Ireland, Britain, Africa and America; and one of the most profound thinkers, across a range of subjects, with the nimblest pen, whom I have encountered.

His years at the *Observer*, even though they involved the editor, Donald Trelford, and myself as his deputy in a perpetual switchback ride, were a delight to me. Conor was, more literally, no mean switchback rider himself. He came with his second wife, Maire, and young family, to have lunch with us one Easter Monday, and we took them to Hampton Court fair. Although ten years younger than he, I was only willing to keep up with the more uproarious children on some of the less fearsome rides. Conor, fortified by more wine than I, funked nothing. When he emerged, with their son and one of ours, from a cage mounted on a wheel, they looked greenish, he quite unperturbed. I suggested that if such cruel and unusual punishment had been inflicted on terrorist prisoners in our native land, they would have had a case worth taking to the European Court on Human Rights.

Our new editor-in-chief's concept of the editorial function was nearer to socratic dialogue than to conventional Fleet Street practice. He saw his role, apart from his own writing, as being to stimulate internal debate. He was by turns argumentative, serious and funny. He circulated a memorandum in his first week, arguing that our editorials – many of which I wrote – were too middle-of-the-road, even suffering from what he called 'muzziness'. He invited responses.

Those older *Observer* hands who had not yet taken his measure decided not to bother. I wrote a reply in defence of the 'middle style' of leader-writing, which I had learned on the *Manchester Guardian*. This derived ultimately from Addison and Steele, and was intended always to reason with readers whom we assumed to be at least as intelligent as ourselves, rather than to lecture them. It was for the *Daily Express* to thunder: 'Let there be no doubt', when there was every reason for doubt. For us, calmness was all. This was a style which another old *Guardian* man, Malcolm Muggeridge, had satirised in the comment that any leader-writer without two hands – 'on the one hand, on the other hand' – would be silenced. Conor was pleased with my memo, and insisted on circulating it also, hoping to draw others into the debate. The more reticent English decided this was not a sport for grown-ups. They were manifestly puzzled by these two loquacious and disputatious Irishmen, drawn from different parts of the island, yet equally reluctant to abandon a position once they had taken it up.

The editor-in-chief was clearly the decisive figure in deciding what the *Observer* should say editorially about the election. He worried away not only at the international issues, on which he had considerable expertise, but also about the political personality of Margaret Thatcher. Soon after he took up his post, she had asked him to see her, to seek his views on Ireland. As a key figure in an Irish government which had left office quite recently, and as author of one of the few worthwhile books on the crisis in Ulster, he was clearly worth listening to. He found, like many before and after him, that it was difficult to get his views across to her. He worried about how domineering her style of government might be.

My preoccupation was different. I was obsessed with Britain's economic malaise, but found it hard to believe that, in a free society with a strong trade union movement, any solution which excluded some form of incomes policy was feasible. Jim Callaghan had staked his career on trying to create such a voluntary policy. Although he had suffered an appalling winter of failure, the Prime Minister had just produced a new concordat with the unions, still to be tested. I thought he should be given another chance.

The debate in the office ran for three weeks, with 'holding' editorials – in the 'middle style' – examining the pros and cons of each party's ideas, but not giving a verdict. The bookies' money was heavily on the Conservatives, and I suspect that the *Observer*'s ultimate support for Callaghan caused the American owners – who were not oblivious of

which party was likelier to allocate the next oil exploration contracts in
the North Sea – great annoyance. But towards the end of the campaign,
Conor suggested we go one lunchtime to a church on the opposite side
of the Thames from the houseboat at Chelsea where he then lived. I
wondered if a Catholic agnostic and a Presbyterian were to pray about
the final editorial judgement in this jewel of an Anglican church.

Instead, as we emerged from examining its architecture and interior
decoration, he said quietly that, unless I disagreed violently, he would
be disposed to support Callaghan. As he knew, that was what I wanted
to do, so we had an amiable sandwich together, and I returned to the
office to draft the leader. This process continued right until the end,
with others submitting drafts of sections they were concerned with. One
of these began: 'Herewith some purely informal thoughts as to how we
might arrive at a "vote Labour" conclusion – not one I would necessarily
endorse personally – with a reasonable degree of scepticism and due
allowance for the counter arguments.'

This was a masterpiece of the counter-puncher's art, and many of its
arguments survived into my final draft. I was to circulate this to the
College of Cardinals who comprised the *Observer* editorial conference,
and I suspected it would have a tough passage, for most of my colleagues
had accepted the 'time for a change' argument. But before this final draft
went out, Conor had advised me that he would draft a few paragraphs,
addressed particularly to Margaret Thatcher's leadership.

It was these which caused the row. The editor-in-chief, whether by
design or because he had accepted a previous engagement, was not at
the final conference. The political correspondent, Adam Raphael, an
old friend of mine, whom I had helped recruit to both the *Guardian* and
the *Observer*, commented that I had veered from my usual temperate
style in this rather *ad hominem* (or, rather, *ad feminam*) dissection of her
political character. The paragraphs were, indeed, different: no middle
style in them. I explained that these were 'by another hand'.

In the final hours, everything was refined, changed, changed back,
and finally put to bed, if only because the printers could wait no longer.
Many newspaper readers may be amused to know how much journalistic
anguish goes into an editorial opinion, of which they will take precious
little notice when they come to vote. That year, the voters came down
decisively for Margaret Thatcher. But with hindsight, I suspect that
Conor Cruise O'Brien's perceptive paragraphs about her highly per-
sonalised style of politics may have been more important than my
workmanlike examination of how the economy might be put right. No
one has put it right yet.

26

TRUE BELIEVERS V. WETS

In this book I have taken 1975–6 as the date of my watershed, the period when both Conservative and Labour Parties made a decisive break with the post-war consensus. It was 1979 which cemented the new politics into place. After the arrival in Downing Street of Margaret Thatcher, everything was changed; even if politicians and journalists like myself, who had grown up, or old, in the ideas of the post-war era, 'cast many a longing, lingering look behind'.

Labour left-wingers who believed the Callaghan government lost its way during the IMF crisis in 1976 were almost relieved at defeat. I doubt if they, or indeed if many others outside the inner circle of Thatcher confidants on the right of the Conservative Party, realised what an ideological government hers would become, and remain.

If I had to describe in a single sentence the prevailing mood among the non-ideological majority in Margaret Thatcher's shadow Cabinet, it would be this: 'Because of the vagaries of our party's electoral system, a rather inexperienced woman has been elected leader; but the country does need a change of direction, and our duty is to help her preside over that, yet to stop her being carried away by curious dogmas and failing to respond to real events.' In other words, they were traditional Tories, guided by Burke's belief in 'circumstances', or Macmillan's in 'events', as the determinant of political action, rather than by dogmatic theory.

Such critics completely underestimated the reaction against previous Conservative policies which she and those closest to her had undergone. They misjudged her determination to have her way. They underestimated the ruthlessness with which, in the most patient and well-judged manner, she would weed out those leading Conservatives who opposed her. They overestimated the power of a world recession, or the threat of the SDP, to slow her down. Inevitably, most of my accounts of this period came from those who had doubts about this new direction in policy. I found their more pragmatic views congenial. But in the light of history, and of their misjudgements, I can see why Margaret Thatcher called them 'Wets'. For eleven years she was to run rings around them.

Yet nobody armed with hindsight is entitled to be too censorious about the Wets. A sane and decent man like Willie Whitelaw was caught on the horns of not one, but several dilemmas. First, as runner-up to her in the leadership election, and having accepted the post of deputy, he had a soldierly sense of loyalty, accentuated by respect for her gender. He found her prepared to take advice from him either privately or in a small gathering – for example, he was influential in reshuffles. But on semi-public occasions (in which category ministers now included full Cabinet meetings, since these tended to be leaky), she liked to show her determination and decisiveness.

Second, although Whitelaw was on the liberal wing of Conservatism, he thought she had the best chance of keeping his party in office; and since he was a strong believer in the private enterprise system, he was especially concerned to keep out of power a Labour Party which was making ever more strident noises about public ownership. When the effects of the first budget began to erode the Tory lead in the polls, Whitelaw tended to think it was because people 'didn't like coming out of hospital', and that the new economic climate was uncomfortable to many. He hoped they would be happier when the income tax cuts came through, to compensate them for higher VAT.

Then he had to make a judgement about the new Prime Minister's character. His belief was that she would prove ultimately to be a prag-matist. This was a comforting view shared by most of the leading Wets, at least for the first three or four years. I suspect this was as much a matter of their own temperaments as of judgement. They were convinced that in order to win and keep power in a democracy, political parties had to adjust to events. They were simply incredulous at the thought of Margaret Thatcher lashing herself to the mast, putting wax in her ears to exclude the siren voices, and sailing through the vortex of the worst economic storm since before the war. Yet, with limited exceptions, this is precisely what she did.

Whitelaw and those in the first Thatcher Cabinet who thought like him were horrified at the growing level of unemployment, which a combination of international circumstances and the government's own economic policies produced. In varying degrees, that was the position of Lord Carrington (Foreign Secretary); Lord Hailsham (Lord Chancellor); Peter Walker (Agriculture); Jim Prior (Employment); Francis Pym (Defence); Michael Heseltine (Environment); Mark Carlisle (Education);

George Younger (Scotland); Norman St John-Stevas (Leader of the House); and Ian Gilmour (Foreign Office spokesman in the Commons).

Around her, the Prime Minister had a group of ministers – derisively called 'true believers' – who were convinced that Britain could be rescued from its economic malaise only by a decisive and swift change in direction. This consisted in relying on tight control of money as the only sure defence against inflation, a rejection of wages or prices policies, a low income tax regime to foster enterprise, reduced public spending, and in general a running-down of the role of the state, especially in industrial intervention. Keynes was out, Hayek and Friedman were in. The key figures in this group were Geoffrey Howe (Chancellor); Keith Joseph (Industry); John Biffen (Treasury Chief Secretary); John Nott (Trade); and David Howell (Energy).

John Nott, an intelligent and amusing, if prickly, man, was perhaps the clearest exponent of the mood when they took office. After the 1979 budget, which switched the burden of taxation sharply from income tax to VAT, he acknowledged that it would have been possible, as critics suggested, to space these changes out over a parliament. But since their aim was to mark a change in direction in the British economy, the Prime Minister had been right to become decisively involved in the budget, and to stand firm. This was what the Heath government had failed to do.

What was refreshing this time, according to Nott, was that Margaret Thatcher was sticking to her guns, and doing what they all believed in. He wouldn't want to be in politics if you didn't make a serious attempt to do this. John Nott was an impassioned radical. His own fiscal dream was of a country in which income tax was abolished, and VAT raised to fifty per cent, with zero rating for essentials. (No, newspapers were not essential, he smilingly told me.) He was impatient of the constraints of politics, and eventually left government and parliament for the City at the height of his political career.

The unions were a key to much of Whitehall's thinking under Margaret Thatcher. The Winter of Discontent had undermined the Callaghan government, and ministers were unanimous there must be a decisive shift in the balance of power between management and unions. There was less agreement about how this should be brought about, how far the law should be changed, or how much the government ought to rely on negotiations with the industrial partners. Jim Callaghan's final months in Downing Street, when he had got from the unions a new industrial concordat, promised more rational behaviour.

Jim Prior, the first Employment Secretary, had devoted much of his time in opposition to repairing relations with the TUC, after the bitterness at the end of the Heath government's three-day week, and its unsuccessful appeal to the country on the theme 'Who governs?' Prior favoured a gradualist approach, with a minimum of legislative change. Even some of his allies on the Tory left wanted more radical action to tame the unions than he did.

It was the new government's wider economic policies, and especially their effect on unemployment, which worried the doubting ministers. Margaret Thatcher conducted five rounds of public spending economies in sixteen months, at a period of growing world recession. Some ministers believed in the old Keynesian principle of contra-cyclical spending on public services and infrastructure. Norman St John-Stevas acknowledged John Nott's point that if she was to have any hope of achieving an incentive effect, they had to make a sharp change in fiscal policy. But he believed these to be the largest public spending cuts in history, and blamed those ministers who insisted on sticking to the monetary targets in circumstances where this was not appropriate.

The Wets complained that there was no debate of politically sensitive decisions in full Cabinet. In the autumn, for example, Jim Prior was taken completely by surprise by the second increase in prescription charges since the Conservatives came in. The Cabinet had gone through other changes meticulously, but because he had not checked the final draft of the Treasury statement, he had not even heard about this proposal until someone told him it had been announced in the House. His conclusion was that his colleagues were going mad, and that they risked making the government look hard-faced, and turning off the voters.

Ian Gilmour, the most intellectually distinguished of that generation of Wets, lunched with me on the day after interest rates were raised to the staggering level of seventeen per cent – because the ten per cent inflation which the government had inherited was now up to more than seventeen. Gilmour worried about economic dogmatism, but admitted he was also oppressed by the lack of an immediate alternative policy. Even as early as that first autumn he did not have much hope that Margaret Thatcher's policy was working.

The doubting ministers believed the Prime Minister was not hearing a contrary view from her inner circle. Complaints about how she ran her government began almost at once. These usually drew a contrast with Ted Heath. He normally waited till the end of a discussion before summing up, and it was not always clear until the minutes appeared what his view was. He was an old hand, and had observed the ways of earlier Prime Ministers.

By contrast, Margaret Thatcher gave her opinion right at the outset, and left others to challenge her. The Wets assured me that they did so. Jim Prior's principal praise of her in those early, fraught days was that her Cabinet produced more vigorous and open debate than Ted's had done. But this was not the type of debate which led to amiable and easy agreement. Norman St John-Stevas acknowledged the difficulty, so early in the new parliament, of arguing against the monetarist policies which had been in the Conservative manifesto. But he was confident that, once the Prime Minister's economic policies ran into trouble, the Cabinet's natural majority of pragmatic Tories would begin to assert more control. After all, it would soon be only three years before they started preparing for the next election, which was when politics took over from philosophy. In the meantime, however, he noticed that it was proving difficult for ministers to stand up to her, and some were having a hard time; it took them so long to get her to accept a point.

In the light of Nigel Lawson's later relations with Margaret Thatcher, his reputation in those early years is interesting. As Financial Secretary to the Treasury, he was not yet a member of the Cabinet. But the Wets blamed Lawson for providing the ideological drive which alarmed them. They believed the Prime Minister half wanted to be her own Chancellor, and relied on Lawson's economic know-how to interfere. Prior found him a hard man, who didn't understand the real world – a long-standing criticism of economists by those whose expertise lies in industry.

Of the Wets, only Jim Prior had an economic department to support him. By the autumn of 1979, he was begging other economic ministers to leave themselves scope to respond to worsening world conditions. But Geoffrey Howe publicly rejected U-turns, and at the 1980 Conservative conference Margaret Thatcher launched her famous 'the lady's not for turning' slogan. Jim concluded sadly that both Labour and Tory Parties were 'on an ideological trip'.

His argument was that public spending was a quicker way to produce jobs than cuts in personal taxation. He had been against the scale of the VAT increases, and rightly worried about the effect on an already dangerous wage round of the four points these added to the Retail Price Index. He was scandalised when he found that expenditure cuts on prudent councils like his own in Suffolk would lead to a newly built old people's home being put into mothballs. He also argued that the government must remain free to seek an incomes policy of some kind if inflation combined with unemployment became nasty enough. At that time, strange as it may seem from subsequent events, Geoffrey Howe was periodically attracted by the German system of 'concerted action' involving government, industry and unions in talks about what the economy would bear.

The ideological weight in the opposite direction came from Keith Joseph. He had been senior partner in Margaret Thatcher's revolt after the 1974 election defeats, but was temperamentally unsuitable to be leader. Even ministers who disagreed profoundly with Joseph spoke well about him to me. They found it hard to reconcile the decent, kind, slightly diffident, and, some said, naïve man they knew with his unbending economic opinions.

He was sceptical, for example, about the unemployment figures, saying that it was a false reading of these which had panicked the Heath government into its U-turn. Keith Joseph reckoned that the vacancies figure understated the real situation by a factor of three or four. Notoriously, he had said that he only discovered after he came out of the Heath government that he had not been a Conservative at all, but 'a sort of semi-socialist, seeking shortcuts to Utopia'. Ted Heath, in turn, used to speak of 'the traitors, Thatcher and Joseph'. He was bitter because they had failed to resign from his government, though they disagreed with its policies, but had disavowed these soon after the 1974 elections.

Joseph rejected all of what he called 'vulgar Keynesianism'; regarded government schemes to create employment as 'Dead Sea fruit', responsible for destroying as many jobs as they created; and believed politicians were not qualified to say where new jobs would come from. He believed these *would* appear if the government eschewed any policies aimed at greater equality of income or wealth, which were bound to reduce enterprise and the prosperity of the country – and therefore of the poor among others.

Yet although this makes Keith Joseph sound more dogmatic than Margaret Thatcher, he was also much more self-doubting. A colleague described him to me as a very good listener, who actually took in new thoughts – not a universal trait near the top of government. Sometimes his practical sense told him to depart from what theory indicated. It was Keith Joseph who was responsible for industrial interventions in the early years of Thatcherism. For a time these allowed the Wets to claim that events were moving the government in their direction. Help was given to British Leyland, British Coal and British Steel.

27

MARGARET'S UMBILICAL CORD

By the winter of 1979–80, less than a year after Margaret Thatcher's government took office, it was in the grip of economic crisis, raging inflation and rising unemployment. Ian Gilmour observed that if a government came in saying its highest priority was to cut inflation, it was not a great achievement to have doubled it.

The Prime Minister had inherited from Labour in May 1979 an inflation rate of ten per cent, with more in the wages pipeline. Before the spring budget of 1980, the increase in the Retail Price Index was above nineteen per cent, and it passed twenty soon afterwards, eventually peaking at 21.9 per cent in May 1980. Towards the end of the parliament, with employment rising to levels unseen since the thirties, inflation was forced down to single figures. But before that the government had suffered political trauma.

As fierce debate broke out in the Conservative Party and the Cabinet, the Prime Minister displayed the unbending posture which was to win her the title of 'Iron Lady' – and not only among Soviet Communists. The shadow of Ted Heath's U-turn lay dark on her mind. By March 1980 she was informing a nervous Conservative audience: 'If I am told this [her economic policy] would endanger the chances of a second term of office, then I tell you here and now that I will take the risk.'

As things turned out, the risk was not a real one. The Labour Party was in the most self-destructive mood in its history. Soon it was to split, with Roy Jenkins and other Social Democrats forming their own party, and joining in an alliance with the Liberals. The political opposition to Mrs Thatcher was divided and demoralised. One of the unresolved questions of history is whether, without that bonus, as well as her victory in the Falklands, voters would have allowed her to continue her economic experiment for two more parliaments.

Margaret Thatcher still believed in her ability to articulate the feelings of ordinary people, and especially the woman in the High Street shopping queue. This was a great political strength. Tom King maintained this did not cause her to reject more expert advice; it was simply the knowledge against which she bounced the experts' views. The point where frustration engulfed her, he believed, was when civil service advice reflected what she saw as the hopelessness of British attitudes.

Even her Tory critics were awed by this umbilical cord to the kitchen sink. Francis Pym, as different in background from Margaret Thatcher as could be imagined, hoped she realised that the support of such women was now at risk. She would be judged in the next election by how prices and unemployment had moved before then. As it turned out, other factors not to be foreseen were to prove more significant.

A dispute over spending on defence, which caused Pym to threaten resignation as Defence Secretary, was symptomatic of the distrust new policies were causing. He even believed the Prime Minister had encouraged him to go on a visit to China which coincided with the budget, so that he would be out of the country at her worst time. This was the beginning of a long-running disagreement between them, which caused her to move him, first from Defence, and then out of the government after the 1983 election. From very early on, Margaret Thatcher began to display determination that her authority must not be challenged.

Her style of government was a subject of permanent fascination to her ministers. They had never met such a bossy woman. Could it be that, once she enjoyed supreme power, she simply reacted in an over-masterful manner to their patronising attitude to a woman leader? Margaret Thatcher had quickly moved away from the *prima inter pares* doctrine of premiership. There were times when she seemed unable to treat her colleagues as grown-ups, much less as equals.

There was permanent tension between Jim Prior and her over relations with the trade unions. She perceived that the unions were unpopular with the public, even with some of their own members, and she did not share his belief that they could be brought to a more cooperative mood through discussion, with a minimum of legislation. She only got the legislation she wanted when Norman Tebbit succeeded Prior as Employment Secretary. The Prime Minister and her close advisers saw the unions as a challenge to the authority of the state. It was an attitude they were to apply later to local authorities.

Indeed, the Thatcher governments became increasingly intolerant of other centres of power or influence in a plural society. They would argue that they acted – whether against unions, councils, doctors, police and prison officers, or teachers – on behalf of citizens at large, and specifically of consumers. Only the lawyers, it seemed, could resist ministers' radical zeal. They adjusted their wigs slightly, and watched their lucrative gravy train roll on, as litigation grew more and more expensive.

In the government's first year, it was the frightening rise in inflation which caught the headlines. Ministers had grossly underestimated the effects of their determination to leave wages entirely to the free play of the market; they had given an expensive election promise to honour pay awards made in the public sector by Labour's Clegg Commission; and they had ignored the cost of their own 1979 budget, the unpredictable result of ending controls on foreign exchange transactions and on domestic borrowing, and the burden of higher oil prices. This new Conservative government had come in with revolutionary aspirations, but had failed to realise that not all the consequences of revolutions can be foreseen.

The contrasting attitudes of two ministers, John Nott and Peter Walker, underline how deep the internal fissure ran. Nott was the most fervent among the group of 'true believers' close to the Prime Minister. His fear was that this government, like Conservative predecessors, would let itself be talked out of its beliefs. He was, for example, vehemently against any form of incomes policy. If the government stuck to its monetarist policies, wage-bargainers would get the message.

John Nott was a master of the extravagant style of making a serious political point, and I enjoyed his company. He used to profess deep suspicion of the civil service. Because he believed that ministers were in permanent danger of becoming prisoners of their civil servants, he would have liked to see the Prime Minister conducting an experiment along lines adopted in Australia and New Zealand, where ministers all worked in one building. British ministers should be told to work in their rooms at the House of Commons, so that they could spend most of their time talking to each other, and having meals together. They would summon their civil servants over when they needed to see them. He believed this would make for a more political government.

Nott's anxiety that Whitehall might talk the government out of its ideology was not his alone. At first Margaret Thatcher would not allow a junior minister to deputise at an important Cabinet committee, if his chief was not able to attend. She feared the junior minister would argue a civil service brief, and that no real discussion or compromise among ministers would be feasible. John Nott did not spend as much time reading Whitehall briefs as his colleagues. He observed that the German Chancellor, Helmut Schmidt, had the same habit, and it had not done him much harm politically.

His self-confident political attitudes rested on his belief that, almost regardless of what happened to the economy, the Conservatives could not lose the next election. His reasoning was that all over the West there had been a move away from collectivism, and he assumed this would have a ten-year life. He thought the Labour Party, which by then was busily tearing its unity and credibility in shreds, would put its affairs in order in a couple of years' time. But Labour would not win voters back to democratic socialism in time for the next election.

By contrast, in early 1980 Peter Walker took a gloomy view of the government's popularity. He was worried about the probable reaction of working people to what was about to hit them in the following three months. The government was determinedly reducing subsidies, so council rents, rates, gas and electricity prices, school meals, transport fares, and the general price level were all certain to rise sharply. There would also be higher mortgages: although the Wets might jeer at Margaret Thatcher's non-ideological softness towards this key group among her supporters, higher interest rates made larger mortgage bills inevitable. Geoffrey Howe's first budget had reduced income tax, but the price in indirect taxation and higher payments for public services now fell to be paid. The public did not like it.

Walker was different from the other Wets in feeling that he did have an alternative economic strategy to the Thatcherite model. As an economic minister in Ted Heath's government, he had the self-confidence to argue this. His policy was government intervention in the economy. He had grown up in the Tory Party of Butler, Macmillan and Heath, and he was not happy with a doctrinaire hands-off policy. He used to declare that the north-east of England would have been a more awful place if it had not been for the interventionist policies of Hailsham, Macmillan, Heath and himself. Peter Walker ridiculed any thought that businessmen, faced with high interest rates, with inflation touching twenty per cent, and against a background of world recession, were likely to invest without government encouragement.

Peter Walker's seniority in politics gave him a bland tolerance, which lasted throughout his service in Margaret Thatcher's governments. He rarely took a personal view of their differences on policy, maintaining that there were no 'nasties' in the government. The Prime Minister was a nice person who wanted to do the best she could for Britain. But she had surrounded herself with economic ministers – also nice people – who were shackled by the Treasury view of life. Jim Prior was regarded as the man who looked after the human relations side of economic policy (as if all economics is not concerned with human behaviour, which is merely *reflected* in the indices!).

Ian Gilmour worried that the economic ministers were 'in the grip of a belief, a very dangerous thing to be'. When Robert Runcie was enthroned as Archbishop of Canterbury, and delivered what Ian regarded as a commonsensical sermon, he playfully wrote a letter welcoming him as a card-carrying member of the Wets.

'One Nation' Tories worried that the Conservative Party would become again what it had been in the thirties, the party of unemployment, of seeming to be on what one called 'an anti-working-class tack'. They had not become Tories to support the nineteenth-century ideas of Birmingham industrialists like the Chamberlains. The only growth the government was likely to get from all the social pain would not be in manufacturing, but in property speculation. If my description of Wet attitudes suggests an internal opposition to Thatcherite ideas which was articulate, but ineffectual, I think that is fair.

With high interest rates and an overvalued pound, British manufacturing suffered savage erosion in the early Thatcher years. The country had its first deficit in manufactured goods since the Industrial Revolution. The received wisdom of the period was that the jobs lost there would be replaced by new ones in service trades. Once, after a television interview with the Prime Minister, when she invited me to stay on for a drink, I asked for examples of how she thought this would come about. She cited an entrepreneur she had met the previous week, who wished to take over Battersea power station to turn it into what we both then knew as 'a Disneyland', but subsequently learned to call a theme park. (This was a project which did not come to pass.)

The following day I was having lunch with the Economic Attaché at the United States Embassy, and recounted this conversation. He looked at me in genuine astonishment, thoughtfully laid down his fork, and exclaimed: 'But gee, John, you can't all make a living opening doors for each other.'

Unemployment rose more sharply during 1980 than at any time for half a century, by almost a million to more than 2.1 million. By the end of that parliament, it was to pass 3 million. Ministers acknowledged to me that only changes in the methods of calculation kept it even as low as this; opponents said the real figure was around 4 million. As more and more people lost their jobs, politicians with longer memories, notably Edward Heath, Jim Callaghan, Willie Whitelaw and Francis Pym anguished, in public or in private, about its social effects.

The fact that unemployment rose so sharply looked like a reversal of the policy followed by all recent administrations, ever since Churchill's wartime coalition accepted Beveridge's view that to maintain full employment was one of the primary functions of government. But the change was not as preconceived as that makes it sound. David Howell, a former *Daily Telegraph* leader-writer who was in the inner circle of economic ministers, was one of the earliest to voice the theory that the nature of unemployment had changed. It was a less acute personal problem than in the thirties, with improved benefits, and also because of changing patterns of family life, with full-time and part-time jobs, and one and a half or two earners. As the eighties passed into the nineties, and high unemployment became endemic in many areas of Britain, this theory seemed to me to become ever less convincing.

The dogmatists in the government simply believed that employment was a residual, an effect of decisions taken in the market-place, by wage-bargainers among others. The fact that the government as employer seemed often to surrender to strong unions, such as miners, power workers and railwaymen, and become tough with the weak, did not appear to daunt those who held these theories. After the excesses during the Winter of Discontent, Margaret Thatcher had all but written the unions out of her morality play, though she probably would not have gone as far as Enoch Powell, who took a mechanistic view of the labour market. With pre-Friedmanite monetarist rigour, Powell had once pressed his argument that unions had little influence on inflation with a memorable description of them as 'innocent as lambs, pure white as the driven snow'.

The TUC was not Margaret Thatcher's favourite baa-lamb. She showed no interest in consulting the unions about the economy, believing that they were not interested, like other pressure groups, in working within the system, but simply wanted a chance to alter government policy. But the Prime Minister was dedicated to the belief, which after recent events had great popular support, that the balance of power in industry must be sharply changed. The unions, by their restrictive attitudes, had made managers afraid to innovate. She was determined to change that. Implicitly, if only unemployment could bring the unions to heel, she would let unemployment rise. It remains among her monuments.

The dissenters within Mrs Thatcher's government maintained their belief, or hope, that for all the anti-U-turn rhetoric, she was enough of a pragmatist to respond to events. As the crisis deepened, and the government's unpopularity with it, the level of interest rates became for them an important indicator of her behaviour.

Francis Pym and other ministers who had links with industry were receiving alarming messages about the malign effect that the hoist to seventeen per cent had on investment, so they were relieved to see the rate steadily reduced again. The Treasury made these reductions at times when, by the strict criteria of monetarism as it was then understood, reductions seemed imprudent. In the new monetarist establishment of academia and Whitehall, a fierce debate began about the criteria by which the tightness of monetary policy might be judged. Margaret Thatcher allowed herself to be convinced it was by then too tight, hence the lower interest rates. Other actions which ran against the grain of ideology were the industrial rescues of British Steel and British Leyland. Keith Joseph presided over these with apparent agony, and the non-monetarists complained that this robbed the government of the political credit for sensibly pragmatic decisions.

These and other divisions in the Cabinet were freely reported in the newspapers. So much so that the Prime Minister's press secretary, Bernard Ingham, warned her early in 1980 that party in-fighting was damaging her government's public image, and preventing him doing his job properly. Many years before, as news editor of the *Guardian*, I had been responsible for bringing Bernard to London as an industrial correspondent. He had been a fine reporter, never sparing himself in pursuit of news. He took the same spirit of loyalty to his Whitehall service, for politicians as diverse as Barbara Castle, Tony Benn and Margaret Thatcher.

Bernard was single-minded, to the verge of being blinkered, about conflicting points of view. He wrote for the Prime Minister a daily summary, originally a page and a half in length, of the principal issues of the day, as he judged them from the newspapers. Once he had decided that leaks were doing her harm, I could believe he would have given her an irascible account of the behaviour of her erring ministers, especially those who talked to people like me. Of course, he himself had once been just such a persistent journalist. Poachers and gamekeepers!

Bernard was fiercely protective of his new boss. He was proud that she had decided to appoint him after a thirty-second acquaintance when she toured the Department of Energy. As criticism of the government for its monetarist ideology grew fiercer, under the frightening weight of the recession, he shied away from the thought that Margaret Thatcher was a monetarist. He preferred to describe her as a more practical person, one who thought in terms of good housekeeping and not spending more than you earned.

Right at the beginning of her period in office, Bernard Ingham believed the Prime Minister had the capacity to be flexible rather than dogmatic, although she was determined her government would attempt to do the things it had been elected for. What depressed her, as it depressed him, was that she suspected the dissident ministers were not really arguing about timing and method of change, but that they had fundamental doubts about the policy itself. In this Margaret Thatcher and her press secretary were right. Nobody who talked as often to the Wets as I did could accept that divisions in the Cabinet were merely about the *pace* of change.

28

THE SDP, BBC AND ME

My transition from journalism to broadcasting coincided, most inconveniently for me, with the more significant transformation of Her Majesty's opposition from one major party into two. During the later period covered by this book, there are two seminal events. One is Margaret Thatcher's election as Conservative leader; the other, the decision by Roy Jenkins, David Owen, Shirley Williams and Bill Rodgers to lead an exodus from the Labour Party.

I have written before about the launch of the SDP, and the subsequent creation of an Alliance with the Liberals (in *The Thatcher Years; a decade of revolution in British politics*). Because I had been studying the British Labour movement for so long, I felt better qualified than most to understand the consequences of that cataclysmic event. In this and following chapters, I shall draw on that earlier account, but for a wider purpose.

I was inhibited then, because of the impartiality imposed by my job as the BBC's political editor, from explaining why, both then and now, I regarded the decision of the Social Democrats to break with Labour as an historic and tragic mistake. An inevitable tragedy, perhaps, but a tragedy none the less, because for two decades it deprived Britain of an alternative government, by preventing the healthy swing of the electoral pendulum which has been the greatest strength of our democracy.

Not that the lot of Labour's right after 1979 was enviable. With the cement of office removed, the party's factions slid into a battle to the death. That tragic conflict is encapsulated in my memory in two encounters with Shirley Williams. The first was at the beginning of the summer parliamentary recess of 1980. She gave a party at her house in Hertfordshire, attended by leading Labour moderates and by journalists. As she showed Madge and me to the door at the end of the evening, she said with a sad smile: 'You have just witnessed the wake of Labour's old establishment.'

Within days, she, David Owen and Bill Rodgers issued their first document distancing themselves from Labour's new leftward direction. This pushed them gradually into alliance with their old political friend, Roy Jenkins, who in November 1979, while still President of the European Commission, had called in his Dimbleby lecture for the creation of a radical centre in British politics. By the spring of 1981, all four had broken with Labour and formed the Social Democratic Party.

The second memory is of a party at our house the following year, after the die was cast. Most of the guests were Conservative, Labour and Alliance MPs and journalists. As I pursued my hostly duties, dispensing food and drink, I noticed only that the guests seemed to be mingling well, and nobody was standing alone. Only late in the evening did Shirley playfully draw my attention to a strange phenomenon.

'John, how clever!' she said. 'You've got a Labour room and an SDP room.'

Our modest establishment would have made such planning difficult, even if we had thought it desirable. But there was something in what she said. For while Tories and journalists were casting their conversational nets in every direction, all the Labour people had gravitated to one room, and all the Social Democrats to another. It reminded me of the segregation by gender which happens spontaneously at too many Irish parties. As the departing guests walked to their cars, a few Labour and SDP people exchanged pleasantries across the psychological peace line. But the emotional division was already deep.

The story of the SDP and the Alliance will be the subject of the next chapter. But first we must consider what caused the division in the Labour Party; a division which kept far from successful Conservative administrations in power throughout the four parliaments which followed.

The IMF crisis of 1976 sowed the seeds of Labour's civil war, for it created a policy vacuum on that party's dominant centre-right wing. Nobody resigned, but the Callaghan government's change in direction provoked from the left the most corrosive charge in the Labour lexicon: betrayal. The left believed Labour governments since 1964 had betrayed socialism. Indeed, ever since 1931, when Ramsay MacDonald entered coalition with the Conservatives, Labour has suffered from an immanent expectation of betrayal by its leaders.

What destroyed Labour's unity was an excess of ideology on the left and an absence of fresh political thinking on the right. Tony Crosland, the great hope of those who believed Labour could be at once socially radical and electable, had died prematurely in 1977. This was a political as well as a personal tragedy, for he might either have become leader when Jim Callaghan retired in 1980, or returned to his role as the philosopher of democratic socialism, providing a political framework to set against the fundamentalist ideology of Tony Benn and the left. Crosland shared the views of both Harold Wilson and Jim Callaghan about the task of a Labour leader. Callaghan once cajoled a rebellious young MP, Neil Kinnock: 'Look, I'm just trying to keep the show on the road.' Crosland defined that aim further: to keep the party together; hold the middle ground against ultras of left or right; and shift and adapt to changing circumstances, whatever the cries of betrayal.

He used to complain to me that colleagues persistently told him he must save Labour from living off the intellectual capital of his 1956 book, *The Future of Socialism*, by bringing his philosophy up to date in a new tract. His response was characteristically combative: 'I'm too bloody busy running a major government department; let them do the new thinking.'

Crosland had weaned Labour away from belief in 'Clause IV socialism', based on public ownership, to an alternative which relied on economic growth and redistribution of wealth through the taxation and social security systems. After the IMF crisis, this policy was in disarray. Crosland accepted the IMF cuts in public spending only in order to preserve the government's life. Fundamental thinking about the efficiency of British industry, how to avoid inflation and stop-go, and how to gain popular support for social justice was more urgent than ever.

Overwork and exhaustion probably contributed to Tony Crosland's death in 1977. Two years later, other senior ministers in the Callaghan government left office exhausted. They had endured minority government, the unaccustomed strains of a pact with the Liberals, and the Winter of Discontent. Only after three months of rest did Jim Callaghan realise how tired he had been. The Queen had sympathetically commented to him on how relentless the Prime Minister's life had become. Callaghan noted wryly that Margaret Thatcher was young and fit, and was revelling in her work. But by then, he thought, he himself would have been fit enough for it again.

What revived Callaghan is an interesting reflection on the strains – I believe unnecessary strains – the British system now imposes on Prime Ministers. As leader of the opposition he was able to go home and have a full night's rest, which is important for a man aged sixty-seven; whereas in Downing Street he had normally worked his way through two despatch boxes at night, and continued his toil between seven and nine in the morning, preparing for the new day's meetings.

Jim told me he had assumed a newly defeated Prime Minister would be unpopular, but had been encouraged by the reception he was getting: when he emerged from a West End cinema, the crowds had applauded him. In fact, Callaghan's rating in the polls when he went into opposition was the highest of any politician in Britain. I suggested to him that he should think hard before giving up his leadership, but he believed he would be too old, at seventy-one, to fight the next election. I murmured about Churchill not becoming Prime Minister for the first time, in 1940, until he was sixty-six. Jim Callaghan said wisely that the world had changed since those days.

He intended to remain leader only long enough to preside over the inquest on election defeat, and to smooth the path for Denis Healey to succeed him. I put to him what I saw as his party's problem: that unless they could find a solution to Britain's chronic tendency to low growth, and therefore remove the principal obstacle to Labour's ideal of greater equality, they would tear themselves apart over internal problems. He agreed with this analysis. Young people might join Labour because they disapproved of Margaret Thatcher, but they would soon want an answer to the issues I had raised with him.

Jim Callaghan returned to the subject we had often discussed, incomes policy. Its breakdown, after considerable success, had probably done more than anything else to defeat his government. He recalled that a quarter-century before he had not thought there was much in it, and said I had been one of those who had convinced him of its importance.

When Labour lost office, what its leading figures desperately needed was time to recharge their political batteries, by thinking hard about policy. Instead the left, outraged by the actions of the Labour government, immediately plunged into a battle to change the way in which the party was controlled, with the intention of revolutionising policies for the future.

The leading figures of the 1970s Labour governments were, by any standards, a remarkable collection of contrasting talents and personalities. Under both Wilson and Callaghan leaderships, three powerful ministers on the centre-right – Tony Crosland, Roy Jenkins and Denis Healey – had circled each other. Now Crosland was dead. Jenkins, towards the end of his term in Brussels, inevitably became something of a King Over the Water, especially after he raised his radical centre standard.

It did not help that there was no love lost between Jenkins and the man universally expected to succeed Callaghan, Labour's third former Chancellor, Denis Healey. Healey was a political loner, a private person within a strong marriage, and his principal handicap in 1979 was to be cast, inevitably, as chief apologist for the late Labour government.

On the left was Tony Benn, who combined the seniority conferred by office in every Labour Cabinet since 1964 with a role as *enfant terrible* of the National Executive Committee, where he strained to the limits the doctrine of collective responsibility in pursuit of what he saw as greater internal democracy. Standing between him and Jim Callaghan was Michael Foot, who since agreeing to take office in 1974 had developed a role as guarantor of the left and fixer of the Liberals.

The man who was doing most fundamental thinking was Tony Benn. If there was an intellectual gap on the right, he set out to ensure this was not true of the left. I have never been able to accept the cliché version of Benn as a near-demented figure, for he has a fertile mind, and a clarity of expression which others ought to envy. But the vigour of his ideological drive, and the ruthless efficiency with which he and others conducted the campaign for constitutional change, were undoubtedly a major irritation to those Labour leaders who feared their party would fly apart.

In my judgement, Tony Benn and those who worked with him share historic responsibility with the Gang of Four for Labour's disastrous split and its consequences. On both wings, these men and women believed with great passion in what they were doing. They were finally incapable of compromising with each other.

During the years after the 1979 defeat, I had many fascinating conversations with Tony Benn. What makes him interesting to a journalist – and often infuriating to political colleagues – is a free-ranging imagination, which fights free of institutional inhibitions. He clearly felt liberated in opposition by his return to the back benches, and surprised me by arguing that the great merit of the British system was its ability to dismiss governments.

He had reached the comforting conclusion that the British people had been right on every occasion they had done this since the war. They had dismissed Churchill in 1945, Attlee's government when it was exhausted in 1951, upheld the Conservatives when they were doing well in 1955 and 1959, put Labour in tentatively in 1964 and firmly in 1966, and dismissed them in disgust in 1970 and again that year. (I felt like apologising to him for the fact that the *Observer*, partly under my prompting, had advocated Labour's re-election.)

Benn maintained that the IMF crisis had exploded the social democratic belief that you could run the country simply on the basis of high public expenditure. The left-wing alternative relied on more public ownership, deep scepticism about the European Community, and a move towards protectionism, to counter unemployment, which under Margaret Thatcher had grown to frightening levels.

His political analysis was that there were three political blocks in Britain: the monetarist right, the corporatist centre, and the democratic socialists. For him, the last group were those members of the Labour Party who shared his views. When I challenged the word 'corporatist' as pejorative, he made clear that he defined the centre as stretching from Jim Prior through Jo Grimond to Denis Healey, Shirley Williams and Jim Callaghan. He saw the battle in the Labour Party as being between those who wanted to diffuse power and spread it downwards, within the party and the trade unions and to the population at large, and those who wanted to operate through deals with the TUC and CBI.

Without finding his arguments persuasive, I have always felt that the media gave a caricature of Benn, rather as they did of Enoch Powell. Both have muscular minds. Both find difficulty in admitting, I suspect even to themselves, that they occasionally act from political expediency rather than principle, perhaps because they are more fascinated by the theoretical arguments than by practical ones. Since this book takes a critical view of political ideologues, it seems only fair to acknowledge the virtues of two leading ideological practitioners. I must, however, confess that I find this easier to do because they have been prevented from pursuing their ideologies into Downing Street.

Another characteristic of Tony Benn which may surprise people who do not know him is that he is among the best-mannered among senior politicians. One morning I spent two hours talking to him at his house over many cups of tea or coffee. So many that, before leaving, I visited his lavatory. When I came out, he was standing in the middle of Holland Park Avenue, sheltered from a heavy rainstorm by his umbrella, trying to find me a taxi. Few Privy Councillors would be so personally considerate to a journalist.

For Tony Benn and the left, the constitutional struggle for control of the Labour Party was at least as important as their differences on policy. But to follow that struggle in detail now would be tedious. Much of what happened then was to be reversed or changed beyond recognition during the leaderships of Neil Kinnock, John Smith and Tony Blair. At the time, however, it was important, for the quarrel split the Labour Party. What Jim Callaghan and his allies on one side, and Tony Benn, supported by organisations such as the Labour Co-ordinating Committee and the Campaign for Labour Party Democracy, on the other were struggling for was the soul of Labour.

The proposed constitutional changes were about how Labour chose its leader, how far constituency parties could control and remove their MPs, and who should write the election manifesto. Decisions on these questions had to be taken under a voting system that was profoundly unsatisfactory. Although I believe Labour's trade union connection keeps its political feet nearer the ground than they might otherwise be, ever since my arrival in London in 1957 I had been writing articles calling for reform of the block vote. Nobody on the right, which then controlled that vote, had taken much notice. Indeed, at the time Hugh Gaitskell found these thoughts subversive.

Since the early seventies, when the right finally lost any remaining control of these block votes, the leadership had grave difficulties at Labour's policy-making annual conference and, more seriously, in the National Executive Committee, which runs the party month by month. Both Harold Wilson and Jim Callaghan had to deal with suspicious and hostile majorities there. In government, they would largely ignore NEC decisions. In opposition, however, this was much more difficult, and it caused rows.

Even after I stopped being a labour correspondent in 1963, I had maintained my contacts in the unions, as well as developing more parliamentary ones. In my conversations in both parts of the Labour movement in 1979, I discovered mutual hostility, even contempt. This derived largely from disputes over the Callaghan government's incomes policy, and specifically its final five per cent norm. But the union leaders, who were being asked to find money not only for Labour's depleted funds, but also for its new headquarters in Walworth Road, regarded the party as administratively incompetent.

The left's struggle to impose its will on the Labour Party, and the dramatic events leading to the departure of the Social Democrats, came at a turbulent time for me, personally and professionally. In November 1981 I resigned as deputy editor of the *Observer*, and became political editor of the BBC. After years of worthwhile, but wearisome Fleet Street politicking, I returned to reporting, with a slightly nervous sigh of relief, wondering whether I would still be able to do it, and in two new media, radio and television.

Madge and I had an idyllic week in Venice between my *Observer* and BBC stints. Most acquaintances think of any departure from print journalism to broadcasting as a carefully worked out career move, based on a judgement that the electronic media are gradually assuming the influence which newspapers once had. In reality, mine had a more mundane explanation. In half a century at work, I have only had four employers, and apart from the decision to leave Belfast for England, none of the moves has been planned.

During my time at the *Observer*, we had already fought off take-over attempts by James Goldsmith and Rupert Murdoch, whom the editor, Donald Trelford, and senior staff did not think were suitable owners of a great liberal newspaper. Earlier in 1981 Atlantic Richfield (or ARCO as it had become known), whose shareholders had run out of patience, sold the paper to Tiny Rowland of Lonrho. There was a clear conflict of interest between Lonrho's extensive commercial interests in Africa and the reputation for independence which the *Observer* had established by its stance during the period when new black states were emerging. The foreign affairs specialists felt strongly about this. But most journalists on the paper also saw many other reasons why Rowland would be an unsuitable proprietor.

I drafted the senior staff's evidence to the Monopolies Commission, opposing the take-over, and together with Adam Raphael, the political correspondent, gave oral evidence. The commission ruled against us, though it recommended supposed safeguards, including independent directors. When Tiny Rowland and the editor met to negotiate about these, I was invited by Trelford to attend, together with representatives of the office National Union of Journalists chapel, of which I was also a member.

It was a dispiriting occasion, with Rowland and his directors high-hatting not only their prospective employees, but also the Department of Trade officials who were supposed to be holding the ring. We had been kept waiting about two hours before the Lonrho contingent arrived for the meeting, and this dragged on until 2.30 a.m. Sometime after one o'clock, on a point of detail where Rowland's arrogance became unbearable, my Irish temper snapped. He and I had a blazing row.

When proceedings ended, he slowly came round the table, shook hands with the editor, then with me, adding with a flash of his astonishingly cold smile, that he very much looked forward to working with me. This did not strike me as a relationship which would be of long duration. The next morning the BBC, totally unaware of my personal drama, telephoned to ask whether I would be interested in becoming their political editor. Although we modern Presbyterians do not subscribe to a seventeenth-century view of predestination, I made an exception in this case. The time had come to move, so I jumped before I was pushed.

The *Observer* printers, soon to change to new technology after centuries of hot metal working on one of the world's most historic printing sites in Blackfriars, saw me off in style. I was probably the last senior journalist in Fleet Street to be 'banged out'. To an extraneous, but moving skirl of bagpipes, the printers thumped their metal rules, in a wild cacophony, on the metal-topped tables, or stones, on which we had made up so many leader pages together.

I was sad to leave behind thirty-six years in print journalism, the last quarter-century of them in London, but at the age of fifty-four, I probably needed a new challenge. When Jim Callaghan congratulated me on the move, I replied that I had decided I had one more job in me. With ex-Prime Ministerial authority he replied: 'Don't be a bloody fool! You've years of work in you yet.'

Before news of my BBC appointment became known, I had a brisk exchange of views about the *Observer* take-over with the current Prime Minister, Margaret Thatcher. It was towards the end of a Buckingham Palace garden party, when Madge and I were talking with a former teaching colleague of hers, Clare Jones, an Irish international swimmer, and her husband, St John Pike, former Bishop of the Gambia.

As the Prime Minister was heading for her car, Denis Thatcher spotted us, and she came over to speak. After introductions had been made, the purpose of her diversion became clear. She fixed me with a stern eye, and said: 'I do find it odd that journalists on the *Observer*, who feel free themselves to write whatever they think, become so agitated when a man who has a bit of money, and believes he has something to say through the media, takes over their paper.'

She waited for a response. I spoke – convincingly, I hoped – about the difference between the roles of journalists and proprietors: we might get things wrong sometimes, doubtless did, but at least we did not have to worry about extraneous business interests, as Tiny Rowland did.

She listened with reasonable patience to this exposition of the journalist's priest-like role, then interjected sharply: 'Yes, I see all that. But do you have to have all these editorial safeguards?'

Although I respected personally several of the independent directors whom the Monopolies Commission had required Rowland to accept, I did not believe they would be able to restrain such a self-willed proprietor. So I put the free-market part of her mind at rest: 'In my opinion, the editorial safeguards are not worth a damn.'

The Prime Minister wisely decided this had gone on quite long enough, and took a cheerful farewell of us all. Years later, Bishop Pike, a profound and holy man, recalled this conversation with a twinkle, and said he had been astonished by the vigour with which we conducted our discussion. I could see why his morning preference on Radio 4 was for *Prayer for the Day*, rather than the occasionally more controversial *Thought for the Day*.

If departure from the *Observer* had been a result of proprietorial strains, my transfer was not stress-free at the other end either. The BBC's Political Unit, of eight correspondents, served both radio and television, and so did not quite know who its bosses were. We were the first bi-medial unit, before the phrase became fashionable in the nineties. From time to time the two media fought over our services, in a disorganised way. But more often the television side were arguing that the unit should be split between the two media.

Apart from this long-running unease, my new BBC colleagues at Westminster had been through an unsettled period, and were not ecstatic to see the appointment of a Fleet Street executive, who I suspect they thought would not be overly keen on hard work 'at the coalface'. I knew I could prove that wrong, but I also asked advice from Robert Carvel, the veteran political editor of the *Evening Standard*. He replied: 'You've been appointed to this job. Now you've got to get yourself elected.'

It was wise advice. I had done a lot of broadcasting in the previous quarter-century, but always as what producers call, 'a guest'. Work on the BBC staff was very different, for it involved much technical knowledge I did not possess, and which I relied on my new staff to teach me. I worked hard to fit in, and they were generous and helpful in return.

29

THE LOST LEADER

What made the constitutional debate within the Labour Party more bitter was that its national membership had changed. Even such a tolerant man as Merlyn Rees found his visits to some constituency parties depressing. The London Labour Party, in particular, contained some foolish people: he was depressed by one debate he witnessed, about whether members ought to share their cars with each other in the name of socialism. Merlyn predicted that such follies would provoke a trend against Labour in London and the south, which might keep them out of office for a very long time.

At the cutting edge of extremism was the Militant Tendency, a Trotskyist sect which had adopted a policy of 'entryism', with a view to controlling the Labour Party. Its principal method of achieving this was an ancient Marxist one: boring or antagonising ordinary members. These, unsurprisingly, did not relish being denounced as 'Neanderthal fossils', so they began to stay away from their local Labour Parties.

I could never understand why Tony Benn did not worry about Trotskyist infiltration as did others, even old left-wingers like Michael Foot. Benn explained that he thought talk of a revolutionary, anti-parliamentary left in Britain was myth. The communist base in industry had diminished, and under Margaret Thatcher union power was eroding quickly. He was content to deal with Militant not by expulsions, but by making Labour more socialist, and increasing its membership.

Where Tony Benn's radicalism seemed to me to falter was in confronting what was wrong with trade unionism, and the doubtful democracy by which union leaders controlled the Labour Party. He did say that of course he was not defending the block vote, but he seemed to envisage a gradualness in tackling it, and giving power to the grassroots, which was not consistent with his general radicalism.

At one long session in his house, he told me he was not just interested in getting governmental power, or this job or that, but in working to change the Labour Party and therefore the shape of British democracy. He was then fifty-five, and although he did not necessarily intend to retire at sixty-five, nevertheless after that age he would tend to be transformed into an embryo elder statesman, so he proposed to devote the eighties to this task of change.

In my judgement, Tony Benn was at once brilliant and blinkered. He was so blinded by the frustration he had felt during the Labour governments in which he served that he never quite resolved the dilemma facing politicians of his talent: between being a practical political leader seeking power to implement what he believed in, and the inspiring, but less disciplined role of political visionary.

In Labour's struggle, both over party organisation and the leadership, the right was less well organised than the left. Whereas the myriad organisations on the left, though bewildering in their alphabetical incontinence, showed remarkable discipline and unanimity in achieving their objectives, the centre and right suffered from that prima donnaism which is the affliction of political organisations where too many members have recently held, and lost, senior office.

Denis Healey has always been rather contemptuous of the importance of organisation by leadership candidates. In the 1976 contest, he relied essentially on his team of Treasury ministers. After Labour's 1979 defeat, noting that he seemed at one time not even to have a regular secretary, I asked whether he was getting organised this time. He assured me he did have excellent intelligence information.

With Jim Callaghan's knowledge, a group of younger right-of-centre ex-ministers under Denis Healey's leadership was trying to prevent the Labour Party going off the rails. Its membership varied, depending on the purpose, but leading participants included Eric Varley, Roy Hattersley, Bill Rodgers, David Owen, and Shirley Williams, who had lost her seat in the general election.

At best, this might have been a star-crossed operation. But to make it more difficult, these were a group of individualists, several with short fuses, all with their own ambitions for the future, having to descend from the well-structured work they had done as ministers of the crown to the scrabble of persuading half-interested trade union executives – with whom they had recently been in conflict over pay policy – that it was vital they send sensible delegates to party conferences. All found the adjustment difficult.

The temperamental differences in the group of moderate ministers erupted in a row between Denis Healey and Bill Rodgers. In Hugh

Gaitskell's campaign to reverse Labour's commitment to unilateral nuclear disarmament in 1960, Rodgers, then a young general secretary of the Fabian Society, had been a key figure in organising the counter-revolution. Healey expected him to do the same job again. He described Rodgers to me as a man of ability, with real expertise in organising votes for a cause within the Labour Party.

But one day when I met Bill Rodgers he was incandescent with fury. Healey had returned from a visit abroad, and had blown his top at all the younger members of the team for failing to get more organisational work done in his absence. He had apparently concluded that Rodgers no longer wanted to undertake what was an onerous chore. When Bill Rodgers resents such a comment, he is not remiss in letting the accuser know this. The rights and wrongs of this dispute were something I was unable to fathom. The characters of the two men ensured a stormy relationship. I have known and liked both of them for many years, but there is a streak of arrogance in both which spelled trouble.

At that time, Denis Healey became alarmed about Trotskyist infiltration, and also about the tolerant attitude the legitimate left was showing to the Militant Tendency. It was Healey, when he was international secretary at party headquarters after the war, who had persuaded the then general secretary, Morgan Phillips, to proscribe the Communist Party.

As leader of the centrist group trying to keep the Labour Party together, it behove him also to look towards its other flank. He did not then believe Roy Jenkins would get a centre party off the ground. Looking at Europe since 1945, he noted there had been no successful defection to the right from any of the socialist parties, and he did not think there could be here. It depends, of course, on whether you define 'success' as eventually gaining power: in that meaning, Healey proved to be right. But the Alliance's creation divided the opposition from 1981 onward, and turned out to be a decisive event for everyone on the non-Conservative side of the political fence.

By the autumn of 1980, the quarrels over constitutional changes and the leadership were becoming intermingled. Even before the disastrous 1980 party conference in Blackpool in October, Shirley Williams, David Owen and Bill Rodgers had written an open letter in the *Guardian*. This gave warning that if Labour's NEC pursued its present course, they would be interested in forming, not a centre party, but a new democratic socialist party, committed to conscience and reform.

Shirley had earlier denounced the centre party that Roy Jenkins conceived at the end of 1979 as likely to have 'no roots, no principles, no philosophy and no values'. Even as late as the 1980 conference, she was disposed to fight on within the Labour Party. But not long afterwards she became so disaffected that she announced she would not accept nomination as a Labour candidate. David Owen declined to stand for the shadow Cabinet under Michael Foot's leadership.

Blackpool was worse than any Labour moderate had foreseen. The conference called for Britain to withdraw from Europe and for unilateral nuclear disarmament. The results on the constitutional issues were a mess, and had eventually to be referred to a special conference at Wembley in January. But before that, Jim Callaghan had decided he had done all he could do for the party he had served for so long, and he resigned.

Denis Healey, expected by friend and foe alike to succeed as leader, gave his political obituary. He had learned a lot while serving under Callaghan, who had been very good as Prime Minister in getting his way. It had been fascinating to watch how he decided early on in a Cabinet dispute what objective he wished to achieve, and then to observe how he set about getting it. Healey said if historians dealt harshly with Callaghan's premiership, that would be unfair. Healey argued that he had done well, considering he had been required to lead a minority government at a time when Labour's trade union allies were in such a dreadful state.

Michael Foot was eventually persuaded to stand for the leadership as a unifying candidate, and although Jim Silkin and Peter Shore, who had already declared their intentions to stand, remained in the first ballot, Foot became the left's principal standard-bearer. Shore took Foot's late change of mind with characteristic good humour.

For a time, with the right wing supporting Denis Healey, Peter Shore had seemed his only serious rival. He was usually thought of as a man of the left, but like many such categorisations, this was simplistic. In Labour's constitutional rows, he was drawn in to support the moderate group. People kept telling me, not always with approbation, that 'Peter is an old-fashioned patriot'. In part, this was because of his Euro-scepticism.

But Labour supporters of Irish unity, who included many right-wing figures, also found his attitude on Ulster tiresome. One, displaying scant knowledge of Irish affairs, described him as 'an Orangeman'. By this, presumably, he meant that Peter Shore perversely believed in the United Nations principle of self-determination, rather than the imperialist principle that such matters are best decided by superior minds in London.

To me, he seemed like a thoughtful Labour radical, who judged issues on their merits as he saw them, rather than by whether they fell into categories of right or left. He remained opposed to the view, then becoming fashionable, that ownership of industry did not matter. Although a firm supporter of a mixed economy, he worried about giant firms in semi-monopoly positions, and argued that it had never been honest to aim at equality without discussing public and other forms of ownership.

With Michael Foot in the contest, Denis Healey's prospects became less certain. Immediately after the 1979 election defeat, Tom McCaffrey, Jim Callaghan's closest aide, had warned me that Healey would be the strongest candidate for the first year, but that after this his star would fade. This was prophetic, though not necessarily in the way McCaffrey meant. I suspect he believed a new generation of leadership hopefuls would soon emerge, including David Owen and Roy Hattersley.

In the event, by the time the election took place, Labour MPs, who were to have the choice of leader for this one last time, were demoralised by the changes the left was forcing. Knowing that they inevitably faced compulsory reselection in their constituencies, enough of them concluded that Michael Foot was more likely than Denis Healey to provide them with a quiet life. They elected Labour's first left-wing leader of the post-war period by just ten votes, 139 to 129.

One of those who persuaded Michael Foot to stand was Neil Kinnock. He was fond of the older man, believed he would hate the job of leader, and didn't like asking him to do something unpleasant. But he believed that Foot might just beat Healey, whom he regarded as divisive. This was my first acquaintance with Neil, who struck me as an independent left-winger, even then inclined to scoff at the pretentiousness of the left's 'umbrella organisations'.

What rang an alarm bell for the future was his attitude on defence. I had been struck by remarks he had made in an *Observer* profile, excoriating his boyhood hero, Aneurin Bevan, for having sold out at the 1957 Labour conference on unilateral renunciation of nuclear weapons. This was Nye's famous speech about not sending a Labour Foreign Secretary 'naked into the conference chamber'.

I was at this conference, while Kinnock was fifteen at the time. He felt it was one of the turning points in Labour history. I deduced that his enthusiasm for Michael Foot, Bevan's disciple and biographer, derived from the profound distress Foot had expressed about this 1957 speech. It was a subject which returned to haunt Neil Kinnock. A principal reason he never became Prime Minister was that his abandonment of unilateralism came too late to carry conviction.

A month or so after Michael Foot was elected leader, I had an uncharacteristically gloomy lunch with Roy Hattersley. He had been hoping and expecting that Denis Healey would succeed Jim Callaghan, and believed he would have made a formidable Prime Minister. Denis retained hopes throughout the 1979 parliament that Michael would not stay in the job until a general election, and that he himself might still get the leadership. But others now thought time had run out for 'the best Prime Minister Labour never had'.

Roy Hattersley found this depressing. Although he liked Michael Foot personally, as nearly everybody does, he did not think he could be elected Prime Minister. This was not just because of differences on policy, notably Europe and unilateralism, but because Foot was not sufficiently engaged on the central economic issues to be a good parliamentary performer at question time and the opening of debates, when he would have to say what he would do in government. He was more a '9.30 at night man', a winding-up speaker who could destroy a government's case with his wit and passion. But under Margaret Thatcher, as Roy Jenkins noted, parliament had changed, and such speeches were of less importance.

Hattersley's second worry was that, even if Margaret Thatcher did enough damage to Conservative unity to lose a general election, Labour would still be in an impossible position. They would have been elected on a programme that a Cabinet containing Healey, Shore, Rodgers, Owen and himself in reasonably senior positions would not be able to implement. Local parties would then begin refusing to reselect moderate MPs, there would be attempts to discipline ten or so members of the government, and the Labour Party would really fly apart.

Despite his gloom, Roy Hattersley never seriously contemplated abandoning Labour, even though in his darker moments he believed it might be in terminal condition. There was nowhere else he wanted to go politically. He remained a democratic socialist, and what he wanted was the old Labour Party, with the left wing always there, but always in a minority. I told him that Tony Benn believed the right must get used to being in a minority. Roy acknowledged the justice of this argument, and said he realised he was asking for a return to a happier past.

But despite this bleak analysis, his attitude to the Social Democrats had changed. He now believed that his old friends were about to defect. He believed they were taking a profoundly mistaken course, and one that was damaging to people like himself, on the moderate wing of the Labour Party, who wanted to fight on inside. He became determined to avoid sharing platforms where he might be associated with a 'Gang of

Three pronouncements'. The 'old Labour establishment', of which Shirley Williams had spoken to me, was falling apart.

Roy Hattersley crossed his personal Rubicon when Shirley Williams wrote to him, praising as intelligent and rational an argument he had advanced against the left at a meeting between the shadow Cabinet and the NEC. But surely, she wrote, he now realised he was not dealing with intelligent and rational people, and that they must be fought. The implication was that he should join the Gang of Three. Roy Hattersley had decided the fight must continue inside the Labour Party, and though he considered writing a careful reply, Shirley's letter was never answered. The basis of trust had eroded.

30

KING FROM OVER THE WATER

After Michael Foot defeated Denis Healey for the leadership of the Labour Party in November 1980, Her Majesty's opposition was on a dizzying roller-coaster, and so was I. My closest Labour acquaintances were offering me rival analyses of the future, and it was more difficult than ever before to decide whose judgement was likely to be right.

The four future leaders of the SDP were by now semi-detached from Labour, in Roy Jenkins' case, much more than that. With a special conference of the Labour Party at Wembley on 24 January due to wrestle yet again with its constitution, it became important to understand their intentions.

On 13 January Adam Raphael, political correspondent of the *Observer*, and I had lunch with Roy Jenkins, who had finished his stint as President of the European Commission, and was now free to devote himself full-time to British politics. On the same day I spoke on the telephone with Shirley Williams and Bill Rodgers. Shirley made clear to me that while the Gang of Four had decided they must do nothing which would make the Wembley conference worse than it showed every sign of being, they would not settle now for a fudged solution.

She expressed scorn of the trade union block vote and what she called the Tammany method of selecting delegates. I recalled to her that when I had been writing articles against the block vote in the late fifties, there had been few salutes from her wing of the Labour Party, which from time immemorial had relied on just that system to defeat left-wing constituency delegates, and retain control. Her reply was that they had always known the block vote was not perfect, but only during this crisis had they discovered that union leaderships did not even know who paid the political levy, and who was therefore entitled to a vote.

She expected the conference to go wrong for the leadership, and said she and her friends would then have to take decisive action. Clearly this was to be a turning point in British politics. After the division in the opposition which they were contemplating, I asked, what possibility would there be of any government other than Margaret Thatcher's? She answered with a question: 'Can Labour be elected?'

Shirley acknowledged that unemployment would damage the Tories, but said oil revenue would make the country feel more prosperous. She told me of a conversation she had had with a Cabinet minister – admittedly, in his cups – who had predicted that unemployment would allow Labour to run up big majorities in Scotland and the north, but added: 'Why do you think we are giving money to British Leyland?' Ministers had considered the benefits of rescue operations for industry in those parts of the country which were politically sensitive. She understood a discussion had taken place in Cabinet which had offended some of the Wets because it was so cynical in its attitude to the pork barrel.

The telephone call with Bill Rodgers provided an interesting retrospective view about the speeds at which he, Shirley Williams and David Owen had moved away from their Labour allegiance. Bill was in sad mood. He had been lying on his back for a couple of weeks with a strained muscle. At lunch later, Roy Jenkins murmured that the illness might be a bit psychosomatic, but then all illnesses were, weren't they? Having just survived the surgeon's knife myself, I was not so sure about this proposition.

Politics apart, this had been a gloomy winter for me. After a hard-working sabbatical month in the United States, I returned on a flight delayed for a whole day, and following endless hassle about whether we would arrive home in time to meet a French exchange boy, I had an eruption of my duodenal ulcer. This happened at the TUC in Brighton, and put me out of action through some of the most turbulent weeks in modern British politics.

My convalescence provided one of my few bright spots that year. Conor Cruise O'Brien, anxious that I should not be tempted into any work, suggested I should read only light novels. Characteristically, he meant Walter Scott, whom he prescribed as the literary equivalent of calves' foot jelly. Later, while I was trying – not for the first time – to convince myself I find Scott satisfactory, a university friend of one of our sons visited us. She took one look at the pile of books beside my sofa, enquired how long I would be off work, and then exclaimed: '*War and Peace*! Tolstoy! You must. Who knows, it may be your last chance to read it.'

Trying to ignore her implicit assumption about my life expectancy, I took her advice, and never looked back. It was splendid convalescence reading, convincing me that there was a political world outside that I wanted to return to. Sometimes in the months that followed, I wished I hadn't bothered. The Labour Party was tearing itself apart, and some of my oldest friends in politics and the trade unions were on different sides.

Bill Rodgers was certainly anguished at breaking with Labour. But apart from all the wrong directions he had seen his party taking, he had just had a disagreement with Michael Foot over what he would do in the new shadow Cabinet. It was only years later, after I had written about this disagreement in *The Thatcher Years*, that I heard from Bill Rodgers' standpoint a fuller version of what happened. Unlike David Owen, he had decided to run again for the shadow Cabinet, hoping that Labour might still be saved from within. More than 100 MPs voted for him. Before the results were known, he wrote to Michael Foot saying he assumed he would not want Rodgers, who opposed unilateral nuclear disarmament, to remain defence spokesman, and that he wished to express a strong preference for industry or, failing that, trade.

Rodgers explained that he wanted both to be conciliatory and to stake a claim to an area of policy he regarded as crucial to Labour's future. These were posts from which he hoped to build bridges to the legitimate left, and restrain what he called 'the wild men'. Rodgers recognised that the right now seemed to be in a minority, but he hoped Foot would want to avoid a split from the right, which would be far more dangerous than those previously feared from the left.

Foot's reply, according to Rodgers, was that he had already promised industry and trade to others. Instead, he offered health, then Northern Ireland, and – I think after Rodgers' decision to leave Labour had been mentally made – regional affairs. Bill rejected these offers, and remained for a brief time as an uncomfortable freelance shadow minister. It was obvious he had been affronted, though he was to receive a visit at home from Michael Foot before he finally decided to leave Labour.

Until the beginning of that year, Bill Rodgers said, he had been the most cautious of the Gang of Three, but as he lay in bed he had time to convince himself how unpleasant it would be to live with the Labour Party until the next general election and beyond, going to selection conferences and professing a passion for it that he no longer felt. He remained strongly anti-Tory and anti-Thatcher, but found it hard to believe a combination of Michael Foot's leadership and Labour's current policy directions would provide voters with a convincing alternative, or a satisfactory government.

Rodgers believed that the defeat of Denis Healey had removed the last chance of an effective struggle against Bennite constitutional and policy changes. Michael Foot seemed to have his mind set in the late fifties: he disliked Bill Rodgers because he saw him as a Gaitskell acolyte, and he hated the dead Gaitskell still, as the man who had stood in the way of his hero, Bevan.

Nor did Foot understand that the issues he himself felt strongly about – defence, public ownership and the unions – might make Labour incredible as a government. These issues, and above all unilateral nuclear disarmament, were to prove a problem for the Labour Party for another decade, under both Michael Foot and Neil Kinnock. It was hard to see how Foot could have compromised on such a long-standing conviction as that on nuclear weapons. But Bill Rodgers thought that, as an alternative indicator of his will to satisfy the right, he might have used his influence with the unions to change the voting system in the electoral college to one member, one vote. Instead, he had failed to do anything.

Bill Rodgers explained Shirley Williams' change of mind since the Blackpool conference by the absence of any straws of hope to which she could cling. Like him, she viewed the prospect of abandoning Labour with horror. But Shirley had had years of experience as a lonely voice on the National Executive, and after she lost her seat in the House, and the comradeship which propinquity provides, the Executive meetings gave her a depressing experience of what contemporary Labour politics were like.

David Owen, by contrast with the other two, had originally been critical of Roy Jenkins' Dimbleby lecture and of Bill Rodgers' own speech in Abertillery, in which he had effectively given the Labour Party a year to set its house in order. But Owen's disillusionment had gathered speed in the previous six months, and he had now passed both his colleagues like a rocket.

At our 13 January lunch, Roy Jenkins confessed to Adam Raphael and myself that he had been up and down in his moods in the year since he gave the Dimbleby lecture. The immediate reaction to that had been good, but the response after a Press Gallery speech in June had been less encouraging. Adam Raphael said his analogy in that speech with an aircraft which might crash at the end of the runway had left doubts about his conviction. Jenkins acknowledged this with a grin, saying he didn't know why the mind worked in this way, but one's inner thoughts often came out.

I had not seen much of Roy Jenkins during his term in Brussels, but this remark at once reminded me of what made him such an attractive politician. Many years before, Reggie Maudling had predicted to me that Jenkins would never lead the Labour Party, though he murmured that he was a civilised man, and ought not to be punished for liking a decent claret. Whatever doubts a journalist might have about the political direction Jenkins was taking – in my case, more than doubts – his conversation was refreshing because of its uninhibited honesty. Not for him the false optimism that deceives nobody, but undermines trust!

Since I wrote most of the political editorials at the *Observer*, I tried to get from him some idea of what the policies of a new party might be. While I wrestled away at this, Adam Raphael, whose prime responsibility was for news, remained patient. He was more convinced of the third party project than I was, and I suspected might be a bit impatient that I was giving its progenitor such a hard grilling. But he said benignly later that I had been right to try, but had received little enough concrete by way of response.

I had just been reviewing a Fabian Society book of essays in memory of Tony Crosland, and advanced the theory that the right of the Labour Party remained divided between Jenkinsites and Croslandites. Crosland was about equality, so what was Jenkins about? He acknowledged that he had been alienated from his oldest friend for a time, though was glad to say that they had come closer again in the final year of Crosland's life. In part, the division had been about Europe, but also about trade unions and other issues.

I kept trying to pin Roy Jenkins down on equality, which Crosland had erected as the socialist banner. This was in place of the left's preoccupation with public ownership, which had tripped up their old friend Hugh Gaitskell. Crosland's definition of equality was not merely equal opportunity, or even redistribution of incomes, difficult as these were to bring about. He had written: 'We want a wider social equality, embracing also the distribution of property, the educational system, social class relationships, power and privilege in industry – indeed, all that was enshrined in the age-old socialist dream of a more classless society.'

This was a radical view, which struck a chord with me – as it was to do, many years later, when John Major used to talk to me about classlessness, before he became Conservative leader. It turned out that he, like everybody else, had his own ideas about what classlessness means. Paradoxically, coming from Ulster, which is generally regarded as a conservative part of the country, what has struck me most forcibly about English society is its obsession with class. The contrast may just be because in Belfast and its environs there is a tiny aristocracy, and a smaller upper middle class than in London. Whatever the reason, the difference was startling.

It was not a Marxist obsession that class governed everything which influenced me. Rather, I noted with amazement an implicit belief among many middle-class people that the prevailing class system would exist indefinitely: no breakdown of barriers by improvements in education; no changed pattern of employment; no resistance to creation of a huge underclass, increasingly alienated from society. Such attitudes had long seemed to me to be one reason for Britain's industrial failure in the latter part of the twentieth century, a symptom of the thrombosis in industry and society.

Roy Jenkins' answer to the equality question was that Crosland had placed too much faith in public expenditure. During the Labour government, Jenkins himself had famously declared that public spending was taking too large a proportion of national wealth, though during the Thatcher years I understood that he had come to the conclusion that this was not Britain's basic problem. He remained a Keynesian, or a neo-Keynesian – 'whatever that means', as he said with his customary frankness. For him it consisted mainly of being deeply sceptical about monetarism in its dogmatic form, a believer in necessary interventions in industry, and in a lower parity for the pound. He returned to equality later, saying that of course he thought a government should lean in the direction of greater equality; enough forces were pulling in the opposite direction to make that sensible.

I did not have a chance to talk at length with the fourth member of the Gang of Four, David Owen, until after their die was publicly cast. The occasion of the break with Labour was its special conference at Wembley on 24 January. This had to decide on the composition of an electoral college for future leadership contests, which had been left over from the disastrous annual conference in Blackpool in October. The Wembley meeting, predictably in the Labour mood at that time, turned out to be another disaster. I spent a tense Saturday there, for I discovered that I was still weary after my ulcer operation, and found the rush of a big political story, when we were hemmed in by early Sunday newspaper deadlines, a strain.

It also turned out to be an extremely complicated event. No democratic institution in the world, except perhaps the American House of Representatives, where procedure is an art form, can take its decisions in a more bizarre way than the British Labour Party. The debate went on in the usual barn of a conference hall, and was notable for Michael Foot's decision not to attempt to give any real lead to his rebellious troops. But what mattered was not the speeches so much as the manoeuvrings which went on during the midday break in the hotel where most of us had lunch. I had a snack with Merlyn Rees, who told me that, from the moderates' point of view, everything was going wrong. Strange happenings were going on in one of the bedrooms upstairs.

No, not sex, the usual preoccupation of Sunday newspapers! This was more serious, and only slightly less titillating: the orchestration of trade union block votes.

To describe how it went wrong would, after this passage of time, be otiose and wearisome. It might, even still, attract the writs for libel which were freely threatened at the time. Suffice to say that some of the union leaders who wanted to help the moderates had given advance commitments about what they would or would not support. Even though the motions before the conference had changed, these commitments were considered irreversible.

Out of this monumental chaos, Labour emerged with an electoral college which gave forty per cent of the votes to the trade unions, and thirty per cent each to Labour MPs and the constituency parties. Beforehand, the NEC was proposing an even division of the votes among the three sections. The right had hoped it would be fifty per cent for the MPs. Even Moss Evans, leader of the left-leaning Transport Workers, believed that with unions then unpopular, it would be better if those who worked day by day with the candidates, the MPs, had the strongest voice. The outcome at Wembley could scarcely have been worse.

Roy Jenkins and his three colleagues met the following day at David Owen's house in Limehouse, and produced a declaration bearing the name of that upwardly mobile area of London. This established a Council of Social Democracy. Nobody doubted this was merely a vehicle for the launch of a new party. Within two months, Shirley Williams had resigned her seat on Labour's NEC, and David Owen, Bill Rodgers and ten other Labour MPs had resigned that party's whip and were coordinating parliamentary tactics with the Liberals.

I lunched with David Owen a few days after Wembley and Limehouse. Oddly enough, I had a similar experience to one recorded by Roy Jenkins in his book, *A Life at the Centre*. I wrote at the bottom of my note of our meeting: 'I found David a much more attractive and interesting person at this lunch than ever before. Is he moderating his arrogance?' Let me add hastily that I have no doubt he also has had occasion to complain of my own arrogance. Especially during my broadcasting years, the task of holding the balance among the political parties was an impossible one, and when David Owen complained, which he did often, without much concession to understanding or tact, I did not invariably retain an air of total sweetness and light.

I was not alone in noticing the contrast between his Dr Jekyll and Mr Hyde. His natural friendliness and good sense seemed to assert themselves in inverse ratio to his political good fortunes. He is not the only politician I have encountered who was nicer when he was losing than when he was winning. Doubtless my own liking for an underdog, compared with a natural journalist's instinct to challenge those who prosper, may have been a factor.

Like his three companions, David Owen realised their new venture was full of risks. For a man who had been the youngest Foreign Secretary since Anthony Eden in the thirties, it was a brave, probably a rash step. The seeds of a later quarrel, which successively destroyed his relationships first with Roy Jenkins, then with David Steel, were already apparent at our discussion in January 1981. It concerned the new party's relations with the Liberals.

David believed that before the Gang of Three had made up their minds about leaving the Labour Party, Roy Jenkins had got himself rather close to the Liberals. He thought David Marquand – the former Labour MP, an ex-*Guardian* colleague of mine, and Jenkins' assistant in Brussels – had been influential in pulling him back towards social democracy. At that stage, Owen was still talking about creating a new socialist party, effectively the old Labour Party in exile. It was because he did not want too close links with the Liberals that he was urging Shirley Williams to become leader of the Social Democrats. He had told Roy Jenkins this.

What struck me about David Owen at this time was that, freed from office in a major party with well-established traditions, his mind ranged freely, and did not bother overmuch about practicalities. It may seem a strange comparison, but there were similarities between his style of conversation and that of Tony Benn. They had become so radical that they wanted to examine every political god for its feet of clay. This makes for exciting politics, but is not easy for others to live with, particularly in a party leader, as the SDP was to discover.

The most surprising part of his conversation was about party alliances. Although he was not ruling out an electoral deal between the Social Democrats and the Liberals – which was the only course the more earth-bound Roy Jenkins thought realistic – Owen considered it possible the SDP might join in a government with Labour. I suggested it would be difficult for them to do this after they had fought an election on a platform which said Michael Foot's Labour Party was wrong-headed. His reply was that Foot certainly could not be leader of such a government.

This would have meant the Social Democrats serving in a government led by Denis Healey. Their leading figures then in the House, David Owen and Bill Rodgers, had voted for him in his narrow defeat by Foot, but in that period of their deep disillusionment with Labour they had certainly not been notable for vigorous campaigning on his behalf. If he had been elected Labour leader, they would have stayed in the party, though Bill Rodgers already had great reservations about Healey. Could they really serve under him in government? True, David Owen had urged moderates both inside and outside the Labour Party not to be too harsh with each other, since they might have to work together again. But personal relations became strained, and tough things were said in both parties. This was really a civil war, and these are always the most cruel.

The most interesting thought that this talk with Owen had planted in my mind was that, depending on the lottery of electoral arithmetic, not all Social Democrats regarded the Liberals as their only possible partners in government. In a conversation with Denis Healey a few days after the SDP had been launched in March, with a media hype unprecedented in British politics, I raised the subject with him. I rehearsed Owen's argument without disclosing its origin. The new party, I said, having fought against Thatcher and Foot, would not accept either as leader of a government in which SDP leaders could serve.

Healey realised at once that I was repeating what I had heard from somewhere inside the Gang of Four. He recalled he had already said publicly he could conceive working with the SDP after the general election, but added tartly that it was too early for him to accept nomination from them for leadership of the Labour Party.

That meeting with Denis Healey took place on 31 March 1981. The following day, Tony Benn announced a challenge to him for the deputy leadership. This election, the first under the new electoral college system, ran right up to the party conference in Brighton that October, and deepened Labour's divisions.

31

A SPLIT CHANGES EVERYTHING

What was a single story has now become two. In the years that followed before the 1983 election, Labour and the Social Democrats were really fighting each other to become Her Majesty's opposition in the next parliament. Neither had a realistic hope of forming a government, though the SDP's remarkable success in early polls and by-elections raised false expectations.

With the Gang of Four and other Social Democrats gone, the remaining Labour moderates had an even tougher fight 'on their hands. In conducting what was a life-and-death campaign to keep the Labour Party alive, they suffered many frustrations. Healey and Roy Hattersley both complained to me that their organisation, Solidarity, was short of money. Hattersley found they were attracting thousands of supporters to meetings up and down the country, but had not the resources to provide a follow-up organisation.

As he travelled around, he was appalled by what Labour supporters were seeing on regional television stations: first, all these sensible, middle-class Social Democrats speaking, and then after the commercial break, a group of left-wing crazies. People wrote to Hattersley after his meetings, and referred to such broadcasts: 'We agree with you, but it's no use with that kind of people in the Labour Party.'

Oddly, the Rowntree Trust refused an application for funds from Solidarity, although it had apparently been giving money to pay the salary of an official of the Bennite Labour Co-ordinating Committee, and was now contributing also to the SDP. With the liberal press overwhelmingly enthusiastic about the SDP, the beleaguered Labour moderates had a distinct feeling that the *bien-pensants* were beginning to write them off. While newspaper hacks wrote witty political songs, and sang these on the SDP special train as it careered round Britain for their remarkable peripatetic conferences, the Alliance began to taste like the flavour of the future, with Labour very much the flavour of the past.

The SDP's bandwagon of success in those early years was astonishing. One opinion poll actually showed the Alliance enjoying fifty per cent support, with Conservatives and Labour sharing the rest. But by-elections were what really established the third force in British politics. In June, only three months after the SDP launch, Roy Jenkins, displaying political skills as an election candidate which shrugged off any fear he might remain a remote international statesman, came close to snatching an astonishing victory in the safe Labour seat of Warrington. September brought a revivalist Liberal Assembly in Llandudno, at which he and Shirley Williams were welcomed into a new joint fold, at one of the most rousing political meetings of the post-war period.

That liaison preceded a Liberal gain from the Tories in Croydon North-West in October, and led on to Shirley Williams' return to the Commons in November, when she won Crosby on a remarkable swing from the Conservatives, with the Labour vote collapsing. Then came Roy Jenkins' second challenge, at Hillhead in Glasgow in March 1982.

I went to that contest. Covering by-elections for television is less enjoyable than reporting them as a newspaper journalist. To form any sensible view of what may be going on, I have always found it essential not only to talk to candidates and organisers at their headquarters or hotel, but also to observe what reception they get from voters, in market-place or doorstep; otherwise you are at the mercy of spin-doctors. But in broadcasting there is a straight clash of interest between cameramen and reporter. Three months into my new job, I was not sufficiently 'converted' to reconcile myself to this inhibition.

As Roy Jenkins' cavalcade swept him through a shopping-mall, and Shirley Williams exercised her skills in human contact by a prolonged wrestling-match to win a single vote, I would become fascinated with the debate. But no sooner was a worthwhile comment going into my notebook than an anguished cry of 'John, you're in shot!' would ring out. The 'language' of television news ordains – heaven knows on what principle of logic! – that while it is useful to have pictures of myself and other journalists listening intently at press conferences, it is death to see us listening in on a conversation during a canvass. How could any self-respecting baby allow itself to be kissed with me looking on?

When I did arrange to talk to Roy Jenkins privately, over coffee in his hotel, this was, as usual, enlightening. My visit was well on in the campaign. This was an election he had to win, otherwise he would scarcely arrive back in the Commons in time to be leader of his new party. But by then, even before the invasion of the Falklands, life for the

Social Democrats was becoming more difficult. Bill Rodgers' negotiations with the Liberals over the allocation of parliamentary candidacies
had taken the sheen off the Alliance's image as the 'nice guys' of British
politics. Here they were having to indulge in rough politics, just like
older parties.

For this and other reasons, their national support in the opinion polls
was lower, and Roy Jenkins detected this cold wind on the wintry streets
of Hillhead. By this time he must have been fully aware of my reservations
about the decision of the Social Democrats to break with Labour, but
that did not inhibit him. He made no bones about saying wryly that he
was not at all certain he would win, though obviously he still hoped he
could do so.

In the event, a series of huge public meetings enabled him and his
three colleagues to put their message across directly to a large proportion
of the voters, and he won by a margin of seven per cent over the
Conservative. He himself recognised, however, that the easy ride which
the Alliance had so far enjoyed was now over, even before the Falklands
gave Margaret Thatcher a chance to present herself as a national leader.

With Roy Jenkins back in the House, he and David Owen contested
a leadership election in June 1982. It was one of those early occasions
when I discovered what a transformation in my habits the move to the
BBC would now dictate. The SDP was announcing the voting figures
in the upstairs hall at its headquarters in Westminster. This came during
our six o'clock television news, so it was arranged that the producer
upstairs would read these into my earpiece, and I would announce them
live on air.

With the SDP's *penchant* for manufactured drama, the two candidates
were to arrive immediately after the announcement, so most of the party
workers and newspaper correspondents stayed in the street to meet them,
and I had to grab them for live interview. I found myself not only
announcing the result to the millions watching television, but to about
200 people, many of them old newspaper colleagues, in the street. Six
months into my television career, the audience at home now seemed to
me normal, almost non-existent. I found the live audience in Cowley
Street much more intimidating.

While the Alliance enjoyed its early triumphs, Labour moderates
toiled on in contrasting gloom. Denis Healey was as near to despair over
defence policy as a naturally exuberant man can ever come. Michael
Foot, who had been on all the Aldermaston marches against nuclear
weapons, was determined to oppose American cruise missiles in this
country, and to abandon Britain's own nuclear deterrent. He told me he

was not a pacifist, and did not believe voters would support a pacifist party, so he could conceive remaining in NATO and possibly increasing conventional arms.

He was equally determined that Britain must come out of the Common Market, and had even voted on the NEC against holding a second referendum before doing so. This added to the anxieties of Roy Hattersley, an enthusiastic pro-European, as well as a supporter of collective defence, and made him wonder whether he might eventually have to go to the back benches. I pointed out that this would place him in the same dilemma that Roy Jenkins had faced in the early seventies: if he stayed off the front bench because of Labour's stance on Europe, he would be saying to voters: 'Vote for a Labour government: it's good enough for you to vote for, but not good enough for me to serve in.'

At times of crisis in any party's life, there are no easy choices, and I have often felt that those of us who watch from outside ought to be less censorious. Ought the Tory Wets to have resigned from the first Thatcher government, which many of them regarded as a disaster? Ought the Labour moderates to have followed the Gang of Four into the SDP? The history of opposition politics in the three general elections after the split do not suggest that was the answer to their dilemma.

In the early part of 1981 when the SDP was launched, I was still at the *Observer*. I found myself, not for the first time, swimming against a prevailing tide, which affected the *Observer* as much as the *Guardian*. This was an unhappy period, which ended only when I took my vows of political chastity on joining the BBC in November 1981. Throughout 1981 and beyond, opinion among liberal academics and journalists was running strongly in favour of the SDP and the Alliance. Many psephologists indulged in an orgy of obituary-writing about the Labour Party. This did not finally peter out until voting patterns in the early nineties made it look ridiculous.

I believed that such academics — some of whom were advising the SDP about fundamental changes they detected in British society — were profoundly mistaken in their judgements, and remained so for many years afterwards. This view was based on my own analysis of the changes in British politics, at what I have called the watershed of 1975–6. What was significant was that the crusades which Margaret Thatcher and Tony Benn launched around that time, in Conservative and Labour Parties respectively, were *reactions* against what had gone before.

Both believed that for much of the previous forty years, since the coalition government during the war, and through successive party administrations since then, the policies followed had been essentially consensual. They were what was called 'Butskellism', an amalgam of the names of Tory and Labour Chancellors, Rab Butler and Hugh Gaitskell. Reggie Maudling once said he could not think of a single policy issue on which he disagreed with Gaitskell. In our conversations, he certainly did not appear to believe all his opponents had cloven hooves.

In sharp contrast, Thatcher and Benn both wanted to put what later came to be called 'clear blue water' between the two major parties. One feared 'the ratchet of socialism'; the other the ratchet of capitalism. The Social Democrats seemed to be riding reactions then setting in against both Thatcher and Benn: against the monetarist policies of the government, which were causing apparent rebellion in the Conservative Party (though that proved to be a false dawn); and against the fundamentalist antics in the Labour Party, which turned out to be a transient, though a tortuously long, phenomenon.

I doubted whether it was possible for the Alliance to establish a new politics on the basis of a reaction against a reaction, rather than on a clear programme of its own. Early success came because it caught a mood of disillusionment, both in the political class, and among the general public also. But was this more than a cry of pain over a long-standing *Angst*, the failure of modern governments to deliver in the mid-twentieth century the economic success British people had come to consider as their birthright in the Victorian age?

I waited to be convinced that the Alliance would invent radically new policies, or indeed discover a permanent constituency in the nation, which would enable it to win power. Over the years since then, first as Social Democrats, then as the Alliance, and more recently as Liberal Democrats, the third party has struggled to find that elixir. In the process, its policy stances have wavered unconvincingly between right and left. A third party has an urgent need to pick up votes from wherever they seem to be coming loose. Tactically understandable, but not the foundation for a political revolution.

In my attitude at this time, I realise that I was influenced posthumously by the thinking of Tony Crosland, who believed it was impossible for a party of reform to be based on a negative. Long before any Labour split was contemplated, Crosland had foreseen the problems people of his political leanings would face. He wrote of his fears that the traditional Labour right 'lacks a truly radical appeal, and often seems insular, class-orientated, conservative and middle-aged'. In a memorial essay, his political assistant, David Lipsey, filled this out: 'Crosland grew increasingly out of sorts both with what he saw as the conservative pragmatism of post-Gaitskell Labour leadership and the fluffy liberalism of other colleagues, who saw rights of homosexuals and membership of the European Community as a sufficient dose of radicalism to last a decade or two.'

A prevailing theme of Alliance pronouncements was to denounce the 'two old class-based parties'. This seemed to me to miss the point. Shirley Williams had been right, when she was still a Labour MP, to worry that any new party would be without roots. Political parties need ideas, and constantly to renew their thinking. But they also need roots.

The Conservative Party aspires to be a national party. The social base of its leaders, MPs, and local luminaries may illustrate its reverence for both hierarchy and property, but that does not make it a purely upper-class or middle-class party. The ability of the Tories to win wider support will always be encapsulated for me in a small incident when I was entertaining Jim Prior at the Athenaeum. An elderly waitress told him the political maxim she had been taught by her father, a police sergeant: 'The Tories have money, so they know how to look after your money.'

Labour, as its name indicates, has origins in the working class. Its foundation by the trade unions may have lumbered it with an indefensible voting system, from which it is taking a long time to struggle free. But the union link has made Labour's political leadership more aware of the needs of have-nots in British society. The zeal with which Conservatives dispersed council estates indicates that they, at least, understood the political strength such a class base gave to Labour.

In 1981 the Alliance began to ride a mood of antagonism to these parties. In retrospect, one significant failure was to win over only a single Conservative MP, Christopher Brocklebank-Fowler. Like so many of the Labour defectors, he lost his seat at the 1983 election. Many other Tory Wets spoke enthusiastically to me about the opportunity the SDP gave them to pull their own party back from its right-wing ideological trip. But no more than that.

Roy Jenkins, whose fine biography of Asquith made him acutely aware of what happened in the twenties and thirties, often worried that history would repeat itself. I believe it has done. The quarrel between the two great Liberal leaders, Asquith and Lloyd George, made opposition to the Conservatives between the wars almost futile. That division in Liberalism, then still the principal non-Tory party, ushered in two decades of Conservative rule, interrupted only briefly by minority Labour governments. Now it happened again: Thatcherism was established in government for a generation, while the opposition quarrelled with itself.

Those right-wingers who stayed on in the Labour Party had an unrewarding battle for the remaining years of the 1979 parliament. For the first time in his political career, Roy Hattersley could foresee circumstances in which he might not stay as an MP until he was sixty-five, and would earn a living writing instead. He said presciently that it had taken ten years to subvert the Labour Party, and would take ten years fully to restore it. Hattersley loves politics, so he was determined not to give up easily.

By 1993, when after three more election defeats he did announce his retirement from the Commons, his beloved Labour Party was in much better shape. Would it not have recovered earlier if the Social Democrats had remained to fight alongside him, Denis Healey and others inside the party? The SDP answer is that only their departure, and the electoral retribution for Labour which followed, have forced it to change.

What proved to be the initial turning point in Labour's internal battle was when Tony Benn challenged Denis Healey for the deputy leadership in 1981. The defection of the Social Democrats alerted Michael Foot to the danger threatening Labour from the right. He was seeing Roy Hattersley often, and asked him what the consequences would be if Benn were elected. Hattersley replied tersely: 'Terminal.' Foot challenged Benn to run against him for the leadership, but this challenge was not taken up.

Some unions and constituency parties told Healey that if Tony Benn defeated him, they would disaffiliate from the Labour Party. He believed about half the shadow Cabinet would not stand for re-election in November. After his vain attempts to avert the departure of the Social Democrats, and the so far successful effort to hold Labour together in face of that schism, he began to believe his party would break up if he did not defeat Benn.

It was, as Wellington said about Waterloo, 'a damn'd close-run thing'. At Brighton in October, several large unions defied strong grassroots support for Denis Healey, thus further discrediting the block vote. Despite this, he won by a whisker: 50.426 per cent to Tony Benn's 49.574. The fight-back by the moderates was more decisively successful in elections for the NEC, where the left suffered its most severe reverse for twenty-nine years. The leadership was back in control, though there were still many battles ahead. Under Neil Kinnock's leadership after 1983, the hard left was almost wiped out in NEC elections.

The Healey victory itself, though narrow, was important. Neil Kinnock played a crucial, if reluctant part in bringing it about. He led a group of dissident left-wing MPs, who voted for John Silkin in the first ballot, but could not bring themselves to vote for either Benn or Healey in the second. In such a tight result, every vote was decisive. So were these abstentions, and the left roundly abused Kinnock for his action.

Denis Healey was not finding service under Michael Foot congenial. Having accepted the job, his position was like Willie Whitelaw's – needing to be loyal, but no more able than his Tory counterpart to conceal his impatience with his leader's attitudes and actions. It particularly irritated him, at a time when Labour was fighting for its existence, that Foot often voted with the soft left on the NEC.

Healey always retains his sense of fun, and drew my attention to a Garland cartoon in the *Sunday Telegraph*, showing him about to take an axe to a tree labelled 'The left wing'. Foot was depicted as saying: 'Woodman, woodman, spare that tree; when I was young, it sheltered me.'

The other battle which the Labour leadership eventually had to fight was with the Trotskyists. Expulsion of Militants was a slow business, fraught with legal difficulty. This involved, paradoxically, the individual rights of people who *were* members of the Labour Party, and claimed *not* to be members of the Militant Tendency, because it did not have members, only unpaid newspaper sellers. What moved Michael Foot to overcome his libertarian scruples, and act, was the large number of letters he received from Labour people all over the country. These complained that Militant members were moving into local parties, with carefully worked-out resolutions, keeping the meetings going till late at night, then carrying their resolutions, and afterwards abusing anybody who spoke against them. He told me this was changing the nature of the Labour Party.

However quickly Michael Foot adjusted the rebellious attitudes of a lifetime, his personal poll rating remained low. There were constant rumours throughout 1981 and 1982 that he would resign, either through ill-health, or deliberately to allow Peter Shore to succeed him, or even to accept the inevitability of Denis Healey's leadership. At times, Healey nursed hopes that he would get another chance to become leader, for he suspected Foot knew he was not electable as Prime Minister.

With rumours so rife, Michael Foot proved himself more of a jungle animal than his scholarly demeanour suggested. In September, after yet another story appeared in the press about his imminent departure, he immediately telephoned Roy Hattersley to tell him there were no circumstances in which he would give up the leadership: he was anxious that nobody should begin campaigning under a misapprehension about his own intentions.

As Foot's deputy, Healey had become better acquainted with his wife,

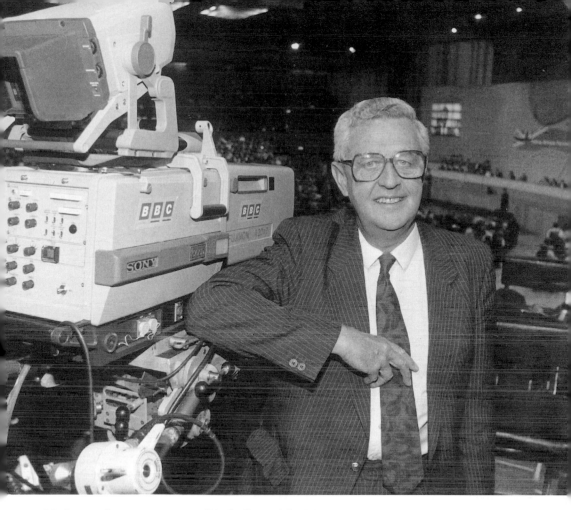

My last conference season as political editor of the BBC.

Clement Attlee, the first of
my prime ministers: 'Got y'
notebook?' – his sentences fell
naturally into paragraphs.

Harold Macmillan: he baffled
the union leaders with reminiscences of the Great War.

The upstairs, downstairs of a
labour correspondent's life.
George Woodcock of the
TUC (top left) and Reginald
Maudling, the Tory Chancellor,
almost in agreement.
Right: learning the realities
of a miner's life.

Harold Wilson, the pragmatic prime minister.

George Brown, a plan that failed.

Gibbard
BBC Television "On The Record": 26 February, 1989

Tactical wisdom from a master politician: 'Always try to write the first draft. They may mess it around a lot later, but something of your ideas will survive.'

An editor and his deputy. Alastair Hetherington and I agree – much of the time.

Opening up the newspaper world to my younger sons, David and Michael.

Two brief reigns: Ted Heath with a youthful Douglas Hurd, sets out on a voyage to Europe – and to a U-turn at home. Jim Callaghan held a minority government together for three years.

The cheerful Chancellor: 'This job's a bugger. Would you like a swop?'

The Lady who was not for turning –
until it was too late for her.

Willie Whitelaw, wise old man of the Thatcher governments.

Nigel Lawson and Geoffrey
Howe in conference: their
resignations led to Margaret
Thatcher's downfall.

The man they thought
most likely to succeed.

Jill Craigie, the film-maker and historian of the suffragettes. Healey liked her, and suspected she now regretted helping to persuade her husband to stand as leader. Roy Hattersley had a different impression. He believed Foot when he said he wanted to remain leader, and to win. He thought Jill was equally determined: she was even getting him to dress more carefully. Peter Shore, a closer friend of the Foots, was certain Michael intended to fight the general election. As that date approached, the rumours subsided.

So the battle lines for the 1983 election were set. While Margaret Thatcher did a virtual lap of honour, the two oppositions were in a deadly war: the Alliance versus a Labour Party led not by Denis Healey, but by Michael Foot. Healey's attitude to the Gang of Four varied from person to person. He regarded Shirley Williams as a great loss to Labour, and still retained residual hopes of winning her back. He blamed David Owen for letting him down, because he had been ambiguous during the leadership election (though as Owen has recorded, he and Bill Rodgers took the precaution of completing their voting papers in the presence of witnesses). He simply did not like Roy Jenkins. He did like Bill Rodgers, but found him a bit Boy Scoutish – doubtless a scar from their earlier quarrel over the right's campaign to counter the left-wing drift.

The two decisive figures in the Labour schism were Denis Healey and Roy Jenkins. Their mutual antipathy has always puzzled me. It cannot just be that they were both ambitious for the same offices. After all, in every political party from time immemorial, men and women have managed to coexist with that obstacle to friendship. These two have known each other since they were at Oxford before the war, but never seem to have become close friends. Considering both their intellectual eminence and the fact that they had common post-war roots on the right of the Labour Party, this is surprising.

Their political attitudes are similar, but they never seem to have become political allies. Roy Jenkins once said he had known Denis Healey since he was aged twenty, and he himself was eighteen. Over seventy per cent of matters, not only of politics, but of general cultural and artistic interest, he was happy to concede that Healey knew more than he did. The trouble was that Healey would not even defer to him on the remaining thirty per cent.

Both men were hard-working when engaged on something they judged worthy of their talents. On the other hand, each had a streak of arrogant idleness, which resented time spent on boring political tasks. Healey felt this about constant wrangling on the NEC, and used to take his pile of European and American newspapers along to its meetings, so that he could catch up with that day's contribution to his voluminous file of press cuttings.

Jenkins felt comparable boredom during his second term at the Home Office, when he was disillusioned with British, and especially Labour politics. Merlyn Rees, who succeeded him as Home Secretary, inherited an elaborate press-button telephone, which allowed him to talk directly to officials around his new department. Experimenting with this, he inadvertently overheard a member of his private office speaking to another civil servant: 'This new man is a workaholic, not like the old one.'

These minor incidents are just a symbol of the mood in the early eighties of two able and sane men. Both were deeply frustrated by the impossible political situation into which events had thrust them, at what ought to have been the zenith of their political careers. Whatever the explanation, their failure to find a way of working together was a huge factor in giving Margaret Thatcher a free electoral run.

32

MARGARET CRACKS THE WHIP

The most traumatic year in the history of Margaret Thatcher's governments was 1981. Not until nine years later, when she was finally removed from Downing Street, was her leadership so much under question. Indeed, this was the first time when grumbling backbenchers talked of running a stalking-horse candidate against her. But she was then at the height of her powers, and knew how to deal with such insubordination.

Her monetarist policy appeared to be in tatters. There was intense, and increasingly other-worldly debate among monetarists, even about the meaning of the figures on which it was supposedly based. Meanwhile, in the real world, there was high and rising unemployment, continuing inflation, a severe budget, spring and summer riots, and a third party which at one stage frightened Conservatives into believing they might finish up in third place in the next general election. Stephen Dorrell, a young backbencher who was too Wet for Margaret Thatcher's taste, but was to be a rising star of the nineties, raised the fundamental question: If the economy recovered, and the discipline on wages of the threatening dole queue were removed, how would the government fight inflation without an incomes policy?

The Prime Minister's method of taking arms against this sea of troubles was to have not one, but two Cabinet reshuffles. These were no mere cosmetic attempts at 'freshening up the face of the government' – the classic PR man's description of what such exercises are for. Rather this was a ruthless move to impose her authority on an increasingly rebellious crew. It certainly succeeded in changing the terms of political trade within her subsequent administrations. After 1981, most of Mrs Thatcher's ministers knew that if they went too far in defying her authority, she would sack them.

Over the Christmas recess, she licked her wounds, after the defeats and retreats of the latter half of 1980, when her inner circle of economic ministers had to give way on both the scale of cuts in public expenditure and on intervention to save industries or firms in danger of extinction. The majority in her Cabinet, the men she had dubbed Wets, began to believe that underneath her shell of ideology, she was really the pragmatic politician they had always hoped she would turn out to be.

For her part, the Prime Minister had decided her Cabinet opponents were taking too many liberties with her authority. They made no secret of their belief that she herself often failed to accept the Cabinet responsibility she demanded from others. In radio and television interviews, she would make policy without having first consulted the relevant minister, and had been known to reopen disputes that they thought had been settled in Cabinet. In her memoirs, Margaret Thatcher was to plead a cheerful 'guilty' to some of these charges: she found this the only way to get things moving in the direction she believed was right.

The Prime Minister became agitated when others adopted a similar free-booting style. The principal victim of her January reshuffle was Norman St John-Stevas, her flamboyant Leader of the Commons. He was among the most articulate of the Wets, arguing in an easily decipherable code that her economic policies were going wrong, and needed to be changed. Stevas was one of the first to become worried about the challenge of the Social Democrats. He feared that the government's harsh policies might siphon Conservative votes off to them.

What probably stung her more than Stevas's speeches were his private jokes at her expense, which often ended up in the newspapers. This was not necessarily his intention. The truth is that it is impossible to make a good joke in the Palace of Westminster, even to political friends, without its becoming public property. The House of Commons is like a closely knit village community, and the velocity with which its gossip circulates greatly exceeds the velocity of money circulation, as prescribed in monetarist theory. I have myself made a joke or advanced a theory in the Members' Lobby, and had it retailed back, with embellishments, within a couple of hours (sometimes deflatingly attributed to A.N. Other). It always reminds me of that favourite introduction to scandal stories in tabloid newspapers: 'Tongues were wagging in this sleepy Blankshire village last night, as . . .'

Stevas's friends were staggered by his dismissal, for it was the first evidence of the Prime Minister's steely determination to have her own way. Peter Walker thought she could have retained him, after giving him a warning that she did not think her Leader of the House should adopt such freelance positions. If she had done that, he was confident that Norman would have avoided careless talk 'for at least a week'. He and others believed their departing friend had been a good Leader of the House, building up the select committee system. He had also given a touch of colour to the government. They regretted her action.

An unstated reason for Norman's fate was that Margaret Thatcher wanted a new post for her Defence Secretary, Francis Pym, and the leadership of the Commons carried the necessary seniority. Pym was a formidable Tory figure, who had served in Ted Heath's Cabinet, and represented, like his friend Willie Whitelaw, his party's One Nation strand. His instincts were of loyalty, but during the turbulence over public spending in 1980, he had resisted some of the cuts the Treasury wanted to impose on the armed services. At one meeting of the Overseas and Defence Committee of the Cabinet, attended by the leading figures in the government, including the Prime Minister, Whitelaw, and the Foreign Secretary, Peter Carrington, Pym told them that he was convinced the line he was taking on defence spending was right. The government could go in another direction if it thought that proper, but it would have to do so without him.

Pym, a stickler for the rules of the game, believed that in making his position so clear he was abiding by these. Until then, however, Margaret Thatcher had not had to cope with such determination. Pym got much of what he wanted in that spending round, but since her policy demanded that she obtain more reductions in public spending, and especially in such a high-spending department as Defence, she determined to move him.

The meeting at which she did so was tense, but friendly. When she asked Pym to be Leader of the House, he pointed out that there had been many changes among NATO defence ministers, as well as a new administration in Washington. He argued this made it more important that there should be some continuity in Whitehall. She acknowledged the importance of what he said, but told him she must exercise her right as Prime Minister to have this change. Pym's acceptance of that authority was helped by two facts. First, he believed his successor, John Nott, though more Thatcherite than himself, would have to fight to defend the services' budgets. Second, the fact that Pym was to take over as chairman of the Legislation Committee of the Cabinet added to the interest of his new post. Committee chairmanships are one of the little extra sweeteners with which Prime Ministers make jobs seem more important: thirteen years later, John Major was still using the same stratagem.

Margaret Thatcher, however, was storing up future trouble between herself and Francis Pym. At the time of this new appointment, he hoped the government's economic policy was beginning to move in the direction he wanted. Like other Wets, he took recent Keith Joseph announcements to indicate that Margaret Thatcher and he were reconciled to a measure of intervention in industry. Pym was anything but a strident Wet; indeed, in any other administration he would have ranked as a very conforming Conservative. He did not want a change of economic strategy, since he believed Britain needed to move back to a more efficient market economy.

But he saw the problem as getting from here to there: in opposition, Keith Joseph had been too much of a theorist, and Pym believed he was now having to temper theory with the effect of real events. That was what this most traditional of Tories thought politicians were for. His view of the Prime Minister was similar. He had no doubt that her deepest ideological instincts were the same non-interventionist ones which had made Keith Joseph look so unhappy when he was announcing more money for the steel or car industries. But Francis Pym, for his part, was equally unhappy at the prospect of 3 million unemployed. He retained a belief that she was enough of a practical politician to realise she would have to bend to events, and do something about this figure.

This was a misunderstanding of the Thatcher character shared by a very different kind of Conservative, Peter Walker. When, at the party conference in 1980, the Prime Minister had delivered her famous squib, 'the lady's not for turning', he had winced, for he believed painting oneself into a corner was something no political leader should ever do. Walker thought gloomily that the government was not even getting credit for what he saw as a desirable change of direction.

The argument was this: Keith Joseph, instead of wringing his hands when he announced more money for British Leyland, ought to have pronounced it to be the happy result of success in the first stage of the government's policy: inflation on the way down, trade unions cooperating, two new Leyland models coming forward, so he was 'investing in success'. Instead, even with more public money coming soon for British Steel, higher public borrowing at a time of recession, a public sector pay policy in place, and a determined effort to get interest rates down, Margaret Thatcher was half clinging on to what Walker saw as monetarist nonsense. He believed she should be claiming credit for a change in strategy intended to deal with the recession.

Jim Prior had the same worries about the government's failure to take credit for industrial intervention, which he believed would improve its public support. He had squirmed when colleagues told him about Keith Joseph's performance on television, sweating and taking a long time to answer questions. This was an accurate description of how this conscientious intellectual suffered publicly over the apparent change of course. But the chasm which divided him and Margaret Thatcher from Jim Prior represented more than style.

During the previous week's economic debate, Prior had sat on the Treasury bench while a new Conservative backbencher uttered what he regarded as right-wing nonsense. He was therefore startled to hear the Prime Minister and her Industry Secretary uttering frequent 'hear, hears'. When the backbencher sat down, Mrs Thatcher told Joseph: 'I regard him as one of the most promising of our young men.' Prior was doubtless intended to hear this. He concluded that the doctrine remained unchanged, but that Margaret Thatcher was divided in her own mind, because she was politician enough to know she had to do something more to win the next general election.

The Prime Minister normally pushed her economic policies through Cabinet with the help of the 'True Believers' – Geoffrey Howe, Keith Joseph, John Nott, John Biffen, and David Howell. But she had taken care to ensure that the dissenters were represented on relevant committees. Jim Prior and Peter Walker were on the Cabinet's two economic committees: E, which dealt with week-by-week decisions, and ES, which was intended to take a longer-term view. Apparently no Minister of Agriculture before Walker had been on these committees, and his department was delighted at its enhanced importance.

The difficulty for the two ministers was that they could never decide how much notice the Thatcherites took of their arguments. The Wets had a nasty suspicion that all the ministerial advice Margaret Thatcher was paying attention to came from a monetarist direction. Peter Walker thought she would have been wise to expose herself to six-hour, no-agenda discussions with groups of ministers at Chequers. These would have encouraged ministers to throw ideas around, without feeling that their whole future depended on everything that was said. The trouble about that theory was expressed years later by a member of another Thatcher Cabinet, Malcolm Rifkind. The acerbic Scottish lawyer could not escape the suspicion that the Prime Minister awarded marks for the soundness of each minister's basic philosophy.

The Wets did have great expectations of the 1981 budget, though they had been refused any general Cabinet discussion on economic strategy in advance of it. But they deceived themselves into believing that circumstances – that old Tory word of Edmund Burke's again! – would dictate a new thrust in policy. The CBI was calling for more expansion, and Jim Prior, who had already been allowed to provide vacancies for 800,000 unemployed people in new Youth Opportunity and Job Replacement schemes, joined in fervently. His political judgement was that the Conservatives could not win the next election unless they could bring unemployment down from the 3 million it was fated to reach, probably to below 2 million. But this was only possible with a certain amount of cosmetics in pulling people off the register through such schemes as Prior had introduced.

Before the budget, Jim Prior sent a paper to Geoffrey Howe, urging him to combat unemployment through a more relaxed fiscal stance, injecting £1.8 billion into the economy. The Wets believed events had moved sufficiently in their direction to make such arguments worthwhile. They hoped the long-expected launch of the SDP would work on their side.

In retrospect, it is difficult to understand what a huge threat many Tories feared this third force would represent to their own party, rather than to their principal opponents, Labour. True, Margaret Thatcher herself, at the depths of Labour's disarray, declared to me in an interview that 'the Labour Party will not die; Labour will *never* die.' This might seem like a remarkably generous tribute to opponents in trouble, until you remembered how nervous Conservatives were about the Alliance.

Michael Heseltine, on the other hand, displayed his customary shrewdness in assessing politics at grassroots level. I once asked him whether he now regarded Labour or the Alliance as the Conservatives' principal electoral challengers. He affected great astonishment about my supposed metropolitan isolation from life outside London, and went on to argue that while both Tories and Labour had great organisations throughout the country, the Alliance existed much more strongly in the consciousness of the London-based media than it did in many regions of Britain.

Some dissenting Tory backbenchers saw the advent of the SDP as an opportunity. One, who was to join the Cabinet after Margaret Thatcher's time, freely speculated to me that the Social Democrat danger might enable Tories to replace her as their leader. If the Alliance held the balance in the Commons after an election, he hoped they would refuse to accept her as Prime Minister. In those circumstances, he would favour an enabling Bill to allow Peter Carrington to renounce his peerage, and take over as leader of a coalition or minority Tory administration.

He had a quotation from Macmillan of the obscure kind party intellectuals delight in: the Conservative Party was best led from the left of centre by a man whose instincts were to the right. I was not quite sure what it meant, but I wrote it down. This MP, however, after also playing with the names of Francis Pym and Jim Prior, made it clear he would have been prepared to accept anyone, even another Thatcherite like John Nott, if that was the way to force a change. This, it turned out, was only the first of many pipe-dreams about the leadership I heard during the Thatcher years.

The Cabinet meeting on budget day, 12 March 1981, came as a terrible shock to the Wets. Geoffrey Howe was taking £2 billion in higher income tax, £2.5 billion through indirect taxes, with added burdens on employees' national insurance contributions, North Sea oil and bank profits. Peter Walker, who had attended about ten pre-budget or mini-budget meetings during Heath's premiership, and three under Thatcher, had never been at such an extraordinary occasion. Apart from his doubts about the content, he thought it had been handled with great political naïveté, for too few influential ministers had been squared in advance. To take such a tough line when the country was already in deep recession would be, at best, politically controversial.

One minister told me that, with only hours to go before the budget was opened in the Commons, and with no hope of changing it, the Cabinet had been split down the middle. There is a conflict of evidence here. Geoffrey Howe claims that the leaders of the Commons and Lords, Francis Pym and Peter Carrington, were on his side. My ministerial informant, on the other hand, said with somewhat loaded judgement that 'all the men of weight and experience were on the same unhappy side'. The usual Wets, he claimed, including Carrington and Pym on this occasion, were joined by ministers such as the territorial Secretaries of State, George Younger (Scotland) and Nicholas Edwards (Wales). On the other side were the inner economic group who, so far, had no apparent doubts about the policy. In addition, Willie Whitelaw, whatever his reservations, played his usual loyal role in summing up on the side of a Prime Minister he had agreed to serve as deputy.

The Wet ministers were angry at the budget's almost conscious punishment of their own successes during the previous winter, in arguing against the Thatcher–Howe line. But their judgement of the Conservative Party was that plotting against the Prime Minister and her policies would be self-defeating. Nevertheless, Jim Prior, Peter Walker and Ian Gilmour breakfasted together at Prior's house the day after the budget. Rumour said the Chancellor was determined to fight back against his 1980 defeats over spending cuts, and that more cuts were coming. The growing pragmatism of Margaret Thatcher, about which there had been much theorising in the previous few months, evaporated in the heat over this budget. The President of the CBI called it 'at best a brush-off, at worst a kick in the teeth'.

Even though the dissident members of the Cabinet did not take part in active plotting, those whom the budget had angered saw an intriguing political situation developing. A couple of days after the budget, I noticed that Peter Walker spent Prime Minister's question time not in his seat on the Treasury bench, but standing behind the Speaker's Chair. This clearly caused some amusement to opposition MPs gathered in the same useful vantage point, and there was a certain amount of mutual ribbing.

Walker, however, was not contemplating what their jibes implied: a move across the House, either to the Labour Party or – what had been considered by a few Conservative backbenchers – the SDP. He was just keeping an eye on how his own Tory colleagues were reacting to Margaret Thatcher's answers on this first appearance since the budget. Some journalists thought that, among Cabinet members, Walker was the most possible recruit to the Social Democrats, though I never believed that remotely probable.

He was, however, concerned about the threat to his own party that the SDP would represent, if voters wearied of government economic policies. He also hoped that the SDP would help him in the task he had imposed on himself and like-thinking colleagues: to drag the Conservative Party back to the political centre. Once when I expressed some scepticism about the public's addiction to centrist politics, he said: 'It's what the people want, John. It may not be what *you* want, but it's what *they* want.'

Although at this time I was still deputy editor of the *Observer*, rather than political editor of the BBC, I jokingly expressed surprise that he thought I had any other than a priest-like role. He replied with a grin: 'The trouble is I have been reading you for the past twenty years.' Peter Walker was one of those politicians who really did not care when a journalist's political views were different from his own. I have always thought this a much healthier attitude than when journalists are expected to be – and when some allow themselves to become – apologists for the ruling clique in any party. This was one unfortunate consequence of intolerant attitudes during Hugh Gaitskell's Labour leadership and Margaret Thatcher's Conservative one.

An already turbulent political year became more turbulent when riots broke out in the inner cities, first in Brixton in April, then in Southall, the Toxteth district of Liverpool, and the Moss Side district of Manchester in July. Margaret Thatcher strenuously denied that these had anything to do with unemployment, but in both the opposition and the discontented sections of her own party this view was contested. Immediately after the budget, I had written a leader in the *Observer* arguing that to pile deflation on existing recession was to risk jeopardising the social cohesion of a nation that was now multiracial. The riots all too soon seemed to confirm that fear.

What concerned me was that the persistence of unemployment in this recession represented a new peril to a whole generation of young working-class people. If a young man moved from a not particularly inspiring education to a dole queue, with a brief intermission in a work experience programme which did not lead to a job, he might lose the habit of work. I had seen in the more economically deprived areas of Ulster how easily a neighbourhood can drift into an unemployment culture. This has since happened in depressingly large parts of the United Kingdom as a whole.

The Home Secretary, Willie Whitelaw, whose daughter lived in Brixton, knew how unpopular the police had become in some ethnic communities. I told him about an *Observer* colleague, white and middle class, whose children in south London had become hostile to the police. Whitelaw had heard too many similar stories from MPs to disregard them. He set out to cajole the Metropolitan Police into having more black policemen. With unemployment high, the police could get plenty of recruits, so this meant positive discrimination in educational standards.

Willie Whitelaw was worried about unemployment. Politically, he was sure it was hitting the government in cities and towns, even when it was *fear* of losing a job, rather than actual unemployment which worried people. If only the government could restore hope to people who were fearful, it might reduce the electoral damage. He had little expectation that the unemployment total would be rapidly reduced. He found it hard to think, in the depths of the recession, from where the Treasury could ask the Cabinet to cut more public expenditure.

Even if some of the Wets were critical because Willie retained for private meetings with Margaret Thatcher his reservations about policy, I found it impossible to think he was other than a frequent voice of sanity in a government driven too much by ideology. On the riots, Whitelaw did not take the simple law-and-order line which some Conservatives would have liked. But he did not accept either that unemployment was the principal reason for disturbance on the streets. He noted that many of those arrested for riot offences were in steady jobs. Whitelaw appointed Lord Scarman to conduct an enquiry into Brixton, which provided insights into what was going on, and made important recommendations about policing.

The truth is that most riots in Britain that summer and subsequently have been a complex mixture of bad race relations and insensitive policing, set against a number of deprived inner city backgrounds. When MPs discussed the rioting, I concluded that over-simplification was, yet again, likely to prove the enemy of sound judgement. The instinctive reaction to such a social crisis was to divide into camps encapsulated in the slogans 'Law 'n' order' and 'Society is to blame', with one group salivating, like Pavlovian dogs, for the swish of the birch, and the other salivating for the swish of the social worker's apron. I wrote at the time:

> Young people are not simply 'rioting against unemployment'; but unemployed teenagers living in areas of bad housing spend more time on the streets; since some of them indulge in theft or 'hustling', all of them attract more police attention, otherwise known as 'harassment'.
>
> The *casus belli* of a youth war therefore lies in unemployment, bad housing, the breakdown of morality and of family/school discipline, a more rebellious attitude to authority in this generation, over-reaction by the police, the violence of youth culture, of some rock music . . . The list trails on to infinity.

I had been travelling in the United States in 1966, the 'long hot summer', when one American city after another erupted in riots involving principally young blacks. The British disturbances of 1981 for a time looked remarkably similar. The riots gradually subsided, but the underlying social problems have, if anything, grown worse. Years later, when I was making a television film about unemployment, I found that the culture of family deprivation running through several generations, which is what I had always feared, had finally arrived. It manifested itself not in great urban riots, but in a depressed and depressing way of life, where petty crime and what the American ghettoes taught us to call 'hustling' are the normal way of supplementing state benefits.

It looked more immediately threatening back in 1981. On 23 July, in this atmosphere of social crisis, the Cabinet held a discussion about public expenditure, which Margaret Thatcher later described as one of the bitterest of her term. What angered her was that the balance of debate had shifted against her. John Nott and John Biffen, both previously extremely dry in their economic views, began to think the cuts were going too far. Nott had been thought of as a possible successor to Geoffrey Howe as Chancellor, if the latter – as was persistently rumoured – was appointed to the Woolsack on the retirement of the Lord Chancellor, Quintin Hailsham.

In the event, Hailsham stayed on in that job until 1987, when he was eighty. His wife had been killed in a riding accident in Australia, and Margaret Thatcher, with that personal kindness which made colleagues excuse other foibles, thought he would be happier if he were fully occupied. He and Peter Thorneycroft had become her two political father-figures in that first Cabinet. By the summer of 1981, both Thorneycroft and Francis Pym, the two men responsible for getting the government's case across, in the country and at Westminster respectively, had fallen out of favour because of their doubts about her politics.

There were rumours at the time of the July meeting that the Prime Minister would like to be rid of Geoffrey Howe, because she believed his presentation of the expenditure cuts had been inadequate. Nott was critical of the Treasury performance at this boisterous meeting, and so exploded any chances he might have had of becoming Chancellor. A colleague described his intervention as 'devastating': he said he knew Geoffrey had been away from London, and that naturally he could not have had any part in preparing the paper for the Cabinet, which was the worst Treasury paper he had ever seen. As Defence Secretary, Nott had accepted defence cuts which made his predecessor, Francis Pym, look very cautious. But then he had asked for a lot more money to spend, thus rapidly running down his personal capital with the Prime Minister.

Over that difficult summer, she pondered on the balance of the Cabinet. Then she acted decisively, in the most significant reshuffle of her whole period in office. She dismissed three Wets, Christopher Soames, Ian Gilmour, and Mark Carlisle. Peter Thorneycroft retired. Jim Prior was exiled to Northern Ireland, to make way for Norman Tebbit, who was to pursue a tougher anti-union line. Two other committed monetarists, Nigel Lawson and Cecil Parkinson, became respectively Energy Secretary and party chairman (with a seat in the Cabinet). The Prime Minister was back in control.

In December 1981, Jim Prior wryly noted that the spending round which followed the reshuffle had been less turbulent than had seemed certain at its preliminary airing in July. This was partly because the Treasury had proved less combative, but decisively because of the Cabinet sackings and appointments. He felt the Cabinet now contained too many placemen. Clearly the new ministers, Lawson, Tebbit and Parkinson were not placemen: they were more decisively Thatcherite than that. What was true was that after the September reshuffle, her Cabinets contained many more ministers who were content to run their own departments, and not become embroiled in general disputes over economic policy. After just two years in power, Margaret Thatcher had cut the Wets down to size. From 1981 onward, her authority was never seriously challenged again, until near the very end.

The Indian summer of revolt came in Blackpool in October. I have never attended a stranger party conference than that one. (Sadly, I missed the great 1963 Tory conference in the same resort, when Macmillan retired, and the leadership contest was conducted almost in public.) Tories quarrel publicly less often than Labour, but when they do, it is with relish. In the conference hall itself, even such a popular figure as Willie Whitelaw had a hard time in resisting demands for the restoration of hanging. His task was not made easier when representatives saw that the Prime Minister was applauding pro-hangers. When a young speaker abused Ted Heath, and the audience cheered, Willie wished, with *esprit d'escalier*, that he had walked off the platform.

But the real battle came over the economy. In varying shades of coded language, the government's policy was attacked by Jim Prior, Francis Pym, Peter Walker, Michael Heseltine, Ian Gilmour and Norman St John-Stevas. The Wets were not prepared to give up the debate, even though some had been sacked, and most others knew they had lost. Among government loyalists, the response was not to turn the other cheek. The favourite venue for most of the fringe meetings at which dissident speeches were delivered was a restaurant called the Lobster Pot. When at a party I mentioned to the wife of the Chief Whip, Michael Jopling, that I had just been to this hotbed of dissent, she replied sweetly: 'We call it Traitors' Gate.'

33

FORTUNES OF WAR

I moved from the *Observer* to the BBC at the end of November 1981, thus arriving in the new world of broadcasting just a few months ahead of the most unexpected event to engulf a British government since Suez: the invasion of the Falkland Islands by the Argentinian military dictatorship, and Margaret Thatcher's subsequent war to recover them. This produced a remarkable victory, in a campaign conducted 8,000 miles from home. Inevitably it also brought the death and suffering on both sides that wars always bring.

In domestic politics, the victory transformed the Prime Minister's standing. Before the Falklands, she had been a beleaguered figure, presiding over a deeply divided government. This had little economic achievement to show for all the pain it had inflicted in unemployment and public spending cuts. Only disarray in the Labour Party appeared to be saving her from certain electoral defeat. Even that safeguard looked likely to be removed after the new Alliance of Liberals and Social Democrats had won a series of sensational by-election victories.

It is true that the political pressure on the Conservatives had eased slightly even before the Argentinian invasion, because Margaret Thatcher was by now very aware of electoral considerations. She had at last acknowledged that economic indicators allowed a softening of her stance on public spending. A skilful and more emollient budget had taken the sting out of internal opposition. But a series of Gallup Poll figures show that her dramatic change in fortune was by no means secure until military victory cemented it in place.

When I moved to the BBC in November, the Conservatives were in third place, with 25 per cent, compared with 43 for the Alliance and 28 for Labour. After the budget in March 1982, and just before the invasion, Labour and the Alliance were level-pegging on 33 per cent, with 31 for the Tories. After victory in June, the government had soared to 45, with the Alliance on 28 and Labour on 25. The Falklands had transformed Margaret Thatcher's status from that of struggling politician to national leader.

By the end of June, Jim Prior, her most persistent critic on domestic matters, acknowledged that the political effects of her great triumph would last longer than he had at first thought. What we journalists called the Falklands Factor had been converted into a Leadership Factor. Only a few continued to demand to know how her government had allowed the Falklands to be lost in the first place. Early in 1983, even an ambiguous report on this from a politically divided commission under Lord Franks did not arouse public anger again.

Jim Prior generously observed that she deserved her triumph, because he could think of no other Prime Minister since 1945 who would have carried out such a hazardous expedition. He now assumed the Conservatives would win the election, a view that had been uncommon when Tories first realised they would have to enter that contest with 3 million people out of work. He was determined that from then on he would avoid rocking the boat. The Conservatives' internal rebellion was effectively over. The Alliance felt the first chill of disappointment in local and by-elections.

When the Argentinian junta invaded the Falklands on 2 April 1982, I was still a BBC greenhorn. Quite quickly, I learned one lesson about my new status: we became part of the controversy, not because of anything done by the Westminster staff, but because some Conservative MPs took violent exception to a *Panorama* programme which examined British domestic opinions on the crisis. When I went down to the Members' Lobby that evening, not having seen the *Panorama*, or had any responsibility for its preparation, I was immediately assailed, quite rudely, by a group of about six MPs.

Although I politely explained to them my ignorance of what they were complaining about, and suggested they write to the Director-General, several persisted in working off their indignation on me. I had come to Westminster, after many deviations on the road from Belfast, to report politics, not to be a 'representative', much less a whipping-boy. So I said firmly that I had explained what they ought to do, adding with unwonted formality that I had not been introduced to several of them, so I would bid them good evening. After I left, a couple of them sought me out to apologise.

The politics of the Falklands presented a real dilemma for broadcasters, among others. The country was united in believing that the Argentinians were in the wrong to deny the islanders their right to self-determination.

But an important debate developed, principally within the Conservative Party, about whether a negotiated settlement was possible. This continued as the Task Force set off on its long journey south.

For journalists, this was not quite a repeat of Suez. Twenty-six years earlier, I had watched with admiration as Alastair Hetherington and David Astor, two editors for whom I worked, took lonely and unpopular stands to ensure that public debate was sustained. In the Falklands case, though there was some American ambiguity, the rightness of Britain's case was not seriously challenged. What was at issue was the best tactics designed to get the invaders out. The new Foreign Secretary, Francis Pym, who had been moved from Defence when Peter Carrington resigned, had hopes that his own and Washington's cooperation with Peruvian mediation might solve the crisis without bloodshed.

So these were important disagreements, and four months into my BBC career I was painfully aware how difficult it was to reflect the national debate fairly in media whose inevitable needs were for sharp pictures and sharp edges. But it seemed to me that the freedom to report this debate was not the least significant difference between British democracy and the Argentinian junta. However unpopular it might make us in some quarters, the BBC had to reflect the turmoil I observed in the Commons lobbies.

Fortunately the Prime Minister, in balancing the War Cabinet, appointed her comparatively new party chairman, Cecil Parkinson, to be a member. He proved a self-confident and intelligent spokesman for the government, mostly in informal and non-attributable briefing. He certainly made it possible for political reporters like myself to give a more balanced day by day account of the internal debate. It was then also that I first learned the value of that aspect of the Lobby system which I think important. This is the part shamefully ignored in programmes and books obsessed with the activities of Sir Bernard Ingham and other Downing Street press secretaries.

Access to the Members' Lobby allows an assiduous reporter to canvass the opinions of a wide variety of MPs in a short time. In a fast-changing diplomatic and military scene, this was invaluable. Readers may wonder why MPs could not simply say what they believed 'on the record'. Some did. Others noted the experience of Sir David Crouch, a senior Tory, who argued at a backbench committee the case for negotiation, and was booed and hissed for his pains. The best way for me to find out the balance of opinion was to talk to as many as possible myself, on Lobby terms – that is, on the understanding that their names would not be used – and then to form a judgement.

I estimated towards the end of April that up to one-fifth of Conservative MPs wanted a diplomatic settlement on the best terms Francis Pym could negotiate. But the Conservative right was fearful that the more pacific wing of the party would make the running in the media, and sixty of them put down a motion warning the government against 'a sell-out'.

The Cabinet, after the shock of losing the Falklands, and in the process losing through resignation the Foreign Secretary, Peter Carrington, and his Foreign Office team, was in some disarray. It was a dramatic political story, and one effect of that is to loosen tongues. It became easier for myself and others to find out what was going on in Cabinet and Cabinet committee meetings where official secrecy, Privy Councillor's oaths, and the much-battered code of collective responsibility often inhibit frankness. One of the more enlightening moments came when I learned that Norman Tebbit had reported to the Cabinet advice given to him by a Labour left-winger, Stan Newens. He was said to have told Tebbit the government ought to get in and finish the Falklands campaign before the opposition began to have doubts.

If the Falklands established Margaret Thatcher as a national figure, it also slowed down the Alliance momentum. Roy Jenkins found during local elections in May 1982 that he was addressing smaller audiences than at any time since he returned from Brussels to launch his crusade for a third force in British politics. But this did not mean that the Prime Minister's Conservative critics had abandoned their private policy doubts.

Traditional Tories began again to hope the economic debate within government was moving in their direction. There were backbench campaigns about failure to uprate unemployment benefit fully, and about attempts to tax social benefits. The Treasury was forced to give ground. The Prime Minister even encouraged local councils to spend money on capital projects. Although the rhetoric remained tough, the government was putting money into threatened firms which it believed could be saved. The Scottish Secretary, George Younger, who was fighting hard for the steel industry, believed that Thatcherite economics were being modified by politics, and had been known to murmur, with a glance back at a famous decision of the Heath era: 'Upper Clyde Shipbuilders is alive and well, and living at Downing Street.'

Ministers on that side of the argument found Willie Whitelaw a valuable ally. If he came down in a minister's favour, it was eighty-five per cent certain that his cause would prevail. Undoubtedly the most outspoken of the Tory traditionalists since Christopher Soames was sacked had been Jim Prior, though some colleagues thought the short fuse of his temper was a disadvantage. Prior himself was still worried that the Prime Minister was putting the government at risk, and complained that critics had stopped standing up to her in Cabinet.

One who did, apparently, was John Nott, previously a Thatcher ally. When the government was formed in 1979, Denis Healey told Nott that he would be Chancellor within a few years, but this ambition was thwarted by Geoffrey Howe's long stint at the Treasury. When Nott entered politics, he had given himself just fifteen years away from business. By 1982, he was serving out the remainder of that period. Margaret Thatcher and he had worked closely together during the Falklands, but their economic views now diverged. One minister told me that in his later years in Cabinet, Nott rarely spoke outside his own brief, except to quarrel with the Prime Minister. He soon announced that he would not fight the next election, and left the government at the beginning of 1983.

Peter Walker continued to plough his lonely furrow at Agriculture. He had occasional sharp exchanges with the Prime Minister and her Chancellor. He once told them, during a major row over agriculture spending, that if they wanted a different policy, they needed another minister. When the Treasury suggested that his department must bear a heavier share of public spending cuts, as the Department of Industry had already done, Walker wrote a tart reply, enquiring whether they had thought of bringing British industry into line with British agriculture which, under his regime, was contributing heavily to the balance of payments.

But Walker had no doubt that Margaret Thatcher's decision to put ministers such as Francis Pym, Jim Prior and himself in jobs which demanded much travel was a deliberate act to keep them away from much of the internal debate at the centre of government. He could not forget that in the Heath Cabinet, when he had been a close lieutenant of the Prime Minister, Thatcher had never once challenged the then Chancellor, Tony Barber. From time to time he became fed up. When, after another rumbustiously independent performance at the 1982 party conference, there were rumours that he would be sacked in January, he was heard to murmur: 'Why wait till January?'

But Margaret Thatcher knew Peter Walker was still one of the big beasts of the Tory jungle, and she did not want him on the back benches. So he remained in her governments until he himself chose to go, just six months before her own dismissal. He used to speculate to friends what might have happened to British politics if Ian Gilmour and himself had led fifteen Tory MPs into the SDP. It would certainly have made that body look less like a Gaitskellite Labour Party. In choosing to ride Peter Walker with a loose rein, Margaret Thatcher had wisely taken note of that risk.

Relationships between the Prime Minister and Michael Heseltine, who moved from Environment to Defence when John Nott resigned, remained distant. She had been impressed by his efficiency in running the Environment Department, and the order he gave to his permanent secretary that no new staff, right down to secretaries and liftmen, should be taken on until they knew what everybody already on the strength was doing. She even encouraged other departments to adopt his management methods.

In some ways, Heseltine was Thatcher's ideal businessman-minister. He was not a conventional Wet, because he would have been sterner in cutting public spending in one area in order to spend more elsewhere. But both before and after the 1979 election, he had told her that her economic strategy was wrong, and would not work. He had doubts about whether a government could win an election with 3 million unemployed, though he took comfort from the state of the opposition. Occasionally he would grimace at the thought of what Jim Callaghan might have done to Margaret Thatcher at question time if he had remained Labour leader: 'I *did say* the Rt Hon. Lady's policies would not work. We had our troubles, but essentially we were trying commonsense solutions. Instead, she gives us *theories*. "Labour not working"? [A reference to a 1979 Tory election slogan on unemployment.] Well!'

So Michael Heseltine had no difficulty in discounting press rumours that the Prime Minister might make him party chairman or even Chancellor. He felt that friends of Downing Street in the newspapers were constantly sniping at him, that colleagues were adept at leaking tendentious views, and that her reported remark, 'Michael is not one of us', accurately described her attitude to him. In fact, he believed she had put him at Environment to keep him out of the government mainstream. It was a remarkable aspect of Thatcher governments that so many ministers felt they were outlawed.

In Michael Heseltine's view, the departments that mattered were the Treasury and Industry, and no non-believer would be allowed near these. He was not to reach Industry until John Major became Prime Minister and had won an election, and even then he found his interventionist instincts challenged by Thatcherites such as Michael Portillo.

Through all the remarkable events surrounding the Falklands War, the threat from the Alliance, and the continuing debate over unemployment and government economic policy, an old refrain was heard again: about Margaret Thatcher's personal style. Heseltine continued to worry about the dangers of her impetuous decision-making. He believed that if a minister could reach her before her mind was made up, and persuade her to use what he acknowledged to be her formidable reasoning powers, the results were better.

Another minister, not attuned to a feminist age in which such things are not said, whispered that his Prime Minister 'argued like a woman'. Challenged to define this phrase, he said she would trawl for the most specious – that was his word – arguments to support her case. His remedy lay in persistence. He found her quite intimidating to argue with. If a minister gave ground, she would simply overwhelm him. But if he kept on, she would eventually listen, and once she accepted his case, would support it enthusiastically.

If this all sounds like an irrational, even improbable way of conducting government business, I can only say that I heard similar descriptions from enough different ministers down the years to leave me in no doubt about its essential accuracy. Where I think the stories may inadvertently be unjust to Margaret Thatcher is that she apparently has a remarkable ability to take in information and argument from others, even when she is talking herself. Not all ministers realised this, and some became discouraged.

Another example of the strange style in this government was Downing Street's behaviour over Jim Prior's legislation for a Northern Ireland Assembly. At the 1922 Committee, an MP accused the Prime Minister herself of being unenthusiastic about this measure, though it was pointed out to the critic that she had signed it. But her influential PPS, Ian Gow, was certainly hostile to it, and two Thatcher allies, Cecil Parkinson and Norman Tebbit, expressed doubts about using a guillotine against their own right-wing MPs. However, the left in the party became indignant about these Thatcherite doubts, and warned that if the whips used kid gloves on the right when they rebelled against a minister like Prior, they themselves would rebel over social benefit legislation. During Margaret Thatcher's leadership, the Conservative Party became irretrievably divided into two factions, and it remained divided after she departed.

In the middle of 1982, my life took another interesting turn. Although I was enjoying the BBC, I undoubtedly missed print journalism. So I was pleased when Russell Twisk, editor of the *Listener*, the BBC's magazine, now sadly defunct, offered me a column. I wrote in the first of these that although I had recently forsaken the primrose paths of newspaper leader-writing for the rigours of Reithian impartiality and the new arts of script-writing and compression, 'perhaps just an occasional obeisance at the Caxton prie-dieu wouldn't turn me into a pillar of salt'. I found that broadcasting was an art of brevity, so a licence to use relative clauses again was welcome.

At the same time, I was writing an article for the *Dictionary of National Biography* on George Woodcock, my old and greatly admired friend at the TUC. Among his papers, I came on his lecture to the British Association not long before his death, in which he had warned of the bleak prospect for employment if cooperation between unions and government on incomes, the cause to which he had devoted so many years, broke down: 'Neither the employers nor the trade unions could or would be willing to hand over their responsibilities or their powers to the state, and compulsion has been shown to be impracticable. The most likely alternative to cooperation is that governments will have to modify their commitment to maintain a high level of employment.' As the unemployment figure passed 3 million, nobody could say they had not been warned.

By the time Margaret Thatcher called the election in the summer of 1983, inflation had fallen to 4.6 per cent. This compared with 10.3 when she entered Downing Street, and a peak of almost 22 per cent in 1980. But she had only achieved this because, over her period in office up till then, unemployment had risen by no less than 141 per cent, to the highest level since the war. This had appalling results in output, national wealth, public services, and worsening crime. It was scarcely surprising that trade union negotiators were not pushing wage claims.

Geoffrey Howe, cautious as ever, hoped by 1982 that unemployment would soon be past its peak, though he acknowledged how difficult it was to predict the course of worldwide recession. (In the event, this was only to be the first of several peaks in unemployment in the eighties and nineties.) Howe was nearing the end of his chancellorship. Despite all vicissitudes, he argued that the Tories had three things going for them that had not been there towards the end of previous parliaments. The party's NCOs were not moaning, but saying 'carry on'; businessmen, who had argued vociferously at the 1982 party conference for short-term concessions for their own firms, still believed the government's long-term direction was right; and the trade union legislation was popular, even among many trade unionists. Later, he was to enhance his party's already strong chances of victory in 1983 by a popular pre-election budget.

His own ambition to be Foreign Secretary became clear to me at this time. For several years now, most of my political lunching companions had been speculating when he would become Lord Chancellor. Geoffrey Howe is not a frank talker, but he is a disarmingly honest politician. Once when he began a sentence defining the reason why he was in politics, I waited, through force of habit, for some grandiloquent claim, which is the casual change of such conversations. But the sentence ended by saying that he was a politician because he had not been able to face the prospect of being a judge, spending a lifetime pronouncing on other people's disputes. He was willing to admit that no lawyer would turn up his nose at the Woolsack, but he clearly did not want it until his chance to be Prime Minister had gone.

Howe had enjoyed being Chancellor, but knew he must move. He had previously contemplated the usual lawyer's route to the Home Office, but by this time preferred the Foreign Office. The negative reason was that a series of talented Home Secretaries – Rab Butler, Henry Brooke, Reginald Maudling, Roy Jenkins and Willie Whitelaw – had tried to scale the peaks of prison and other reforms, and had found the task extremely difficult.

The positive reason was to have long-term reverberations in Conservative politics: Geoffrey Howe was keenly interested in Europe. In the light of subsequent events, his analysis of the electoral aspects of the European issue is full of irony. At that time, Labour was anti-Europe, but Howe believed the public would worry about the bad effects on employment if Britain withdrew. The Alliance, he said, was Euro-fanatic. That left the Tories as the party who were in favour of membership, but would protect British interests. It was not an uncomfortable position to be in for the 1983 general election.

At the time of his move from the Treasury to the Foreign Office, I put Geoffrey Howe down as 'a quiet zealot' – not over Europe, but generally. His mild manner deceives many people. He had been a relentless pamphleteer and controversialist since his early days in the Bow Group. A conversation with him rarely revealed secrets to a journalist, but he was a stubborn advocate of his own and the government's case. He was still, and remained for many more years, ambitious to be Prime Minister, though the fact that he was so close in age to Margaret Thatcher made him doubt whether he had much chance of succeeding her. But the Foreign Office, quite apart from his developing interest in Europe, provided him with another useful training-ground, if the road did happen to lead to Number 10.

As the election approached, and with the opinion polls showing the Conservatives well ahead, almost out of reach, the possibility of a radical manifesto was in the minds of Thatcher loyalists. But a Think Tank report advocating a root-and-branch reform – meaning reduction – in the welfare state was leaked, and the alarm bells started ringing. The Prime Minister finished up with a manifesto which was much less definite than she would have liked on subjects like rates, education vouchers and spending on the social services.

The state of the world and British economies left the problem of public spending levels unresolved. The population was ageing. The cost of the welfare state and other public services would continue to rise. With fewer people in work, the same taxes raised less revenue. The problems of industrial competitiveness and wage inflation were deferred, rather than solved, by the recession. More and more Third World countries were joining the queue for industrialisation. If an economic miracle was not in sight, the most fundamental review of the welfare state since its foundation at the end of the war seemed inevitable.

But Margaret Thatcher remained cautious throughout that election campaign. Whenever challenged by reporters with a suggestion that she intended to cut this or that benefit, she would give a firm denial. A couple of years later, when I was preparing a report for television on Norman Fowler's welfare state review, the civil servant briefing me kept referring to 'pledged benefits', and showed me a list with dates on it. Almost all of these fell within the period of the election campaign, and were a product of her press conferences. Afterwards I used to joke to newspaper colleagues that their proprietors ought to have sacked them for failing to extract an undertaking from the Prime Minister that there would be no imposition of VAT on newspapers. For that year she showed herself a hyper-cautious election fighter, not willing to sacrifice a single vote to unconsidered radicalism.

34

AN AGE OF BANANA SKINS

By comparison with what went before, and what was to come after, the 1983 election and the parliament which emerged from it were dull. Two incidents stand out in my memory: the IRA bomb in Brighton, which came close to killing a large part of the British Cabinet; and the Westland affair, that strangely irrelevant event in which Margaret Thatcher created the enemy who eventually destroyed her.

However unimportant the Westland Helicopter Company was in the great scheme of things, the debate about its affairs raised again what was anyhow an obsessive theme of Conservative conversation: the Thatcher style of government. There had been few complaints about this when she was the victor of the Falklands, but when things went wrong, her domineering ways grated. Arguably it was her style which ignited the slow fuse that eventually led to her downfall.

Between 1983 and 1987, much did go wrong. This became known as the Parliament of Banana Skins. No sooner was the largest election victory since 1945 in the bag than inflation, mortgages and unemployment all rose, and the government had to cut public spending. As she has since acknowledged, it looked as though the Prime Minister had 'cooked the books' during the election.

The following four years brought unrelated misfortunes which were grouped under that generic term, banana skins. Cecil Parkinson, joint architect of victory, had to resign after he fathered an illegitimate child. Following the most cursory consultation, Margaret Thatcher's friend President Reagan invaded Grenada, of which the head of state happened to be Her Britannic Majesty. A junior minister encapsulated this casual humiliation in the words: 'The Yanks kicked sand in our faces.'

More seriously, the Prime Minister ran into criticism from within her Cabinet, again because of Reagan, when she gave him permission to use British bases for an American air attack on Libya, to punish its support for terrorism. At one Cabinet before the raid, when Geoffrey Howe uttered a mild note of caution, a minister told me that Margaret Thatcher treated him abominably, gave a long monologue saying this was all Reagan could do, and that she hoped this would not be a Cabinet of appeasers. 'The rest of us,' he said, 'just kept our heads below the parapet, hoping we could soon get on to discussing milk quotas.'

But the incident weakened her. Willie Whitelaw had called Reagan a most uncomfortable and dangerous ally. My informant himself was appalled by Thatcher's behaviour, and by her attitude towards advice, scepticism, the whole Baldwinesque style of politics in which he believed. This minister confessed he would like to be rid of her, but did not think there was much chance. In the event, she got rid of him before her own demise. And the American raids did appear to reduce Gaddafi's appetite for terrorism.

On the night that American bombers attacked Libya, but before the news was known, I already had an important story on my hands: the government had been defeated in a vote on Sunday trading. But when I telephoned Broadcasting House with my report for the midnight news, they told me about the raid, and asked me to deal briefly with shopping hours. I went down into the Members' Lobby, which an hour before had been buzzing with excitement over the first defeat of the Thatcher era, and found it almost deserted. A few government whips were still there. It was clear they understood, in the words of an old Irish song, that misfortunes never come singly.

In this parliament, Margaret Thatcher faced a new leader of the opposition. The weekend after Labour's 1983 election defeat, Michael Foot and Denis Healey both announced their resignations. Although less than seventy-two hours had passed since the close of polls, it quickly became clear that supporters of Neil Kinnock had lined up enough votes among the trade unions to defeat his principal opponent, Roy Hattersley. According to the new rules, the election campaign dragged on from June till October, but the result was never in doubt: Kinnock became leader, Hattersley his deputy.

Roy Hattersley, like so many able leaders in both parties, before and since, knew that his chance of the top job had gone for ever. I had dinner with him and his wife Molly on the evening when the leadership election result was formally announced, and he gave me as a memento of his campaign a small penknife of steel from his native Sheffield.

The overwhelming industrial event of the parliament was the miners' strike, which lasted for a year, from the spring of 1984. It was the one subject on which I encountered absolute unity in my conversations with

Tories: the government had to win. Not all of them relished their leader's rhetoric about Arthur Scargill as 'the enemy within', a domestic version of the Argentinian dictator, General Galtieri. But on the substance of the dispute there was no dissent. This was the long-delayed battle on the issue of 'Who governs Britain?', which had defeated Ted Heath ten years before. The government was determined to win, at whatever cost in domestic bitterness or in the future of the coal communities.

For the Conservatives, a political bonus from the strike was that it caught Neil Kinnock in an impossible position. He was MP for a mining constituency, with a weight of tradition which said he ought not to oppose trade unionists engaged in a dispute. Yet he knew Scargill had made a fatal error in dodging the ballot vote which ought to have preceded a strike.

On the day of his election, Neil Kinnock had imposed a new discipline on the Labour Party. With the Alliance only just behind them in the popular vote in 1983, they were ready for his stern words. He warned them against self-indulgent diversions, and proclaimed that only single-minded pursuit of power would bring them success. In his ruthless defeat and expulsion of the Militant Tendency's Trotskyists, he showed himself the most effective party manager Labour could have hoped for during this impossible period in its history.

By the end of the 1983 parliament, Neil Kinnock believed he was about halfway through his efforts to put the Labour Party in good order again. In London particularly, there were still a number of Labour people who were self-indulgent – his greatest term of criticism – not serious about politics, but very serious about themselves. His view, he told me, was that the time when a Labour leader could deal best with such people by ignoring them had passed around 1980, perhaps earlier. He was tough with such members, not because he enjoyed punishing dissidents, but because he had to make Labour a serious contender for power. Stern and effective party management was the most impressive aspect of the Kinnock leadership. It is doubtful if the Labour Party would have survived as a major player in British politics without him.

The trouble was that Neil himself was conscientiously committed to one item of policy that was to prove unacceptable to voters: unilateral nuclear disarmament. He wanted rid of Polaris and of American bases, and spoke of building up conventional forces, though he conceded that this would run him into trouble with the armed services. Kinnock's stance on defence worried his deputy, Roy Hattersley. So did his initial opposition to Europe. Hattersley discovered that Kinnock was a nice man to work with, a good public performer, and with an uncanny ability to make the Labour Party work. He concluded that his leader's interest lay more in presentation than policy-making. But Hattersley was in a state of semi-permanent despair over the part of Labour's policy that Kinnock cared most about. He suspected the party's defence stance was an inevitable vote-loser.

When he told Neil Kinnock of his anxiety, the response was: 'Don't worry, kid. It'll be all right when we're in government.' Did this mean he would change the policy? Most shadow ministers with doubts concluded that Kinnock was relying on detente to solve his dilemma. Finally, in the following parliament, it almost did, but by then his credibility with the voters was fatally damaged, for the 1992 election, as well as that of 1987.

During the 1983 parliament, the opposition lived constantly with the expectation that a divided vote between Labour and the Alliance would make another victory for Margaret Thatcher almost inevitable. Until the 1987 election gave Neil Kinnock decisive public support against David Owen and David Steel, nobody could be quite sure which party was to form the official opposition. In that period, a Labour frontbencher said they might have to reconcile themselves to losing once more. Even he did not realise the length of the ditch into which the opposition had dug themselves.

What the nation lost through opposition divisions was a proper debate, leading to an electoral decision, between the political theories which divided Margaret Thatcher from both Labour and the Alliance. She believed in hands-off government, even when unemployment looked worrying. She held that a government must simply – if only it *were* simple! – reduce inflation, lower interest rates, cut taxes on industry and others, create a good climate for enterprise, and leave businessmen and workers to make room for more employment. The opposition parties, to greater or lesser extent, believed in Keynesian reflation measures, preferably practised on a worldwide scale.

Because of continuing quarrels between Labour and the Alliance, that debate was never properly joined. If Labour had its troubles, the storm-clouds which were to engulf the Alliance after its 1987 defeat were already on the horizon. The Liberals had always hoped that the SDP would deliver dissident Labour votes, while they would perform their historic task of mobilising unhappy Tories, whenever the government ran into its periodic troubles. To their surprise, they found that the Social Democrats, now under the leadership of David Owen, who had replaced Roy Jenkins in 1983, were winning support not from disgruntled Labour voters, but from Conservatives.

They ought not to have been surprised. The SDP membership, unlike most of its original MPs, who had lost their seats in 1983, was very different from that even of the Labour right. Many had previously been uncommitted politically, some were former Conservatives. One Liberal surmised that the new party's social mix was dictated by its system of collecting subscriptions by credit cards, which were then uncommon in working-class areas.

David Steel's relationship with David Owen, despite the public relations hype to the contrary, was never an intimate one, such as he had enjoyed with Roy Jenkins. They were of the same generation, for one thing, and the Liberals thought Steel would have to be top man, because his was the larger party. They were also of different temperaments. Steel used to acknowledge that the difficulty in winning over Labour dissidents arose in part from Labour's change in leadership, from Foot to Kinnock. But he also believed David Owen was alienating Labour voters, and observed tartly that at a time when there was a revolt against Thatcherism and the Thatcher style, it was odd that Owen had become the hero of the *Express* and *Sun*. Like Margaret Thatcher, he was assertive and very sure of himself.

A liberal-minded Tory thought David Owen's mistake was to divide the segment between Thatcher and Kinnock, then raise a finger to see which way the wind was blowing. The Labour Party was in trouble, so the obvious thing for an Alliance leader to do was to take over that side of politics. Instead, Owen looked like 'the best Conservative Prime Minister we don't have'. The Alliance's weakness was that it had the sheet-anchor neither of ideology nor of class commitment to prevent drift and destructive argument. Its faults were the obverse of those in the older parties.

Michael Heseltine's was the most traditional view of all. He thought David Owen had made a historic mistake in breaking with Labour and losing that power-base without creating a viable alternative one. He asked me to reflect on what a Labour front bench would look like if it consisted of Healey, Hattersley, Kinnock, Owen and Williams, among others. It was a thought that had occurred to me.

Conservative conferences in the two years after the 1983 election were occasions of high drama. The first, in October 1983, was dominated by the Parkinson affair. The question of whether or not he would have to resign ran right through the week, overshadowing more mundane news. Although Parkinson received a warm enough reception for his speech on industry, a single encounter convinced me that his fate was sealed. When I spotted a woman MP who was close to the grassroots of her party, I sat down beside her, and asked: 'What do you think?'

She had no doubt what I was talking about, and replied simply: 'He'll have to go.'

She reminded me of a Roman emperor, giving the thumbs down sign over the stricken gladiator, but I was grateful to have her judgement of how Conservatism's powerful female voice would go.

Later that evening, the one before Cecil Parkinson resigned, I found myself sitting on one bed in his room, while he and his wife Ann sat on the other. It was a small room, and became rather crowded when a party adviser and a press officer joined us. It is only on such occasions that a journalist sees how modestly even middle-ranking Cabinet ministers are treated by conference organisers. I was engaged in a complex turf battle with ITN about who would interview him, and when. Cecil, understandably, was more concerned with the fight to save his political career. It was the first time I had met his wife, but even this brief encounter, in embarrassing circumstances, helped the next morning, when the BBC newsroom wakened me from deep sleep at 5.30, to alert me about a *Times* article by Sara Keays, which further undermined him. I phoned the Parkinsons' room, and Ann, retaining a tough-minded dignity, told me all she could.

Cecil resigned a few hours later. It was a busy day for broadcasters and others, at the very end of a busy conference season. That year the BBC had decided to send their television news presenters on the seaside circuit. As I prepared my *Nine O'Clock* package, Sue Lawley was hammering out her own script for the introduction to the programme on a neighbouring typewriter. For a reason which now escapes me, I had unwisely decided, on the occasion of the leader's speech, to refer to Margaret Thatcher's ever-immaculate coiffure. Knowing that some people find difficult my pronunciation of terminal 'r', whether in English or French, I was quietly rehearsing it to myself. After the third 'coiffure', Sue could take no more. Without looking up, she said kindly: 'John! Why not try "hair-do"?' When she heard my pronunciation of that word, she probably wished she hadn't bothered. On the other hand, I have always found the English wrong-headed in their determination to ignore the way our language is spelled.

The 1984 Conservative conference was an altogether more sombre affair. Personally, I was hanging on that year. In February, I suffered a massive heart attack in the BBC room at the Press Gallery. If I had to have a coronary, this was a wise choice of venue, as I reached the Westminster Hospital within minutes, which probably saved my life. I had a by-pass operation in April, and returned to work, gently, in July, with stern warnings about lifestyle and working hours.

Throughout the autumn conference season, I was ostentatiously obedient: early to bed, a brisk morning walk along cliffs or promenade, careful eating. It was in the course of going early to bed that I encountered Norman and Margaret Tebbit. Norman thinks this was on the night of the bomb; I suspect it was on the previous evening, the Wednesday, in part because Margaret Thatcher says that on the Thursday night Norman was helping to write her speech.

Whoever is right, I met the Tebbits as we departed around midnight from one of the late-evening parties which, even for a convalescent political editor, are an essential place for gathering news. Margaret Tebbit went to bed, while Norman and I settled down, on a couch on the landing outside their room, for a last chat. His final words were a warning that if he wakened his wife, I would be to blame.

When the bomb went off, I was asleep in the Metropole, the next hotel along the promenade. As ambulance and fire engine bells convinced me this was a major incident. I put on trousers, a jersey and a raincoat, and descended to a scene of great confusion. Guests from the Grand, in pyjamas and dressing-gowns, were in the Metropole lobby. When I knew what had happened, I went to find BBC colleagues. Because the police feared further explosions, they would not allow us into our offices in the conference centre, so preparations for the morning programmes had to be made in casual encounters on the promenade.

Somebody told me there was a camera crew at the police station, to which it was thought the Prime Minister had been taken, for safety. I joined them, and sent in a message to her that we would like an interview for *Breakfast News* and the *Today* programme. This was at about 4.30 in the morning. She appeared soon afterwards. Looking back at the tape of that interview, I have often been struck by the contrast in our appearances. Fortunately the shots of me were taken from behind. Even so, it is the only time I have appeared on television with a day's beard stubble quite apparent. Margaret Thatcher had used her time in the police station to restore her usual immaculate appearance.

Her Special Branch bodyguards were nervously keen to get her into her car as quickly as possible. The police were still worried that there might be further attacks on members of the Cabinet. But the Prime Minister was determined to give full attention to her interview with me, for she recognised the need to get a public grip on what had happened. At that stage she had no knowledge of the casualties. Even when I had asked her all that seemed sensible in these circumstances, and as minders hustled her towards the car, she turned to ask if I had everything I needed. Not for the first or last time, I noted mentally that Margaret Thatcher, even under the most appalling personal strain, was a supreme political professional.

Friday was an emotional day at the conference. Five people had been killed, including the wife of John Wakeham. Many others were injured, among them Margaret Tebbit, who was paralysed. The Prime Minister made a brave, defiant speech. What I found equally moving were the messages of support, sent to a Tory conference by the opposition parties. Democratic politics can be a fierce business, but when terrorism seeks to destroy it, disagreement fades into its proper proportions.

My day, which began well before dawn, continued through a long series of news bulletins, ending with the *Nine O'Clock*, after which a colleague drove me to our home in Surrey, where I arrived about midnight. The following week I had to telephone the Westminster Hospital for my next out-patient appointment. I spoke to the senior staff nurse, a woman in her early twenties, about the same age as our second son, but who for a couple of weeks had been a figure of towering authority in all her patients' lives, as we struggled after a weakening operation.

When we had made my date with the consultant, she turned to events in Brighton: 'I saw you interviewing the Prime Minister in the dark. What time was that?'

Sensing her tone of disapproval, I confessed that it was 4.30 a.m.

'Then I saw you on the *Nine O'Clock News*,' she continued and, offering me a technical way out: 'Was that pre-recorded?'

I acknowledged that it was live.

'So what time did you get to bed?'

I said about midnight.

'Well, John, that's not the way we told you to behave.'

I murmured that attempted assassination of the British Cabinet was rather a special event, but she sounded unconvinced.

When I met the consultant, I told him of the conversation. He laughed, and replied: 'Mr Cole, doubtless many of our patients are behaving just as foolishly as you. But if you insist on doing this in front of a television camera, my staff will give you stick, and they're absolutely right.' One of the fascinations of journalism is the sense of constantly living in different cultures. Never was I more conscious of this than when trying to reconcile the requirements of the BBC with those of the NHS.

Margaret Thatcher was frustrated during the 1983 parliament because her manifesto had not been as radical as she would have liked. Retrospectively, she blamed the caution of Geoffrey Howe, whom she had put in charge of its preparation. But others thought she herself was careful not to take risks. Persistent high unemployment inevitably caused ministers to look at the cost of social benefits, but the Prime Minister's instinctive caution conjured up the row which would follow cuts. Peter Walker used to conclude that it was her rhetoric which was strident, rather than her behaviour.

Others were less sure. Jim Prior, exiled to Belfast, eventually left the government in 1984, at his own request. He had been fed up with Margaret Thatcher for a long time, his wife Jane even more so. In opposition, Prior had done a lot of work to reconcile the trade unions and the Tories, but now he saw his colleagues heading off in quite a different direction. Len Murray was trying to woo the TUC towards a 'new realism', but Jim Prior thought the government's attitude was wasting that initiative: no minister was trying even to keep in touch with the unions.

As a man brought up in the Macmillan–Heath age of Conservatism, he was particularly anxious about unemployment. But his belief that the Prime Minister took no notice of his views about matters outside Northern Ireland was confirmed when he raised it in Cabinet. Prior said they needed a general philosophical discussion about where the government was going on unemployment. Quite politely, she told him that they had one of those every week. Bernard Ingham maintained that Thatcher would never have sacked Prior, because she liked people who spoke up in Cabinet, and that ministers who complained she did not listen were guilty of being too timorous.

Backbenchers blew hot and cold about their leader. One told me that, after an all-night sitting, he had been in the Commons tearoom with several weary colleagues when she arrived to cheer them up and thank them for their efforts. They were all greatly flattered, as she settled with her coffee at their table. The trouble was that, instead of listening to their views, she gave them hers, in an uninterruptable monologue. Yet he was full of praise for her ability to remember wives' and children's names, ages, health problems and so on. She was personally considerate, and politically implacable. When I told this story to another young Tory, he said nobody but the subservient would have been in the tearoom so early in the morning, and that Margaret Thatcher was 'like everybody's mother-in-law, talking and not listening'.

Even in this period, when her authority seemed beyond challenge, ministers also expressed their doubts to me about her style of politics. One thoughtful fellow said that, like him, she was a product of the post-war grammar school and Young Conservative generation, but that he had grown out of this, while she had not. She represented the *petit bourgeois* tendency in Conservatism which he hated. He went on to accuse her of arguing *ad hominem*: she would look at a Whitehall paper, and say: 'Ah! That's Snodgrass. I knew him at Education. He's unsound, not one of us.' He himself tended to think that people were what their intellects were, and therefore to judge each argument on its merits. He found the Prime Minister inclined to *feel*, rather than to *think* her way through problems.

Right-wing ministers, who had no doubt that Margaret Thatcher was leading the Conservative Party and the country in the more ideologically driven direction that they wanted, nevertheless nursed doubts about her style. One said that the qualities which had previously made her popular – decisiveness, a willingness to speak out, certitude – were now working against her, because they made her seem bossy, and bossiness was a negative factor when things were going wrong. He concluded that her popularity would be restored when the government contrived to have fewer mess-ups.

The minister whose attitude to Margaret Thatcher came to matter most was Michael Heseltine. Because of his detachment from her, he tends to be classified as a Tory Wet, but this is a misreading. Heseltine believed the government had sold the pass on its convictions when it dodged the issue of spending on the welfare state. When the history of the government came to be written, he thought the pledges about these benefits which the Prime Minister had given during the 1983 election, after the leak of a Think Tank report, would be regarded as its gravest error. The result had been a historic missed opportunity: the great growth of North Sea oil revenue in the eighties would have allowed the government to educate the British people away from their propensity to consume more in wages and welfare benefits than they produced; and thereafter to create the New Deal politics in which he was interested: the use of public resources to generate wealth and jobs and to revive the inner cities.

Even before his resignation in January 1986, Michael made no secret of the fact that he was 'not one of us', that he had an entirely different vision of Toryism from his chief. Despite his seniority, he had no close relationship with her. He was disillusioned with the way the Cabinet was run, believing that she packed the key committees with Thatcherites. He observed some ministers remaining behind after meetings, and assumed there would be a further gathering, to which only those who were in a conspiracy with her would be invited. He found pointless the discussions about economics in full Cabinet, since there was no virtue in going over the same issues four or five times, when she had no intention of changing course.

Perhaps Michael Heseltine's resignation was in the stars from a long way back. When it eventually came, during the Westland affair, it was at a time which was personally inconvenient for me (not to mention for HM government). The debate within Cabinet had been rumbling on for weeks. It was a difficult story to cover for radio and television, because nobody was saying anything on the record, in the House of Commons or anywhere else. So we were left with unattributable briefings from the various factions, which are all right for background, but of limited use without foreground.

Early in January, I went to Belfast to cover fifteen by-elections. All the Ulster Unionist MPs had resigned in protest against the Anglo–Irish agreement. It was bitterly cold weather, but we had gathered a lot of good material for our filmed report, and when the thunderbolt struck, we were heading to a rendezvous with another of the candidates. I was in the first of two cars, driven by the cameraman, while my producer was behind with the sound recordist. Suddenly I saw her jump out of the rear car, when we were stopped at a traffic light. She ran up and knocked frenziedly at my window. When I opened it, she barked at the driver: 'Heseltine's resigned. Drive to Broadcasting House.'

The cameraman, followed by his sound recordist, did two of those tyre-abusing U-turns which earn nervous looks in Belfast. Both cars headed for the BBC's Northern Ireland headquarters, and within minutes I was making my first broadcast. Since only one cameraman was present in Downing Street when Michael Heseltine performed his famous walk-out from the Cabinet, I did not feel at great competitive disadvantage. But, after a couple of broadcasts for various outlets, I hurried to the first aircraft for London.

When I contacted the office on the car telephone from just outside Heathrow, I learned that a special television programme to cover the Heseltine news conference was due to begin in under half an hour, and that they would like me in the studio at Shepherds Bush. The hire-driver saw this as a challenge, and screeched to a halt outside the Television Centre just as they were going on air. As he disposed of my suitcase, I hurried to the sixth floor, where the editor of Television News removed my overcoat and pushed me into the studio.

While John Humphreys was introducing the programme, I slid in beside him, out of camera-shot, and allowed the make-up woman to perform the magic trick of making me look cool and calm, in time for him to ask me his first question, of the 'tell-us-what-this-is-all-about' kind. It was at such moments that I realised my move from newspapers to broadcasting had not been a foolish mistake. At fifty-four, as Jim Callaghan observed, I had needed a new challenge, and now at fifty-nine, when the adrenalin was pumping, even around my damaged heart, I felt a few miles were still left in my engine.

The Heseltine news conference, which I watched in the studio, and then explained to the audience, was one of the most dramatic any of us could remember. Here was a powerful minister who had, literally, walked out of the Cabinet. At this distance in time, the rights and wrongs of the helicopter industry are not the issue. During Westland, Alan Clark thought it just possible that a Prime Minister like Baldwin, who often did not begin work till lunchtime, might not have known what was going on. But he could not credit ignorance in such a hands-on character as Margaret Thatcher.

Michael Heseltine's resignation was only a symptom of the grumbling weakness of an otherwise impregnable Prime Minister: she was rubbing more and more people up the wrong way.

Most ministers had come to accept her masterful way of treating them as a law of nature, or at least a trait of character which would not change. It became a joke among them. During the 1983 election, I had done weekly interviews with the party leaders. Margaret Thatcher's all too easily became a recitation of her previous night's speech. One morning I had noticed a paragraph in the *Financial Times*, in which an unnamed Tory backbencher said: 'Margaret is like a headmistress. She bosses us all around.'

At a particularly arid moment in the statistical desert, I quoted this to her. Eyes flashed, nostrils flared. 'Well!' Two of the most influential people in her life had been headmistresses, women who knew what they believed, and said what they knew. The flow continued for two minutes. I then ended the interview, and she became nervous about what she might have said. Only when Sir Gordon Reece assured her that it was satisfactory did she relax. So the Prime Minister was not without self-doubt, at least as far as her public image was concerned. But her increasingly ruthless behaviour towards those who stepped out of line was now legendary. Not only had there been a clear-out of Wets during her first government, but immediately after the election victory in 1983 she had sacked her Foreign Secretary, Francis Pym, hitherto thought of as a possible successor from the traditional Tory wing.

Francis Pym invited me round to his flat soon after his dismissal. What specially offended him was that, during the election campaign, they had travelled back together from a summit in the United States, and she had made no mention of her intention. Coming out after our talk, I met the Leader of the Commons, John Biffen, who was going in to express his regrets to Pym. Neither of us foresaw that John, whose not-too-well-concealed doubts about Margaret Thatcher caused Bernard Ingham to describe him as 'semi-detached' from the government, was to be dismissed in similar circumstances four years later.

Even Bernard, whose loyalty to the Prime Minister was not to be questioned, had been known to observe that although she had earned great respect from her party for her abilities, there was not a lot of affection, and this could be a weakness if things ever went wrong. In 1984, that was a prescient observation, though it did not come to fruition until four years after the Westland affair.

Michael Heseltine's resignation was only the beginning of a political crisis which almost toppled Margaret Thatcher. She had a couple of gruelling debates in the House, and lost her Trade Secretary, Leon Brittan. Many thought he was left as scapegoat for the improper leaking of a letter from the Solicitor-General, Patrick Mayhew, when the blame really belonged in Downing Street.

Whatever the truth of that, for a time the Prime Minister was chastened. Early in February, a minister assured me that her style had changed, though he prudently added: 'whether temporarily or not'. A feature of her governments had been a steady stream of admonitory minutes addressed from Downing Street to departmental ministers. These had now dried up, and in Cabinet and its committees she was even sitting back and letting others talk, instead of setting a firm line at the outset of a discussion. Kenneth Baker was heard to observe that there were many more meetings, and therefore a lot more paper to read. Others deduced that her determination to lead from the front had disappeared, and there had been proper collective discussions on inner cities, local rates, and Northern Ireland.

One colleague volunteered the information that Margaret Thatcher looked depressed and hurt, and that the feeling was personal as well as political. She was sad she had not been able to protect those close to her. But his worry was that in her distress, she had developed a more general feeling which was politically dangerous. This was that Britain was not taking the opportunities she had given it, indeed did not want them. She had said that the enterprise culture, on which she had pinned such hopes, was not working, and that the education system was a disaster. She wanted tax cuts, but the public did not give these such high priority.

This feeling that the country was letting her down had strange echoes of how Ted Heath had felt in the bleaker moments of his government. One of the problems of ideology-based politics is that the public often declines to conform to the ideology. There were those Tories who thought Margaret Thatcher's time for departure might be near, but a shrewd observer inside the Cabinet told me that he simply could not see Willie Whitelaw, John Wakeham, the Chief Whip, and Cranley Onslow, chairman of the 1922 Committee, telling her this. There was still much support for her at the party grassroots, and also a feeling among ministers and MPs that 'to cut down the biggest tree in the forest' would leave the Tories with a dreadful gap.

35

THE ARROGANCE OF POWER

In the slow decline and harsh fall of Margaret Thatcher, she emerges as a classical tragic heroine, a monumental figure in twentieth-century British politics, brought down by *hubris*, by fatal flaws in her character. After her third general election victory in 1987, she developed an arrogant sense that she was politically immortal. In truth, the cracks appeared almost at once. They were later to develop into the connected chasms in which her leadership perished: the poll tax, the economy, and Europe.

She remained a driven personality. After her narrow escape from political destruction during the Westland affair in 1986, ministers believed she was running her government in a more collegiate way. But just before the election, I concluded there had been no permanent change. She was back on a personal high. I was told in an awed whisper that, in the three weeks before the campaign began, she had driven through the Cabinet radical policies on education, housing and – fatally – local government finance. It would normally have taken about six months to discuss these, and put them in the party programme.

Margaret Thatcher was determined not to repeat the mistake of her second term, when she had too cautious a manifesto for her taste. She believed third-term Tory governments tended to run out of steam. She remembered Harold Macmillan's after 1959 – in which she had her first junior post – as drifting, purposeless, without her sheet-anchor of ideology. Although the 1987 manifesto, like most of the genre, was the work of many hands, a meeting of Nicholas Ridley and other Thatcher familiars in Downing Street set its radical tone. Opting out of schools, the attempt to break down local councils' grip on rented housing, and the changes in the health service were all given impetus by what critics called 'the true believers' within the government. Not everyone thought this wise. A junior minister whispered conspiratorially: 'The manifesto doesn't matter as much as they think. They talk about the nanny state.

I'm an old-fashioned Tory who believes there are some things only the public sector can do.' But that was not the prevailing wisdom at the top.

Ministers believed they were certain to win the election. Labour shadows, still unhappy about their unsaleable defence policy, and aware of the damage done by quarrelling in the early eighties, privately suspected they were going to lose. The Home Secretary, Douglas Hurd, by now emerging as a senior figure on the Cabinet's consensual wing, was nervous about the speed with which Margaret Thatcher had taken the new radical policies through. The community charge – what was later, as the poll tax, to become the explosive charge that helped to destroy her – caused him particular concern. Hurd believed the poll tax would be very difficult to sell.

In retrospect, this may sound like a masterpiece of understatement, but at that time it was perceptive, for many leading Conservatives had been seduced by that most dangerous phrase in politics: that 'something must be done', in this case, about local government rates. Two other powerful figures were signalling what a dangerous course the government was embarked upon: Michael Heseltine from outside, Nigel Lawson within. But the Prime Minister ignored them.

Her mastery of the Cabinet again seemed total. Yet there were signs of overreaching, and of obsessions, like that with 'presentation', which had long infuriated such serious-minded elements as Lawson and Nicholas Ridley. For example, the election campaign produced a nervous eruption on what was called Wobbly Thursday. Yet despite one maverick opinion poll, the Tories were in no danger of defeat. This panic developed in the course of a ludicrous battle between rival spin-doctors, Tim Bell and Saatchi and Saatchi; and their ministerial patrons, Lord Young and Norman Tebbit. Bitter infighting about something that barely mattered clouded victory. I could not help wondering what impression this public relations nonsense might have made on Margaret Thatcher's distinguished predecessor, Winston Churchill. He was so aloof from PR that he would not allow his press secretary to have an office in Number 10, but made him sit in the Foreign Office, across Downing Street.

This row gave a sour taste to the post-election announcement that Norman Tebbit was retiring from government, though he had told the Prime Minister of this decision before the campaign began. Lord Young, who appeared to be Margaret Thatcher's flavour of the month, became Secretary for Trade and Industry, and would have liked to succeed Tebbit as party chairman. Willie Whitelaw convinced the Prime Minister there would be a conflict of interest between his work with companies and his control of Conservative Party finances. David Young had made the mistake of trading too heavily on his reputation as a Downing Street favourite. When he failed to become chairman, his political fortunes ebbed, and two years later he returned to industry.

The incident had wider implications. Margaret Thatcher's critics had always said she conducted her government like a court. Those who did not share her ideology predicted that 'Thatcherism' would not necessarily survive the passing from the scene of its eponymous heroine. One said when she was gone, Conservatism would resume its previous course, like a great river rolling towards the sea. Later, he was less sure there would be a counter-revolution. But the question remained: how many leading Conservatives had genuinely been converted to what was an entirely new philosophy for their party, and how many were mere courtiers? Like most human projects, the long-term fate of 'Thatcherism' turned out to depend more on events, including events beyond its control, than on ideology.

Courtiers or not, Margaret Thatcher's ministers saw their reputations oscillate wildly. Another example of this was John Moore, whom she made Health Secretary, with the difficult task of conducting the National Health Service review. Moore took too seriously some overheated press reports that he had become the natural heir to the Prime Minister, since no other suitable candidate had emerged from the Thatcherite wing of the party. This apparent vanity left him with too few allies when a mixture of ill-health and inexperience ran him into trouble.

The Prime Minister's approach to the health service review was both radical and ideological. She wanted to introduce market principles. Kenneth Clarke suspected that when she thought about the NHS in her bath, she might wish she could privatise it, but realised only a less drastic plan was politically acceptable. In contemplating American practice, she was running against the grain of the public, which had always assumed that the NHS was one of the finest post-war British achievements, and that American health care – as President Clinton later asserted – was far from satisfactory. But a cherished Thatcherite belief prevailed even among traditional Tories like Clarke: public services were in permanent danger of becoming producer conspiracies against the consumer. The medical and nursing professions were held to be part of that conspiracy.

John Moore made himself vulnerable by criticising his predecessor, Norman Fowler, for not planning a radical enough review. The Prime Minister liked that, because she had removed Fowler from the job for just that reason. What she did not like was the eruption of a rash of press stories about underfunding of hospitals. John Moore was eager to establish his credentials as a minister who could be relied on to be tough on public expenditure, even in his own department. Most politicians reckon they can safely assume that the Treasury will provide this steel, and that they are wise to fight their own corners. Moore failed even to go to Star Chamber to win more money for health. When the row broke, a colleague cruelly said his back was so much against the wall that his elbows were penetrating the bricks.

Kenneth Clarke, who eventually took over his job, did not make the same mistake. Although he was suspicious of producer-lobbies, he thought of himself as the kind of consolidating Tory Margaret Thatcher needed to save her from her ideological obsessions. Clarke was determined not to fall into the same trap about resources as Moore had. Contemplating the 1988 public spending round, the new Health Secretary said cheerfully that the Prime Minister would not be able to sack him that year, so soon after his appointment. He had no intention of picking up his cards in the poker games with the Treasury until the last moment. Clarke's arrival signalled more combative ministerial discussion of the health review.

Margaret Thatcher was widely held to be a bad listener. When the government was under heavy criticism about the coming shape of its NHS reforms, Cranley Onslow, the discreet and loyal chairman of the backbench 1922 Committee, took a delegation to see her. He indicated that Dame Jill Knight, a senior member and an expert on health, would open their presentation. The Prime Minister immediately cut in to give her own views. These lasted for twenty-five minutes. Delegation eyebrows were discreetly raised. When she had finished, Onslow resumed, politely but firmly, where he had been interrupted: perhaps Dame Jill would begin now? The Prime Minister apologised, explaining that the NHS review was very much in the front of her mind.

In view of her own argumentative disposition, it was fortunate that she appointed a political toughie like Kenneth Clarke to succeed John Moore. However fallible the outcome, he at least stood up to her. John Major, who as Chief Secretary, Chancellor and Prime Minister, was the only person to be involved in all the years of debate about changes in the NHS, has an amusing perspective on how Margaret Thatcher and Kenneth Clarke approached these discussions: they were birds of a feather, in that neither listened to the other. In fact, the new health team – Clarke, David Mellor and Edwina Currie – consisted of people who did not find listening as easy as speaking.

The Prime Minister's personal style had always tended to be fussy. Whitehall iconoclasts privately referred to her as 'Mother'. Guests at Downing Street receptions were often surprised to see her rearranging curtains or opening windows, a task other hostesses at this level might leave to the staff. But as Denis Thatcher once philosophically observed to my wife, Madge: 'She'll not be satisfied until she's got the curtains the way she wants them.'

On the Saturday after the election, when she summoned David Waddington from Lancashire to be appointed Chief Whip, she advised him on where to park his car, apparently fearing the poor man would be bewildered by the Trooping of the Colour ceremony, which was taking place on Horseguards Parade, behind Downing Street, that morning. A man who was to have the onerous task of dragooning recalcitrant Tory MPs through the lobbies might have sorted out his logistics without such high-level assistance. But ministers often noticed that she was far more considerate about their personal and family problems than about the political pitfalls they might face.

Her total mastery of government and party produced a herd-like tendency among Conservatives to look to her for a lead on almost everything. One minister described scathingly how, during a supposedly free vote on televising parliament in 1985, about thirty Tory backbenchers had hung around, watching 'for her to pick up her handbag' and head – as was predictable – for the 'No' lobby. The thirty followed, as he put it, 'like a row of ducklings'.

Three years later, against her wishes, the Commons voted to be televised. By then, Conservative MPs were less willing to take her lead than in the past. That was a sign of the times. Arrival of cameras in the Commons has had many effects, some good, some bad. My own opinion is less that of a broadcaster than a democrat: it seemed simply impossible to deprive the citizens of Britain of a chance to see their elected representatives in action, when it was technically possible for their proceedings to be available in people's homes. How broadcasters and politicians have used that facility is another matter.

MPs derived great amusement from the advice assorted television experts gave them. One minister conjectured that the principal beneficiaries of the system would be osteopaths and hair-weavers, the former because members would get stiff necks from looking up towards the cameras; the latter because bald spots would have to be covered up. He assured me that whips were urging backbenchers to get in the 'doughnut' behind the minister. This meant two PPSs in the second row behind the Great Man or Woman, and four backbenchers in the third row, nodding assent for the benefit of the cameras.

The trivial-minded may care to observe how often, on tele-worthy occasions, a well-groomed woman frontbencher, on instructions, is to be found sitting beside the relevant minister or shadow. Party managers, like newspaper editors, apparently believe that women are still better box-office then men. Margaret Thatcher would have subscribed to that. In the event, televising of the Commons probably helped, rather than damaged her, for she handled the new medium with her usual assiduous competence.

In that 1987 parliament, one minister described her as being 'on a permanent self-confident high'. Another, normally a conformist, startled me by saying she was the only Prime Minister who had 'moonlighted as leader of the opposition': she indulged in semi-public criticism of her ministers. Right until the end, when her future was in doubt, Alan Clark maintained that many ministers were simply scared of her.

Her tendency to argue from first principles became the subject of Cabinet jokes. Ministers blessed their stars that Willie Whitelaw, rather than the Prime Minister, chaired the committee on AIDS. One said that her instincts would have led them straight back to Sodom and Gomorrah, whereas Willie never let discussion stray much beyond the Elephant and Castle – home of the Health Department.

Yet some found her style at once astonishing and endearing. A senior member of the Cabinet arrived at lunch laughing that he had just heard 'the shortest speech ever made in this or any Cabinet'. It was by Tom King, Secretary of State for Northern Ireland, who had introduced a detailed paper about the Belfast shipyard, Harland and Wolff.

He began: 'Prime Minister, you will recall ...' She cut in to say: 'I recall everything about Harland and Wolff ...' and then proceeded to give her own views, before allowing him to say anything more. In the end, I was told that King got most of what he wanted, but it seemed a strange way to conduct serious business. Amusing as my informant found the story, it raised for me in acute form a problem about Margaret Thatcher's attitudes. In my childhood in the thirties, Harland and Wolff had been the largest single shipyard in the world: the Clyde collectively was a more important shipbuilding centre, but on the Queen's Island, we had the biggest firm, and we were proud of that.

In the post-war era Belfast learned painfully that change and decline were inevitable. What worried me was that Margaret Thatcher's certitude about Harland and Wolff's troubles was just a symptom of her indifference to the historic traditions of British manufacturing. The country paid dearly for this, as serious balance of payments deficits reappeared towards the end of the eighties. Once great industrial bastions seemed to have no resonance for her, because they were associated in her mind with two principal bugbears, trade unions and Whitehall's industrial rescues.

In the case of Northern Ireland, there was an added problem. She seemed to have a total lack of feeling for a province that was remote from her own background. Perhaps she experienced a rare sense of guilt that she had conspicuously failed to apply her principal political stock-in-trade, the 'smack of firm government', in a province where it was really needed. Controversies about public ownership or privatisation, fixed or floating exchange rates, or markets within the health service are less important to ordinary citizens than the right to live free from a terrorist threat to life and limb.

Margaret Thatcher had a reputation among ministers for leaving to others problems she thought insoluble. One who worked closely with her on Ulster once told me her principal interest in the province was the safety of English soldiers serving there; 'English', rather than 'British', he said. This was a proper concern, of course, but he added that she found it difficult to take a broader political view of events there. The stalemate which followed the Anglo–Irish Agreement flowed naturally from the Prime Minister's failure to use her boasted political antennae, as she implicitly admits in her memoirs.

At the lunch where I heard of the Tom King incident, my guest also astonished me by saying that if she had not been Prime Minister, she would have been a typical woman Conservative, making the tea at association meetings, sharing their prejudices, with a woman's certainty, and finding it difficult to move from any stance she had taken up. Political prudence prevented him saying anything like that in public (even if, with his High Tory origins, political correctness might have provided no obstacle). This was an enlightening view of Margaret Thatcher from a close observer, even an admirer.

Her approach to politics was described by another uninhibited pre-feminist as 'very womanly'. She had been shocked by an interview she had heard on the radio, in which an Asian woman had described how her children were bullied at school. This apparently did more than acres of Home Office minutes to interest her in racial problems. But she was never keen to take a public role in race relations, and Douglas Hurd used to call on the help of the Prince of Wales for that, and on Princess Anne to visit prisons.

Accounts of her increasingly uninhibited conduct were reaching me from all parts of the Cabinet. John Major, then a comparatively junior member, but a sharp observer of the characters of his elders, was full of praise for the skills of Douglas Hurd, who could express his reservations about policy with wit and charm, and without causing a split – which I took to mean an explosion from the Prime Minister.

But Hurd himself, who had become a reluctant admirer of Margaret Thatcher, saw it somewhat differently. He believed she retained residual suspicions of men such as Kenneth Baker and himself who had been close to Ted Heath. He had noted in Cabinet and at committees that she appeared to have good lateral vision, and would say from time to time: 'I can see from the Home Secretary's expression that he's not happy.' Hurd light-heartedly concluded that he would have to learn to control his features better.

Critics were divided in their own minds about the balance sheet of Margaret Thatcher's merits and defects. There was no doubt about her supremacy. Some worried about what the American Senator J.W. Fulbright once called 'the arrogance of power'. One MP said sardonically that with a majority of 100, she could, if she wished, legislate for the Slaughter of the First-Born ('We could carry that on the pay-roll vote.') I suspect some of her ministers will still be debating on their death-beds whether they ought to have resisted more, or helped her more. Most saw both sides of the account.

Nigel Lawson, even when they were in what proved to be terminal disagreement, saw her as the first British Prime Minister since Churchill to emerge as a star on the international stage. He acknowledged that her gender had helped in this, for Golda Meir and Indira Gandhi had also achieved greater prominence than their male colleagues. Lawson laid his finger on one important truth: because she had been Prime Minister for so long, this inevitably created a different relationship with ministers. By then, only Geoffrey Howe and Peter Walker had received their pro-motion to the Cabinet from anyone but her.

Once I met Nigel Lawson at Lord's, where in a brief respite from his chancellorship he was watching cricket with his young son. I told him that Mrs Thatcher thought it a good idea before holidays to load off on to her ministers' desks as many major government papers as she could. The look Nigel gave me had a touch of St Sebastian about it.

36

GOING ON AND ON AND ON

The tenth anniversary of Margaret Thatcher's arrival in Downing Street was due in May 1989, and she was suffering from the erosion of time. Despite her sensible attempts to give this date as little attention as possible, inevitably it cast a long shadow. Talk about when she would retire, and who might succeed her, began almost as soon as the 1987 election was over. However much politicians may deny it, they think often about career prospects.

The Prime Minister had given me her own forthright views on retirement in an interview on 11 May 1987, the day she announced the general election. Such set-piece interviews at the start of elections are often boring. Party leaders understandably want to launch their campaigns with a strong burst of propaganda. But Margaret Thatcher made some remark which left me an opening to ask, with ostentatious concern for her age, whether this would be her last election (as it would be mine). Oh, no, she assured me, she intended 'to go on and on and on'.

I knew I had a good news story, which would interest politicians as well as general viewers and listeners. There was only one camera in Downing Street that day, shared between BBC and ITN. When that is the case, after the Prime Minister has departed interviewers record what are called 'cutaways'; that is, repeat those questions likely to be used in the edited version. Michael Brunson of ITN listened as I repeated my 'Will this be your last election?' to her now empty chair. He wrinkled his nose. Michael had been unlucky to be first in to bat that day, otherwise he might have been able to induce her to repeat this little gem.

The Prime Minister later regretted using this phrase. She told Kenneth Baker, her party chairman during the leadership crisis, that it led to her being called arrogant. She clearly did not sense this danger at the time, for in the spring of 1988 she developed the theme, telling Brian Walden she intended to continue until a new generation of potential leaders emerged. This caused anguish among the more immediate hopefuls.

In the new parliament, a strong feeling emerged that there was a log-jam in the government. The two senior men, Sir Geoffrey Howe and Nigel Lawson, had been in their posts at the Foreign Office and the Treasury throughout the 1983 parliament, and they were still there. Howe was enjoying his travels and negotiations, and Lawson delighted Tory MPs in 1988 with a major tax-cutting budget.

Yet it was disputes with these two senior ministers which were to destroy Margaret Thatcher's political career, as well as theirs. Geoffrey Howe later accused her of rupturing this once solid troika at the head of her government by testing the relationship to destruction 'in pursuit of an ideological obsession'. Her main preoccupation had always been to stop her government being blown off its ideological course. She believed carelessness about ideology had been Ted Heath's fundamental error. Yet as a Prime Minister who wanted to win elections, she combined ambition to stick to her political theories with caution about losing Conservative votes.

In that third term, her instincts seemed to desert her. She sought, for example, to achieve incompatible objectives in economic policy: she liked a strong pound, both for reasons of prestige and to keep inflation down; yet she was often reluctant to accept rises in interest rates, which her Chancellor thought necessary, but which would be unpopular with mortgage-payers.

These were issues which turned into a running battle with Nigel Lawson, the one figure in her government who was prepared consistently to take her on. By the late eighties, Lawson was in conflict with her over the European Exchange Rate Mechanism (ERM), indeed over the whole ideology of fixed or floating exchange rates. In that context, he was buttressing his economic policy by shadowing the Deutschmark, to her growing annoyance. On inflation and interest rates, they moved around each other in an increasingly frenzied *pas-de-deux*. And then there was the poll tax, on which Lawson had been the only senior minister who carried his long-standing opposition into open debate in Cabinet.

The Chancellor was an instinctive gambler, yet with formidable in-tellectual equipment for the job she had given him. He shared the Thatcherite ideology, but was more prepared to let experience influ-ence the application of ideology. Above all, having done the work, and been exposed to a range of international opinion, he was not pre-pared to bow the knee to what he saw as prejudice.

John Smith once remarked that the Chancellor was 'a clever fellow'.

But he encapsulated the downside of Lawson's character by disclosing why he found him irritating. Lawson tended to say, not that he disagreed with Smith, or even that his opponent was wrong, but that he 'did not understand'. If the Labour man was offended by a sense that he was being patronised, the effect such an attitude must have had on Nigel Lawson's boss may be imagined. Margaret Thatcher can scarcely have been unaware of what he thought, for Lawson has never been either a hypocrite or a good actor. He once convulsed the Cabinet by praising an international finance ministers' meeting: there had been no bank governors or prime ministers present, so everybody had known what they were talking about.

Apart from the Prime Minister herself, Lawson is the decisive figure of the Thatcher years. For me, he was also the most interesting. Like his leader, he had come to the top in politics with a strong ideological commitment. He also had a mission: to be Chancellor of the Exchequer. Kenneth Clarke used to joke: 'Nigel has never really liked politics, but has concluded that they are a necessary, if disagreeable preliminary to becoming Chancellor of the Exchequer.'

But by 1987, Lawson did not intend to stay as Chancellor for another four or five years. He had a young wife, Thérèse, and small children. The job entailed very hard work and long hours, which he felt was unfair to her, since she could not share in the satisfaction that he had from achieving his political objectives. He was one of those rare politicians at the higher level who have windows of sanity about their rights to a personal life.

The Chancellor also felt that his job was not well paid, at least by the standards he might achieve elsewhere. This was unfair both to his wife and their children. There had been much talk, as there often is about Conservative ministers with young families, that Lawson would go off and earn a higher salary in the City, and it was true that he felt a strong need to make more money. It became clear to me, however, that this was not an overwhelming preoccupation. He still felt political ambition, though he once reminded me he had been longer in journalism than in politics, and suspected he would not miss it when he left.

At that time, politicians and journalists usually scoffed at the thought of Nigel Lawson as party leader. My own view was that he ought not to be ruled out of the lists, particularly as the Tory right had no obvious candidate. I had known Nigel Lawson since his days as City editor of the *Sunday Telegraph*, and since there had never been a journalist-Prime Minister – if you exclude Churchill – I had a sneaking hope that his time might come. Politically, he was a gambler, and would have made the commentator's job more interesting.

Occasionally I asked him about this, but the furthest I ever got was a confession that if the entire Cabinet fell down dead – a tragedy which I suspect the phlegmatic Lawson would have borne with more equanimity than most – he was not prepared to say he would push the crown away. But he wasn't exactly doing anything about it, was he? This confirmed observations I had from others: that the Chancellor could not be bothered cultivating a coterie on the back benches, did not suffer fools gladly, and did not display any of the other symptoms of leadership aspiration, like a persistent craving for refreshment in the tearoom, that hotbed of leadership intrigue.

Yet the absence of any plausibly right-wing candidate to succeed Margaret Thatcher kept my doubts alive, and they were aroused again in 1988 when I heard that Nigel Lawson was to be seen more often in the Members' Dining-Room and in the Smoking Room. Surely the gastronomic attractions were not equal to those of his club, the Garrick? The answer seemed to be that Lawson found Westminster more convenient from his house and office; and perhaps that he was beginning to find the company of at least some of his fellow-politicians congenial.

But I came to believe that what now really interested him in politics was the possibility of becoming Foreign Secretary. Colleagues were increasingly impressed by the knowledge the Chancellor showed in his interventions in Cabinet. This was especially true in international affairs, which told them something about his ambitions. Again, he was cautious about this, maintaining that he spoke at Cabinet from his experience in international finance ministers' conferences, without ulterior motive. He and the current Foreign Secretary, Geoffrey Howe, had worked closely together, both when Lawson was a junior minister at the Treasury, and in the Cabinet. They were to collaborate even more closely in the later dispute with Margaret Thatcher over the Exchange Rate Mechanism.

In 1987, Lawson did not know what Howe's personal timetable was, for the simple reason that the Foreign Secretary himself did not know. Most ministers were waiting to see whether Margaret Thatcher would prepare to call it a day in the summer of 1989, after ten years in office. Howe still hoped he might succeed her, and the accepted wisdom of the time was that he had the best chance of doing so. Certainly, until he believed she would stay on too long for him to have a realistic hope of becoming Prime Minister, he was not ready to contemplate the Lord Chancellorship, a post for which many were tipping him.

Lawson's colleagues believed the international contacts he had made as Chancellor would be a valuable start to diplomacy. The more critical thought the Foreign Office unsuited to his personality. 'He lacks the capacity for empty politeness that diplomacy requires,' said one, who had himself mastered that dubious skill. Lawson's PPS, Nigel Forman, one of the shrewdest economic minds on the Tory benches, laughingly described the Foreign Office as an Eventide Home for Retired Chancellors. Others, by contrast, regard it as a waiting-room for Downing Street, citing the careers of such diverse characters as Anthony Eden, Alec Douglas-Home and James Callaghan.

Lawson was not the only man who wanted to be Foreign Secretary. Douglas Hurd had more obvious, long-standing qualifications – ex-diplomat, Ted Heath's political assistant during the European entry negotiations, opposition spokesman on Europe, junior minister at the Foreign Office. At that time, Hurd was so burdened by his workload as Home Secretary that he was not able to take as full a part as he wanted in the political work of the government. He was surprised, and I suspect a bit upset, to hear that I believed Lawson had FO ambitions. Did I *know* that?

On the other hand, unlike most others, Hurd did not dismiss out of hand the thought of the Chancellor as a future Prime Minister. Lawson, he once reflected, had the journalist's quality of quick reaction, without great depth, which was needed for Number 10. As that thought sank in, forty years of my life crumbled into dust.

37

NIGEL TELLS HER SHE'S WRONG

With the new parliament, the Chancellor's tasks had become more testing. A new velocity in his quarrels with the Prime Minister cannot have improved his concentration on the job in hand. But his speech to the first Conservative conference after the election did not conceal his belief that he was every bit as much responsible for victory as she was. The British economy, he believed, was in its best state since the Second World War. Among his critics, the word 'arrogant' had attached itself to Nigel Lawson, but for the moment he was flying high.

The fissure between them eventually engulfed both Prime Minister and Chancellor. Their dispute concerned his wider economic judgements, their ideological differences over exchange rate and monetary policy, and over Europe; and, crucially, whether the pound sterling should be in some fixed relationship with other European currencies, notably the Deutschmark. To make matters worse, as Nigel Lawson wrestled with them, the government as a whole faced a gathering political crisis over the poll tax, a subject on which the Chancellor never wearied of telling the Prime Minister she was mistaken.

Even when stock exchange crashes round the world in October 1987 took the gilt off his economic gingerbread, Lawson was determined to show Tory MPs that if the prosperity that gave them election victory ran into the sands, it would not be his fault. In November, when I talked to him, he was still determined to have a tax-cutting budget in the spring. Before he left the Treasury, he wanted to go into the history books as author of the decisive budget of the later Conservative years. The one he introduced on 15 March 1988 banked more than any before or since on the theory that enterprise would only flourish in a low-tax environment.

When the Prime Minister first heard the scale of the tax cuts he proposed to make, she was nervous. Their wider disagreements began long before the budget, but they developed into a feud in the months following. This, however, was a case of *post hoc* rather than *propter hoc*: she was enthusiastic at the time about most of the measures he announced. He intended the budget to be one of the seminal political events of the decade. Like most budgets, it has been more controversial in retrospect than it was, at least among Conservatives, at the time. The backbenchers who wildly waved their order papers on budget day did not foresee the years of recurring inflation, high interest rates and disastrous trade gaps which were to follow.

Lawson was breaking with tradition by introducing a large tax give-away *after*, rather than *before* an election. This appeared to clash with the cynical advice which that pillar of Irish–American propriety, Joe Kennedy, once gave to his son, Jack, when he was campaigning for the Presidency: 'Don't buy one vote more than's necessary, Jack; I don't want to finance a landslide.' But this budget was not as politically altruistic as might appear. By removing all higher rates of tax except forty per cent, and bringing the standard rate down to Geoffrey Howe's target of 25p, Lawson pleased his own party, but left a long gap before the next election, during which kindly oblivion might obliterate public memory that these tax concessions had gone to an already privileged section of the population.

The budget infuriated Labour, which accused the Chancellor of looking after the Conservatives' better-off supporters, and being careless about both the poor and the broader national interest. The budget speech had to be interrupted by an adjournment of the House, following disturbance among first Scottish Nationalist, and then some Labour members. This was the first time this had happened since Arthur Balfour, as leader of the opposition, graciously asked for an adjournment during Lloyd George's 'People's Budget' in 1909. After the Chancellor had been speaking for the first three hours, Balfour saw he was exhausted.

Nigel Lawson's admirers believed he had put the Conservatives in a good position for the future. Although it might look bad that the tax cuts coincided with effective reductions in some social benefits, the latter had always been planned for after the election, while reduction in higher tax rates was considered politically prudent only in the first year of a parliament. They argued that the Tories would be able to devote the succeeding three budgets to helping the working poor. One MP added, with a touch of cynicism, that the nearer to the next election this help was given, the better.

Behind the scenes, all was not well. Arguments between Chancellor and Prime Minister about the exchange rates had run right up to the day when he was completing his budget speech. He regarded her behaviour as inconsiderate. Their relationship was by now almost beyond repair. Indeed, when Nigel Lawson went to Buckingham Palace for the Chancellor's usual pre-budget audience with the Queen, he told her it would probably be his last, as he was finding Margaret Thatcher impossible to work with. Her Majesty's response is not recorded.

Shortly after the series of spectacular world stock exchange crashes that had culminated on Black Monday, 19 October 1987, the day jitters engulfed the City of London, I had lunch with the Chancellor. He dismissed the fear that they might herald a slump on the scale of that in the thirties. But like other finance ministers, he was sufficiently concerned to loosen monetary policy.

There was a paradox in Nigel Lawson's attitude to markets, and to an extent the Prime Minister shared it. With the benefit of hindsight, even those dedicated to the dogma that 'markets must decide' might have foreseen that after the ending of exchange controls, computerisation of world stock exchanges, and the changing pattern of credit which followed 'Big Bang' in London, markets would behave in a less predictable manner. From the Chancellor's standpoint, often less rationally. A sceptical observer once said of Margaret Thatcher that while she believed in theory that the market must decree what happened, this applied 'only if the market decides what she thinks is right'. Even true believers found it difficult to discern a pattern of rationality.

It has all become even more irrational since then. Good news for the rest of us often seems to be bad news for the markets: as worldwide recession ends, and unemployment falls, institutional investors at once fear that renewed inflation will bring higher interest rates and lower profits, so they drive down the value of both vulnerable currencies and the stock markets. There must be a better way to organise the world's finances.

Nigel Lawson, whose daily work was dominated by market irrationality, described the 1987 crash as 'absurd'. He was understandably reluctant to accept that those who live and swear by the markets must be content to die by them – at least politically speaking. Lawson often inveighed against their refusal to look beyond the end of the week or the ends of their noses. His criticism of 'teenage scribblers' in the City, which he later regretted, did serve to underline his belief that the ideology from which both Chancellor and Prime Minister began was not quite the Laws of the Medes and Persians. He had come to believe that free financial markets needed to be balanced by an agreed system of international cooperation, hence his support for the Plaza and Louvre agreements to manage currencies. Thatcherite critics thought such attempts ran against the whole theory of market economics. Others accepted that this was the only way to avoid a repetition of the thirties.

During that winter of 1987–8, Margaret Thatcher showed increasing tendencies to cling to ideological props. The whole Cabinet, including her, supported the Chancellor's policy after Black Monday, when he brought interest rates down, over a month or two, by 1.5 per cent. Faced by widespread public fear that the world was heading into slump, any Prime Minister would have found this action difficult to resist. But although she did not dissent from his attempt to staunch a loss of confidence among British industrialists, one of her circle pointedly said to me that the reason she liked Alan Walters was because she believed he got his judgements right, and that if he had been available in London, mistakes would not have been made.

That remark was unjust, but it reflected the deeper quarrel between Margaret Thatcher and Nigel Lawson. He had the reputation of being the arch-priest of monetarism in Britain – some said even before Margaret Thatcher, Keith Joseph, or Geoffrey Howe. Now critics were calling him a monetary agnostic. Ideology again clouded that judgement. The truth was that Lawson had leaned far enough out of the ivory tower to discover that, in the real world, and when the unexpected happens, a responsible Chancellor cannot allow preconceived theory to dominate his handling of events. He may still go wrong, but in face of economic turbulence it is unforgivable simply to sit in an ideological bunker.

It was just such obduracy, after all, that had allowed the slump in the thirties, and curdled the economic and social history of Britain for a generation. Practical experience had educated Nigel Lawson beyond theorising, and made him an increasingly complex political economist. When, a year after Black Monday, he and I lunched together again, I commented on the widespread anxiety about what Geoffrey Howe was calling 'inflation revisited'. The Chancellor reminded me, not unreasonably, that in late 1987, like many others, I had been worried about recession. There wasn't going to be one. (As it turned out, there was, but much later than anybody expected, after an unsustainable boom.)

The balloon went up during the summer parliamentary recess of 1988. Britain's trade gap opened alarmingly. I learned that the Cabinet had been warned about this in the spring, under heavier than usual vows of secrecy. They had also been warned that inflation would go up to 5.5 per cent, showing yet again the limited value of Treasury forecasts. Douglas Hurd, whose close interest in economic policy as it affects

politics has always belied his reputation as a holy innocent, concluded
that provided inflation came down again, all would be well politically.
But if mortgages stayed high for too long, and if inflation got worse, the
government would suffer. Inflation was to rise to eleven per cent in
1990.

One factor in this trouble was a credit explosion in the deregulated
money markets, with floods of imports, followed by revived inflation,
and by the need for higher interest rates. Mortgage-holders – with whom
Margaret Thatcher believed she had a symbiotic relationship because of
her policy of selling council houses at cheap rates – began to complain
that higher mortgage payments were wiping out their gains from income
tax reductions.

Another factor was wages. Unemployment under Margaret Thatcher
was now higher than any previous post-war Prime Minister had thought
conceivable. Yet there was renewed anxiety that excessive pay increases
would fuel inflation. Those who thought Britain's deep-seated economic
malaise had been cured by a combination of recession, high unemployment, trade union laws, privatisation, and Whitehall's policy of strict
non-intervention in industry were seeing their illusions shattered. Or
ought to have seen this.

I have little doubt that in the summer of 1988 the Prime Minister was
tempted to move her increasingly independent Chancellor's hands away
from the economic levers. Some Tory MPs pondered how the deteriorating economy fitted in with the Thatcher/Lawson disagreements
over exchange rates, interest rates and managed currencies. But the
messages sent from the backbench 1922 Committee were unequivocal.
Both directly and through the Chief Whip they gave their opinion that
Nigel Lawson had been the architect of the 1987 election victory just as
much as herself, his 1988 budget was a brilliant success, and whatever
their disagreements about economic theory, she was to leave him where
he was. It is a measure of growing doubts about her man-management
that a similar message came from the grandees about Geoffrey Howe,
whose disputes with the Prime Minister were also growing more acri-
monious.

The opposition was delighted that the Tories were now suffering from
the divisions which had done both Labour and the Alliance/Liberal
Democrats so much damage in the recent past. A Labour MP said to a
Conservative acquaintance, in mock earnestness: 'Have you heard about
the Monopoly Commission's ruling? Apparently our monopoly of rows
and splits was illegal. You're allowed to have them now too.' Nobody
could have guessed how deep and long-lasting those divisions would

prove. Though as the quarrel over Europe has continued, I have often thought of Chris Patten's comparison with the damage the nineteenth-century Conservative Party inflicted on itself over the Corn Laws.

38

A BLIP OR A CRISIS?

Before the clouds piled up in the second half of 1988, Nigel Lawson's popularity with Margaret Thatcher's MPs was one reason she did not confront him earlier over an economic policy about which she has been bitterly critical since they both left office. In my last conversation with her, just a fortnight before she was removed from Number 10, she made clear how bitterly she regretted the inflation then afflicting her government and the nation. 'Never again,' she said grimly. She did not have the opportunity to prove that determination.

Although she accuses Lawson of ruining her government's reputation by allowing overheating in 1988 and subsequently, he in turn claims that she was sometimes reluctant to raise interest rates when he thought this necessary. However often the Chancellor recited his rubric about interest rates — that they would remain 'as high as it takes for as long as it takes' — what Denis Healey used to call sado-monetarists regarded him as a Micawber, running the economy in a rosy glow of false optimism. Nigel Lawson did think the worst would be over in eighteen months. Between boom and bust, it took much longer than that.

Mortgages were at the heart of one disagreement between Prime Minister and Chancellor in which, for a change, he was the ideologue and she the pragmatist. He would have liked to be rid of mortgage tax relief, in order to reduce tax rates further; she would have none of this, regarding mortgage-holders as 'our people'. Her need for votes from the new home-owners apparently overcame any ideological, Reaganesque prejudice against 'tax breaks'.

In those years of 1987–8, when the supposed economic miracle turned sour, the field in which I believe ideology most gravely blinded the government to a dangerous reality was the labour market. One of the weaknesses of Whitehall advice to ministers is that the Treasury has never understood how wage-bargaining works, only how it ought to work in an ideal (i.e. deregulated) world. To some mandarins, it seems, trade unions are still conspiracies to restrain trade, as they were to the judge who transported the Tolpuddle Martyrs.

Whitehall regarded labour relations as below the salt, fit only to be considered by lesser breeds at the old Ministry of Labour. Since that department, in its new guise as the Department of Employment, has also embraced Thatcherite ideology, and so distanced itself from the collective bargaining process, governments have had as little warning of risky movements in wages as of an earthquake. As inflation began to creep up, first Nigel Lawson and then the Prime Minister resorted to variations of the futile process known in America as 'jaw-boning' – trying to *talk down* the level of pay settlements. The Thatcher governments always had an ambiguous attitude to wages. They acknowledged government has a role, as employer, in the public sector, but appeared not to realise that publicly and privately employed people cannot be insulated, for the obvious reason that they compare their pay increases in the pub or at the clothes-line.

Unfortunately, the one man in the Cabinet who understood this did not have great clout at Number 10. Peter Walker, in his Welsh fastness, had long memories, dating from the Heath government, about pay problems. He observed at this time that private employers, enjoying good profits in a booming market, had no incentive to risk a strike and loss of business by standing firm. Of course, unions had not pushed wage claims during the recession of the early eighties, especially when employers were threatening redundancies. Now, with labour shortages re-emerging, he noticed that unions were becoming more assertive again.

Such thinking was anathema to true Thatcherites, who were so hooked on 'money supply' that they would have liked Lawson to prepare to take another penny off income tax in 1989. And if his economic problems got worse? Why, simply tighten the money supply. So far as wages were concerned, the same applied. These ideologues regarded even Lawson's and Thatcher's jaw-boning as otiose. If the Chancellor would simply turn off the sterling tap, employers and unions would see profits and jobs drying up, and soon get the message. Sadly observing this certitude, I recalled the comment of our most pragmatic Prime Minister, Melbourne: 'I wish I was as cocksure of anything as Tom Macaulay is of everything.'

By November, Nicholas Ridley was still arguing that Lawson had put too much emphasis on wages, instead of on money supply. But Margaret Thatcher's ideological soul-mate was by now deeply disaffected about the way economic policy was being conducted. He told me gloomily that if he had a Victoria Cross to award for his government's economic success, it would go to Geoffrey Howe rather than Nigel Lawson.

During the later years of Margaret Thatcher's period in office, she was in triumphalist mood so far as the trade unions were concerned. Especially after the defeat of the miners' strike, British unions were in the doldrums. The prediction many years before by their General Secretary, George Woodcock, had been fulfilled: if they would not reform themselves, government would do it for them. Yet Whitehall had not so much reformed the unions as submerged them. They were still a significant factor in the economy, except that ministers refused to acknowledge this.

This ideological blindness left the British government at odds with almost all other Conservative parties in Europe, as well as with more enlightened employers in Britain. Ministers have discovered to their horror that Europe still believes in tripartism – cooperation between the social partners (industry and the unions) and the government. By contrast, Margaret Thatcher condemned the long-standing German system of *Mitbestimmung*, including worker-directors, as 'Marxist thinking'. A traditional Tory, contemplating events since her Bruges speech in 1988, said: 'This government believes its own propaganda about Britain's success. We're in danger of finishing up as a rainswept island off the coast of Europe.'

It was not just Social Chapter ideas which became unpopular under late Thatcherism. One of her earlier Downing Street advisers, Sir John Hoskyns, later of the Institute of Directors, described collective bargaining itself as a complete anachronism, and hoped that companies were moving away from it. Much later, Kenneth Clarke, in his Mais lecture in 1994, was 'delighted to say that the latest data show that the proportion of employees covered by collective bargaining has fallen by a third'. This, from one of the most sensible and pragmatic ministers to serve in the governments of the eighties and nineties, seemed to me like ideology gone mad.

The opposite point of view on the labour market needs to be underlined, for it became unfashionable during the eighties. In principle, governments in a free and plural society ought not to expect to be all-powerful, or even all-knowing. If they fail to recognise that trade unions are one of the bulwarks of people's rights, they fly in the face of, among other things, this century's experience in the communist countries, where workers had no bodies to protect them, and suffered accordingly.

But in practical terms, ministers faced a more immediate danger. In the words of Walter Pater, they were 'rebels against the fact', trying to pretend that trade unions and collective bargaining did not exist, because they *wished* that this were so. Every time the economy recovered from recession, they were offered proof of the folly of such attitudes. But their own ideological commitment to deregulation blinded them to the facts.

When there could no longer be any doubt that overheating had occurred, and rising inflation was firmly established again, Willie White-law spoke to the Chancellor. He had originally been very suspicious of Nigel Lawson, but this earlier distaste had now turned into admiration. Whitelaw warned him not to pursue his intention to leave the Treasury – whether for the Foreign Office or to repair his family finances in the City – before both inflation and the burgeoning trade deficit had come down again. If he did quit before that, he would be saddled with the same reputation as Ted Heath's Chancellor, Anthony Barber, who had seen his boom followed by bust. It would look worse, a Conservative enemy said, if Lawson's departure took him to 'a mink-lined bolthole in a bank'.

The Chancellor himself remained confident that the economy would recover from what he notoriously described as 'a blip', and that all would come right again, allowing him to leave the Treasury with honour, probably in the autumn of 1989. This date for his departure proved to be right, but the circumstances were not at all what he had envisaged.

Deteriorating relations between Prime Minister and Chancellor derived as much from personal chemistry as from ideology. He was a strong-minded minister, expert in his own subject, who was not prepared to accept the kind of personal treatment from her which others had grown used to. Critics called her behaviour demagogic, but most members of the Cabinet felt they must just let it wash over them. One minister said to me, in admiration rather than censure, that 'only the bastards, Heseltine and Lawson', stood up to Margaret Thatcher.

Lawson certainly did. With drawn breath, other ministers would tell me stories of the encounters between these two supremely self-possessed human beings. I am still uncertain whether to believe as literal truth one which reached me indirectly: of how, towards the end of Keith Joseph's period in government, she once constantly interrupted her ageing mentor, to everyone's embarrassment, until Lawson could bear it no longer, and demanded that she be quiet, which she did, for several minutes.

Having the Prime Minister and Chancellor living in adjoining houses, and with a connecting door, means that even close colleagues do not know how often they see each other. One of Lawson's ministers adopted an old Whitehall joke: that there might be a swing door between the two houses, but it didn't often swing. Enough of the relationship was visible for other ministers to recognise the strains. These sometimes showed in Cabinet. One told me that Lawson, like the rest of them, hated to be interrupted by the Prime Minister; but unlike most of them, he did something about it: he kept on talking, if necessary allowing a duet to develop. He said in admiration: 'Nigel has excellent volume control.'

Everybody acknowledged that he was competent at the technical aspects of his job. He would work in Number 11, his official residence, rather than at the Treasury, so that he could concentrate. This was the job for which his whole life had been preparing him, and he was determined to be very much his own man. There lay the problem. Margaret Thatcher would have liked a hands-on version of her honorific, First Lord of the Treasury. Colleagues close to both believed she recognised his competence, but they concluded that, 'because neither Nigel nor Margaret is a warm person', they could not come close to each other.

Lawson was quite capable of examining his own character. He once said to me: 'I am a very self-contained person', which I think is true. About this time, he adumbrated a constitutional doctrine for relations between Prime Minister and senior colleagues: that they exercise a mutual veto on each other's actions. That also is valid – until the moment of parting. He and Thatcher, though holding many common beliefs, were ultimately chalk and cheese. Lawson is a fully paid-up intellectual, who wrestles ideas into submission. Margaret Thatcher is more like a barrister, who niggles away at chinks in his argument, with an instinctive politician's zeal. It was bound to end in tears.

At the top of Thatcher's political charge-sheet against Lawson is that, through errors in his policies, he threw away her government's successes against inflation. Here, domestic and European politics connect, for so far as she was concerned the villain of the piece was his decision to shadow the Deutschmark. She maintained that failure to let the pound float was to blame for injection of much inflation into the economy. This was what her ideology taught, even if many others thought the analysis simplistic. In her memoirs, she notes that by 1990 the rise in prices was approaching ten per cent. Then she adds a sentence of a malevolence that measures the gulf between her and a man who had, after all, once been among her closest colleagues: 'But by 1990, Mr 10 per cent had departed, and others were left to deal with the consequences.'

★   ★   ★

The quarrel between Margaret Thatcher and Nigel Lawson over fixed and floating exchange rates, and particularly their running battle about British entry into the European Exchange Rate Mechanism, can appear so recondite that readers may scarcely believe it generated such venom. I can sympathise with anyone who finds this subject difficult and does not want to pursue it, but the argument is so fundamental to the final years of Margaret Thatcher's government, and to her removal from office, that it is not to be avoided. I say this with personal feeling, because of an experience which revolutionised my own attitude to how I did my job as political editor of the BBC. It probably turned me into what my sons would call a more 'stroppy' colleague.

Usually on a Thursday, I tried to spend the half-hour before Prime Minister's questions in the Members' Lobby, gauging the mood of MPs. This meant missing whichever team of departmental ministers was on duty at question time. One of the frustrations of a political journalist's life is that he cannot be in two places at once (though that is not unique to our trade). On 10 March 1988, I had read an article in the *Financial Times* by Samuel Brittan, an old friend of the Chancellor. His discussion of exchange rate policy alerted me to the seriousness of disagreements about Lawson's attempt to keep the pound below 3 Deutschmarks. Over the previous weekend, after hectic meetings between Thatcher and Lawson, it had been allowed to rise to 3.05 Deutschmarks on the Monday, but the Chancellor felt if it went much higher his policy would be undermined.

So I made sure to be present for Treasury questions, which came before those for the Prime Minister. As is customary, she did not attend. In the course of his answers, Nigel Lawson said that any further appreciation of the pound against the Deutschmark was 'unlikely to be sustainable'. A few minutes later Mrs Thatcher entered. In replying to Neil Kinnock, she took a markedly different line, finally asserting: 'There is no way in which one can buck the market.' In other words, shadowing the Deutschmark was a mistaken policy.

I learned soon afterwards that Margaret Thatcher regretted putting this so brusquely. Single-minded politician that she was, her target was the man across the despatch boxes from her, Neil Kinnock, rather than Nigel Lawson. But the words were on the record. Just five days before the Chancellor's budget, this struck me as a startling difference of emphasis between the two. I thought I had persuaded the *Nine O'Clock News* of the importance of the story, and went to the Television Centre to prepare the report. But as the evening wore on, the editor's and producer's enthusiasm for the subject steadily eroded.

Let me confess that at this time my own grasp of the technicalities was more tenuous than later events made it. Worse, television graphics were then in their infancy, so far as Westminster correspondents were concerned, and I had no skill in suggesting how such a subject might be reduced to comprehensible visual terms. The man in charge tried to persuade me to switch my attention to an inconsequential development in Ulster politics. At first I resisted, but when he eventually said the Lawson/Thatcher affair was not going to get on air, I weak-mindedly agreed to do the other story.

Oddly, the daily newspapers made less of the Commons exchanges than I had expected. It was not until Sunday that the gravity of the disagreement between the Prime Minister and her Chancellor was spelled out. While I was having breakfast on Monday, the editor in charge of the lunchtime news telephoned to ask whether I would be available to discuss on his programme 'this interesting *Sunday Times* story'. At some damage to my blood pressure, I explained that it *could* have been on the previous Thursday's *Nine O'Clock News*. But I went in, and from then on the story of the Thatcher/Lawson row increasingly dominated the political and economic news agenda.

The incident made me much more aggressive in backing my own judgement about what had to be covered on the news, and occasionally in making myself obnoxious when I did not get my way. I hope it also made me better at explaining to colleagues why some events which appeared boring or abstruse were actually of great importance. I expect we all learned lessons.

The turbulence did not end in March 1988. Month after month, Prime Minister and Chancellor were still at odds, and the opposition was exploiting their differences. On 12 May Neil Kinnock pressed her to say she agreed with Lawson's opposition to a further rise in sterling. She conspicuously failed to do so. Both Westminster and the markets grew turbulent. A Thatcherite MP told me that 'a Grantham upbringing does not encourage the conventional hypocrisy of pretending unanimity where it does not exist.'

It was obvious, however, that the Labour leader would return to the attack the following week. So on Monday 16 May Lawson did go through the swing door to Number 10, to agree a formula which she would use the next day. This acknowledged that the government used both interest rates and intervention to manage the currency. It was further than Margaret Thatcher's ideology told her she ought to go, but the whips told her something more compelling: the message they were getting was that Nigel Lawson must not be forced into resignation, because they could not afford to lose him. It was a message she accepted, but bitterly resented.

Both Margaret Thatcher and Nigel Lawson have written on this subject at great length. With inevitable over-simplification, I shall attempt to summarise their disagreement. This was a debate between what the Chancellor subsequently – and pejoratively – called 'simon pure monetarists' (Thatcher and her adviser, Sir Alan Walters) and an 'exchange rate monetarist', which is what he says experience had turned him into. It is no accident that the occasion of Lawson's resignation was his demand that the Prime Minister should get rid of Walters. He maintained that publication of Sir Alan's academic writings was confusing the markets. Walters was key to the disagreement. He and Lawson appear to me to have been two clever and gifted men, guided by ideology, yet arguing over matters which required the day-by-day practical judgement that only a Chancellor in touch with all the instruments of economic policy had any hope of commanding.

Lawson, while describing himself as one who believed in 'monetarism at one remove' – i.e. through the exchange rate – claims to have adopted a severely practical criterion: which form of monetarism was the least difficult to operate successfully? The story of the early years of the Thatcher governments was of a constant battle to find an index of monetary targets that remained reliable once policy-makers started to use it. Ministers were in danger of running through all the 'Ms' in the motorway network before they found one that led anywhere.

Margaret Thatcher still maintains it is impossible to hold down inflation except by monetary methods. You can either control the money supply through interest rates, or you can have a target for the international value of the pound. But you cannot do both. In their memoirs, each blames the other for reductions in interest rates, which they subsequently accepted had added to inflation.

What made the Prime Minister's relations with both Lawson and Geoffrey Howe so difficult was her ambivalence over the European Exchange Rate Mechanism. She had agreed to the formula that Britain would join 'when the time is right' (or 'ripe': there has been endless debate about which is the original, another piece of mind-boggling semantics). Lawson maintains it was illogical for her to accept this phrase, while simultaneously relying on the advice of a man who thought 'the ERM was the work of the devil', and that Britain should *never* join. Margaret Thatcher herself admits she only accepted even the principle, in 1980, in order to gain the support of the German Chancellor, Helmut Schmidt, in her European budget negotiations.

Constitutional purists within the government complained that the debate about the timing of entry was never properly engaged within the Cabinet itself. It rumbled on, either in carefully selected meetings of ministers, or in bilaterals between Thatcher and Lawson, from 1985 until Lawson's resignation in 1989, and beyond; though by then, John Major and Douglas Hurd were in stronger positions to persuade her to join. For by then also Alan Walters had gone, and her own position within her Cabinet had been weakened by Lawson's resignation, as well as by the 'stalking-horse' challenge to her leadership in November 1989.

As far as Margaret Thatcher, Nigel Lawson and Geoffrey Howe were concerned, this was a debate which gradually poisoned human relations, because none of the three strong characters involved was prepared to give ground. What frustrated Lawson was that he knew in the end she would have to agree to entry. He began to make jokes about a subject which had become political dynamite. At one public meeting, he told a questioner that Britain would join the ERM 'when the time is ripe . . . but that is a matter for the government as a whole, not just for me'. It was a little private joke for his audience of economists. They laughed, and so did the Chancellor. Nigel Lawson was no longer even pretending he and the Prime Minister were in accord. The Thatcher government's internal coherence was breaking down.

39

THE POLL TAX'S ONLY FRIEND

It is not often that you find the key to a tragedy in the indexes of books. But an entry in the index to Nigel Lawson's memoirs subtly reminds readers of how bitter and insoluble disputes which become encrusted with ideology can be. 'Community Charge, *see* Poll Tax', it reads. By contrast, Margaret Thatcher and Kenneth Baker, two of its progenitors, both settle in their books for 'Poll Tax, *see* Community Charge'. Behind the rival orderings of those five words lie years of controversy, as Margaret Thatcher fought for a long-cherished plan to change the basis of local government finance.

What's in a name? In this case, a great deal. The government wanted to convince the public that it was replacing domestic rates with a more just system, under which everybody would pay something towards local services. The Prime Minister was determined this would not be saddled with a title which for centuries has aroused radical ire. Hers was to be a tax on people, rather than on property. Not, however, a local income tax, based on 'ability to pay' – though that was a phrase used in her original pledge in 1974. Conservatives were busily reducing *national* income tax, and did not want to create a new one locally. So they finished up, after much anguish, with a flat rate payment by everyone aged over eighteen, with ever more complex rebates for the needy.

In fact, a poll tax. Ministers' efforts to prevent this name being used in place of the official 'Community Charge' were doomed from the start. Margaret Thatcher might fume and drum her fingers if any minister slipped into the vernacular (though she had been known to stray herself). BBC editors might issue memoranda reminding us of our duty. But anybody who had ever written a headline for a newspaper realised that the briefer title was irresistible. Conservative tabloids adopted it for typographical convenience, as readily as they used 'bid', 'probe' or 'shock'. They used it as often as the most left-wing 'can't pay, won't pay' campaigner. Monosyllabism rules, OK? 'Community Charge' survived principally in official documents.

The dispute over name was only a symptom of her indomitable, stubborn will, after a third election victory, to have her own way on any subject to which she put her mind. Of course, the poll tax was not the sole cause of Mrs Thatcher's demise, but the electoral disaster with which it threatened the Conservative Party lethally undermined her leadership. Backbench MPs, increasingly fearful of losing their seats, knew that while she remained Prime Minister they would not get rid of a tax which was infuriating their own supporters. So when repeated tinkering failed to take the sting out of the poll tax, her fate was sealed.

One of the shrewdest of her backbenchers, who was appalled at his postbag, and suspected that people who had not voted Labour since 1979 were deserting the Conservatives in droves, first alerted me to the seriousness of the Prime Minister's own position. This was fully six months before her fall. He said the officers of the backbench 1922 Committee – the famous 'men in grey suits' – were now taking an effective role in discussions about the tax, and if they found she was not responding, they might move on the leadership.

In the event, this was not the manner in which the end came. The same MP said, with a smile, that 'Michael Heseltine is very available just now.' It was from Heseltine that a direct challenge was to come. The occasion was Geoffrey Howe's explosive resignation statement, and the cause of that was Europe, rather than poll tax. But it was the poll tax which left the Prime Minister vulnerable to the Heseltine challenge.

This remarkable political drama had two stage-sets, which sometimes seemed poorly coordinated. One was the Cabinet, in which, until a very late stage, most of my conversations showed there was much complacency, or misdirected loyalty: 'the worst is over'; 'it was a one-year unpopularity phenomenon'; 'the anger will fade'. And so on. The Prime Minister's political longevity had created a problem for her: she had almost run out of ministers who were prepared to be openly critical, even when she would have benefited from a restraining hand. The political skeletons of those who had taken on this strong-willed woman stretched all the way back to 1979. Willie Whitelaw, now retired, would ask gloomily whether any minister was arguing with her across the whole field of government.

The second scene was the Tory back benches. They reflected much more accurately feelings in the country, where Conservative constituencies were erupting in fury. Indeed, the further I went from the centre of Whitehall power, the more realistic predictions of trouble turned out to be. The Prime Minister's efforts to bridge the gap in perception between the two were ineffectual. In February 1990, just before the poll tax was due to take effect, a junior minister described to me an expedition she made into the House of Commons tearoom – a sure sign that the chief knows the tribe is restless. The description given to me of this visit was that 'Margaret was on transmit, no receive'. This was not what was needed.

The history of the poll tax went back thirteen years, to when Mrs Thatcher, then Environment spokesman in Edward Heath's shadow Cabinet, promised to replace domestic rates by 'taxes related to people's ability to pay'. In the storm of mutual recrimination which followed her defeat, Margaret Thatcher has blamed Ted Heath for insisting on such a pledge, without having worked out what came next; blamed Michael Heseltine for failing to find a new tax when he was Environment Secretary in the early eighties, and for making the system fiendishly complex; and blamed her successive Scottish Secretaries, George Younger and Malcolm Rifkind, for failing to warn her of coming storms in Scotland, where a different law first turned local government financing into a political crisis.

In return, others blame the disaster on what her last Environment Secretary, Chris Patten, used to call her 'unbending and exotic will'. 'Loony left councils' had become her obsession. She did not find unco-operative Conservative ones much better. During her eleven years in office, she put six different men in charge of the Environment Department, and she never ceased to harry them for a solution. In the end, she was given what they thought she wanted, rather than what would serve her best. So she fell victim to her own determination to dominate her government.

The poll tax is an illustration of both Margaret Thatcher's strengths and her weaknesses: a politician who never wearied in trying to solve problems; but one who could not recognise when the time had come to draw stumps. Nobody could doubt there was a problem. Over the years, central government had taken over financial responsibility for so much local council activity that the link between taxation and representation had been weakened. Voter-ratepayers did not know who to blame for either inadequate public services or excessive rate burdens.

Faced with such an unsatisfactory system, which excited her intellect as much as her passions, Margaret Thatcher was not the kind of woman to accept that no solution could be found. Traditional Tories might think, with Disraeli, that they would be wiser to concentrate on lofty objectives like 'the elevation of the condition of the people'. She was a radical. When she forced the poll tax into the 1987 election manifesto, Douglas Hurd, then Home Secretary, at once recognised the political dangers. Later, in the 1990 leadership contest, Hurd was sometimes to be portrayed as a lofty international statesman, unsuited to the muck and brass of domestic politics, innocent of its day-by-day hazards. But in fact, since his time as Ted Heath's right-hand man at Downing Street, he has always kept a careful finger on the political pulse at home.

Hurd saw this proposal's inclusion in the election programme as an unusual combination of prime ministerial commitment and pressure from Scottish Conservatives. He was afraid that the Scottish tail was wagging the English dog. Tories north of the border were facing an imminent – and legally obligatory – revaluation, which they maintained would cause them grave political damage if some reform of the rating system was not introduced. So it was they who most urgently pressed the government for action. As a result, Scotland was given the poll tax first. Scottish Tories paid a heavy price for importuning the government.

Margaret Thatcher could not complain she had no warning of the dangers. Her most formidable critic on this subject also was Nigel Lawson. The Treasury has traditionally been suspicious of the Environment Department, which requires huge sums of money for local government, and yet always has the convenient excuse that it cannot control what councils do. (This is called democracy, and to many Whitehall mandarins is an exotic plant.) But Lawson was a politician as well as a Treasury man, and as early as 1985 he opposed the poll tax, instead advocating a radical reform of the rating system. Even then, in his Cabinet memorandum, he called it 'poll tax': a sign of the increasingly unhappy relationship between him and the Prime Minister. The Chancellor argued that it would be 'completely unworkable and politically catastrophic'.

After her first two Environment Secretaries, Michael Heseltine (1979– June 1983) and Tom King (June–October 1983), had failed to give her a solution, the Prime Minister pressed for action from Patrick Jenkin (October 1983–September 1985). But it was his juniors, Kenneth Baker and William Waldegrave, who were given the detailed task of constructing a proposal. Lord Rothschild, Waldegrave's old boss at the Downing Street Think Tank, is credited – or blamed – for the idea, but it was the two ministers who worked on it for the Cabinet.

Later, as storm-clouds began to gather round the poll tax, a veteran Whitehall insider gave me a highly critical version of what he believed to have happened. Kenneth Baker, he said, had come to the conclusion that the Prime Minister was determined to have something, so decided he might as well have the credit for giving it to her. Baker gained a reputation in government for taking action in a department (Information Technology, Environment, later Education), and then moving on quickly, leaving somebody else to clear up residual problems. It is ironic, in view of this widely expressed criticism, that when Margaret Thatcher was finally sunk, it was he who chose to go down with the ship. His brief period as Home Secretary under John Major was no more than a swansong.

My informant was not so charitable. He maintained that Baker, Waldegrave, and a group of clever advisers enjoyed each other's company, as they worked up the poll tax proposal. Sometimes they would toil far into the night, sometimes play bridge. There was a woman from the Treasury who was an exceptional bridge player. He presented a picture of a group so dazzled by their own ingenuity, even brilliance, that they were blind to the practical and political consequences of what they proposed.

This informant explained one of Nigel Lawson's anxieties: that to anyone contemplating purchase of a larger house, the poll tax would remove the disincentive of a higher rate bill. This would set off a house-price explosion, and so fuel inflation. It was an irony that Lawson himself, by an ill-advised decision to remove multiple mortgage tax relief on a date announced several months in advance, contributed to just such an explosion. 'Social engineering', an age-old charge by Conservatives against their political opponents, can take many forms.

Kenneth Baker maintained then and subsequently that the poll tax proposals he left behind, when he moved from Environment to Education in May 1986, were fatally damaged by the dropping of a safeguard called 'dual running'. He had intended to phase in the poll tax and phase out the rates over periods up to ten years. But the 1987 Conservative conference took an emotional decision against dual running, and called for immediate action. Baker wrote tartly in his memoirs that this conference 'had the illusion that the community charge was so perfect that the nation was thirsting to take it down in one gulp'.

Yet Conservative backbench dissent about the tax began almost as soon as the 1987 parliament assembled. The party's manifesto had clearly foreshadowed what was intended, so Margaret Thatcher was characteristically scornful of such jitters. But she now had about sixty MPs on the Conservative benches who had come from local government. They detected endless dangers: the tax would be difficult, almost impossible, to collect; there was manifest unfairness in presenting similar bills to the duke and the dustman; the voters who were losers would waken up to their misfortune uncomfortably close to the next general election, while the gainers would barely say thank you. Would it not be better to transfer education spending to the Exchequer; or reform the rates; or do something, almost anything, different?

To Margaret Thatcher, retreat was impossible. This was the measure which she had designated the flagship of her legislative programme in this third, more radical term of her government. The painful search for a means to fulfil her pledge on local government finance had run through her years in office like a grumbling appendix.

The new parliament was dominated by poll tax. Neil Kinnock attacked the measure effectively in the Queen's Speech debate in 1987. Michael Heseltine, with the authority of a former Environment Secretary, gave her latest holder of that post, Nicholas Ridley, a roasting at a Conservative backbench meeting, and also did a brilliant critique on the bill's second reading. After two cautious years on the back benches, this was his most significant and open break with the Prime Minister.

Privately, Heseltine was astonished that Margaret Thatcher and Nick Ridley were pushing ahead with the bill, even though they had a mandate for it. As her leading rival, he paid close attention to the detail of what she was doing, for he foresaw a political crisis, and an opportunity. He believed she was wandering into a wilderness of limitless trouble. I concluded that the Red Sea would need to part before Ridley could bring the government out unscathed.

Heseltine was privately critical of the Labour party for having failed to get its act together. But the opposition was having its own troubled debate on a dilemma to which no politician has found a convincing answer. John Smith, as shadow Chancellor, and Jack Cunningham, Bryan Gould and David Blunkett, successive Environment spokesmen, canvassed the respective merits of local income tax, reformed rates, or a hybrid system. One version of this last category caused Kenneth Baker, the most assiduous news editor-manqué of politics since Harold Wilson, to salivate over headlines that would read: 'Thatcher slates roof tax'. But the Prime Minister had her own troubles to keep her occupied.

Labour was vulnerable to government attacks on MPs and councillors, especially in Scotland, for refusing to pay the poll tax. In the shadow Cabinet itself, Donald Dewar, the Scottish Affairs spokesman, criticised Robin Cook for threatening to do this, and Cook had to promise he would not repeat the offence. The opposition's difficulties blunted its attacks on the government, but Conservative MPs were doing its work well enough. At turbulent meetings of backbenchers, the bill had more critics than friends. If the second reading was difficult, the committee stage threatened to be a nightmare.

I had no hesitation in predicting in broadcasts that this was a controversy which would have a long shelf-life, and that the scheme would have to be amended. I was wrong in forecasting that since this reform was a personal commitment made by the Prime Minister long ago, 'the Tories now have little choice but to sink or swim with Maggie'. Her total dominance for a decade had deceived me into forgetting an important law of politics: that nothing is for ever, and that the Conservative Party's treatment of its leaders is based ultimately on a policy of payment by results.

By the time of the parliamentary battles of 1988, any residual illusion that the poll tax represented a remedy for which the nation was waiting had evaporated. I asked my critical Whitehall insider what the balance of forces within the Cabinet was. He replied with a laugh that he was tempted to say it was 'one against the rest, but the one prevailed – as usual'.

This was unfair to the Prime Minister. In fact the only really solid opposition had come from the Treasury, led by Nigel Lawson. John Major, both as Chief Secretary, and later as Chancellor, tried to warn her of the political dangers, but by then the die was cast. She did seek, by agreeing to ever more elaborate amendment of the system, to extract the political poison. The ultimate conclusion must be that the poll tax was irredeemable.

In July 1989, with the row rumbling on, Margaret Thatcher gave Chris Patten his long-merited promotion to the Cabinet. He became Environment Secretary, with responsibility both for the poll tax and for green issues. The Conservatives' disastrous results in the European elections that May had been accompanied by remarkably strong support for the Green party. I attended a garden party in 1989 at Ian and Caroline Gilmour's house in Isleworth, at which wives of Conservative MPs confessed freely that their children were going to 'vote Green' – which they clearly saw as a shocking admission, even at a heterodox political gathering.

Although they presented this as their offsprings' principled support for a cause both of conscience and of fashion, in fact the Greens were the beneficiaries of a protest vote against the poll tax and the government generally. This happened to be a year when the Liberal Democrats were distracted by a mid-life crisis, so the Greens were the natural, if temporary repository for protest. This accidental event gave unusual emphasis to Chris Patten's 'green brief'.

By February 1990, Patten had concluded that his new job would be a fine one if he could concentrate on the green issues, which interested him greatly, and had not inherited the poll tax. He foresaw that its introduction in England and Wales in April would have a bad effect on Tory fortunes in local elections the following month. His pessimism was justified. Even though Kenneth Baker, as party chairman, succeeded in veiling many bad results by concentrating media attention on dubiously achieved successes in Westminster and Wandsworth, Conservatives were swept from control in large parts of England.

But Baker's public relations success had a perverse effect on Patten's 1990 negotiations with John Major and Norman Lamont at the Treasury. Already in 1989 he had endured a hard time in his first spending round with Nigel Lawson. Patten maintained that Lawson, having been against the poll tax from the start, did not see why he should ease its passage by providing more funds. Nigel Lawson strenuously denies this. After fighting off what he found an extraordinary proposal by his old political ally, Nicholas Ridley – that he should postpone the income tax cuts on which he had set his heart for his 1988 budget, in order to subsidise the poll tax – he now faced a new mendicant for funds. Chris Patten came from the paternalist Tory wing of Conservatism, which Lawson's radical instincts despised.

The Chancellor thought that instead of asking for more money, Patten ought to have joined him in persuading the Prime Minister to kill the poll tax, since both of them knew it to be a political disaster. This was a tall order, especially for a new member of the Cabinet; and with a Prime Minister who had taken ten years to include him, the most intellectually distinguished man of his Conservative generation.

After Lawson resigned, Chris Patten hoped to do better in 1990 with the new Chancellor, John Major, and his Chief Secretary, Norman Lamont. But he found their negotiating stance to be tough. Major's political instincts, as well as his Treasury hat, made him sceptical of the scheme's feasibility. Patten's aim was to get money to eliminate as much of the political damage as he could from the poll tax. The Treasury talks might be what Wellington called 'hard pounding', but at least they were conducted in an amiable spirit.

At that time John Major and Chris Patten were still thought of as rivals for future leadership, since Tories assumed Margaret Thatcher would continue for a year or two after another general election victory in 1992. The two men were about the same age. The Chancellor's self-image is caught in a remark he made about his supposed rival: 'Chris is cleverer than me, but less at home in a four-ale bar.' John Major saw himself as an all-round politician, with his own direct line to voters.

Talks under the Prime Minister's chairmanship were a more wearing process for Patten. The underlying difficulty, he believed, was that she did not like and did not understand local government. Indeed, neither the Conservatives nor Labour had ever looked at its finance and organisation together, nor produced a philosophy of local government.

Without any such map to guide her, Margaret Thatcher had returned to a theme which had been a recurring one for her throughout the long debate: new legislation to curb council spending. This was a paradox. The principle of the poll tax was to make councillors directly accountable to those who elected them, by transforming their pattern of taxing, spending and services into a transparent one. But the Prime Minister did not trust the effectiveness of that system, at least in the early years. By the beginning of 1990, she knew voters were blaming either the government or their Conservative council for the higher bills they would be receiving. The system was hurting what she called 'our own people'.

She harped on constantly about the need to retain Whitehall control, through the system of charge-capping (*née* rate-capping). She wanted to introduce more general powers to cap council spending, and Downing Street kept coming up with more and more new schemes to do this. But Chris Patten argued that if the principle of poll tax was accountability, actions which pulled responsibility for the size of council bills back to Whitehall were illogical. He found the way the Prime Minister conducted the whole debate irrational.

The practical problem which worried him was the difficulty of getting the new legislation she wanted through parliament. He feared such legislation would dominate the whole autumn and winter at Westminster, and keep open the political controversy which was inflicting such damage on the Conservatives. Now I knew this was a view which John Major shared. He had an ex-whip's instinct not to offer rebellious backbenchers an opportunity to hang other, and more fundamental, amendments on to a bill intended for a narrow purpose.

But the new Chancellor illustrated the tough-minded political skills he was developing by keeping Chris Patten in the dark about his own views. For a time Patten did not know whether Major shared the Prime Minister's belief in the need for legislation. He suspected the Treasury only pretended to want more capping powers in order to put pressure on him to make a softer financial settlement. Patten liked John Major, but was unsure how Margaret Thatcher's new Chancellor got on with her. It was the question ministers kept asking themselves, until the moment when, after her own fate was sealed, she effectively handed him the leadership of their party.

In the end, the Prime Minister accepted she could do without legislation, though she noted wryly that the target level for average poll tax bills had more than doubled since they were first conceived. Patten breathed a sigh of relief. He was new to the Cabinet, but he was not entirely new to the joys of locking horns with Margaret Thatcher. Before entering parliament, he had been head of the Tory Research Department. Down the years he had been enlisted, as one of the sharpest pens in the Conservative Party, to help with drafting her conference speeches. These brainstorming sessions went on through the night, into the early hours of the Friday morning, and tended towards the fundamental. By 1990, when he was 'recalled to the colours' for the speech, Chris Patten counted it as progress when he found himself 'debating first-year university economics, from first principles' at 3 a.m., rather than 5 a.m. His own attitudes and those of his Prime Minister had always diverged widely.

What is surprising is how most ministers behaved during these drawn-out rows over the poll tax. The only explanation is that Margaret Thatcher's long and dominant premiership had created a new political dynamic – or perhaps lack of it. She was in what turned out to be terminal trouble, yet none of her Cabinet colleagues seemed to be advising her to cut her losses. One junior minister assured me that the Prime Minister was the tax's only real friend. This was not the impression I received from other conversations at the time. They were whistling to keep their courage up.

John Major made no secret of his view that the poll tax controversy had done the Conservatives great damage. He blamed Nicholas Ridley for this, noting that the Cabinet were all getting on well together 'except for one', and that Ridley played his own game in bilateral talks with the Prime Minister. Major suspected that even in Downing Street his influence was fading, because of his part in the poll tax.

In Nicholas Ridley's final, disappointed days in the government, this once powerful keeper of the Thatcherite flame was proving a bugbear to several colleagues. Chris Patten criticised him for sniping at Major, because Ridley himself had wanted to be Chancellor; and of sniping at Patten, because he had previously been Environment Secretary. When I asked whether Ridley was intervening in discussions about the poll tax, Patten twitted me for naïveté: that was like asking whether someone had interfered over the Black Death. Its new custodian clearly felt the tax ought to be a communicable disease.

The solution to this disaster did not come until after Michael Hesel-

tine's challenge had driven Margaret Thatcher from office. Some Conservatives remained convinced to the end that her attempt to make
everybody pay for local services was right, and ought to be supported,
at whatever political cost. John Major's PPS, the right-wing Tony
Favell, was one such. He knew how unpopular the proposal was in the
Conservative Clubs of his political base in the north-west. These had
been founded more than a century before, at the time when Disraeli
gave the vote to the working class, and they reflected their origins. Favell
stuck to his guns, and lost his seat.

40

THE MUSIC STOPS FOR GEOFFREY

Long before Margaret Thatcher was driven from office, she was fatally undermined by a spreading belief in her party that, over her long years in power, she had gained in arrogance and lost in judgement. Her treatment of Sir Geoffrey Howe and Nigel Lawson, her two most senior colleagues, confirmed what errors about policy had already suggested: she had replaced the political savvy which is needed to hold a government together with a stubborn omniscience.

Throughout this parliament, she was in conflict with both ministers over British membership of the Exchange Rate Mechanism, though, as we have seen, that issue overlapped with wider economic policy. The stories of the two men's departure from the government intertwine. It is impossible to treat them in chronological order. The crucial breaking point for Geoffrey Howe – his removal from the job he loved, Foreign Secretary – came before Nigel Lawson's resignation. So I will describe first why Margaret Thatcher determined she must have Howe out of the Foreign Office. Lawson's break with her comes in the next chapter, and the events leading to Sir Geoffrey's resignation from the government, and her downfall, in Chapter 45.

Personally, Howe was in the more difficult position of the two men. As well as his policy differences with the Prime Minister, they both had to live with the fact that (a) he wanted to succeed her; and (b) she did not want him to. Most Conservatives regarded him as heir-apparent. His membership of the Heath government, his candidacy for the leadership as long ago as 1975, his role in reshaping Conservatism in opposition, his service as Chancellor in the tough early days of the government, and his stint as Foreign Secretary: all these made him a formidable aspirant. His colleagues saw him as courteous, unflappable, and a man who looked reasonable on television.

Nor had he allowed his heavy travel diary as Foreign Secretary to isolate him from the Conservative Party at home. He was at pains to tell anybody who would listen that he managed to keep in touch with the Tory grassroots. He imposed on himself annually ten regional tours on behalf of Conservative Central Office. He took care to visit Scotland and Wales every year, and went to each of the English regions every second year.

Beneath Geoffrey Howe's quiet manner is a driving and ambitious man. Once I wrote a column in the *Listener* giving a list of possible successors to Margaret Thatcher. They were drawn from the younger generation, for I had been influenced by the Prime Minister's remark to me about 'going on and on and on'. So I omitted Geoffrey's name. When my wife and I were invited to Sunday lunch at Chevening soon afterwards, our host took me aside, and gently made clear that he still regarded himself as a candidate for the top job.

Yet despite his popularity, Tories in the know were beginning to write Geoffrey Howe out of the script. Alan Clark ruminated that politicians at the top level had a shelf life. Because of Margaret Thatcher's long period in Number 10, this had run out for many who had been tipped as successors before Howe. One younger minister said cruelly: 'I have the sense that the music stopped for Geoffrey some time ago.' What made it stop was the antagonism Margaret Thatcher now manifestly felt towards him. Not only did she treat him harshly in Cabinet. She was dropping hints that there was nobody in her own generation she thought fit to succeed her, and would carry on until a new generation emerged. She wanted somebody with more sceptical views on Europe.

The other great subject of Westminster speculation in 1988 and 1989 was about who would succeed Nigel Lawson as Chancellor. John Major made a shrewd assessment: that the Prime Minister did not have 'a reserve Chancellor' at her disposal. She was soon to put that right, to his own advantage. I believe that Major saw that appointment coming a long way ahead. He did not foresee that Lawson would go so soon. He believed, and hoped, that his mentor at the Treasury would remain there until this fresh outbreak of inflation was over. But this future Prime Minister had begun to plan his own political future. His musings were not confined to the famous canal trip he and Norma had with an old friend, the Tory MP Robert Atkins, and his wife, when they first dreamed of Number 10. His personal modesty was always shot through with ambition, and he had a keen eye for his next career step.

Ministers I talked to at this time were full of stories about the deterioration in relations between Thatcher and Howe. Friends reflected sadly on how quickly human attitudes can change. As Prime Minister and

Chancellor, these two had often stood together, embattled against a largely Heathite Cabinet, maintaining the new thrust she wanted in economic policy. Even in 1983, when Geoffrey went to the Foreign Office, never her favourite department, she expressed delight because at European Councils she at last had by her side a man who was expert in, and fascinated by, the detail of the negotiations she took so seriously.

Like many political marriages of convenience, this one seemed to have been made in heaven. John Major noted that Howe remained polite, dogged and unsquashable. But the Prime Minister knew he wanted to succeed her, and perhaps detected a trace of impatience. Michael Howard's view was that she had never got on with any Foreign Secretary, because she was suspicious of diplomacy. Whatever the reason, by 1987 their colleagues were reporting to me that the Thatcher–Howe relationship was now dreadful. When he was giving his foreign affairs reports at Cabinet, her irritation was obvious. Of course, her underlying annoyance was about the content of what he, and the Foreign Office, were saying. But his manner also had come to grate on her, and she would grow agitated when she thought his mumbling was not audible to ministers further down the table.

He had a 'dogged-does-it' attitude to her interruptions that was reminiscent of Thackeray's Dobbin. He would allow her to go off on a long, demotic disquisition on some subject he had raised, and then would say, without open rebuke, but with undertones for those who had an ear for them: 'And now, Prime Minister, we must *decide* about . . .' These two, who had been as close as any two members of the early Thatcher governments, were gradually falling out of love with each other.

Geoffrey Howe's notorious tendency to mumble could not be blamed for a more general discontent in the Cabinet. Ministers complained to me that the Thursday meetings were becoming boring. This seemed a strange observation to make about what, to a journalist, is the apex of national politics. But ministers explained that the formal meetings had lost interest because so much was settled either in committee or in one-on-one meetings between Mrs Thatcher and departmental ministers. Cecil Parkinson used to while away the time on Thursdays by reading his press cuttings.

The detail of how the rumbling row over the Exchange Rate Mechanism eventually erupted is part of Nigel Lawson's story. For our purposes here, it is enough to say that when the Prime Minister returned from the Madrid summit at the end of June 1989, she was seething with anger. This had been generated by the pressure the Foreign Secretary and

Chancellor had put on her beforehand to give a clear indication when Britain would enter the ERM. Back in Downing Street, she told an intimate: 'My Foreign Secretary said if I didn't commit myself to a date, he'd resign. Well, I didn't commit myself, and he hasn't resigned. What sort of Foreign Secretary have I got?'

But there was more than that behind the reshuffle which followed on 24 July 1989. Because of the events leading up to Madrid, she now knew, if she had doubted before, that Nigel Lawson was in profound opposition to her doctrinal beliefs on exchange rates, and that his views were as little likely to change as her own. She reflected on who would replace him if he resigned. As John Major had noticed much earlier, she had no reserve Chancellor sitting on the bench. Absence of suitable substitutes generates unease in either a football manager or a Prime Minister.

Events leading up to the reshuffle were remarkable. Mrs Thatcher seemed to be on a psychological high. She had been to Paris for a G7 meeting, and to be a reluctant celebrant of the bicentenary of the French Revolution. She marked this vivid occasion in the national life of our ancient neighbours, in an interview with *Le Monde*, by lauding *Britain's* Glorious Revolution of 1688, adding a sly reminder to the French of Edmund Burke's unflattering thoughts about *their* revolution.

When she was back home, chance took a hand. At Prime Minister's questions, the Speaker selected to ask a supplementary question a Tory backbencher, 'returning from a good lunch' (as it was put to me). According to an indulgent minister, he jumped up and said the first thing which came into his head. But she read into it unintended subtleties, and concluded that Geoffrey Howe and Nigel Lawson were again plotting against her. Soon after the incident, she said to a close colleague: 'I'd better have a little reshuffle.'

It was more than a little one. The Defence Secretary, George Younger, and the Industry Secretary, Lord Young, wanted to leave the government. John Moore, a right-winger whose name had once been floated in the newspapers as her eventual successor – a premature flattery which he took too seriously – had never recovered from his rough period at Health and Social Security, so she asked him to stand down. Cecil Parkinson was switched to Transport to replace Paul Channon, who was also dropped.

But though these were extensive changes, they did not bring about the revolution the Prime Minister really had in mind. She had moved John Wakeham, her former Chief Whip and confidant, from being Leader of the House to replace Cecil Parkinson in charge of Energy, including the tricky privatisation of electricity. Wakeham had not enjoyed his Leadership as much as his stint as Chief Whip. Colleagues also thought he had been less influential in this higher position than he had been before. The explanation gives the flavour of a government which was now being run very much like a court.

Margaret Thatcher, though a puritanical worker, enjoyed political gossip. When Wakeham had been Chief Whip, she would invite him round to Number 10 in the evening, to hear – as a colleague put it – 'who was doing what to whom' in the House of Commons. Prime Ministers are able to spend much less time there than other members, or even ministers. They quickly get out of touch with the mood in an assembly which can, after all, either sustain or overturn their governments. As she kicked off her shoes and enjoyed a glass of whisky, John Wakeham, with information from more than a dozen whips, was the right man to tell her what was going on. With the friendly malice that is the salt of politics, my informant conjectured that John was not averse to inventing non-existing problems, and promising to solve them. After his promotion from the Whips Office to the Cabinet, Wakeham did not have so much interesting gossip to pass on.

The sensation in this reshuffle was what happened to his old job as Leader of the Commons. Reshuffle days are difficult for evening newspaper and broadcast journalists, because the official list is invariably delayed until after 6 p.m., for diverse reasons. Once during John Major's premiership, for example, Downing Street put a telephone call through to a skiing restaurant at the top of an alp, and asked to speak to Michael Ancram, a junior minister at the Northern Ireland Office. Since every British skier had heard the enthusiastic proprietor's announcement that the British Prime Minister was on the line, Ancram judged it prudent to ask if he could ski down to his hotel before taking the call in greater privacy.

From such accidental circumstances are the frustrating delays of reshuffle days made. I discovered this early in my broadcasting career, so with the BBC's lunchtime and teatime bulletins in mind, I always made sure that my colleagues and myself got around, in person or by telephone, to places where we could build up some picture of what was happening, long before the names came out officially.

On this occasion, I was due to do a live report for the one o'clock television news from the outside broadcast point in Downing Street. I left my office at about 12.40, but because I have always had a cavalier belief in my ability to meet a deadline, I dropped down into the Members' Lobby of the House, to check if there were any developments. What I learned there convinced me yet again of the value of giving priority to news-gathering over concern for the nerves of broadcasting colleagues, who never feel safe unless everyone is standing on his or her chalk-mark ten minutes before the programme begins.

In the Lobby I quickly learned, from someone who was in a position to know, that the Prime Minister had told Geoffrey Howe she wanted him to leave the Foreign Office, and had offered him the Leadership of the House. When she saw his unfavourable reaction to that, she suggested that he might prefer another post. This was the Home Secretaryship, a post then held by Douglas Hurd. If Howe had preferred that job, Hurd would have been offered the Leadership of the Commons instead. At this tense meeting, the Prime Minister parenthetically gave Geoffrey her opinion that Douglas was the best Home Secretary her government had ever had. She might have been wiser to say it to him. Howe asked for time to consult his wife, Elspeth, and other colleagues.

A few other journalists picked up the Howe story, but none of these had as early a news outlet as myself. So I arrived, somewhat breathless, in Downing Street, to break this remarkable piece of news. Not, as it turned out, only to BBC audiences, but to most members of the Cabinet. Ahead of a reshuffle, quite senior ministers have pathetically complained to me: 'You people know far more than we do.' Downing Street officials are as zealous as their chief in keeping other Whitehall departments in the dark.

When I returned to the Commons after a hasty snack, Douglas Hurd was there, checking whether his job had really been offered to Geoffrey Howe. He had felt for some time that his Home Office duties took up so much time that he was not able to play a full part in the general political work of the government, so I am certain he would have accepted an offer to lead the Commons. But the way in which he learned about this possible change was not conducive to comradely relations within the government. Margaret Thatcher apologised to him later, as well as she felt able to do. Her explanation was that when she saw Geoffrey Howe's frown at her suggestion he should be Leader of the House, she offered him the Home Secretaryship.

The unfortunate way in which Douglas Hurd learned of these events was not the fault of the person who alerted myself and others to Howe's departure from the Foreign Office. All he said was that Leadership of the House was 'not the only job' Howe had been offered. In a hurried walk from the House of Commons to the cameras in Downing Street, I had just sufficient time to deduce the only possible alternative. No other post was senior enough for Howe to be asked to consider except the one great office of state he had not held, the Home Secretaryship.

There is no easy way to dismiss someone, but colleagues observed that Margaret Thatcher was becoming an ever less reluctant butcher. Even her friends believed she might have retained Geoffrey's loyalty if she had taken him aside well in advance of the changes, said what a wonderful stint he had had as Foreign Secretary, but added that she needed him as Leader of the House in the period of preparation for the next general election. Howe remained a workaholic, full of ideas, and David Waddington, the Chief Whip, thought he ought to have been given a role in drawing up the manifesto. But he judged their relationship now to be dreadful: the Prime Minister did not conceal the fact that Sir Geoffrey bored the pants off her. How they had worked together for so long was a mystery to him.

The humiliating manner in which Geoffrey Howe was removed from a job he still enjoyed set burning in him a taper of resentment. Fifteen months later, this exploded in the resignation speech which ended her leadership. His period as Leader of the Commons was not a happy one. But in the reshuffle of July 1989, Margaret Thatcher had other fish to fry as well.

If Howe was to be removed, most politicians would have agreed that Douglas Hurd, by temperament and experience, was made for the Foreign Secretary's job. She thought otherwise. Hurd had been Ted Heath's political secretary when he took Britain into the European Community. He shared the Foreign Office's enthusiasm for Europe. She had painful experience of how similar enthusiasm – in Peter Carrington, Francis Pym and Geoffrey Howe – had clashed with her own instincts. She was not yet sufficiently weakened to have to turn to Douglas Hurd. Anyhow, she had wider considerations in mind than the conduct of foreign policy.

On reshuffle days, I have always found it useful to keep constantly on the move, taking in not only the usual lobbies, corridors, tearooms and bars where we meet MPs, but also the courtyards and outside passages where ministers are to be found. Or even ministerial drivers, who have their own cheery, if not invariably reliable network of information: 'My minister says he won't need a driver, so he's either "out" or he's going to Northern Ireland' (which would entail a police driver).

In an afternoon sweep outside the palace, I encountered John Major, waiting for his car at Members' Entrance. It was then 3.30 p.m. He enquired eagerly what I had heard. I told him, and we savoured the implications of the remarkable events concerning Geoffrey Howe and Douglas Hurd. Major, as number two at the Treasury, had talked with me in recent months about his need to gain experience in a department of his own. He had been a junior minister at Social Services, and though it was widely rumoured that John Moore would go, he hoped not to be sent back there, since he did not think that department would have much exciting work in the immediate future.

Within an hour of our conversation, he was Foreign Secretary, a post well beyond his expectations. Lady Thatcher's explanation of this promotion in her memoirs is that she wanted to give the Conservative party a selection of candidates with relevant experience to succeed her when she retired. Her intention then was that she would depart during the following parliament. John Major needed to hold one of the three great offices of state – Foreign Secretary, Chancellor, or Home Secretary – if he was to have a chance of competing with what she calls the 'talented self-publicists' who would be his rivals.

Margaret Thatcher's explanation of planning so long in advance for a succession to herself in the nineties cannot be taken simply at face value. It is true, but not the whole truth. Prime Ministers, like editors, managing directors, and bosses generally, are more concerned with what happens during the period when they are in charge than in any hazy hereafter. If the vacancy for a Tory leader had happened at the time she intended, instead of through her involuntary expulsion from Downing Street, John Major would have been well able to look after himself, though obviously her endorsement would have been a substantial help, even then. Because the vacancy occurred in 1990, that endorsement became essential.

I believe there was a more immediate reason why she made him Foreign Secretary – as it turned out, for just nine weeks. Mindful of the bruising encounters she had recently had with Nigel Lawson, she realised that her Chancellor and she might soon have to part. With his promotion to the Foreign Office, John Major suddenly became better qualified for the post of reserve Chancellor – a 'situation vacant' whose existence this prescient ex-whip had noticed a year and more before.

41

TWO OLD FRIENDS DEPART

In judging a politician, it is important to understand what his self-image is. John Major's is that he excels in the personal skills he learned in local government and in the Conservative whips' office at Westminster. He has always prided himself on knowing what is going on across the whole Westminster village. Throughout his political career, he has been modest about his intellect, though in fact it is a muscular one.

When he was Chief Secretary, John joked to me that everyone at the Treasury had an Oxbridge first except himself and the man who made the tea; and he wouldn't be too sure about the academic status of the man who made the tea. Yet he believed he had both common sense and presentational skills, which he had been told were what really mattered in a Chancellor. This comforting piece of advice, to a man whose own education had ended at sixteen, came from Denis Healey (Balliol and the Treasury). Healey has always expressed disdain for the concept of economics as a great mystery.

By the time Major was promoted to the Cabinet as Nigel Lawson's deputy in 1987, the Chancellor's troubled period had begun. His disagreement with Margaret Thatcher over fixed versus floating exchange rates was at the chrysalis stage, but the world stock markets crisis in October 1987 opened a second front between them, for it set him off on the course of expansion that led to renewed inflation.

By the middle of 1988, the Conservative Party at Westminster believed a reshuffle at the top of the Cabinet could not be delayed for more than a further year. Nigel Lawson's intention to leave the Treasury, either for the Foreign Office or the City, set the ministerial gossips thinking about his successor. The names they discussed with me may seem excessive in number, but it is about par for the course when politicians grow excited about a big job.

Cecil Parkinson's appointment as chairman of Star Chamber, the

Cabinet committee which tries to settle disputes between spending ministers and the Treasury, set off speculation that Margaret Thatcher might be about to give her long-time favourite his first really big job in government. This had been deferred five years earlier because of his resignation after the Sara Keays affair. Parkinson was a confidant of the Prime Minister. She often telephoned him at weekends or in the evenings, and asked him to go either to Chequers or Downing Street for a general political chat. He has always bitterly resented the suggestion that his 'in' with Number 10 reflected her soft spot for handsome, well-dressed men. He *did* wear monogrammed shirts, but this began as a joke when a Tory whip, Spencer le Marchant, chided him for being a fop, and said: 'You'll be wearing bloody monogrammed shirts next!' That, according to this old-fashioned Tory, was a custom common only among people he called 'yoiks'. Parkinson had a shirt made with his initials on, and came to like them.

He maintained Margaret Thatcher promoted him because, in all the jobs she had given him, from party chairman to Energy Secretary, he had performed effectively. Some colleagues were critical of the way he was handling the privatisation of electricity, and doubted whether he had the weight to be Chancellor, though Nigel Lawson at one time thought of Cecil Parkinson as his likeliest successor. John Major, whose own long-term ambition was for this post, believed Parkinson's appointment to Star Chamber was being talked up too much, and that while he had the same umbilical cord to the C2 voters as the Prime Minister, his was not a first-class intellect, like Nigel Lawson's.

Few doubted who Margaret Thatcher would really like to appoint as Chancellor: Nicholas Ridley, a political soul-mate, or 'true believer', as non-Thatcherites derisively called him. (Traditional Tories have their own counter-ideology to Thatcherism, a suspicion of enthusiasm and dogma, deriving from Pitt, Burke and Salisbury.)

Ridley had been a driving force behind many of the proposals in the radical 1987 election manifesto. John Major believed the Prime Minister certainly liked him better than almost anybody else in the government, and that he had the intellect for the job. But Major, who was clearly astonished by Ridley's aristocratic disdain for much that went on around him, nursed a suspicion that one day he might decide to chuck up politics, and go fishing.

Margaret Thatcher's favourite minister had another disadvantage. He had total contempt for presentational skills. Ridley once quizzically asked me whether I realised that his predecessor as Industry Secretary forty years before would have expended seventy-five per cent of his time and energy taking policy decisions, and twenty-five per cent explaining them to parliament and the public (including, he derisively implied, the media). Now the percentages were the other way about. On that day, he had already been to Brighton to make a speech, he had to open an exhibition at Battersea, and he was devoting lunchtime to me! This was clearly not his preferred set of priorities.

'Presentation', though often an obsession at Conservative conferences, was a Ridley bugbear. Once when we were waiting to record a television interview, my producer suggested that he might like to put out his cigarette, and in order to defuse any suggestion of bossiness, made her little joke: it was National No Smoking Day.

Nick Ridley exploded: 'National No Smoking Day! Bloody nanny state!'

I interjected: 'Now, now, Nick, be careful. Edwina will get you!'

Mrs Currie was then the junior minister at Health, and the antithesis of Ridley in her assiduously cultivated media profile, as in most other ways. He revealed that his London flat was in the same block as hers, and claimed that he left his cigarette ends and fast food packages outside her door. The thought of this fastidious aristocrat eating fast food, much less behaving in such an anti-social way, beggared belief.

He was not the only minister to find Edwina's style over the top. On the night she joined the government, I broke the news to Douglas Hurd, while we were waiting to appear on *Newsnight*. His first reaction was a startled 'Oh, my God', but by the time she arrived at the television studios a few minutes later, he had recovered sufficiently to offer a congratulatory embrace.

So if not Parkinson or Ridley, who? John Major believed Leon Brittan would make a good Chancellor, but predicted that he would not come back into the government. At the time of his resignation over Westland, Margaret Thatcher had indicated that he would hold office again, but Nigel Lawson got her psychology right. He foresaw that she would not make Brittan a minister again, because he reminded her of the Westland crisis, the worst moment in her premiership. Soon afterwards, the Prime Minister appointed Brittan to the European Commission. Even an admirer like Alan Clark took that as evidence of her ruthlessness.

Another former Chief Secretary who might be a candidate was John MacGregor. Critics wondered if he was good enough at seeing the wood from the trees. One murmured: 'If you put him down a hole, he's like a ferret, and will get things done. But if you put him in a field, he's like a rabbit, and doesn't know which direction to go in.' Of Kenneth Baker, colleagues suggested that Margaret Thatcher would never let him near the Treasury, because he was a spender, or as one sweepingly put it, 'didn't know about money'.

That left the current Chief Secretary, John Major. His own modest opinion was that it was too soon for him to be promoted within the Treasury; he was still on a learning curve. John admired Nigel Lawson's intellectual ability in wrestling with complex technical decisions. But he believed Lawson had much more than that to offer Margaret Thatcher. His whole life had been a preparation for the job he was doing now, and the government's reputation rested on his skill. With the close-in view of a deputy, John Major detected what others had missed: that Nigel Lawson was an astute political animal, with his finger in pies all over the government.

That combination of qualities set Lawson on course for an inevitable rivalry with Thatcher. This was not a conventional rivalry, of a younger politician wanting an older one's job. More dangerous than that, this was a rivalry of the mind, between two able and dedicated people who both believed they knew what was best for their party, government and country. As Lawson grew to match her in experience, their common stubbornness was fated to lead to trouble.

John Major hoped Lawson would stay on as Chancellor until he had got the economy back on course, after the 'blip' which began in 1988. This would also have the personal advantage for Major that the vacancy would come at a time more propitious for him. At that time, Major was popular with people on all sides of the Commons, though Gordon Brown, who shadowed him as Chief Secretary, confessed that he himself became more guarded in their relationship after one incident. When both were due to speak in a debate on public expenditure, Major told Brown this would be low-key, as he had nothing much to say. The Labour man was therefore surprised to find himself being roughed up during his own speech by half a dozen Tory backbenchers, and suspected the Chief Secretary had deployed the skills of an ex-whip to arrange this.

Behind all this speculation about who might become Chancellor, a power struggle was developing among the three senior members of the Thatcher government. What made the Prime Minister unhappy in 1989 was that Geoffrey Howe and Nigel Lawson were on the same side, both opposed to her over European policy. Ministers blew hot and cold when describing Margaret Thatcher's attitude to the Community. Douglas Hurd, one of the Cabinet's most convinced Europeans, used to take comfort from her growing knowledge of foreign affairs. She had an astonishing capacity for absorbing the details of European negotiations, which increased her self-confidence. What was more, while she had not liked the way Giscard d'Estaing patronised her, she liked his socialist successor, François Mitterrand, and she was more experienced and sharper than Helmut Kohl, so *she* patronised *him*.

But Hurd saw the Prime Minister as being in her heart a British nationalist. Her colleagues might now be spared the tirades on the subject to which she had formerly treated them, but her underlying attitudes remained unchanged. Chris Patten, another pro-European, classified her approach to the subject as 'visceral'.

Nigel Lawson, not instinctively a Euro-enthusiast, but with an intellectual's detachment, detected a difficulty for Britain. He saw the Community as a coalition, in which individual governments had to make compromises. Most continental politicians were used to this, whereas British ministers normally had a majority in the Commons, and therefore made their own decisions operative. Lawson believed we had to get used to compromising, winning some arguments, and losing some. It was a truth that John Major was to learn painfully when he became Prime Minister.

Geoffrey Howe and Nigel Lawson had come to the conclusion that Britain could no longer go on saying that we would join the Exchange Rate Mechanism 'when the time is right [or ripe]'. Lawson had been an influential figure in international attempts to restore something of the stability of the Bretton Woods fixed exchange rate system, through the Plaza and Louvre agreements. He had got himself into ill odour with Margaret Thatcher through his decision to hold sterling steady by shadowing the Deutschmark, but he fervently believed that greater stability for the pound was essential. Howe was also a strong supporter of attempts to revive managed exchange rates, and believed the ERM was part of that endeavour.

For party as well as governmental reasons, senior ministers now felt an urgent need to present a united front on Europe. Nigel Lawson, despite his own less than fanatical support for the European ideal, had concluded that Britain's trading and economic future lay there. He also worried because, as long as we stayed out of the ERM, the markets tended to conclude that the government did not care if the pound was devalued. As Margaret Thatcher resisted, entry became increasingly important to him.

Before the Madrid summit in June 1989, Howe and Lawson put pressure on the Prime Minister to name a date for going in. She reserved her position. The Foreign Secretary accompanied her to the summit. Finance ministers were not invited on that occasion, but a few days before Madrid, the Chancellor grimly assured me that he would be closely in touch with what was going on there. The crunch was approaching.

Lawson's battle over the ER M was not only with the Prime Minister, but with her economic adviser, Professor (now Sir) Alan Walters, who had returned to Downing Street in the summer of 1988, against his opposition. He liked Walters personally, and did not deny the Prime Minister's right to have independent advice, just as she did on foreign policy. The trouble was that the professor not only had trenchant views on monetary matters, but as a high-profile academic had published his analysis widely. The markets rightly concluded that his writings represented the advice Walters was pouring into the Prime Minister's ear. That left them wondering what the government would do next. This uncertainty made the markets nervous, and the Chancellor's job more difficult. While Lawson thought it inconceivable that Britain could stay outside the ERM, Walters hoped the system would collapse under the strains the French and Italians were then feeling.

The Chancellor had the comfort of the Prime Minister's assurance that she wanted him to stay at the Treasury after the reshuffle. He understood Geoffrey Howe was also to remain as Foreign Secretary. I confirmed this assurance from other sources. Lawson, now in embattled and tough mood, conceded that he might conceivably remain Chancellor until the end of the parliament. Although he thought inflation and the trade figures would come back under control, he recognised the wisdom of staying until that improvement was well under way. It would, as events turned out, have been a long wait.

This was not a dilemma he found easy to resolve. Once, when giving me a lift to the Commons, he surprised me by saying. 'You've been around a long time, John. What would you advise?'

I replied that I found the whole profession of politics so interesting, and the City, about which I knew little, boring, that I could not imagine anyone preferring the Square Mile. Anyhow, I had watched him and John Smith patently enjoying themselves in a battle in the Commons the previous week. But I could see that, from his point of view, unless he was aiming to be Prime Minister, or retained his interest in the Foreign Office, he had strong family and financial reasons for getting out of politics.

It was hard not to admire the way the Chancellor kept his nerve during these bruising battles with the Prime Minister. One day I was having lunch in a Westminster restaurant with the Labour frontbencher, Jack Straw, when Nigel and Thérèse Lawson came in. Subsequently, I learned that this was a day when he was at loggerheads with Margaret Thatcher. The Lawsons were placed at the next table to us, so Jack and I talked incessantly in order not to intrude into what I would guess was a 'cheering-up' lunch. I could not help wondering whether the tee-shirt his wife was wearing would be visible from Number 10, if she put it out on a clothes-line. The jolly slogan Mrs Lawson sported read: 'I'm the boss.'

John Major proved to be more prescient than anyone else I talked to about how the Prime Minister would break the log-jam in her Cabinet. On two occasions he expounded what proved remarkably like her eventual solution: that she should make either Geoffrey Howe or Douglas Hurd, probably Howe, Lord President of the Council, Leader of the Commons, chairman of Star Chamber, and coordinator of home policy – a sort of Rab Butler figure. Major thought the government was in danger of having a hard-faced image, and believed Howe in such a role might put that right by his inventive approach to social policy, which went all the way back to his Bow Group days.

I have often wondered since whether John Major's remarkable fore-sight was really inside knowledge. Others close to the Prime Minister floated similar ideas before me, but with less apparent confidence. Major was undoubtedly close to Margaret Thatcher at that time, but not, I think, senior enough to be told directly what she had in mind about the future shape of the top of her Cabinet. And unless he is an exceptional actor, when I met him halfway through the 1989 reshuffle he was genuinely perplexed about what he would be asked to do next.

The other explanation is that he had the acute instincts of a political professional, and kept his ear very close to the ground which contained most of the secrets – the whips' office and contiguous territory. An old patron of his, John Wakeham, formerly Chief Whip and then Leader of the Commons, certainly knew by the time of the Madrid ructions with Howe and Lawson that the Prime Minister was beginning to foresee the Chancellor's resignation, and decided to get Major into a suitable post from which to succeed him.

The Conservative Party was anxious about Europe in the summer of 1989. It was not yet such an obvious threat to the Tories' legendary instinct for party unity as it became in 1993, during the Maastricht rows, and since, but at the time the trouble seemed bad enough. They fought a negative campaign in the European elections, and for the first time since Margaret Thatcher became leader, she suffered defeat in a nationwide election. She was shaken, and even told ministers the time had come to 'calm it', that is, not take too many new policy initiatives. But as the minister who told me this observed, it was doubtful whether she was capable of taking her own advice.

For many younger politicians, her attitudes to Europe were becoming ever more uncongenial. The Bruges speech in 1988 had offended pro-Europeans. One grew vehement when he discussed it with me, saying it sent policy off in exactly the wrong direction. He claimed there had been a first draft by Charles Powell, which was 'awful', then a Foreign Office draft, and the Cabinet Office had pulled these together. I asked another minister, just before the European election defeat, what were the real reasons for her doubts about Europe. He replied succinctly: 'She thinks they are a bunch of wankers.'

The Cabinet majority were reluctant to involve themselves openly in a dispute about which Margaret Thatcher felt so strongly. Lawson was sufficiently worried about the quarrel over Alan Walters to consult the Home Secretary, Douglas Hurd, and he received sympathy from him and Kenneth Clarke. There were many subjects on which Hurd and the Chancellor did not agree. But as a novelist, and connoisseur of the human condition, Douglas Hurd found that, for his own taste, he had too many 'saccharine people' around him in government, and appreciated Nigel Lawson as one of the salty ones. In Lawson's final year, these two oddly assorted characters met regularly in private.

Nigel Lawson had now been engaged in this long and frustrating struggle with Margaret Thatcher since 1985, when she flatly refused to consider early British membership. He hoped, but was by no means confident, that Geoffrey Howe's presence at her side in the Madrid council chamber would exercise a modifying influence. She had appeared to endorse in the Commons the pro-ERM remarks Lawson made before the Treasury Select Committee. He was not convinced that this meant she would go as far as he wanted at Madrid, which was essentially to set conditions for British entry which made it likely within two or three years.

Yet Lawson thought she now knew in her heart that a decision on the ERM would have to be taken soon. This judgement was proved right early in the subsequent chancellorship of John Major. But the furthest Nigel Lawson could go in his estimate of her position before Madrid was that she was thinking deeply about the subject, but had not yet reached a conclusion. At the time, the two tense meetings at which the Foreign Secretary and Chancellor warned the Prime Minister they might have to resign were kept secret.

It was a year later that a right-wing junior minister delightedly explained to me that they had told her 'unless she signed on the dotted line at Madrid', they would resign and make a very public row. That, he said, was why she had sacked Geoffrey Howe. From other sources, I learned that the Prime Minister thought she had better break up the alliance between Howe and Lawson, which was threatening to defy her. But if she had foreseen that Lawson would resign so soon afterwards, she would surely have left Howe at the Foreign Office. Conceivably, such a respite might have saved her job.

The rot really started for her when Nigel Lawson did eventually resign on 26 October 1989. I had left Westminster early that evening to write a script for *On the Record* at the old Lime Grove studios of the BBC. Madge and I were due to go on to a party for Alastair Hetherington, the former editor of the *Guardian*, who was retiring from the chairmanship of the Scott Trust, which owned the paper. A researcher in Lime Grove suddenly shouted 'Lawson's resigned'. He had a reputation for practical jokes, so colleagues invited him to shut up.

But I hurried to the tape machine he was reading from, and in minutes was in a taxi to the news studios a mile or so away. Others at Westminster were scrambling the news on to the air. My job was to provide the background to what, for many people who had not followed Lawson's quarrel with Thatcher, was a bolt from the blue. I had to keep on broadcasting, on one radio and television programme after another, during the rest of the evening. Alastair's farewell proved to be one of many social occasions on which my telephone calls kept promising I would arrive any moment now. I never did.

Nigel Lawson's resignation was a result of the Prime Minister's growing determination that she must not be challenged, even on the comparatively minor matter of her economic adviser. Only two days before, a minister as close to her as Cecil Parkinson still believed she would not force the issue. But for her, Walters represented ideological commitment, unpolluted by political considerations. That was important to Margaret Thatcher. So she lost her Chancellor because he believed Walters now had more influence with her than he did. Walters himself resigned that same evening. Her economic adviser's past writings had caught up with them, and the schism between Prime Minister and Chancellor had become too publicly obvious for a proud man like Nigel Lawson to bear. John Major became the new Chancellor.

42

THE FIRST STALKING–HORSE

With the economy in the doldrums, the Conservative Party in growing electoral panic over poll tax and the cost of mortgages, and the row involving the Prime Minister, Lawson and Howe rumbling on above and beneath the surface, a gradual erosion of Margaret Thatcher's standing had begun.

She remained powerful within her government, but she was becoming isolated and embattled. To talk of 'Life after Maggie' was no longer *lèse majesté*, and most of my political lunching companions gladly did so. A gap had been left in her defences by the retirement of her loyal deputy, Willie Whitelaw, who suffered a stroke at the end of 1987. Willie was the complete pragmatic politician. His worldly wisdom and skills in party management had saved her from many a banana skin since 1975.

Margaret Thatcher herself felt Whitelaw's departure keenly. When she visited him in hospital, she said, almost unbelieving: 'But Willie, you've *never* been ill.' It was the end of an era. In Cabinet, she had to change her method of dealing with difficult problems. Previously, it had been: 'Willie, shall we refer this to E or E (A)?' (the names of two Cabinet committees). Now, she would greet some deadlock with the words: 'Oh, I suppose I'll just have to do it myself.'

Now that his mediation had gone, ministers found it prudent to clear in advance with Number 10 any controversial proposals they wanted to bring before Cabinet committee. The Prime Minister's network of control, operated principally through Charles Powell (even though he was supposed to be her private secretary only for *foreign* affairs), was widely feared. A friend of hers once advised me to note that she had now been in post longer than even the most senior civil servants, and was notorious for promoting them – or not – according to their attitudes, as much as their abilities. The Sir Humphreys found hers a cold climate.

Many ministers thought her more of an enigma. As the terminal crisis of her leadership was building to its climax the following year, however, John Major urged me to note one advantage she still had: that her Cabinet colleagues *liked* her, because although she could be infuriating, she was also personally considerate. By that stage, it was clear that he was as near to being her chosen heir as anyone had ever been.

Others tended to emphasise her infuriating traits. Sir Patrick Mayhew, a Tory from an older school, found her behaviour with colleagues astonishing. He once observed that she saw herself as an Ellen Terry, one moment a defiant Boadicea, the next holding her head in her hands and saying they had all betrayed her. Meanwhile, ministers sat 'like a row of stoats', reminding themselves that she was a woman, and must be treated courteously, and differently from a male Prime Minister.

Mayhew was torn between anxiety and admiration. As a traditional Conservative, rather than an ideologue, he had his doubts about whether the public still retained an appetite for perpetual revolution. He grumbled that some people were always wanting to dig up the roots, when what was needed was a little pruning. On the other hand, he gave credit to Margaret Thatcher for having made beneficial changes in Britain, for having turned the country round, whereas previous Conservative governments, notably Macmillan's, had merely presided over decline, doubtless calling up the most apposite Greek and Roman precedents and allusions to show why it was inevitable. Sir Patrick's attitudes encapsulated neatly the 'yes, but . . .' attitude of many in her government.

What lost the Prime Minister the sympathy of some colleagues was the brusqueness she showed towards them in the presence of others. Even an admirer told me that a minister bringing in a proposal often had to endure unfair argument. She tended to say: 'Who on earth produced this load of rubbish?' The minister might be tempted to reply: 'Well, you've been bloody badly briefed too'; but of course he did not, and only if he had the strength to dig in could he hope to win her over.

Sometimes the brusqueness turned to rudeness. I was told that with two fellow-lawyers, David Mellor and Kenneth Clarke – both of them QCs, and therefore nominally senior to her in their old profession – she had used the same put-down, on separate occasions, when disagreeing with their arguments. She enquired whether they had been at the Chancery Bar. When the reply was in the negative, she pronounced that this was just as well, otherwise they would have starved.

When this happened to Mellor, *esprit d'escalier* told him he ought to have said something rude back, and walked out of her government. Because he had not done so, he felt emasculated. But later he was present when she played the same trick on Kenneth Clarke, and Mellor found himself laughing at the repetition. It is in such ways that what is 'done' and 'not done' in politics evolves. Margaret Thatcher as Prime Minister was a radical force in manners, as well as in policy.

Clarke was one of the few ministers who stood up to her in the semi-public forum of Cabinet. He told her, from the depths of his personal experience as a Nottingham Forest football fan, that the football membership scheme on which she was insisting was a nonsense. She was very reluctant to give it up, but after a mauling in the House of Lords, it was changed beyond recognition. A reaction seemed to be setting in against certitude and ideology. Virginia Bottomley, not normally a woman to make political jokes, was heard to convert 'Thatcherism' into 'Thatcherwasm'. Her promotion to Cabinet rank came after the change in Prime Minister.

Right-wing ministers still believed Thatcher's ideological thrust was correct. Nicholas Ridley, the greatest 'true believer' of all, now at the Department of Trade and Industry, was disappointed that she did not risk making him Chancellor when Nigel Lawson resigned. Yet she saw him as her ideological touchstone. At the DTI, he remained an opponent of all interventionism. He once confessed to a colleague that in his department he had 'damn all to do, and 12,000 people to help me do it'. John Major detected that Ridley's disappointment over the chancellorship had made him more detached in his attitude to Margaret Thatcher. Others on the right accused her privately of running a Heathite government. Ridley now suspected that she was no longer a vote-winner. Some thought she knew this herself.

The Prime Minister had other strong allies in Cabinet. Cecil Parkinson, still close to her, believed right into 1990 that she had no intention of retiring. She made it clear to him that her revolution was not nearly complete. But it was now only a small group of ministers whose ideological soundness she fully trusted – Ridley, Norman Lamont, Peter Lilley, when he joined the Cabinet, and Parkinson himself. She probably saw John Major, even then, as being much more 'political' than she was.

A feeling of isolation afflicted her, just when, with the Iron Curtain crumbling, she sensed a new destiny ahead. Now that Ronald Reagan had retired, she told confidants, the ideological drive in Washington had weakened. If she allowed Britain also to run out of ideological steam, the former communist countries of Eastern Europe would look unavailingly to the West for a guide.

The reader may detect here the *folie de grandeur* which ministers complained of in her final years in power. The reality has turned out somewhat differently from her vision. In the years since Margaret Thatcher retired, economic hardship has followed the bungled liberalisation of markets in Russia and other countries of the former communist empire. This must raise questions about the simplistic view that all they needed was overnight imitation of a Western economic model. Britain's experience over many centuries of open trading was not easy for the peoples of Russia, Poland or Hungary to absorb so swiftly.

Those closest to the Prime Minister's moods detected that she felt increasingly unhappy both abroad and at home. As reshuffle time came round, Cecil Parkinson observed that, while in previous years ministers had been sitting on the edges of their seats in case they should be dropped, now she herself, after the resignations of Lawson and others, was waiting anxiously to see if anyone else would want to go, when she needed them to stay.

But after the July reshuffle, there was no sign that she intended to reduce her isolation by giving Geoffrey Howe the kind of role as Deputy Prime Minister that Willie Whitelaw had occupied. Ministers like Douglas Hurd could see the advantages if Howe were allowed to replace Whitelaw. When he presided at the Cabinet's home policy committee, there was a rational discussion in which younger ministers with well-developed political antennae, such as Kenneth Baker and Kenneth Clarke, joined in. It seemed that everyone relaxed more when she was not presiding.

But the Thatcher/Howe relationship had deteriorated too far for her to regard him as she had Willie Whitelaw. When he began to speak in Cabinet or committee, although she would allow him to continue, she sometimes closed up her file, and did not take much notice of what he was saying. A close Thatcher-watcher asked whether I had noticed how she seemed to pass ministers as on a moving pavement or escalator? Men such as Francis Pym, John Biffen, Nigel Lawson, John Moore and Geoffrey Howe appeared for a time to be close to her, and then events moved them away. It was at about the same time that colleagues began to notice how close she was now coming to John Major. Only a couple of years previously, he was one of the junior members of her Cabinet. Suddenly, he was Foreign Secretary, then Chancellor, and beginning to be regarded as heir-apparent.

Talk of a stalking-horse candidate against the Prime Minister grew through that autumn of 1989, producing fevered discussion about who might succeed her if she was forced out. Michael Heseltine, for three years the King over the Water, was now converted into the Man to Stop.

Everybody agreed he had played his backbench cards with great skill. He had been loyal to the government, except on issues like the poll tax, where he could take a leading role in a popular rebellion, and remind Tory MPs that events now justified his own earlier scepticism as Environment Secretary. One minister was full of admiration of his cleverness in ending one anti-poll tax speech in the Commons with a sharp attack on Labour, so that he would be able to sit down to Conservative, rather than Opposition cheers. Michael Heseltine was the complete politician.

A year earlier, as the government's economic troubles gathered, Heseltine had foreseen what Jim Callaghan used to call 'an interesting political situation'. He conjectured that if the economy remained bad towards the end of 1989, Margaret Thatcher would not want to retire. Yet if Labour got its act together, she would be under pressure. In those circumstances, he had a speech in his mind, which he would make to the Tory Party conference. This was just ten minutes long, and set out his vision of Conservatism. Even the stage-managers of that notoriously stage-managed assembly would not refuse him permission, since a refusal would cause an even bigger row than the speech.

In the event, it was Sir Anthony Meyer who challenged the Prime Minister in 1989; Michael Heseltine's opportunity was to come a year later. He had believed that if she did not retire in 1989, she would find herself forced to go on into the next parliament. Heseltine and his wife, Anne, both suspected that Denis Thatcher would have an important influence on the Prime Minister's decision about retirement. Both had considerable respect for the way in which he played his difficult role as his wife's political consort.

The respect they felt for him may have arisen originally from a small incident at a Downing Street reception. Anyone who has attended these knew that Margaret Thatcher liked to combine the roles of Prime Minister and careful, rather fussy, housewife. On one occasion, when Anne Heseltine was a guest, her hostess assumed the duties of waitress at the buffet, and loaded her plate with more food than the slim Mrs Heseltine could comfortably face. As his wife moved on, Denis Thatcher took in the situation at a glance, murmured, 'You don't want all that lot', and taking the plate away, left her to choose her own food.

Denis Thatcher's admiration of his wife was genuine and manifest. She was the kind of leader Conservatives like him had been waiting for all their lives. He particularly admired what he saw as her great courage in making her deeply sceptical Bruges speech, which colleagues had advised her against. He even argued that it would 'change the course of history'. A minister once surmised that what made Margaret Thatcher so immune to doubt about her opinions was the fact that at the end of a day she and Denis would retire to the flat above Downing Street and, behaving like grassroots Conservatives of the right, wonder why on earth the government was behaving so foolishly.

Denis Thatcher's relations with journalists were usually guarded. At a party conference, when I arrived late at a party, he enquired what had delayed me. I said I had been appearing on the *Nine O'Clock News*.

He asked, rather pointedly: 'And what have you been saying about us tonight?'

I outlined the bland report I had done on some uncontroversial subject.

Absent-mindedly, he said: 'Of course, everybody at the BBC's a Trotskyist.'

Startled, I answered: 'I beg your pardon?'

He was equally surprised that I should be surprised: 'Oh, nothing personal, old boy!'

I assume he thought Trotskyism was one of those unpleasant personal diseases that can happen to any of us.

43

JOHN MAJOR'S RISING STAR

John Major did not enjoy being Foreign Secretary. In light of his subsequent career, it is hard to know whether it was good or bad fortune for him that he spent only nine weeks in the job – between Geoffrey Howe's removal from the Foreign Office and Nigel Lawson's resignation as Chancellor. Douglas Hurd, though he would have liked the job himself, generously decided that Major was 'a star'. This was the Home Secretary's favoured accolade for younger colleagues. He applied it also to Chris Patten, who had been brought in to face the poll tax débâcle.

Hurd particularly admired the skill with which Major handled the Prime Minister during a heavy piece of American lobbying. President Reagan, surprisingly, telephoned her himself about a low-level problem, a European broadcasting directive, which seemed to exclude non-European material. After what Hurd thought was a marvellous Major performance at the Council of Ministers, Thatcher was able to tell the President that the directive had been going to go through anyhow, but that Britain had won a clause – 'where practical', or some such. Hurd believed the reason Major was able to handle her well was that he did not feel the same frustration as, in recent years, Geoffrey Howe had suffered.

But John Major quickly grew contemptuous of the less admirable aspects of diplomacy, and specifically of European foreign ministers. He found these a more unlikeable bunch of individuals than you were ever likely to meet elsewhere. If they stabbed you in the chest, he concluded, that was because they had missed their target, which was your back. This was in interesting contrast with his view of the finance ministers of the Community, whom he had met as Chief Secretary, and was to know better as Chancellor. Major found them congenial. Once, when we were lunching together after he became Chancellor, he was praising the finance ministers. I said he would probably not remember a contrasting remark he had made about the foreign ministers. He surprised me by replying at once that he had described them to me there, at the Athenaeum, 'just before our soup arrived'. This casual feat of memory, reminiscent of Harold Wilson in his heyday, impressed me.

Some of the drafts which the Foreign Office wanted him to send to the Prime Minister horrified him. He asked if this was they way they usually minuted Margaret Thatcher, and was told that it was. Personally, he would not have sent them to the under-secretary in charge of pensions, much less to a Prime Minister, and especially this Prime Minister, whose own doubts about his new department were notorious. John Major felt if the Foreign Office had to deal with Charles Powell at Downing Street, it served them right.

Margaret Thatcher's suspicions about the Foreign Office are legendary, though they have not always resulted in any very effective control of its policies. At times she seemed to regard it as a free-standing institution, independent of government. South Africa provided one example given to me. She had been persuaded, reluctantly, that British military attachés ought to be withdrawn. Some time later, a Foreign Office minister, accompanying her at a meeting with an African statesman who complained about Britain's record in opposing apartheid, was astonished by the reply. First she ticked off what had been done: the Gleneagles agreement, no arms sales, and so on. Then turning to the FO man, she added: 'And *they've* withdrawn military attachés, whatever good that may do.'

When Nigel Lawson resigned on 26 October 1989, John Major was switched back to the Treasury as Chancellor, and Douglas Hurd achieved his long-term ambition by becoming Foreign Secretary. Even then, the Prime Minister was reluctant to appoint Hurd: Prime Ministers do not necessarily want round pegs in round holes, if they do not like the hole in the first place. It was suggested that Tom King, who had only moved to the Department of Defence nine weeks before, should be given the Foreign Office. But the new party chairman, Kenneth Baker, held out for Hurd to have the job.

For her own sake, this was a sensible decision. She had been seriously weakened by her Chancellor's resignation, so to put two of her ablest, and now most senior ministers in the posts they coveted was a minimum precaution. But the irony is that Douglas Hurd and John Major immediately set aside any jealousy or suspicion their recent treatment might have created between them, and formed an alliance as solid as that between Nigel Lawson and Geoffrey Howe. And for the same purpose: to convince the Prime Minister that Britain's future lay in a closer relationship with Europe, and that there was little she could do to stem the tide.

But they determined to handle her with a delicacy that their more senior predecessors had wearied of: no great rows, but gradual persuasion to achieve what they thought right. Douglas Hurd understood her reservations about his pro-European stance, and believed what she needed was reassurance, rather than confrontation. Rows did not achieve their purpose, and they did lose elections. This is a wise political saw, though one which the Conservative Party has found impossible to apply to its European wound.

John Major had always admired Douglas Hurd's polished style in Cabinet, and observed that as Foreign Secretary his approach to Margaret Thatcher was superbly effective. The new Foreign Secretary was more self-critical, and confessed he had not always been so successful. When he had been Minister of State at the Foreign Office, he had made the mistake of arguing back. But he decided that the methods of Geoffrey Howe's earlier period had been right: he simply waited till she had finished her tirade, and then resumed what he had been saying.

It is remarkable how unanimous Margaret Thatcher's ministers have been in treating her as a force of nature, almost a volcano, who had to be propitiated by those living on the slopes below. From time to time ministers would assure me that she respected those who stood up to her, that she liked to be argued with. But comparatively little solid evidence has emerged that such arguments were fruitful in changing her mind. In the final analysis, it is difficult for outsiders to judge; and insiders are, *ex officio*, pleading a case.

I can only say that personal experience has not convinced me that Margaret Thatcher finds it easy to acknowledge the legitimacy of alternative views. Once, in a group discussion with other broadcasters, I was asking what I thought were merely sharp questions about her government's controversial changes in education and health. After a few minutes' ping-pong across the table, she fixed me with her aggressive blue eyes, and said: 'You don't believe a word of it, do you?' I resisted the temptation to give the conventional suspect's reply: 'You done me bang to rights, guv.' Instead I said that my job was to ask questions.

The Hurd–Major partnership had to confront the Prime Minister with the issue she found most unpalatable: the Exchange Rate Mechanism. The balance of politics in this debate had changed drastically since her rows with Geoffrey Howe and Nigel Lawson. From early in 1990, John Major concluded he would be able to persuade her. Peter Walker thought political prudence would prevail over ideology.

A harsher critic quoted Beaverbrook on the later Lloyd George: he no longer minded in which direction the bus was going, so long as he was still in the driving seat. Margaret Thatcher was now worried about the security of her leadership. Lloyd George had another lesson for her. He once gave his view of the perpetual tension between ideology and politics by asking an election candidate, who had what he called 'a free trade conscience', whether his campaign was intended to get him to Westminster or to heaven. By 1990, Margaret Thatcher's dilemma was almost as sharp as that – though whether there is a monetarist heaven seems doubtful.

So far as ERM entry was concerned, John Major himself was satisfied by the spring that what was left of the conditions affecting other countries, especially the removal of exchange controls, did not matter a fig: they were more or less fulfilled. What mattered was inflation. From my knowledge of what he thought at the time, it is unjust to suggest that the Chancellor was a soft touch in negotiations for Britain's entry. For a long time Margaret Thatcher had been committed in principle to joining. She herself concluded she would have to do so, since industry and the press were all against her, and she was running out of support. Despite this, in her memoirs she accuses Major of playing the same 'cracked record' that she had found so unmelodious when Nigel Lawson was the disc jockey.

The problem was that her declared policy and her ideology pointed in opposite directions. What she really wanted her new Chancellor to accept was precisely what had led to the breach with the old one: that he could not use the exchange rate in his steering of the economy, but would concentrate on money supply alone. Her belief was that John Major was 'drifting with the tide'.

As I read these words of hers, I recalled a conversation she and I had about the televising of parliament, which she was resisting long after parliamentary opinion had changed in favour. I gave my opinion that the tide was running against her, but she replied tartly that I should remember that tides went out as well as coming in. It is true that the fashionable tide in favour of ERM membership, which had been flowing ever more strongly, was eventually to ebb. But not until long after Margaret Thatcher had lost office.

John Major knew the government faced a tricky choice: between going in fairly soon, though not at once, in order to have influence in shaping Stages 2 and 3 of the Economic and Monetary Union; or to wait outside, to show that Britain was not an easy touch, and negotiate against Stages 2 and 3, as our price for entering the ERM. One

Eurosceptical attitude guided him: no Prime Minister or Chancellor could stand at the despatch box, say the government was surrendering the powers of parliament and the existence of the pound to a European bank, and hope to survive.

Even more Euro-enthusiastic ministers recognised that EMU was a long way in the future. But Kenneth Clarke was in near-despair that Britain might yet again be missing the boat over the ERM. What worried Norman Fowler was that the public might become bored by Tory rows. As early as December 1989 he scented the troubles which would engulf John Major as Prime Minister, and himself as party chairman, in the European election disaster of 1994.

Douglas Hurd and the Foreign Office wanted to join the ERM during the second half of 1990, which was what eventually happened. Even in early 1990, the Chancellor was less unreservedly in favour of early entry. He used to observe that for him entry was no easy option. You might go in, and find within three weeks that you needed to devalue, and that the others might not want to let you. He did not even accept that Britain would necessarily have a good first six months, followed by possible trouble. The effects of membership were simply unpredictable. It could mean higher interest rates; or *revaluation*; or a period of immediate bumpiness. It was eventually to prove even bumpier than that for John Major.

So the new Chancellor was by no means a European idealist. In fact, there was then, and has been ever since, a strong conflict of evidence about his deepest beliefs on the European project. Colleagues tend to see what they want to see. A determined pro-European, unsurprisingly, concluded he was a determined pro-European. Another minister called him 'a genuine agnostic'. The truth is that John Major's instincts were so much less ideological than Margaret Thatcher's that Tories found them hard to fathom. They had grown accustomed to her style. He never engaged in the same intellectual wrestling-matches that she and Nigel Lawson used simultaneously to love and hate.

John Major's straightforward belief was that the Conservative Party and British industry did not want the country to be left behind developments in Europe. The European fissure in Toryism, about which Chris Patten had warned me long ago, was growing deeper, and the long delay over the ERM was becoming its San Andreas fault. Major saw the need to avoid an eruption. It was no more complicated than that.

Peter Walker believed substitution of John Major and Douglas Hurd for Nigel Lawson and Geoffrey Howe had reduced Margaret Thatcher's freedom of action. She could not sack Major. If he went to her one

night and said they had to join the ERM, or he'd go, she would have
to give way. Geoffrey Howe, now largely excluded from these discussions,
observed the same trend with grim satisfaction. He would see victory
for the policy he had long wanted, but would not himself be in at the
kill.

By April, John Major noted that the newspapers no longer contained
the steady drip of stories about Margaret Thatcher erecting new conditions for entry. Since Lawson's day, the Treasury had always been
hypersensitive about the operations of the Downing Street press secretary,
Bernard Ingham. The new Chancellor believed that, at last, Douglas
Hurd and himself, clambering like soldiers in Flanders over the stricken
corpses of their predecessors, had got the Prime Minister squared to
accept entry: genuinely 'when the time was right [or ripe]'.

The announcement of Britain's entry came on 8 October 1990. The
news reached me at a most inconvenient moment, when I was preparing
my report on the final day of the Labour Party conference in Blackpool.
I had to hand that over to a colleague, race down the motorway to the
BBC's offices in Manchester, and tackle the political side of the ERM
story with inadequate information, and pictures sent down the line from
London. To add to a sense of disarray, the only lip-microphone available
reduced the volume of even my voice to levels that were almost unfit to
broadcast. It seemed like a symbol of an unhappy chapter in Britain's
European politics, a chapter that was not yet ended.

Margaret Thatcher had recognised that her isolation over Europe
could endanger her leadership. But from time to time her deepest
ideological instincts overcame her normal political caution. She seemed
simply unable to stop herself offending those Tories who wanted to be
at the heart of Europe. A fortnight before her downfall she was still
arguing vigorously in private against going any further in European
economic integration. She was particularly hostile to talk of a single
currency, saying the Community had not thought its way through the
subject, simply made a declaration. She was still firm in her ideological
belief: the market must be allowed to decide. The poorer countries in
Europe would have to realise that the transfers of resources to sustain a
single currency were simply not going to happen. Anyhow, she concluded dismissively, she could not get it through parliament. She was
already flirting with the idea of a referendum, which was to offend even
some normally reliable supporters within her Cabinet.

This chapter in the history of Thatcherism has a strange epilogue.
Some time after Britain entered the ERM, Nicholas Ridley told John
Smith that Margaret Thatcher had only gone in with the intention of

coming out at the earliest reasonable opportunity. Smith found this an astonishing confession for him to make to a political opponent. But Nick Ridley was never a conventional politician, and though his prediction was not fulfilled in the time-frame he conceived, nor under the same Prime Minister, nor even while he was in the government, Britain did conclude its long travail over entry with only a brief period inside.

44

THE BUNKER MENTALITY

After Nigel Lawson's resignation in October 1989, I realised for the first time that Margaret Thatcher might not remain Prime Minister until the next general election. What first aroused this suspicion was a conversation on 1 November 1989 with a strong supporter of John Major's, who regarded himself as being on the Tory left. He said: 'The time has come for our wing of the party. We've got her boxed in.'

Later that month the stalking-horse challenge by Sir Anthony Meyer began the destabilisation of the Prime Minister. Although she won overwhelmingly, sixty Tory MPs withheld their support, either by voting for her opponent or abstaining. Her campaign manager, George Younger, had to tell her that a large number of others had only given her their support on a probationary basis.

Even before the Meyer challenge, both Younger and Peter Carrington had advised her to take a cool judgment as to whether or not she was likely to win the next election, and then to decide when to retire. Margaret Thatcher was quite uninterested in such advice. Younger concluded gloomily that she was unlikely to follow the example of Harold Wilson, and go voluntarily. Wilson, he reasoned, was interested in holidays in the Scilly Isles and in golf, whereas the only subject which fascinated Margaret Thatcher was public affairs.

George Younger also urged her to resist the bunker mentality, which afflicts all long-serving leaders, by changing her staff. He particularly suggested she should move Charles Powell and Bernard Ingham out of Downing Street. Powell gets mixed reviews from the insiders. Margaret Thatcher's last Foreign Secretary, Douglas Hurd, achieved a reasonable relationship with him. He judged that most strains between Downing Street and the Foreign Office came from the Prime Minister's off-the-cuff remarks in answer to supplementary questions, which Bernard Ingham tended to emphasise at his briefings, rather than to play down.

Hurd considered Powell to be one of the most competent civil servants he had ever encountered. As her private secretary for foreign affairs, he could produce, within an hour, a marvellous minute of a meeting with a foreign leader. What offended others was that Powell's language was authoritarian. Successive principal private secretaries, nominally his seniors, deferred to him, because he had so much more access to the Prime Minister. She had come to rely heavily on both Powell and Ingham, with whom she was comfortable. So she ignored Younger's advice.

The final rupture with Geoffrey Howe and Nigel Lawson inflicted a personal, as well as a political blow on Margaret Thatcher. Intimates reported she was 'a bit down', which in this context meant deeply anxious and depressed. One believed she had been close to resignation after Lawson went. Willie Whitelaw, who still kept in touch with events, judged her to be shaken both by the results of the Meyer challenge to her leadership and by Lawson's resignation.

As 1990 dawned, he foresaw trouble for her that summer, especially if both economy and political prospects remained gloomy. There might be pressure for her to go, which Whitelaw, at that stage, thought would be a mistake, since she had a better chance of winning a general election than any other Conservative leader. Later events were to alter his opinion. Another old adversary, Peter Walker, detected a change in her character. He thought her principal remaining objective was to win elections, and that she would adjust policies as necessary. For all their differences, Walker regarded her as a skilful politician, and clearly hoped pragmatism was at last peeping through the iron curtain of her ideology.

The view I had reached was less comfortable. It was that by Margaret Thatcher's third term, events had irreversibly moulded her character. Her fight to win the Conservative leadership in 1975, her uphill struggle to impose her ideology on a Heathite team, her persistent feeling that the system was determined to frustrate her reforms had produced a political leader driven not just by ideology, but by an immanent sense of being right.

She now believed that she knew better than almost anyone what was right and what was wrong; and not just about mainstream political subjects such as the economy. If she devoted enough of her own energy to any subject, she thought she was likelier to reach the correct conclusion than those who had laboured longer in that field: ministers, bishops, football administrators, police, lawyers, social workers. This is a description not so much of an ideology as of a mission. Missions make for great triumphs and great disasters. As the 'economic miracle' turned sour,

Tory MPs worried about her political persona. Admirers continued to admire, but the more doubting began to speak of her as insensitive, narrow, humourless, with growing signs of arrogance, intolerance, even megalomania.

The party chairman, Kenneth Baker, believed she had picked herself up after her depression at the turn of the year, partly through her own remarkable work-rate. Because of the gathering political crisis, Baker was now as close to her as any other minister. He had become an important political figure in his own right, and for a time was one of four or five ministers spoken of as a possible successor. Indeed, since Geoffrey Howe's eclipse some thought the serious contenders were Hurd, Heseltine and Baker.

The Prime Minister recognised in Ken Baker the kind of fertile political mind and dynamic presenter of policy that a government in trouble desperately needed. More sniffy ministers might laughingly call him 'the Kabaka', and complain that to hear him at the Tory conference declaiming a purple passage from Shakespeare's *Henry V* was painful to people of discrimination and taste. Party conferences are not places suited to people with weak stomachs for well-cooked corn. The post of Chief Barker to the Conservative Party can vulgarise the most fastidious, as even the saintly Chris Patten discovered.

If Ken Baker was to be a leadership candidate, proximity to the Prime Minister had both advantages and disadvantages. Critics said he had never stood up to her enough. This applied particularly to his previous job, Education Secretary. During that period, one minister had so mis-understood my observer status as to urge me to tell Ken she could not sack him, and that he ought to list for her which of her changes in education he could accept and which were intolerable. As reporters at the *News of the World* say, in more lurid circumstances, 'At this stage I made an excuse and left.'

By the spring of 1990 Baker was uncomfortably aware that her troubles, notably over the poll tax, were offering a golden opportunity to a serious rival, Michael Heseltine. Despite his reputation as a parliamentary loner, Heseltine was now lunching and dining with MPs from all parts of his party. He was especially encouraged by hints that right-wingers might accept his ambiguous claim to have been 'a Thatcherite before Thatcher'. What some at least on the right now thought desirable was 'Thatcherism *without* Thatcher'.

As undeclared candidates shaped up in this unthinkable leadership election, what struck them was the changed political complexion of the Conservative Party in the Commons. Because it had been led from the right for more than a dozen years, there were many more right-wing MPs. It is one of the uncomfortable paradoxes of politics that, at roughly the time when an ideology has lost the first bloom of youth, and is displaying its downside, the party which nurtures it has just begun to catch up. As Margaret Thatcher's leadership moved toward its close, the Tories might have been better served with fewer of the new intake from the right. Neil Kinnock and his successors would later face a similar problem, on the other wing of their party.

But aspirants to the Tory succession had to deal with the party as it existed. Not only Michael Heseltine, but Kenneth Baker knew he had to get votes from right-wing MPs. When someone commented to Baker that the right did not have a candidate, he quipped: 'What about me?' A strange aspiration for a man whose origins were in more traditional Toryism. But another candidate whose name was barely mentioned in the spring of 1990 was drawing the same lesson from his study of the modern party. John Major, once a member of the 'Blue Chips', a group of young Wets from the early years of Thatcherism, also knew that anyone who wanted to lead the Conservatives now needed votes from the right.

Tories believed they were facing their toughest general election challenge for almost twenty years. One MP said he had never received such a hostile postbag as on the poll tax, and that Conservatives throughout the country were experiencing similar hostility. There were three counts against Margaret Thatcher: the public thought she had been there too long; after eleven years Britain's problems remained unsolved; and the poll tax had been a mistake.

As rows over this dribbled damagingly on, rumours about another leadership challenge in November 1990 burgeoned. A junior minister, fresh from canvassing in the May elections, sadly acknowledged that she was no longer a vote-winner, and enjoyed little affection on the doorsteps any more. The C1s and C2s were turning against the Conservatives on bread-and-butter issues. Backbenchers were now saying openly that if they could move to a new leader without damaging internal strife, they would do so.

I learned in early spring about what one of the participants called 'an Establishment plot'. Alan Clark had been asked the previous year to be prepared for what would happen if a bad result against Sir Anthony Meyer forced Margaret Thatcher's resignation. A plotter told him there had to be a 'stop Heseltine candidate', and asked if he was willing, as a Minister of State from the right, to nominate Douglas Hurd. Nicholas Scott, a Minister of State from the left, would second him. Clark agreed to do so, provided the Prime Minister had gone voluntarily, and not been pushed by the 1922 Committee.

How serious was the Establishment plot or – more accurately, if less dramatically – this contingency plan? Alan Clark, as his *Diaries* reveal, is not inclined to undervalue his own significance in the development of great events. What became clear when the Prime Minister actually had to step down a year later, is that the Establishment is now less important for such purposes than it thinks. Instead, the old verities of right and left, of political ambition, ancient antagonisms, friendships and hostilities reassert themselves. But the story does illustrate the febrile mood in the winter of 1989–90.

Douglas Hurd himself heard about this story, but dismissed its importance. He and Kenneth Baker had discussed Margaret Thatcher's troubles, and had agreed it would be better for the Tories if they could keep her in post: the turbulence of change would be too damaging. Michael Heseltine also heard of the supposed Establishment plot, and sadly concluded that Tristan Garel-Jones, the influential Deputy Chief Whip, might be involved. He was surprised by his 'stop Heseltine' activities, because they had always been friendly. So he philosophically concluded that by running Hurd as a caretaker, Garel-Jones's aim must be to keep the leadership open for his close friend, Chris Patten, or for John Major. In the eventual contest, Garel-Jones continued to back Hurd. The Major camp also concluded that his objective in this was to promote the long-term interests of Patten.

Through all this, Michael Heseltine behaved with great circumspection. His strategy remained what it had always been: to say nothing which could be interpreted as disloyal. By following that policy ever since he left the government, while making clear his own views on Europe, industry, poll tax and other issues, he had encouraged the proactive Heseltine group to grow in numbers, and eroded the reactive group. If he did anything active against Margaret Thatcher, he reasoned, it might encourage his supporters, but it would also mobilise his opponents. Heseltine's underlying belief, which was confirmed by events, was that the man who wields the dagger rarely wins the crown. In the end, like Harold Wilson in 1960, he was deprived of the luxury of choice, and had to challenge her.

But in early summer, he still claimed not to be under any great pressure to do so, since most of his supporters accepted the logic outlined above. Yet his instincts told him she was in such deep political trouble – in a Cabinet minority of one or two on poll tax, for example – that someone would challenge her, or that she would go before that challenge occurred.

He remained on the *qui vive*. But he felt happier about his own future than he had done at any time since he left the government. He said to friends the worst position he would gain in a leadership contest was second. The logic of this was important to his career: he had always believed that any new leader would bring him back into a good Cabinet post. He had no illusions that Margaret Thatcher would do so. The wounds on either side had gone too deep.

Were there any signs that the Prime Minister herself contemplated retiring before the next election? I found none, though one intimate told me that Denis Thatcher once said to him: 'If it were my choice, she would have gone at nine o'clock yesterday morning.' An impish junior minister thought Denis must inevitably be suggesting to her that she should 'chuck it in', so that they could 'sail four times round the world, mostly to golf courses'.

Jim Callaghan had a conversation that pointed in the same direction. At Indira Gandhi's funeral, he found himself standing beside Denis Thatcher at a reception, and told him: 'Mine's a wonderful life. Wherever I travel, I'm treated as a Prime Minister, looked after, meet the people I want to meet. But there are no red boxes waiting to be worked through each night. I can commend it.' To this the Prime Minister's husband replied fervently: 'I can't wait.' Her own view, however, was that she still had work to do, and she did not trust anyone else to do it.

More openly disrespectful ministers said that, although she looked tired, she still occasionally went off on 'ideological rants'. They maintained she did this only to let off steam, rather than in pursuit of policy. One cited an occasion when John Major was explaining what the French and Germans wanted to do about aid for Russia. The Prime Minister thought she was being railroaded, and proceeded to complain to Major, at some length. The Chancellor waited until her rhetoric ran down, and then said: 'I am deeply grateful to you, Prime Minister, for giving me that gentle steer.' The Cabinet dissolved in laughter, and Major's view prevailed.

This was a light-hearted exchange, though it was not the way ministers would have felt free to treat her during most of her time in Downing Street. By now, John Major was closer to her than most. After he became Chancellor in October 1989, he met her privately at least once a week, and sometimes more often. These were not just Prime Minister/Chancellor meetings, but roamed over the whole political scene. The swinging door of Downing Street was now swinging, and so was John Major's career.

In November, he came to lunch with me straight from a meeting with the Prime Minister, who was leaving for New York. This was during the turbulence arising from the Meyer challenge. She had seemed to him reasonably relaxed over rumours about her future, and felt she could control events. John Major certainly wanted her to stay on, as he also did during the Heseltine challenge the following year, because he thought that was best for the Conservatives; probably best for himself as well, since many still considered him too young and inexperienced to succeed.

By then Margaret Thatcher was beginning to relax a little. I heard of one occasion when she breezed into a meeting, slapped her file on the table, and said to the assembling ministers: 'I'm in a dreadful hurry this morning. I've really only got time to explode.' Self-satire had not been a notable feature of the earlier Thatcher years.

In what proved to be her final year in office, a pro-European minister detected a battle between her head and heart on Europe, the ERM, and the whole ideological business of floating exchange rates. Michael Portillo, an emerging figure of the right, not yet in the Cabinet, believed that she remained at heart a free floater, but noted also that she was happiest when the pound was strong, because this showed overseas confidence in the British economy.

The most senior right-winger in the Cabinet, Nicholas Ridley, who had lost influence after being passed over for the chancellorship, now felt free to act as the Prime Minister's ideological conscience. When she sent him to the DTI, he warned her that he intended to range more widely over the whole field of government. The party chairman, Kenneth Baker, nervously thought of him as 'a licensed trouble-maker'. The Chief Whip observed that Ridley was a man with a mission – always a danger to good order within government.

Because of his dealings with Brussels at the Environment Department and now at the DTI, Ridley had become much more anti-Community. He was not advocating that Britain should come out, but was determined we should concentrate on the single market and on freeing financial services. Within the Cabinet, he was increasingly regarded as a loner, though those who worked closely with him admired him. Lord Caithness, one of his ministers, said he would 'walk over glass' for Nick Ridley.

Yet there was a sense that his ministerial career had nowhere further to go. The crisis came when, in an interview with Nigel Lawson's son, Dominic, editor of the *Spectator*, he was offensively critical of the Germans. The row rumbled on into a weekend. It was one of those many occasions when work devastated my family life. On Saturday we were entertaining my niece and her husband, who were making a rare visit from Ulster. But Ridley's PPS, Steven Norris, helpfully kept me up to date with the developing drama by telephone. Throughout lunchtime, I spent most of the time passing these nuggets on to colleagues who were broadcasting that day. By mid-afternoon Ridley had resigned, the family party had to be abandoned, and I went to the studios at Shepherds Bush for the rest of the evening.

The *Spectator* article and the forty-eight-hour wrangle over whether resignation was necessary produced conflicting reactions. Kenneth Baker believed Ridley would have to go. Alan Clark records in his *Diaries* his own characteristic belief that 'Nick's performance was a welcome return to the old doings of the nineteenth century, when major figures of the government could digress giftedly and constructively on the issues of the day, without constantly being hauled over the coals by some wanker in the FCO Press Office.'

He recalls making these remarks to a group of journalists in the Members' Lobby, and records my own objection to this theory: that in the days of which he was speaking, it took three weeks for newspapers to get to Berlin. Other right-wingers took a more anxious view of the affair. Eric Forth, arguing that Ridley ought not to be sacked, said the No Turning Back group felt they had no other representative in the Cabinet. Anyhow, Mrs Thatcher was really a Ridleyite, though she had other concerns, like holding her party together. But he suspected she saw Ridley as one minister able to say what she would have liked to say.

By the middle of 1990, the possibility that Margaret Thatcher herself might have to retire was firmly on the agenda, though the sheer enormity of this proposition still deterred many Conservatives from contemplating it. Some of my conversations had to be conducted on a 'what if?' basis. The front-runners had changed: still Douglas Hurd, for those who wanted a period of calm; still Michael Heseltine, for those who believed Conservatives would want a clean break after Margaret Thatcher; and now John Major, the man she herself had put in good shape for the succession – though when she left, in her own good time. At one stage, even Willie Whitelaw suspected the Heseltine option might attract the party.

Many Tories on the left still cherished the thought that Chris Patten could be their leader, either if Mrs Thatcher stayed a little longer, or if Hurd acted as caretaker. Patten's position was unenviable. As the obvious rival to John Major among the younger generation of Tories, he was held back by the job Margaret Thatcher had given him. Responsibility for handling the poll tax had put him under a cloud. He himself thought the disastrous policy he had inherited had brought the Conservative

Party close to collective nervous breakdown that spring, and added: 'I could have gone the way of John Moore.'

His impossible dilemma convinced me once again that choice of party leaders involves a large element of luck. Often it depends mainly on what happens in the three months before a vacancy occurs: who does well then, or simply is fortunate enough to be in the right place at the right time; or at least not in the wrong place.

By now, the luckier contenders had their eyes on where their leadership votes might come from. The enigma was John Major. The doubts about what his instinctive political position was – which have persisted until the present time – first surfaced then. Many Cabinet traditionalists favoured him, because they believed he came from the left. The Chief Whip, Tim Renton, seemed to suspect this might no longer be true, though he thought Major's real position remained to be proved.

Nigel Lawson, who observed him from closer range than most, thought his successor at the Treasury was, as he told Major's PPS, Tony Favell, the weekend before his own resignation, 'a complete politician'. Certainly nobody would have said of John Major that he was an ideologue; or that like Nigel himself he came into parliament to be Chancellor of the Exchequer, and thought politics was an unfortunate prerequisite of that ambition. John Major loved the game itself.

A close observer of the 'Blue Chip' group said Major's political position was complex. He had not been an original Blue Chip, but when they decided they needed to extend their influence, they had 'spotted' likely people and invited them to join. Major was one of these. My informant said his instincts were 'more Thatcherite' than the others. Another ex-minister thought he supported the Prime Minister principally because he was grateful to her for his remarkable promotions.

John Major and Chris Patten had an interesting relationship. Until recently, these two had been thought of as leading candidates, assuming Margaret Thatcher would retire in the mid-nineties. They clearly liked each other. When I asked Chris Patten if John Major was 'one of us', from his own standpoint as champion of left-wing Toryism, he said yes, in that he had 'decent instincts'. But Major was incredibly tough, and did not inherit the middle-class guilt which those like himself, with a liberal education, had. For example, he did not feel the same need to please the higher education establishment.

On the right, there were doubts about John Major's Thatcherism, though it was assumed he would receive the right-wing votes. From as far back as December 1989 Michael Portillo had been an enthusiastic supporter of Major as the next leader, though when the Cabinet deserted

Margaret Thatcher, he was to be one of the last to try to persuade her to hang on. Many on the right were less sure than Portillo, and remained puzzled about Major's gut political instincts.

Years before, while he was at the DHSS, he had selected as his PPS Tony Favell, a Stockport MP who belonged to the No Turning Back group of right-wingers. This was a shrewd move. Ambitious ministers on one wing of the Conservative Party are wise to keep themselves right by having their 'eyes-and-ears' on the opposite wing. Favell was intensely loyal to Major, and had no fear that, if he became Prime Minister, he would turn his back on Thatcherism. To doubters on the right, he argued that although Major was a social Tory, he was by far the best leader the right could hope for.

This was a time when those of us who passed through Waterloo station first noticed a huge growth in the number of beggars, and grew depressed at what this said about our society. Many of them were young people, others unsuccessful products of the government's Care in the Community programme, which was intended to bring patients out of long-stay hospitals, but with more support than they were evidently receiving. When I suggested to one minister, who had long been critical of Margaret Thatcher, that the government's policies were responsible for the growing numbers of such derelicts, he made a perfunctory defence, and then said bluntly that she would 'like to turn the hoses on them'. What! He immediately explained that this was an exaggeration: it was simply that she regarded such people as a 'police problem'; but the police argued that if there was nowhere else for vagrants to go, it made no sense for them simply to be moved on.

Tony Favell told me if I was worried about the plight of Waterloo's outcasts, John Major was the Conservative leadership candidate who would do something to help them. Although he had taken tough decisions himself as a minister at the DHSS, his politics had a social dimension, and he was concerned about the underprivileged. This was my own impression, from conversations with Major himself. I first heard him talking about 'the classless society' before he ever mentioned it in a speech.

But what were the practical implications? Major maintained that his compassion leaped over the upwardly mobile to lower down the social heap. I think at that time he was probably conducting a subconscious argument with Margaret Thatcher, who was obsessed with the interests of mortgage-holders, her electoral base. He acknowledged that it was bad that high interest rates meant people had to pay extra for their mortgages, but he was more concerned about those in society who had tried, but not quite succeeded, who could not afford a house because of inflated prices. This made him passionately against inflation which, he argued, inflicted greater punishment on the less well-off than on the better-off.

The party leadership was never far from Major's mind, or from that of journalists like myself, since by now I believed a change could not be long delayed. For example, he ruminated about ages: both Ted Heath and Margaret Thatcher had become leader while still in their forties. He and Chris Patten were now in their mid-forties. John would make no move to replace Margaret Thatcher, but he was preparing for contingencies.

By the spring of 1990, having settled into the Treasury, he knew that the economy was unlikely to come right quickly. He hoped the nadir of the government's fortunes might be in May or June, and that better economic indices would be enough to improve Conservative morale and fortify the Prime Minister's standing. Aside from her interests, that would make his own succession more probable. But I began to suspect that, because he could not be sure this economic revival would come so quickly, he would prepare himself for whatever might happen.

Indeed, John Major had never concealed his ambition. Anyone worth a place in the Cabinet ought to think about the next step, provided this is not allowed to corrode the soul. I have little patience with the rubric that ministers sometimes use to journalists: that they 'are very happy doing this job'. This may be true, but it is rarely the whole truth. Anyone who reaches senior Cabinet level without at least fleeting thoughts about the possibility of Number 10, the Treasury, or the Foreign Office may not even be up to his or her existing post. In 1994, once Kenneth Clarke was established as Chancellor, he felt no need to conceal his ambition to succeed John Major.

Only, of course, when the time was right (or ripe), as the saying goes.

45

MICHAEL RAISES HIS STANDARD

I had lunch with Geoffrey Howe the day before he resigned. It was a guarded occasion. My guest was drinking only water, because he had been putting on weight. But he also had a lot on his mind. The following morning, Madge and I flew to Paris for a long weekend there – or so we thought.

Soon after arriving, I telephoned the BBC office to tell David Walter, an old Westminster colleague, that we were in Paris, and would like to meet some time that weekend. When we returned to our hotel after an early dinner, I was surprised that David had called so soon: he was sitting in the lobby, awaiting us. But his motives were not social. When the Howe resignation was announced, the BBC had hauled him out of a concert to find me. David pushed me into the hotel telephone kiosk, where he already had a line open to London, in the hope that I would be in time for the end of the *Nine O'Clock News*.

That did not work out, but we then went to the Paris studios, for a late-night broadcast on *Newsnight*; followed by a few hours' sleep, broadcasts for *Breakfast News* and the *Today* programme, and an early flight back to London. The priorities of news organisations are always strictly practical: the BBC organised our return to London with lightning efficiency: club class only was available, with champagne accompanying breakfast (never my favourite drink at any time of day). It took them some months to recompense me for what I spent on my lost weekend.

Geoffrey Howe was more considerate: a polite note arrived soon afterwards, saying that at the time of our lunch his mind had not finally been made up. He added that, even if it had been, both of us understood that he could not have told me. That, I thought sadly, is life.

The Prime Minister had given her report on the Rome summit to the Commons on Tuesday, 30 October. Douglas Hurd and others worked carefully on the text, which was designed to keep a divided Conservative

Party appearing as united as possible. Then came the question-and-answer session, the period when Margaret Thatcher's stream of consciousness tended to take over from Whitehall caution. As a friend of Hurd's put it later, 'she was bowled a soft ball, and couldn't help hitting it out of sight'.

The following week, an exasperated Cabinet member moaned at the memory of the performance that had driven Geoffrey Howe over the cliff into resignation: 'I have spent fifteen years pretending that she would change. Someone writes her a wonderful statement, like the one on Europe she had last week. Everything was fine while she was reading it. But then a question provokes her, and she leaves the script ... that's when you get what T.S. Eliot called "the beauty of it hot".'

The faces of Geoffrey Howe, Douglas Hurd and John Major, sitting behind her on the front bench, were studies in inscrutability. I recorded at the time that there was no need, so far as this Cabinet was concerned, to maintain the ban which the Commons had imposed on television reaction shots. The stone-faced Presidium of the Soviet Communist Party in the Brezhnev years could not have hidden their thoughts more completely. In Howe's case, this was partly because he had missed her most unrelenting words about Europe. In one of those moments which might change history, Tom King was chatting to him at the relevant time.

When he read *Hansard* the next day, Geoffrey was struck by the great difference in tone between the original statement, which was very measured and, to his surprise, rather pro-European, and her response to questions. In particular, he had not realised at the time how difficult she had made John Major's task. He was persuading other finance ministers to take seriously Britain's proposal for a 'hard ECU' (which might or might not evolve into a common currency). The Prime Minister had given one questioner her opinion that this would not be widely used. She had also said that she had not been as strident in the heads of government meeting as she was in the broadcast interviews afterwards. When I remarked that it would be difficult to be as tough to somebody's face as she had been in these interviews, Geoffrey Howe laughed, and quoted a saying of the Inner Temple: 'Even in affidavits, the truth will break through.'

The Prime Minister's standing was undermined by the resignation of the man who had been her deputy for fifteen months, though in title rather than reality. In public, ministers made calming statements. Douglas Hurd regarded leadership speculation as 'the sort of froth that clears away quite quickly'. John Major had 'no doubt' that she would remain leader up to and after the general election. Kenneth Clarke professed himself 'quite convinced' of that.

In private, ministers were less certain. Many of them had been friends of Geoffrey Howe's for a long time, in some cases protégés; longer than the period during which they had felt any great personal loyalty to Margaret Thatcher. They foresaw turbulence on the back benches, and an almost certain attempt to remove her. This threat to the Prime Minister swiftly replaced Howe's resignation as the main subject of discussion. At once I reported on the television news that the absolute dominance she had exerted over her Cabinets since she confronted and sacked the Wets in the early eighties was now slipping away. I predicted that she would have a hard fight on her hands to hold on to her job. She would fight, because she was an instinctive fighter, but she was now in much deeper trouble than she had ever faced in the past.

Only a fortnight before, when a challenge was just a possibility, I had met the Prime Minister, and been left in no doubt that her combative spirit remained. When I remarked that Bernard Ingham had been making clear that any challenge would be 'most fiercely contested', she fixed me with a baleful glance – as if I intended to put in for the job myself – and said, with flashing eyes: 'Do you want it straight from me?' Less histrionically, she debated with herself whether a challenge would be a good or a bad development: as a sign of disunity it might damage the Tories; but on the other hand, it might lance the boil.

The speed with which the leadership crisis developed dictated a change in my reporting methods. Since I had moved to broadcasting, late in my journalistic career, what were called 'packages' – that is, scripted reports which incorporate clips from interviews by politicians – had been the principal form of our reporting from Westminster. On radio, I also often did 'two-ways' – conversations with the presenter – principally for the *Today* programme. I did these also for *Newsnight* on television.

Senior colleagues told me I was good at 'two-ways', and encouraged me to do more of them. For almost a quarter of a century, I had been accustomed to this format, when I appeared, as a newspaper journalist, mainly on Independent Television. But now, as a full-time broadcaster, I was suspicious of any theory that 'two-ways' could replace 'packages' – which I regarded as 'real' television journalism. Colleagues found our role reversal both amusing and surprising: I was regarded as a broadcaster with a cavalier attitude to pictures, so it seemed to them strange that I should be resisting a move to use me more often as a commentator. In 'two-ways', the words were all-important, since the only picture was of me, often windswept on College Green.

Since then – I think partly as a result of the use of 'two-ways' during the Conservative leadership crisis of November 1990 – these have developed as a much more common form of television journalism. They have become commonplace, and sometimes worthwhile, as a means of reporting from war zones. In my own case, the Thatcher leadership crisis is one of those rare occasions when I am willing to admit I was wrong, and that editors were right to overrule me. 'Two-ways' often enabled me to tell a fast-developing story better.

The reason I am troubling readers with what may seem like a tedious BBC technical debate is that the account of Margaret Thatcher's final days which follows is based heavily on transcripts of my 'two-way' broadcasts. During those hectic days, I did not have time to make notes of conversations: what I learned from these went on the air as quickly as I could get to a microphone or camera. Often I can no longer remember who told me of fresh developments. But a discriminating reader will note the unfortunate result which made me suspicious of 'two-ways' in the first place: the account lacks some of the coolness of judgement, even elegance of thought, which was possible when I had time to write a script.

A principal reason why I never crossed the frontier from my first love, journalism, to a later love, politics, is that I thought my talents were better exercised behind a typewriter than on my hind legs. While I hoped I had some political intelligence and judgement, I had no illusions that I was quick-witted. To watch Harold Macmillan or Harold Wilson at the dispatch box was a valuable deterrent to political ambition. So it was strange that in my later career, I should find myself a surprised victim of spontaneity. With that health warning, the story continues.

When Geoffrey Howe was removed from the Foreign Office in July 1989, his first appearance as Leader of the House had produced an amazingly warm ovation from the Conservative benches. Now the sudden resignation of such a popular figure revived dormant doubts about Margaret Thatcher's style of leadership. She consistently under-estimated his standing in her party. Just before he resigned, she treated him with great brusqueness at successive Cabinet meetings, savaging his plans for the legislative programme. His ministerial friends were scorching in their criticism of her behaviour. For the first time, many Tories began to say she could not win the general election. Margaret Thatcher was suddenly in a crisis of confidence.

The atmosphere remained feverish when MPs returned from their constituencies. In the Queen's Speech debate, she made a fatal mistake in her reference to Sir Geoffrey Howe's resignation by implying that his departure had come more for personal than political reasons. The party chairman, Kenneth Baker, also suggested that the resignation was about political style, not policy. When the Prime Minister claimed that his resignation letter showed no significant difference between his views of Europe and her own, Howe was as angry as a normally placid man can be. In his resignation speech the following week he would taunt them with the thought that he must be 'the first minister in history [to resign] because he was in full agreement with government policy'.

On the Sunday before Howe's sensational resignation speech, I forecast in my *On the Record* commentary that, because of continuing loyalty to Margaret Thatcher among grassroots Conservative activists, no stalking-horse would stand: 'Only a Heseltine challenge can open up the leadership issue . . . the key to Heseltine is Sir Geoffrey Howe. This weekend the former Deputy Prime Minister is drafting his resignation speech with infinite care.'

On Tuesday 13 November, Geoffrey Howe launched his thunderbolt. He raised the very same issue which had caused not only Nigel Lawson, but also Michael Heseltine, her likely challenger, to leave the Cabinet earlier: her domineering style of conducting government business. Her recent deputy wanted to know how could they go on pretending that the government had a common policy on Europe, 'when every step forward risks being subverted by some casual comment or impulsive answer'? And he ended with a transparent invitation for a challenge to her. It was to come, predictably, not from within her Cabinet, but from Michael Heseltine.

The resignation speech produced immediate turmoil in the Members' Lobby. Margaret Thatcher's Tory critics gleefully declared that she was 'already dead in the water', or that 'the game is up for her'. Members of the Cabinet began to say privately that if Michael Heseltine challenged her, she could lose. Once the senior figures came to suspect this, they inevitably began to make their own contingency plans, however discreetly.

Immediately Geoffrey Howe sat down, I learned that Heseltine was 'consulting friends' that evening. There is no more transparent euphemism. So I told the *Six O'Clock News* audience that he would announce his candidature the following day, as he did. I went further at 9 p.m., declaring that the Prime Minister was now in such deep trouble with her party that, although she would not be beaten in the first ballot of the contest against Michael Heseltine, there would be enough votes against her and enough abstentions to leave her gravely damaged. I added: 'People are now beginning to say the unthinkable.'

Although Michael Heseltine still suspected that whoever wielded the dagger would not inherit the crown, Howe's speech left him little option. The whole of his political life in the four years since he had marched so dramatically out of her Cabinet had no other logical conclusion. His announcement was delayed that evening only because he saw advantage in leaving the next morning's headlines to reveal the full gravamen of Sir Geoffrey's condemnation.

On Wednesday 14 November, I received an early telephone call from Michael Mates, MP for Hampshire East, Heseltine's principal lieutenant. He invited me to Michael's house for an interview, in which his candidature would be announced. While Anne Heseltine served us coffee, her husband explained his intentions. At least 100 Tory MPs were urging him to stand, because they believed polls showed he had a better chance than Margaret Thatcher of winning a general election. He promised a review of the poll tax, more enthusiasm about Europe, and a different style of government.

Cabinet ministers were now privately talking about a 'stop Heseltine' candidate. Attitudes to Michael among his colleagues were strange. In his wilderness years, many of them spoke warmly to me about him. Several who proved hostile when he challenged Margaret Thatcher had even said earlier they would be quite happy to serve under him. But within Cabinets, or even shadow Cabinets, an odd chemistry operates. A feeling emerges that 'somebody inside' is entitled to the job, since they have borne the heat of political battle together. Above all, even if their own judgements were that Heseltine might make quite a good Prime Minister, Margaret Thatcher's attitude created a deep prejudice against him. In the end, he destroyed her premiership, but she destroyed his chance to succeed her.

For many months, throughout the traumas of poll tax and European election defeats, Douglas Hurd had been spoken of as 'the Number 11 bus candidate', the minister most likely to take over if the Prime Minister fell, in carefully undefined circumstances. Some thought his lack of economic experience was a fatal flaw, though supporters maintained his manifest intelligence would easily fill that gap.

When Heseltine declared his candidature, John Major was robust in his support for Thatcher. He declared: 'The Prime Minister has been nominated by the Foreign Secretary, seconded by me, we expect her to win, we hope she will win, we hope she will remain leader of the Conservative Party.' Then, lest anybody should be in doubt about his views, he added: 'I hope and expect and am confident that that will be the case.' But privately the Chancellor's friends were taking precautions. If Margaret Thatcher's dismissal became inevitable, they did not want Douglas Hurd to be swept in as a Tory Establishment successor.

At 6 p.m. I reported that while Douglas Hurd and John Major remained totally loyal to the Prime Minister, they were 'obviously reserving their position about what would happen in what they regard as hypothetical and, they say, unlikely circumstances'. (That is the kind of off-the-cuff prose I am not proud of, but these chapters tell the story as I reported it at the time.) What is clear is that, like the prospective alternative Prime Minister, I was keeping *my* mind open to the possibility that she might be gone quickly.

By Friday 16 November, I was convinced that if Margaret Thatcher did badly in the first ballot, John Major, Douglas Hurd, Willie Whitelaw, her former deputy, and George Younger, her campaign manager, would warn her of two ineluctable results: that she risked humiliation in a second ballot against Heseltine; and that even if she survived this, she would be so badly damaged as to face defeat by Neil Kinnock in the general election.

Senior ministers now accepted that, even if she did beat Heseltine, the best she could hope for was 'a lap of honour', before retirement. They would persuade her to retire within a few months. If not, they would at least use her narrow escape to 'tie Gulliver down', in John Major's graphic phrase. But if she continued as a wounded Prime Minister, it could be disastrous for the Tories.

On that Friday, the Chancellor went to the old television studios in the Norman Shaw Building, across from the House of Commons, to give interviews on the latest economic statistics. Any idea that his withdrawal that weekend, first to hospital, and then to his home in Huntingdonshire, was because of a diplomatic illness is misplaced. John Major had been suffering from his impacted wisdom tooth for months, but despite the painkillers prescribed for him, the discomfort and fever now made him look quite ill. His decision to go ahead with the operation was inevitable, though he tolerated the witticism that he was awaiting the nation's call at Colombey-les-deux-wisdom-teeth.

Earlier in the week, Douglas Hurd and John Major had breakfast together. As proposer and seconder, they were not involved in any conspiracy to get rid of Margaret Thatcher. But both shared the Cabinet majority view that Britain's future would best be served by a sensible relationship with Europe. Both were now deeply worried about what she might say and do on this subject, and extremely suspicious of the

influences of old political friends. John Major was especially anxious
about the noises coming to her ears from what he used to call 'the daft
right off-stage'. To me, these noises seemed to be increasingly on-stage.

The anxieties of the Chancellor and Foreign Secretary centred principally on the influence of one of her closest political friends, Nicholas
Ridley, who had resigned after making disparaging remarks about
Germany, but was still close to her; and of Norman Tebbit. When
Geoffrey Howe resigned, she invited Norman to return to the Cabinet
as Education Secretary, but more importantly as one who sympathised
with her scepticism about Europe. He declined for personal reasons: his
wife, Margaret, has been severely paralysed since the Brighton bombing.
But Tebbit remained an important influence.

John Major's position, like that of Douglas Hurd, remained
unchanged: if she decided to stay in the contest, they would continue to
support her. Major hoped her personal considerateness to MPs would
win her sympathy. But simultaneously he was doing his sums. When
journalists told him Michael Heseltine might receive as many as 140
votes on the first ballot, he was surprised. Yet the Chancellor himself
noticed some surprising people showing their heads above the parapet
for Heseltine, and thought this could only encourage others to do so.
Taking 140 votes for Heseltine as a hypothesis, he drew a diagram to
clear his mind as to the probabilities.

There were 372 Conservative MPs who had votes. If you subtracted
140 from that, 232 votes were left, to be divided between Margaret
Thatcher and abstentions. Under the rules, she needed to fulfil two
requirements: to gain 187 votes – fifty per cent of the electorate plus
one; and to beat Heseltine by 56 votes – fifteen per cent of the electorate. If she were to receive just the 187 votes, she would need up
to 45 abstentions from those who could not bring themselves to vote
for either her or Heseltine. John Major did not expect a second ballot,
and he distanced himself from efforts to promote him as a fall-back
candidate.

But because a second ballot would allow other candidates to enter the
fray, all potential leaders and their supporters were eyeing the others, and
calculating who might break ranks. John Major believed that if she were
to win fewer than half the Tory MPs to her banner, or even a little more
than that, her Cabinet colleagues would advise her that she should not
risk humiliation by going to a second ballot. The opposition would
inevitably emphasise how many votes were cast against her. After three
general election victories, none of her Tory admirers, or even former
admirers, wanted her to lose a fourth. In this, naturally, they were

thinking not only about her personal humiliation, but about their party's hold on office.

Most Conservatives expected an uncomfortably close call for Margaret Thatcher. Senior ministers considered what improvements in the conduct of government business they might force on her. They reasoned that surely even she would become more amenable this time. Major, Hurd and the Cabinet's pro-European majority were now determined she must not be allowed to jeopardise Britain's chances of successful negotiations in Europe by making warlike noises in advance of the next summit, as she had done so often in the past. They thought a weak Thatcher victory, which was the best she could hope for, would at least serve to strengthen their own hands.

Most believed that, even if she won technically, the leadership issue would not be over: MPs might give her a narrow victory, in the hope that she would see it would be sensible to go within a few months. That Friday before the first ballot, a mood was growing among the best-informed people at Westminster that, by one means or another, and on whatever time-scale, Margaret Thatcher's long leadership of the Conservative Party was drawing towards its close.

During the weekend, Tory MPs consulted in their constituencies. This was ostensibly about the Thatcher–Heseltine choice they faced the following Tuesday. But they were already beginning to float before the eyes of surprised supporters the names of John Major and Douglas Hurd. Those two were still committed to standing by her, so long as she remained in the contest, but they could no longer close their eyes to what might happen within ninety-six hours.

The Foreign Secretary, facing yet another importunate reporter, declared his hope that the Prime Minister would win decisively on the first ballot. But when asked whether he would rule out standing for the leadership in any circumstances, Douglas Hurd gave the taut, but pregnant answer: 'Against her.' This confirmed that he would not challenge Margaret Thatcher, but left his hands free if she withdrew. John Major was also at pains to say publicly that he would not stand while the Prime Minister remained in the contest, though he also expressed his belief that there would be no second round.

In the event, Major's Friday calculations were upset not by a failure in Margaret Thatcher's support – she actually got 204, rather than just the 187 which represented half her MPs. It was the abstentions which fell far short of what might have been anticipated: only sixteen MPs who were dissatisfied with the Prime Minister refused to vote for Michael Heseltine. That gave him 152, twelve more than had been allocated to him in the journalists' hypothesis. The result for Mrs Thatcher was disastrous: she fell short, by four votes, of the fifteen per cent margin over Heseltine which she needed to win on the first ballot.

46

THE LADY'S CRUEL EXIT

On the Sunday before that first ballot, there was a flurry of interviews by the Prime Minister and Michael Heseltine. She reignited their old quarrel over Westland, saying he had been unwilling to accept Cabinet responsibility. But the challenger took that charge head-on, by raising Europe, on which he claimed to be closer to the views of Margaret Thatcher's two key ministers, the Chancellor and Foreign Secretary, than she herself was. The moment when observers realised how close to her jugular Heseltine's challenge struck was when he savaged her for claiming omnipotence: 'Is parliament not to be allowed to consider these matters? Has the Cabinet no role in these things? That is the essence of the problem – that is why Sir Geoffrey Howe resigned. That is why Nigel Lawson resigned. That is why I resigned – because the Prime Minister feels so strongly on these matters that collective Cabinet responsibility . . . is not acceptable to her.'

The Prime Minister's anxiety in face of his challenge showed in the miscalculations she made. She offended some Tories by saying that Michael Heseltine's views were corporatist, and 'more akin to Labour's'; and when she hinted that there might be a referendum on the single currency, even two of her most loyal ministers, John Wakeham and Cecil Parkinson, had not been consulted, and were nervous about the proposal.

By Monday evening many Tory MPs were keeping their own counsel, and others were promising their votes to both sides. I judged then that Margaret Thatcher was unlikely to emerge from the contest with Michael Heseltine in a strong enough position to carry on for long as Prime Minister. At the end of the *Nine O'Clock News*, having studied every barometric gauge available, I hazarded the guess that if as many as 150 or 160 of her MPs failed to support her, either by voting for Heseltine or abstaining, her position would be hazardous.

The results on Tuesday evening were worse than that. Forty-five per cent of the Parliamentary Conservative Party had turned their backs on the woman who had led them for fifteen years. If she remained in office, this was a gift-wrapped statistic for Labour and Liberal Democrats to use all the way to the next general election. The Tories would enter that election so bitterly divided that victory would be almost impossible.

So although Douglas Hurd and John Major had publicly to endorse her decision to carry on into the second ballot, the ground beneath her feet was shifting rapidly. Some who had voted for her, including ministers, had warned her campaign team and their whips in advance that they would desert if she did not win outright on the first ballot. Cabinet ministers began privately to consider their options. Conservatism's wise old man, Lord Whitelaw, who was to see the Chief Whip, Tim Renton, the following morning, had concluded that she would be wise to withdraw. At Westminster, by bedtime on Tuesday, Margaret Thatcher, absent in Paris, looked to be mortally wounded.

As soon as I arrived at the House on Wednesday morning, Conservative MPs began stopping me in corridors and in the Members' Lobby to tell me that if she persisted in her declared intention to enter the second ballot, they would switch their votes to Michael Heseltine. One even said he had written to tell her this. The Heseltine campaign, inundated by fresh offers of support, believed that if she carried on, victory for their man was certain.

The No Turning Back group, blaming ineptitude in her campaign for her poor showing, were offering to organise it better, and pleading that she should carry on. But as I hurried across to Downing Street for a 'two-way' on the lunchtime news, a Cabinet minister (quoting, unconsciously I assume, from a Victorian ballad) told me 'her time of departure had come', and that he was consulting with colleagues about how to bring this about.

Margaret Thatcher had now arrived back from Paris, and called a lunchtime council of war. As Cranley Onslow, the normally taciturn chairman of the 1922 Committee, left the House to attend this, I learned that he was going to report the views of a sharply divided executive. The Chief Whip was receiving many panic calls. Those whose priority was to 'stop Heseltine' were already pressing Major and Hurd to put their names forward. At 1 p.m., I reported 'a substantial defection' to these two from the Prime Minister's supporters. They remained Margaret Thatcher's proposer and seconder, and therefore undeclared candidates. But beneath the surface, what looked like an American write-in campaign was under way.

Her situation was now desperate. But she emerged from Number 10 on her way to the House in Joan of Arc mood, and told the waiting cameras: 'I fight on, I fight to win.' Difficult to see what other line she *could* have taken, until the moment when she announced her withdrawal. But her defiant remark caused me to be asked at six o'clock: 'John, the rumours ran strong that she would call it a day. What went wrong in the rumour factory?' Doubtless this was not intended personally, though it showed scant respect for reports of trends in the Westminster lobbies I had been giving during the previous twenty-four hours.

My irritation at what I saw as the crassness of that question illustrates a chasm in attitudes among different trades in radio and television. Real broadcasting people – as distinct from late interlopers like myself – have, almost *ex-officio*, a reverential attitude to what politicians and others say 'on the record', even more so if they say it to *them*, in an interview, on *their* programme; or even, in the case of a news programme, if it provides the stunning quote in the headline sequence. For television presenters, unlike newspaper or broadcasting correspondents, an on-the-record comment is, after all, their bread and butter. They do not have the responsibility of reporting in the real world, where politicians' private thoughts are sometimes quite different from what they have to say in public.

The so-called 'rumours' that people wanted her to call it a day were running even more strongly than they had been at lunchtime. In that 6 p.m. interview, I reported that members of the Cabinet were at that moment seeing the Prime Minister individually. This turned out to be the crucial event of the whole election. By then I knew that at least four of them believed she must stand down, and that another five thought it would be better for the Conservative Party if she did. What I confessed I could not know is how far they and others would summon up the courage to tell her their honest opinions face to face. In the event, enough did this to convince her, only a couple of hours after her defiant 'I fight to win', that the game was up.

Many MPs worried that if she did not stand down, their party would be destroyed as an effective political force for several years ahead. This was now a matter of raw electoral survival, an issue which brings out Conservative ruthlessness. Canvassing for a drafting of either John Major or Douglas Hurd began in earnest. One junior minister told me later that, while Margaret Thatcher was still saying she would remain in the fight, a Cabinet member was seeking his vote for Major. He maintained that the whole Treasury team, which included Normal Lamont, the future Chancellor, and Richard Ryder, who was to become Chief Whip, were up and running before the Prime Minister conceded defeat.

John Major himself, convalescing in Huntingdon, agreed again to second her nomination, which Douglas Hurd was proposing. The two men, who had become close friends as they worked together for the previous year, were now emerging as rivals in the battle for the leadership. They had talked, on a contingency basis, about who would have the better chance of defeating Michael Heseltine. Since the eclipse of Geoffrey Howe, Hurd had been thought of as, if not quite heir-apparent, then the man most likely to succeed in an emergency. He was also older.

One of those closest to John Major told me, just after he became Prime Minister, that he had advised him against any agreement to allow the Foreign Secretary a straight run against Heseltine. He had reminded the Chancellor of the unhappy precedent after the Norway debate in 1940, when Lord Halifax had made way for Winston Churchill to succeed Neville Chamberlain. Not a precise, nor indeed a happy historical parallel, it seemed to me, but it certainly showed that while Margaret Thatcher was still clinging to power, her most senior ministers no longer believed in her political immortality. They knew that the right wing – and particularly the group which, as Euro-sceptics, was later to cause both of them so much trouble – was desperately attempting to mount a counter-attack on the Prime Minister's behalf. But the weight of her advice, from Cabinet colleagues and others, spelled *finis*.

Although Major was still uncomfortable from the effects of his operation, he was by no means out of touch with politics. By that evening, the information he received in telephone calls had convinced him that Margaret Thatcher's chances of survival were – to put it mildly, as John Major tends to do – limited. The Chancellor had a divided mind. All the bonds of loyalty to a leader who had promoted his career with such remarkable speed reinforced his own instinct: to support her nomination, for so long as she wanted this. He saw no illogicality in continuing to do so, even though the entrails told him she was done for. Political prudence also counselled him to continue his support, until such time as she released him. John Major knew that she would prefer him as her successor to either Michael Heseltine or Douglas Hurd. He must do nothing to risk that support.

As the Cabinet ministers trooped into her room one by one, journalists had to work hard to find out what was going on. The rooms of the Prime Minister and other ministers are 'behind the Speaker's Chair'. This means they open off a labyrinth of corridors which is out of bounds to journalists, unless they are going to visit a minister or opposition spokesman by appointment. Long after the event, memoirs and reconstructions of the afternoon and evening of Wednesday 21 November have offered accounts of what ministers subsequently believed they did and said.

Once Margaret Thatcher's dismissal had loosened tongues, I picked up much fascinating detail. The most colourful titbit was that before going in to tell her she ought to resign, Kenneth Clarke telephoned his wife, Gillian. He asked her to get his old senior counsel's gown out of mothballs, as he might need it quite soon. I *think* this was Clarke's little joke, though later he believed he would not have gone back to the bar even if he had walked out of the government. By then, of course, he was on the glory trail.

On the day itself, we Lobby correspondents at Westminster had to make a difficult judgement: how far those Cabinet ministers who now believed she should give up the fight might be daunted by her public declaration that she would fight on. By nine o'clock, I concluded that, if they had said to her what I knew they felt, a majority of the Cabinet would have advised her against standing in the second ballot. And if she did carry on, many were offering, at best, reluctant support.

A crucial telephone conversation with a senior minister between the *Six O'Clock* and *Nine O'Clock News* programmes removed my residual doubts. The threat to her continuance in office was now far graver than her colleagues' public positions implied. I would be wise, this minister suggested helpfully, though with meticulous caution, to keep open a part of my mind to the possibility that she would change her defiant stance. He said two per cent of my mind, so that was what I reported. But clearly this man, who always kept himself as well informed as anybody in the government, knew the chances that Margaret Thatcher was finished were much stronger than two per cent.

Others were less convinced. Again, doubtless, the importance broadcasters attach to statements made 'on the record' prompted the doubting question I was asked right at the end of the *Nine O'Clock News*: 'John, is there any possibility that we ourselves have been prey to spoiling tactics and black propaganda, when we try to assess who's doing what in the election?' I felt I was really being asked: 'John, have you been talking nonsense about poor Mrs Thatcher these past few days?' At the end of a long day, I fell back on the kind of BBC-speak I would not normally use.

'No,' I heard myself say, with po-faced solemnity, 'it's always a risk that that should be so, but I am confident that the reporting we've been doing has been based not on wild and extravagant claims, but on proper research by our own staff among Members of Parliament who, frankly, are talking much more freely than they were before.' Only when angry would I have said 'proper research', when I meant simply behaving as reporters, and asking Conservative MPs their opinions.

The next morning I was driving to Westminster when my bleep sounded many times: the BBC, a hydra-headed monster, never does things by halves. The messages told me that Downing Street had announced Margaret Thatcher's resignation. My live report from Downing Street for the lunchtime news was dramatically interrupted by her return from Buckingham Palace, where she had been telling the Queen she would carry on only until the Conservative Party had elected her successor. To frenzied shouts from cameramen that I should 'get down', so as not to spoil their shots of her arrival, I continued my commentary while crouching. Some politicians believe that should always be the posture of journalists when in their presence.

The pictures we had to obtain were of Margaret Thatcher at the final turning point in her political career. Yet the news had moved, cruelly but inexorably, away from her. In the swift manner of such seismic change, the Queen of Downing Street was dead, and the public were left wondering what would happen next. My task now was to help them with that.

As a boy of eight, in 1935, I had been upset by the primitive savagery of the proclamation of the death of George V: 'The King is dead. Long live the King.' Although not an adult royalist, I felt then that I knew the old king intimately, since his head was on most of my pennies. The heralds seemed to take a cavalier attitude to his death, and to a reign that had lasted considerably longer than me. Surely they could not be calling the Prince of Wales King already? (Though in the light of Edward VIII's brief reign, perhaps they saw a special need to be quick.)

Now I was like those heralds, moving on swiftly with the news. A strong tide was already running for John Major. In the way that political minds work, it had begun to run before his predecessor's fate was publicly acknowledged. A Tory backbencher, when asked what kind of leader they wanted, replied: 'Someone, anyone, who can win the general election. Ideology? Who needs it?'

Before Margaret Thatcher faced her final crisis, William Waldegrave used to speculate whether the Conservative Party would want its next leader to be 'painted in poster colours', as she was, in which case it would choose Michael Heseltine; or whether it would prefer someone in 'pastel shades', for which Douglas Hurd or John Major would be more suitable subjects. When Conservative newspapers later complained about Major's 'greyness', I remembered that in those days, 'greyness' was a synonym for calmness.

Whatever the ante-post betting might be, my instincts told me, throughout a weekend when the pressures from the candidates' campaign teams became intense, that it was not the job of the BBC to do anything which might influence the choice by the Conservative Party of its next leader. We should report claims from each camp, but keep our distance from too definitive judgement. I dodged an almost immediate challenge, on air, to tip the winner by saying: 'If MPs haven't made their minds up yet, why should I?'

I did define the motives which would govern their choice: the wish to pick a general election winner. What sank Margaret Thatcher was a conviction among Conservatives that they could not win with her at their head. They just wanted another leader – in some cases, *any* other leader – who would restore their shattered electoral support. That morning, Michael Heseltine's team let me know that, if he were to lose in the second ballot, he was prepared to serve under either of the other two. Later that week, the Major and Hurd camps said the same. The drive to reunite the badly damaged Conservative Party had begun, and would continue, whoever became its leader. The Tories' strength is that they do not allow personal sympathy for colleagues, however elevated, however once revered, to stand in the way of single-minded deter-mination to win and retain power.

Michael Heseltine, with his impressive support among MPs in the first ballot, had a flying start, but he had to win on the second ballot or not at all, for if the contest went to a third round, the votes of John Major and Douglas Hurd were likely to transfer to each other, rather than to Heseltine. But he was, paradoxically, both the favourite and an outsider. He was favourite because it was he who had a launching pad of 152 first-round votes, and he was the man who had given the anti-Thatcher bandwagon such a decisive push. He was the outsider because Thatcher loyalists would not quickly forgive him for his success in unseating her; and because the Cabinet was determined one of its own should take over.

On the evening of Margaret Thatcher's downfall, the BBC's pre-senters invited me to assess her place in history, live on the air. This seemed premature – by about fifty years, perhaps? The furthest I would go was to say that, leaving out the Churchill wartime coalition, hers was one of the three landmark administrations of the twentieth century: the Liberal government of Campbell-Bannerman, Asquith and Lloyd George which began in 1906, Attlee's Labour government after the Second World War, and hers. I added that because she was the longest serving Prime Minister of the century, she had her place in history. What precisely that place was would remain controversial, because her policies had so bitterly divided the nation.

Not exactly a paean of praise, but it was my best judgement at the time, and since.

47

THE BUBBLE ON COLLEGE GREEN

Within twenty-four hours, the Westminster scene was transformed. Although John Major, Douglas Hurd and Michael Heseltine were all careful to pay their respects to the pieties of Thatcherism, that age was being dismantled with the speed which Blackpool or Brighton scene-shifters demonstrate on the Friday a party conference ends. The new variety performance has to begin at once.

But Michael Heseltine, in particular, needed to do what he could to assuage the anger of Margaret Thatcher's supporters. He made clear what most Conservative MPs rationally knew: that his had been a necessary, if painful challenge. In her last year, many of her MPs concluded that she was a certain loser in the next general election. They believed it would be impossible for her to escape from some of the hooks on which she had impaled herself and the government, most notably the poll tax.

That boil had now been lanced. Heseltine claimed, rightly, that his challenge had produced a new mood of unity in the parliamentary party. But he had few illusions that this would be credited to his account. Rather his mood was that of Dickens' Sidney Carton – not just: 'It is a far, far better thing that I do than I have ever done'; but, more *sotto voce*: 'It is a far, far better rest that I go to, than I have ever known.' Not 'rest', as it turned out, but certainly not victory.

Heseltine is a brave, but not a reckless politician. When Geoffrey Howe's resignation speech gave him his long-awaited chance to remove Margaret Thatcher, he took it, because he had little other choice. But he had always known how difficult it would be, in such circumstances, for him to succeed her. He had another objective. By making clear that he, the candidate with 152 votes to his credit in the first ballot, would want the other two to continue in their current posts in any government he led; and, more significantly, that he would be happy to serve under either of them, he assured his return to government office.

After almost five years in the wilderness, whatever happened in the leadership election, Michael Heseltine, the stormy petrel of Tory politics, would be back. Miraculously, through all that time he had remained a significant player in the political game. It was the greatest achievement of that kind since Churchill's in the thirties. Heseltine's exile had followed a resignation for which he got no support in a Cabinet in thrall to Margaret Thatcher. Considering how unforgiving modern politics has become, it is astonishing that he pulled it off.

In this election, he had the lead on one issue: the Tories' most obvious suicide note to the electorate, the community charge, or poll tax. His warnings on this from the back benches gave him a flying start, and he promised 'a fundamental review'. Taxes could not survive unless the public thought them fair, he said. Major and Hurd both realised this was a nettle they also must grasp. The Foreign Secretary had been worried about the poll tax ever since the 1987 manifesto. The Chancellor, as Chief Secretary, had shared Nigel Lawson's and the Treasury's hostility to it. He quickly demonstrated his need, and willingness, to detach himself from Margaret Thatcher, when he complained that the government had been 'bounced into decisions before they were fully thought through, and before we knew precisely how it would affect people'.

The Lawson-Major villain in this dispute had always been Nicholas Ridley, but Ridley was only the whipping-boy. John Major, now that he was fighting for the leadership, could not avoid the strong implication that Margaret Thatcher was also at fault. He and Douglas Hurd both made clear that the changes in the poll tax she had so far sanctioned would not be enough. The post-Thatcher era in politics was being born before our eyes, in a fever of electioneering.

Michael Heseltine's appeal to many Tory MPs who did not necessarily share all his views on policy was that he could save their seats and win the next general election. Opinion polls over the period when only Heseltine and Margaret Thatcher were in the contest had underlined his appeal in the north and among skilled manual workers, who had been slipping away from the Tories. When I put it to him that such polls were highly hypothetical, he retorted: 'You may think it's hypothetical, but to the lads and lasses out in the marginal constituencies, there's no hypothesis about it. They want to win, and believe I can win for them.'

But at Westminster, John Major's bandwagon was already rolling, given a solid shove by Margaret Thatcher's not-very-secret support. That first day, Friday 23 November – when my sixty-third birthday passed me by without time to notice, much less celebrate it – the Major camp claimed they already had 140 votes. He was gaining the support of many MPs on the right, who were distraught that they did not have a candidate from their own wing of the party. He was less convincingly Euro-sceptical than they would have liked, but they had nowhere else to go. Major's attitudes on domestic policy remained enigmatic, but he seemed to lean more strongly towards government help for the have-nots than the right would ideally have wished.

The Heseltine camp were claiming that some former Thatcher voters had moved to them. If this was so, then there was a stronger drift in the opposite direction, because Michael Heseltine's vote of 152 was to melt down in the second round the following week to 131. He had done his job in removing Margaret Thatcher, but like the middle-distance runner who sets the pace in the first lap, was inexorably edged out by the eventual winner.

Douglas Hurd's appeal was to traditional Toryism: his statement that he would place more emphasis on persuasion than on assertion had echoes of what Geoffrey Howe used to say – that while Margaret Thatcher sought to win victories, he tried to gain friends for his point of view. Hurd eschewed any hint of an anti-Heseltine campaign, saying: 'What we need to do is unify this party, which has been scratching and back-biting and doing itself harm. That's got to stop.'

My wife Madge, kindly thinking I had been working too hard for a man with a heart condition, gave me breakfast in bed on Saturday morning. When there was so much interesting material to pore over in the newspapers, this was bliss. But the restful busman's holiday was short-lived, for three campaign managers were on the telephone to me before I had finished the toast. Each proclaimed good news for his candidate. Others were providing the BBC's news coverage that day; I was due to return to the battle on Sunday, when all three contenders were to give radio and television interviews. But I passed on these latest stable-tips, for what they were worth, to the Saturday news programmes.

Sunday was an edgy day for broadcasters like myself, as well as for newspaper journalists who did not want to be used unscrupulously to launch a bandwagon. By then the Major campaign was claiming 150 pledged votes, 'with the numbers increasing all the time'. At a small briefing conducted by Norman Lamont, sceptical press questions seemed to anger him. In fact, he emerged from that campaign as Conservatism's Mr Angry. He savagely attacked his old boss, Nigel Lawson, for daring to support Heseltine. The mood in the Major headquarters, a house in Gayfere Street, just round the corner from Tory Central Office, was by now triumphalist. I have often noticed that in elections the people who know they are losing are usually pleasanter to deal with than those who expect to win. That, I suppose, is human nature.

John Major himself, well above such battles, gave good performances on television, discarding any 'grey man' image when he grew passionate about the National Health Service: 'It saved my life as a baby, it saved my leg when I was in my early twenties. I'm a very strong supporter of the NHS.' Douglas Hurd, wearily defending himself against the charge of being a toff, said: 'Images, images, images! The day when politics is completely dominated by images is the day when it goes downhill.' Michael Heseltine's appeal was to MPs of all political shades who had recognised their urgent need for a new leader: 'I've transformed the fortunes of the Conservative Party. We are now ahead in the polls, and we're going to have a fundamental reform of the community charge. That's not a bad week's work.'

The Tories at Westminster were certainly enjoying this, the most open election for a leader they had ever had. Members of the Cabinet divided their support between John Major and Douglas Hurd; only David Hunt backed Michael Heseltine. Major's team included Norman Lamont, David Waddington, John MacGregor, John Gummer, Ian Lang, Michael Howard, Cecil Parkinson, Tony Newton and Peter Lilley. Hurd had on his side Chris Patten, Kenneth Clarke, Tom King, Malcolm Rifkind, Peter Brooke and William Waldegrave.

It was on the Saturday that Geoffrey Howe and Nigel Lawson angered the Major camp by coming out for Heseltine. Lawson aimed a savage blow at those who maintained that the next leader must come from within the Cabinet. He quoted from the paper he had written in 1985, warning that the poll tax would be 'completely unworkable and politically catastrophic', and added wearily: 'Unfortunately I received no support from any of my colleagues on the committee, and this reflects, I think, a general characteristic of Cabinet government in practice.' He meant Cabinet government under Thatcher, and was blaming others for not having stood up to her. That was why Lawson and Howe were supporting Heseltine, the man who had removed Margaret Thatcher.

Tory MPs had all lived under her shadow for so long that she inevitably influenced how they voted. Many were instinctively supporting her chosen successor, John Major; others opposing him just because they feared he might represent an extension of Thatcherism by other means. By the Monday, one of the unknown factors in the contest was whether her fury against Michael Heseltine, which many MPs found reflected in their constituencies, would deter them from supporting him.

Heseltine's camp knew how fatal this could be to his chances, but hoped his backers would not be deterred by this traditional grassroots loyalty to a leader whose time had passed. Those who looked back to Margaret Thatcher's own successful challenge to Edward Heath fifteen years earlier detected a parallel: local Conservative Associations supported Heath long after his MPs had deserted him.

The three candidates themselves, all determined that they would be in Cabinet together when the leadership election was over, behaved with courtesy to each other. This was not true of their supporters. Denigration – or 'negative propaganda', if you are given to squeamish euphemism – is an essential part of any election, even an internal one. Soon I was hearing from Douglas Hurd's opponents that he had not got the charisma to attract ordinary voters. The whisper against Michael Heseltine was that the antagonism to him in the constituencies would leave the Conservative Party bitterly divided for years.

But the most prescient criticism I heard in the nooks and crannies of Westminster that week was about John Major. This foreshadowed the next controversy that was to engulf the Conservative Party – and one which would put the poll tax row in its parochial place. It was during the leadership contest that pro-European MPs first expressed doubt about whether he was 'sound on Europe'. In part, this was because he was seen as Margaret Thatcher's candidate. The prominence of Norman Lamont, who was deeply Euro-sceptical, as his campaign manager also aroused suspicion. Major himself held meetings with MPs who entertained these doubts about his European credentials. They trooped in, some for ten-minute private sessions, others in groups.

These talks were intended to satisfy doubters that, although he had right-wing support, he was neither a right-winger nor an anti-European. One of those he saw told me the Chancellor had been asked about his statement that proposals for closer European union – what was later to become the Maastricht Treaty – ought not to be brought before Parliament 'in the foreseeable future'. He had explained that this meant not till after the Inter-Governmental Conference. Since this was to conclude its work the following year, some were reassured. Others thought John Major was giving different impressions of his European commitment to different factions, and they voted for Douglas Hurd, as a more dedicated European.

As a candidate, John Major did not put a foot wrong. His whole life in politics might have been a preparation for these days. While the voting was actually taking place, I met him in the committee corridor, where Cranley Onslow and his team were conducting the election. We had a brief chat, but he apologised for not prolonging it, explaining that he still had some doubtful MPs to canvass before the poll closed, but would be glad to have a longer talk with me when it was all over.

I suspect the soon-to-be Prime Minister did not understand when I replied, as we parted, that if what he hoped would happen to him that night actually happened, our next conversation would be less useful to me as a journalist. This, alas, is the truth about journalists' relationships with politicians who become leaders of their parties. Naturally, editors and correspondents are always glad of a chance to meet Prime Ministers, though for some journalists the motivation owes more to self-importance than to any great addition to their knowledge. Such meetings do also serve to provide some impression of a Prime Minister's or opposition leader's mood and morale. But once they reach the top of their particular greasy pole, they no longer have any strong incentive to indulge in the kind of conversation that really enlightens a correspondent about what is going on behind the scenes. Numbers two, three or four in a Cabinet or shadow Cabinet are often less discreet than number one.

For what any political journalist wants to know is how decisions are being shaped, what are the issues within departments or in Cabinet committees, who is likely to prevail, what future policy is likely to be. That, after all, is what our various readers and audiences legitimately want to know, preferably at a time when they might still have the chance to influence the outcome.

A Prime Minister or party leader has different, equally proper concerns. However theoretically devoted to 'open government', he has an interest, sometimes perhaps a duty, to maintain the apparent homogeneity and unity of the collective leadership, to get the decisions in the bag before press and public start sticking their troublesome noses in. Occasionally the veil is allowed to drop a little, but never as much as in 'the dear, dead days beyond recall'. Every Prince Hal must abandon his Falstaffs.

By Tuesday 27 November, election fever had risen higher still. Margaret Thatcher was now telephoning MPs she regarded as still doubtful, to tell them that support for John Major meant continuation of her heritage. When I reported this at lunchtime, a half-hearted attempt was made to deny that such conversations were taking place. But the MP who told me, whom she apparently considered a doubter, was actually a convinced Heseltine supporter, and resented being called out of a meeting to take her call.

Election night produced a scene outside the Palace of Westminster like Vauxhall Gardens when Handel's Water Music was first performed. The television networks had erected temporary studios on College

Green, in the BBC's case the now well-known glass bubble. Television lights, inside and outside, created an atmosphere of excitement. Many political groupies, who could not penetrate those parts of the Commons where the voting and announcement were taking place, regarded this as the next best thing, for they saw an endless string of leading politicians coming over to give their views.

In our programme of live coverage, one of the political correspondents telephoned the voting figures from the corridor outside the room where they were counted: Major 185, Heseltine 131, Hurd 56. Margaret Thatcher was later to remark sadly that the new Prime Minister gained fewer votes in winning the job than she had in losing it. The difference, in the cruel way of democratic politics, was that he was on the way up, whereas she was now on the way out. That made all the difference.

Although John Major was two short of what he needed for an outright win, I knew Michael Heseltine would realise he had no chance in a further ballot. So I immediately told viewers, from my seat in the bubble, that he would soon concede the election. The sentence was barely uttered before he came down to our camera outside his home, and did so. He advised his supporters to transfer their votes to Major in the third ballot, which the rules said was necessary. (In the event, it was cancelled, by common consent.) Soon afterwards, Douglas Hurd appeared to add his congratulations to John Major.

During my years in broadcast news, I had often pined for the greater space of newspapers. Space is especially necessary if your interest is in political ideas, and I had kept myself happy by writing columns for, successively, the *Listener* and the *New Statesman*. But on an evening like this, when everything was happening live in our broadcast, my own job as political editor of the BBC seemed to me to be the best in journalism.

Later, when I finished the last of many reports from outside Number 10, the house lights were on, as a party Margaret Thatcher was giving for her successor got under way. Already John Major had been briefed by officials on the immediate tasks facing him. He had appointed his Treasury press officer, Gus O'Donnell, to move with him. I still had to return to the House of Commons, where a car was to pick me up to go to the *Newsnight* studio in Shepherds Bush, for the final work of a long, but exhilarating day.

As I headed down the street, Margaret Thatcher's parliamentary private secretary, Peter Morrison, came out of the celebratory party. Doubtless he had some personal wounds to lick, for his conduct of the Thatcher campaign was blamed for her failure to defeat Heseltine decisively enough. I think that judgement underestimates the fatal extent to which her hold over the Conservative Party had weakened.

Without any memorable preliminary, Morrison testily informed me that I had been talking a great deal of nonsense during the past couple of weeks. I replied, with matching acerbity, that I had told our audiences the Prime Minister was likely to have to go, and that she had now gone. What he did not seem to comprehend was that such analysis was my job. It was pointless to shoot the messenger. It was equally senseless that I was being praised, with comparable extravagance, by other political *ingenus* who disliked Margaret Thatcher. They seemed to think I had been personally *responsible* for her downfall because they had seen me, hour by hour, *reporting* the crisis gathering around her head. As I walked away from Peter Morrison, I was quietly fuming.

Before I reached the bottom of Downing Street and turned into Whitehall, a steady drizzle had begun. I paused to let a car pass before crossing. Because I was preoccupied with my own thoughts, I had not noticed that it came out of Downing Street. The chauffeur gave a hoot, the window was wound down, and Peter Morrison, courtesy restored, asked whether I wanted a lift to the House. It was the *amende honorable*, but I felt the dignity of the press required me to say I preferred to walk. The rain came down more heavily as I trudged down Whitehall.

The next day was dominated by the formation of John Major's first Cabinet. He faced a delicate task in his appointments, and also in deciding his own answer to the key question: what kind of government was it going to be, a new one, or Thatcherism with a new face? This was a question I was to discuss in a *Panorama* programme the following autumn, after a decent interval for him to settle in. It was a question to which I was unable to find a satisfactory answer then, from the many ministers and ex-ministers I interviewed; and to which John Major has not found one yet.

The stark dilemma facing him was whether or not he could afford to be his own man. The ingredients of that choice could not be less helpful to a man whose training as a whip taught him to take a clear, open-eyed look at political reality. For while it was the departure of Margaret Thatcher which had suddenly destroyed Labour's long-standing lead in the polls, and put the Tories modestly ahead, his own party was deeply wounded, and disrupted by that departure.

How far could he afford to detach himself from the Thatcher governments in which he and his principal ministers had served? Might not the improvement in Conservative poll standing simply be because the leadership drama, which had turned into the greatest political cliff-hanger in a generation, had excited the British public? Perhaps it had brought the Tories uncovenanted benefits from what I called at the time 'a sustained party political broadcast, with only Neil Kinnock's Brahms missing'? The prudent path ahead for John Major was by no means obvious.

The furthest he felt able to go was, inevitably, to bring Michael Heseltine in from the cold; to decide on radical change in local government taxation; and to declare on the steps of Number 10 that he wanted 'a country that is at peace with itself'. The new Prime Minister clearly intended to begin cautiously, rather than to be controversial.

He made only the necessary ministerial changes. There were three key appointments. Norman Lamont, his deputy at the Treasury, and campaign manager during the election campaign, received his award as Chancellor. An intimate told me Major admired Lamont's intelligence, but not his political instincts, which were very different from his own. A more imaginative course would have been to give the chancellorship to Chris Patten, who if the vacancy at the top had occurred later would have been John Major's principal rival to be Prime Minister.

Norman Lamont was quite overtly sceptical about Europe, and his appointment to this key post raised a whiff of the trouble which lay ahead. Trouble over Europe had undermined Margaret Thatcher. Major has never had anything remotely like an ideological approach to Europe, then or since. But by appointing Lamont, he seemed to signal at once that he intended his government to be, in this respect, something like his predecessor's.

Chris Patten went instead to be chairman of the Conservative Party. This proved a coarsening experience for a man more suited to the subtlest work of government than to those of a political barker, though he was to tackle his task with enthusiasm in the run-up to the 1992 general election. Some workaday Conservative irritation with the BBC caused even the urbane Patten to suggest, in his speech at the following year's party conference, that his supporters should jam BBC switchboards. Although his complaints did not concern my own department's work, I felt sufficiently provoked by this uncharacteristic, but irresponsible *jeu d'esprit* to tell him I was tempted to organise a jamming of switchboards at Conservative Central Office. But within ten minutes of this minor fracas, Patten had reverted to type, and was helping me to get a camera crew round some insane restriction by security men.

Michael Heseltine, as Environment Secretary, had the task of dealing with the poll tax crisis. He was first offered the nominally more senior job of Home Secretary. But he recalled how, as a young President of the Oxford Union, he had received Iain Macleod, the visiting Great Man, who asked him whether he contemplated a career in politics, and which office he aspired to. Michael stammered out that he would like to be Home Secretary, but Macleod told him this was 'the graveyard of political careers', and he ought to eschew it. In 1990, when the choice came, Heseltine remembered Macleod's advice, and opted for the Department of the Environment.

What he would really have liked was the Department of Trade and Industry, but John Major had a careful political balance to maintain in a twitchy period for his party, and he knew that such an interventionist appointment would give the wrong signals to the grumbling Thatcherites. So he appointed Peter Lilley, a firm right-winger, eventually giving Michael Heseltine the reward of his heart's desire only after he had won his own mandate in a general election. But in 1990, to tackle the poll tax, which had so depressed Conservative MPs in the dying months of the Thatcher era, was as politically useful a task for his own rehabilitation, as well as that of the government, as this prodigal son could hope for.

One Thatcher-sceptic minister whose star rose on her departure was Malcolm Rifkind. When John Major took over, I learned that he had been in the frame as a possible Home Secretary. He was naturally interested when I told him this, but he professed to prefer the job he got at Transport. Rifkind later became Defence Secretary, a senior job in a Tory government.

The later stages of the government appointments brought me one minor humiliation. John Major had not appointed any women to his first Cabinet, and this produced some public criticism. So television news editors were very excited when, just before the *Six O'Clock News*, Gillian Shephard became the first woman Treasury minister ever. Women's appointments, it is thought, interest viewers more than those of men. I rarely covered a reshuffle during which somebody back at the office did not ask me what was going to happen to Edwina Currie. Beside her, it seemed, the Lawsons, Howes, Majors and Heseltines were mere bit-part players.

I interviewed Mrs Shephard live into the *Six O'Clock News*. Neither she nor I knew at that moment what her precise responsibilities were to be, so questions about money supply or VAT were not feasible. The shaming truth is that, during a reshuffle we would never have interviewed anyone outside the Cabinet if she had not been female. But fired by the perverse feminism which was in the office *Zeitgeist*, I heard myself asking her what she would bring to the Treasury 'as a woman'. To be fair to myself, I did not expect her to reply: 'Well, I *could* always make the tea.'

But it was a crass question, and Mrs Shephard, though patently nervous at her first television exposure in Downing Street, was having none of it. Quite justly, she cut the feet from under me by replying: 'Well, I hope that, *as a person*, I will bring good sense and hard work and dedication to this job. I don't know that I bring anything special to it, as a woman. The Prime Minister was at pains to tell me that there was no question of being appointed as a woman, I was being appointed on merit.'

Collapse of stout party! I floundered through the rest of the interview, and afterwards apologised to her for such a daft question. Seeing my embarrassment, she began to worry that her reply had been rude, which it was clearly not intended to be. Late in my career, this taught me another lesson about television: always to follow my own instincts, rather than relying on somebody else's. Even when, as in this case, I was so weary at the end of an exhausting fortnight that my brain was in automatic gear.

48

A NEW STYLE AT NUMBER 10

The events of November 1990 left the Tories traumatised, yet elated. The mere fact of Margaret Thatcher's removal produced one opinion poll which showed them with astonishing support from fifty-one per cent of voters, though more rational MPs knew how transitory this would prove. Meanwhile, their old leader having been removed, the new leader had to answer a number of delicate questions: What would he do about the poll tax, which had such a large part in bringing Thatcher down? When would the economy revive? Would he be able to unite the Conservative Party on Europe? And could he win a general election which had to be held within eighteen months?

By this time I was sixty-three, and had two years left as BBC political editor. The 'normal' retiring age is sixty, though for too many colleagues in recent years it has been much earlier – at a cost in both personal unhappiness and 'retirement packages' which does not bear thinking about. However, in an Orwellian organisation like the Corporation, the only path to sanity for what is called 'a front-of-camera man' is to plough his own furrow. So since the BBC seemed content that I should carry on till I was sixty-five, I settled in to enjoy reporting this new government, which might be my last.

Soon after John Major became Prime Minister, he went to Washington to meet President George Bush. This was a good opportunity to talk to him during the flight. We travelled overnight, arriving at Andrews Air Force Base at 5 a.m. British time. I interviewed him on the plane and, clutching the cassette given me by the pool cameraman from Channel 4, I looked out for my contact, 'the tallest cameraman in the United States'. This friendly phenomenon took his shots of the Prime Minister landing, recorded my 'piece to camera', summing up what he hoped for from his mission, and then drove me to the BBC Washington offices.

In the subsequent forty-eight hours, I only emerged from those offices to go to the Embassy once, for a briefing on the talks, hundreds of miles away in Camp David; and to bed twice (or perhaps *that* was once – my memory and diary are unclear). On such a mission, if a television reporter has to prepare reports for *Breakfast News*, 1 p.m., 6 p.m., and 9 p.m., the chance of his emerging into the daylight, where things are happening, is not good. For his reports, he must rely on information picked up on the plane and earlier, plus the news footage which pours in from the American networks. Fortunately, the visit contained less news than symbolism.

In those early days, the new Prime Minister enjoyed his airborne drinks sessions with the press. More, apparently, than he did later, after my time as political editor, when relations soured. I made a mock complaint to him: that he had not appointed a single Cabinet minister who was older than I. While I was reconciled to policemen looking younger, and even judges, a whole Cabinet younger than myself was harder to take. He came back with a couple of names, whom I dismissed as comparative youngsters, but he finally convinced me that the Lord Chancellor, Lord Mackay, was my senior by a few months. I had to be thankful for small mercies.

The new Prime Minister was enjoying a honeymoon with his own party. At first, most Conservative MPs were simply relieved at the change in political style. One gently moaned: 'No more ideology, please! Let's just wrap our manifesto around John Major's personality, and ask the people to trust him.' This more laid-back atmosphere spread quickly into the Cabinet Room. One of his staff claimed with delight that this must be the first Prime Minister since Attlee to have the Test cricket scores brought in to him. He had the capacity to make a flippant remark in the middle of a serious meeting, which discouraged pomposity.

Cabinet meetings were much more free-and-easy, even conversational. Unlike his predecessor, Major would allow the minister leading in a subject to proceed without interruption.

Politicians do like a bit of drama, and some undoubtedly missed Margaret Thatcher. 'It was all great fun,' said one. Another amended that: John Major's Cabinet meetings were more *fun*, but less exciting. There was not the same expectation of blood on the floor after every disagreement. A few, however, maintained that Thatcher had more debates in Cabinet, while Major quickly developed a penchant for getting his own way *in his own way*: not so much *Sturm und Drang*, more fixing in advance, carefully selecting the groups of ministers who would discuss a subject. They confessed that this took much longer, but all were at pains to make clear he was no soft touch. He would let everybody deliver an opinion, but then say firmly: 'I prefer these arguments to those, so this is what we'll do.'

At a dinner in January 1991, within two months of becoming Prime Minister, John Major's decision on poll tax became clear to his circle of advisers. Picking up one of the clichés of this long-running debate, he said: 'We've got to get rid of the poll tax. It's unfair that a duke should pay the same as a dustman.' Clichés often *become* clichés because they are true. Soon afterwards, Michael Heseltine, looking out at a snowy February landscape, said happily: 'Well, I've apparently solved the greenhouse effect. Now for the community charge!'

It was not to prove as easy as that, though even previous protagonists of its principles, such as Michael Portillo – whom John Major, in another bout of balancing, had made Heseltine's deputy – acknowledged that the poll tax now consisted entirely of sticking-plaster. The subject occupied many anguished Cabinet meetings. At one, the Prime Minister noticed it was 1 p.m., and said: 'If we don't break up now, they'll say there's a crisis.' Already his subsequent obsession with the media was beginning to show. But he eventually achieved his aim of lancing this boil with only minor Tory hiccups.

In the early days of his premiership, Margaret Thatcher's mood was the subject of much worried comment from ministers I talked with. The Prime Minister handled the relationship with great circumspection. Although she had backed him for the succession, time brought suspicion. She recalled her impression that he had hesitated when she asked him to nominate her in the second ballot against Michael Heseltine. The attitude of the rest of her Cabinet made this irrelevant, but the supposed memory lingered. She gave Major's campaign manager, Norman Lamont, a hard time over what she believed to be his early desertion of her cause.

So Major made sure to talk to her, either in person or on the telephone, and to write letters about subjects which might concern her, especially during the Gulf War. This came during his first three months in office, and was said to be the subject of Thatcher's tactless remark about back-seat driving. The Chief Whip, Richard Ryder, saw her regularly, for long talks, and found her mood up and down. She was recovering from the trauma of her dismissal, but slowly. The Thatcher Foundation, for which her son Mark had over-ambitious plans, did not look as if it could be on such a vast scale as he once envisaged. She did not enjoy the early days of writing her memoirs, though in the end, I think, these proved to be a much livelier read than might have been expected, from an author whose political longevity invited a mere exercise in self-justification.

But her long pre-eminence gave every casual utterance from her a lapidary significance. One minister said bitterly: 'She was always criticising the government when she led it, so why expect her to change now?' There were reports that she had been so outspoken at a dinner party that even her husband, Denis, whose opinions were some degrees to the right of her own, had counselled caution.

There was a long dither in the media about whether or not Margaret Thatcher would remain in the Commons after the election, or take the peerage to which she was entitled. So long as she stayed an MP, there would be Tories who would regard her as 'the Queen over the Water', and wait for – perhaps work for – a restoration. Malcolm Rifkind took a judicial view, suited to a Scottish lawyer: it would be better for the country if she stayed in the Commons, which was the right place for former Prime Ministers; but it would be better for his party and government if she departed for the Lords. Her announcement, at the end of June 1991, that she would leave the Commons produced a collective sigh of relief from ministers.

Nobody was so tactless as to rub Margaret Thatcher's nose in what a disaster her addiction to the poll tax had become for her party, though Douglas Hurd, who concentrated mostly on his Foreign Office duties, but kept a cool eye on the domestic scene, tartly observed she would be as wise to campaign against its abolition as to favour the Black Death. This was the second minister I had heard comparing this 'flagship' of her third term to the plague. On that subject, Conservatives simply wanted a rescue operation. One assured me he was prepared to forget Thatcherite principles, and just throw money at the problem, adding cynically that 'bribery and corruption are back in fashion'.

In March, Hurd praised the European habit of loading much less expenditure on to local taxes. Sadly, I had been away from Westminster during a brief sickness, and did not understand the significance of this. Five days later, Norman Lamont's first budget achieved the dubious coup of paying £140 towards each citizen's poll tax bill, while not giving delighted recipients of this bounty their higher VAT bills until later in the year. This delay did not save the Conservatives from heavy losses in the May council elections, but without it these might have been worse. So far as I was concerned, this was one 'exclusive prediction' I might have worked on, but it eluded me.

Apart from the poll tax, John Major had a delicate task in deciding whether to market his government as a new product, which would wash whiter, or as the well-established firm voters could trust. The *Financial Times*, now emerging as the most wittily independent of the broadsheet papers, put the choice like this: 'It can blame [its past] on a previous government, headed by someone called Margaret Thatcher, who was executed last November, and buried in an unmarked grave. The government is now headed, instead, by a certain John Major, who happened to arrive from Mars at the same time.'

Right-wingers were worried in the first few weeks because the new Prime Minister did seem willing to throw money at admittedly good causes: haemophiliacs, the homeless, cold weather payments. Michael Portillo, not yet in the Cabinet, but a rising leader of the Thatcherites, recognised that in John Major the Tories had a more left-wing figure than her. But by January he reported that the right's worries were dissipating, as the government got on what seemed to them a more even keel.

The Prime Minister and his party chairman, Chris Patten, had to keep their eye on the activities of what Patten would whimsically call 'the Arditi', Mussolini's hard men. These were right-wingers, either ex-ministers or younger members of the No Turning Back group, some of them still in the government. They were said to be so angered by Margaret Thatcher's dismissal that they did not mind if the Conservatives lost the election, and already had scapegoats in their sights (including Chris Patten).

I have often wondered why senior politicians usually refuse to admit to the weariness which afflicts the rest of us when we pretend there are thirty-five hours in the day, rather than twenty-four. Margaret Thatcher was notorious for not needing to sleep, and others began to emulate her by making a fetish of this. When I saw Chris Patten in October 1991, after he and John Major had taken the politically dangerous, but inevitable decision to postpone the election into 1992, he put up no such act.

The official dinner he had been at had gone on so long he was still working at his government boxes the next morning, before coming to meet me at lunch, and he seemed dispirited. There had been a period in March of that year when, ministerial gossip said, John Major himself was dispirited, because everything seemed to be going wrong. Some even talked of his having a nervous breakdown, though I was satisfied this was never a possibility. But about that time he was far from discreet in his view that to be Prime Minister was not the only thing in life. He once confessed that if Douglas Hurd had really wanted the job, he would have been perfectly happy to remain Chancellor, only friends told him he must not make such a deal. (This was a happy confirmation of the Lord Halifax story which one of his friends had told me.)

John Major quickly became irritated by his treatment in the media, and said that because of this, no leader could last more than ten years, since the people grew weary of him. The new Prime Minister, after a miserable few weeks, beset by insoluble problems, thought he would not weep over early retirement. With the honeymoon over so quickly, a life spent at county cricket grounds must have seemed seductive. This belief that he was unfairly treated in the media took many forms. When journalists put to him criticisms of the NHS reforms, he would say if the public did not realise they were a way of getting value for money, this was because the media were not presenting the issue fairly. This circularity in criticism defied reasoned debate, but there was no doubt that John Major felt unfairly done by.

His argument was that Labour was getting away with telling a big lie, because the media interviewed the wrong people, felt no obligation to tell the truth, as distinct from interviewing the sides, and did not ask hard questions of opposition spokesmen, or those NHS professionals who were hostile to the changes. Although I was not responsible for most BBC reporting of the NHS changes, I followed the issues with some knowledge, because Madge was at that time chairman of a Community Health Council, which handled many complaints about the new system. So I knew that this was a row which was not simply 'got up by the media'. But when I pointed out that a recent Gallup poll suggested the Conservatives were not believed on the NHS, this only confirmed the Prime Minister's view that the media were not telling the story properly. Circularity again!

Yet the attitude expressed by John Major is not uncommon among politicians of all complexions. The only occasion when I picked up any personal criticism from him – until a later confrontation just after Britain's exclusion from the European Exchange Rate Mechanism – was in his attitude to the reporting of Prime Minister's question time. His press secretary, Gus O'Donnell, mentioned that John felt the selection of clips was often unfair. I argued that his irritation merely reflected a bad political period for him: if he were ten points ahead in the polls, he would not be concerned with such matters.

Such complaints echo the title of Bernard Ingham's book, *Shoot the Messenger*, only in this case, it was not Bernard's successor, Gus, who was the messenger, but the BBC. Yet I know this is one subject on which fair-minded people can reach different conclusions from the same facts. It goes to the heart of the central problem between politicians and broadcasters, agenda-setting, on which I confess to having more ambiguous feelings than most broadcasters. In other words, I can see the politicians' point, though not the answer to their problem.

The trouble with Prime Minister's questions was that it was only one item in the day's busy news agenda. A half-hour news programme has the greatest difficulty in squashing everything into the time available. MPs naturally use this high-profile period of the parliamentary day to comment on the events which are making headlines. But sometimes they miss the subject which broadcasters are convinced is preoccupying the public that day. I mentioned to Gus that, for example, the matters on which Neil Kinnock, as leader of the opposition, chose to question the Prime Minister sometimes made life difficult for reporters, because they were hard to fit in with the other news. Gus seized on this, and indicated that the Prime Minister thought it was he who should set the news agenda.

There you have the problem: Major would not want Kinnock to set the agenda; and Kinnock would not want Major to do so. Broadcasters believe this leaves them with little choice but to make up their own minds about what is important. This is also what their instincts tell them is the right choice in a democracy. But sometimes they get it wrong, more often through lack of expertise than through malevolence or political bias. John Major and I were to return to this subject at one of the bleakest moments in his premiership.

One unfairness in Conservatives' criticism of their new leader was that they did not make enough allowance for the changed state of the opposition. Ever since Labour's third successive defeat in 1987, Neil Kinnock had skilfully used the alchemy of despair to keep his party united, even on such a grievous subject as Europe. Although the Alliance, stricken since its 1987 defeat by the Owenite split, was not breathing so close to Labour's neck as before, Kinnock convinced his followers that to go on losing elections was shameful neglect of an opposition's prime duty, to provide an alternative government.

Conservatives clung to their belief that Neil Kinnock himself simply was not an election winner. The more generous conceded that he had effected a remarkable transformation in his party since 1983, changing its policies on defence, Europe, public ownership, even the balance between taxation and expenditure. But they used this transformation to accuse him of jettisoning all his convictions, of not believing in anything.

Neil Kinnock was doing much better in the House, and sometimes manifestly defeated John Major, in a way he had not been able to do to Margaret Thatcher. But a minister assured me as early as March 1991 that the issue of the general election would be: 'Fed up with us' versus 'frightened of Labour'. A cynical Conservative, guying his party's pro-gramme, indicated that the public 'didn't give a fig for choice and opportunity', but simply wanted to know what Labour would make them pay personally in taxes. The Tories and their supporting newspapers were happy to oblige with their own estimates of this bill.

John Smith, at this time emerging as the strong man of the Labour front bench, was most Tories' feared alternative to Neil Kinnock, though there was no serious disposition in the Labour Party to switch horses. My growing scepticism about opinion polls was increased by one which purported to show that if Smith replaced Kinnock, Labour would win an election in a landslide. Yet everybody knew the coming election was likely to be close.

The shadow Chancellor showed great reluctance, until just before the election, to offer Tories a fiscal target to shoot at. The current joke was that John Smith's ideal Labour manifesto would consist of a single sentence: 'The Tories are a bunch of rascals', followed by the address of Labour Party headquarters, for donations to funds and help with campaigning. One wit acknowledged that he might grow verbose, and add: 'Trust me!'

With an election imminent, the key Tory relationship was between the PM and his party chairman, Chris Patten. Judith Chaplin (then Major's political secretary, later an MP who died tragically young) noticed that at first they were studiously polite to each other, because Major had deprived Patten of his chance to be Prime Minister, probably for ever. They soon became friends as well as political allies. Both like a joke, and these had been thin on the ground during the Thatcher years.

Michael Heseltine was manifestly pleased to be back. He found Major a cerebral chief, where Thatcher had been emotional, and he revelled in what he called 'proper discussions', the subject on which Heseltine had quarrelled with Thatcher. His method with Major was to seek advance meetings on difficult topics, and not to proceed unless the Prime Minister backed him. Colleagues feared Heseltine still felt he was working his passage, after the mutiny years. John Wakeham, who as an ex-Chief Whip had a fixer's instincts, heard that he found the atmosphere in Cabinet unwelcoming. So he conveyed a message from the Prime Minister that Heseltine should feel free to make speeches across the political range, rather than confining himself to poll tax and green issues. Would the colleagues not resent this? Wakeham assured him they would not.

When I returned from my summer break in 1991, I was told that the BBC wanted me to prepare a *Panorama* about the Tories, before their conference in October. This programme appeared on the eve of the Conservative conference, and examined whether or not this was a new government or just a new Prime Minister. Speeches in Blackpool that week gave me my answer: it was really a continuation of the Thatcher government, though with a kinder face. Tories, understandably, preferred to have it both ways.

Malcolm Rifkind summed up a common view: the new government was at one with Margaret Thatcher on economic management and privatisation (though already some MPs were describing rail privatisation as 'poll tax on wheels'). The main difference was that John Major gave higher priority to public services. He claimed Major as a Conservative, whereas Thatcher was a radical. She once told a Cabinet committee: 'If we do this, it's going to mean a lot of changes, but that's what we're here for.' He said this was not the attitude of a Conservative, who needed to be convinced that change was inevitable. Michael Heseltine believed there was 'no such thing as Thatcherism', only Thatcher; that the personality was the doctrine.

But the new Prime Minister was careful about party unity. An insider told me of his assiduous attempts to keep Norman Tebbit in support of the new government, through a number of breakfasts at Number 10, before the strains over Europe became too great. John Biffen said Major's left-wing reputation had already won him support on that side, but because of the right's doubts about him, he was seeking the Conservative 'point of equilibrium'. Biffen maintained that what John Major stood for was competence in government and in the political skills. But he predicted that gradually people would hark back to conviction politics, to a time when Margaret Thatcher called all the shots.

Alan Clark, with an iconoclasm that even his *Diaries* did not match, felt sure that John Major's real views were not dissimilar to Margaret Thatcher's, or his own. He had sat beside the new Prime Minister when some new issue came up, and his reactions, like Alan's own, were reactionary, in the more derivative sense of that word. From his standpoint, the trouble was whenever Chris Patten, whom he clearly did not revere, had poured a load of Hampstead horse-manure into the Prime Minister's ears, the government's policy was very different from what hers would have been. (For geographical accuracy, the Tory chairman then lived in London SW rather than NW.)

The Prime Minister's own view about the question 'new government or old?' was characteristically down-to-earth. Of course he had to defend the record of the Thatcher decade, but one of the changes he thought had to be made was to do with the free market. There were real people in the free market, and some of them had suffered, so a government had to make arrangements to help them. He believed the people then coming into parliament supported his kind of caring Conservatism, and since there were only about forty Tory MPs with a different view, he would have the bulk of his parliamentary party 'at peace with itself', which is the way John Major likes to think about parties and countries. In this aim, like others, he had underestimated the effects of Europe.

Worse, when he had been in office for a year, he was still awaiting 'the green shoots of recovery', which his Chancellor had been predicting with ever-diminishing persuasiveness. Faced with the fact that Britain was now moving into an unbelievable second decade with between 2 and 3 million out of work, he acknowledged that 800,000 people were now long term unemployed, but argued that a higher proportion were in jobs in Britain than elsewhere in Europe. As for the criticism that many of these were part-time jobs for women, rather than principal family wage-packets, the Prime Minister believed this was what many women wanted. But he still did not know when the feel-better factor would appear. He was relying on a simple conviction that voters did not want a Labour government.

49

ELECTION ON A KNIFE EDGE

In the years when I was a visitor in the nation's living-rooms at nine o'clock most evenings, people often stopped me in the street to enquire what the weather was going to be like. They posed the question with the confidence of sharp-eyed citizens who recognised me as Ian Mc-Caskill, the weather forecaster, another man with a non-Standard English voice and spectacles. Such is television fame! It was my habit at such encounters to spread cheerfulness by predicting sunshine all the way.

From 1991 onward, my casual interrogators had a different question: 'When's the general election going to be?' The answer to that was more surely based: 'When the Prime Minister thinks he can win, or when the final legal date approaches, whichever is first.' With economic recovery stubbornly delayed, and talk of a 'two-dip recession' in America, he was forced into the latter choice.

General elections were always the most enjoyable part of my job, and since this was to be my last as political editor, I was determined to enjoy it. But modern campaigns are an exhausting process, for journalists as for the politicians themselves. They last roughly a month. In 1992, each working day began at 7.15 a.m., with the Liberal Democrat press conference, and continued through Labour's and the Tories', to allow the political leaders to leave on their expeditions to various parts of the country around ten o'clock. For the rest of each day my routine varied: sometimes out in the country, for meetings or interviews, other times rooting round the various party headquarters, in person and by telephone, to seek news of how their campaigns were going.

Apart from weekends, when I slept at home, I stayed in a hotel next door to the National Liberal Club, where the opening press conference took place. I tumbled out of bed early enough to read a few papers, listen to radio or television news, and turn up in time to face a fresh-looking Paddy Ashdown. His day doubtless lasted even longer than ours – in my case, till after either the *Nine O'Clock News* or *Newsnight* – but he had some advantage over me in years, and did not have to look over his shoulder at the silent disapproval of a hospital cardiology department. The BBC eased the strain by providing me with a driver for the duration.

This proved particularly useful when I went to big evening meetings in the north of England. While I was making my final broadcasts from these, the driver, a kindly man called Paul, would find somewhere to buy me a pizza and a couple of cans of beer, and I would consume these, as if they were nectar and ambrosia, while he rolled me back to London and bed. With luck, I would get in a little extra sleep on the journey. Sometimes I feared I might become the first chauffeur-driven lager-lout, though I was too tired to sing.

Paul's presence proved especially fortunate on one night towards the end of the election. I was due to broadcast a final interview with the *Nine O'Clock* presenter live. It was to be from a point outside Conservative Central Office, since I had been covering John Major in Kent earlier that day. With three minutes to go, I was told we had 'line trouble'. I ran to the car, was driven to the BBC's Westminster headquarters a few hundred yards away, warning the editor from the car telephone that I would need lines connected from that building, and finally ran up the two flights of stairs to the studio.

When I had reached it, and the studio manager had attached the microphone to my tie, I decided to devote the minute still available to much-needed recovery of breath, in the hope of convincing viewers I was not about to expire. So I laid my head on folded arms on the table. This image on monitor screens caused consternation at Shepherds Bush. The telephone rang, and an anxious editor enquired: 'Are you all right, John?' I mustered enough breath to assure him I was 'just resting', and thirty seconds later the interview proceeded. Afterwards I made a modest request that equipment checks should take place earlier the next night.

The result of the 1992 election was the most difficult to predict for many years. The government had two main problems. One was that it had been in office for thirteen years, the other that the Conservatives were presiding over their second recession in that time. But right at the beginning, that wise old bird of Tory politics, Willie Whitelaw, gave me his opinion that no election was ever won except on real disposable incomes, adding with a twinkle: 'You may ask why we need politicians.' The Conservative campaign, it soon emerged, was based on that party's classic tactic: to prove that Labour's taxation and expenditure plans would reduce voters' disposable incomes.

There probably was no convincing way for the government to handle the unemployment issue, for the figures had risen alarmingly throughout their period in office. Some ministers unfeelingly heaved a sigh of relief when, during the campaign, the separation of the Prince and Princess of Wales overshadowed bad jobless totals. Despite later reductions, more people lost and were afraid of losing their jobs during this recession than at any time since before the war.

A few days after the election was called, a close colleague of the Prime Minister reported that he was 'in overdrive'. I had noted his zeal, with some discomfort, when I was trying to concentrate on a brief interview I was to do with him, live into the one o'clock television news. While waiting, we had only a silent monitor screen. As I checked over my questions, I was keeping half an eye on this, on the principle that when my face appeared on the monitor, I should speak.

John Major took a more political interest in the silent screen. He read aloud the graphics from Labour's election manifesto, and proceeded to argue with them. John Motson could not have produced a more excited commentary, though for its acerbic tone, it was more Barry Davies. I kept my head down, and forebore to debate anything with my inter-viewee before our time.

The Conservatives decided to concentrate on Labour's taxation poli-cies. At first, this seemed to misfire. John Smith produced a shadow budget which received as much media attention as the real one from Norman Lamont. This was not as peculiar as it may seem, because at that time most tipsters would have expected him to be the next Chancellor, in which case the Lamont budget would have become inoperable. The Tory attack at first concentrated on the losses they said people earning more than £22,000 per year would suffer under John Smith's plans, but this had less resonance than they hoped.

The man who found out why was their Chief Whip, Richard Ryder. Before the campaign began, he had told me that his role in it would be that of 'libero', or sweeper. Ryder, like myself, is a football enthusiast. Indeed, both of us, together with Kenneth Clarke, Roy Hattersley and others, were later enlisted by the *Sunday Express* as 'celebrity reporters', each covering his own football team. My account of West Ham was the furthest from impartial reporting that I hope ever to stray. During the election, Chief Whips are free of the task of marshalling their errant MPs, so can take a roving role in their party's campaign.

Ryder was canvassing in a lower middle-class area of his Norfolk constituency, where he discovered that people earning between £10,000 and £12,000 were quite unfazed by what Labour might or might not do to people better off than themselves. Many of those earning more than £20,000 were probably in safe Tory seats. He and Chris Patten at Central Office concluded that the election would be won and lost among 'Thatcher's children', the manual workers who had deserted Labour in 1979, and never come back. All the parties believed there was an unprecedented number of undecided voters in this group.

The Conservative machine set out to persuade them not to trust Labour. John Smith maintained that eight or nine out of ten voters would be better off under his proposals. Whether he would have been able to get this message across better to the voters if Labour's tax plans had been revealed many months earlier is a question I often debated with him. Smith's view was that an opposition had enough problems without offering early targets for the government to shoot at. No Labour leadership I have known since the 1959 election, and doubtless earlier, has found a satisfactory solution to this electioneering problem.

Throughout the campaign, the two parties flung statistics back and forward, like Great War artillerymen on the Western Front. The Conservative slogan was 'Labour's tax bombshell'. It was to be much quoted against them in the following parliament, when taxes rose under Norman Lamont. But if tax was one campaigning issue for the Tories, the other was Neil Kinnock. They were ruthless in targeting him, because every minister I spoke to in the year before the election had convinced himself that Kinnock could not win.

This tactic reached its climax during the most ludicrous event of the campaign, the War of Jennifer's Ear. It is hard to say whether the parties or the media behaved more foolishly during this. Certainly, the only people who emerged with credit, and appeared to gain some support, were the Liberal Democrats, who determinedly kept aloof from the battle. Yet health was a key issue for Labour. Their party election broadcast sought to dramatise the subject by the method Lord Northcliffe pioneered in the tabloid press of the twenties: human interest.

Jennifer Bennett was a little girl who could not get an operation on her ear done under the NHS, while another child had it done privately. The row erupted when Jennifer's name, which had not been given in the broadcast, appeared in two newspapers. If Labour wanted to use the story to bring health to the top of the election agenda, the Tories were determined to use it to pillory Neil Kinnock as 'unfit to govern'. As one minister told me later: 'It would have been difficult to begin our morning press conference with the words: "Our subject today is Neil Kinnock."' They felt Jennifer gave them the opportunity.

By the time the media had taken firm hold of this juicy bone, the rival health policies had disappeared almost without trace. Conservatives and Labour fought a tied match, over two or three days, about the media-obsessive issue of which of them had leaked her name to the papers. Whoever were the guilty men or women, this was a question scarcely worth the attention of a London equivalent of the *Washington Post*'s Watergate investigative team. I did my best to drag our coverage back to the various parties' plans for the NHS, but I was swimming against a strong tide, in both broadcasting and the newspapers. During an election, as at other times, each influences the other, and a pack mentality develops. This occasionally improves coverage, sometimes the opposite.

Throughout the campaign, public opinion polls vacillated widely, but on the whole favoured Labour. A week before polling day, in what the Tories came to call Red Wednesday – in an echo of their own Wobbly Thursday of the 1987 campaign – Labour appeared to shoot ahead, with polls giving it leads of seven, six and four per cent, larger than either party enjoyed before or after. This caused it to claim its lead was too large for John Major to overtake. That, of course, is part of electioneering: each party tries to create a bandwagon effect, assuming that some voters will want to back the likely winner.

On the evening of the day these favourable polls were published, Neil Kinnock and his whole shadow Cabinet appeared at a huge rally in Sheffield, for which Labour supporters had bussed in from all over the north. Some commentators blame the triumphalist mood there for turning the tide against Labour. Several factors argue against that. The Sheffield rally, though doubtless a triumph of the modern theatrical impresario's art, ran behind time, what with bands, rock groups, opera singers, even political speeches. A BBC colleague who was compiling our filmed report for nine o'clock had a difficult task in getting even the earlier part of Neil Kinnock's speech on the air in time.

I had to do a live interview with the presenter from the gallery of the hall, against competition from rock music, exploding fireworks, and assorted mayhem. It was difficult to concentrate, but this was one of those broadcasting occasions where the best rule is simply to keep talking and hope you are audible and make sense. I reported that the Labour people at the rally were understandably elated by that morning's opinion polls, and by their own great occasion in the hall.

But before I went on air, I had learned from London the result of a later opinion poll, in which the Conservatives were ahead, though only by half a point. Roy Hattersley came to the gallery to ask for any late news, and when I told him this, he wrinkled his nose unhappily. If the tide turned against Labour at the time of this spectacular in its deputy leader's native city, it did so before a trumpet blared or a firework blasted. But the people in the hall did not know this.

Another factor which belies the charge that Labour thought it was home and dry is Neil Kinnock's own private attitude. I had arranged to have talks with each of the three party leaders as they travelled round the country. My meeting with Kinnock was on his aircraft, on the morning of the Sheffield rally. His mood was one of sober satisfaction over the polls, rather than triumph. Indeed, although he argued that very little further movement in his direction would give Labour an overall majority, rather than a hung parliament, he was warning his campaign team against any complacency. With a rugby coach's sternness, he told them they must not take the poll lead for granted, must avoid looseness in their organisation, must 'keep tight and shove'. Soon after our meeting on his plane, he began to detect the tide against Labour.

I saw Paddy Ashdown in a back room of the hall in Leeds where he was to speak. Paddy gave me a sober and sensible assessment of how the Liberal Democrats were doing, acknowledging that there were too many 'don't knows' to make a prediction possible. This was especially true for a third party, which was hoping for a role if the voters decreed a minority government.

I had an interesting insight that night into the virtual reality which is electioneering. This was an early evening meeting, so by the time I was doing my live two-way into the *Nine O'Clock News*, the crowds would be gone. The Liberal Democrats' elaborate stage-set had just arrived from Edinburgh, and immediately after the meeting was to head for Ashdown's next venue, in Bristol the following evening. My producer and I had to persuade the scene-shifters to wait long enough for me to appear in front of the political backdrop.

After our talk, Paddy girded his loins, and advanced up the centre aisle. Music thumped, lights flashed, dry-ice clouds engulfed him – as they had in Edinburgh, and would do in Bristol. He shook hands, waved, advanced to the rostrum, as the final extravagances burst around him. He looked towards heaven, or rather the ceiling of the educational institution where he was speaking. 'Wow!' he shouted, leaving his stolid Yorkshire audience with the warm feeling that it was remarkably civil of them to put on such a welcome just for him.

Two days after the Sheffield rally and my chat that morning with Neil Kinnock, I joined John Major's entourage in a sweep through Kent. He was by then well into his routine on the famous soapbox, and used it effectively at a daytime meeting on a village cricket field. He dealt well with questioners and hecklers, but I suspect what really mattered was the benign influence on his own morale of a style which suited him.

Before the campaign began, Douglas Hurd noted that John Major was more interested in detail and tactics than any Prime Minister since Harold Wilson (whom Douglas, as Ted Heath's political aide, had observed from close quarters in the elections of the seventies). But he was not as obsessed by the media as he had once been, and Hurd believed he would perform well. Sir George Young, a minister with his own marginal seat to defend in west London, thought John was the Tories' best asset, and he hoped Central Office would not tire him out. He did best as the nice chap, confident, calm, looking well, and not flustered. But if there were a few bad polls, and if the Prime Minister was tired, it would affect his performance. This was uncannily like what, at one stage, seemed to be happening, before closer contact with people crowding around his soapbox raised the Prime Minister's spirits.

I travelled with John Major by helicopter on one leg of his journey through Kent. There were six seats: pilot, co-pilot and detective in the front, the Prime Minister, Norma Major and myself in the back. I was placed in the middle, but since I had less than half an hour available to assess his judgement of the campaign, I risked appearing rude by warning Mrs Major I would have to concentrate on John. She was very under-standing.

He impressed me by his willingness not to play games with me, particularly by his confession that this was an election where the parties would have to go right to the wire before the result was clear. I was struck by his genuine puzzlement about the discrepancy between the opinion polls and what he was encountering on his tours. Every time he went out and met people, he came back feeling happier about his prospects. But he admitted that his impression of their warmth was belied by national and some local polls. I was reminded of a similar, though longer journey I made with Hugh Gaitskell thirty-three years earlier, when the Labour leader had been overwhelmed by the enthusiastic reception he received around Britain, yet had lost the election badly.

John Major had similar doubts in his mind. But on his journeyings, he was talking to a large number of candidates and experienced election workers, some of whom he knew well enough to trust their judgement. They claimed there was no correlation between the opinion polls and what they were finding on the doorsteps. Less than a week before polling now, the Prime Minister was still asking himself uncomfortable questions: might his people on the ground be concentrating too much on the canvass of their better areas, and so get a wrong impression? Were they just being polite to a leader they knew was facing defeat?

He was relying heavily on what had become known as the Kinnock Factor: what his party's organisers round the country were telling him was that many people were fed up with the recession, but would not vote for Neil Kinnock. The Prime Minister was sober, rather than euphoric. The only real depression he showed was not about opinion polls, but because his attempt to argue the constitutional issue, particularly over Scottish devolution, but also over the danger of hung parliaments, was being overwhelmed by rows over Jennifer's Ear. He wanted to talk about the dangers of a break-up of the United Kingdom, and felt the election was being trivialised.

Soon after our talk on that Friday morning before the final week, the constitutional issue developed wings. This followed what I regarded as a serious error by Labour the previous day, when it raised the issue of proportional representation at its morning press conference, a week before polling day. This sign of loss in confidence in outright victory did more to arrest Labour's momentum than any supposed triumphalism at Sheffield. In my judgement, no political leader could hope to tiptoe into power, winning votes only if people are confident he has no chance of forming a government. If Sheffield was intended to enthuse Labour supporters, and convince them Neil Kinnock had a reasonable hope of becoming Prime Minister, that seemed a sensible tactic.

When I argue that Labour's worst error in the final week came over proportional representation, the reader is entitled to know that I have long been opposed to its introduction for elections to the British parliament (as distinct from European or Scottish assemblies, where no government is being elected). This view is based on the belief that voters ought to elect a British government, rather than merely electing the representative body from which a government will be formed by negotiation. In other words, that the power to make and unmake government should always be in the hands of the voters, rather than party negotiators.

The debates on this subject easily become convoluted, so I promise not to weary readers with detail. In public discussion it is often assumed there is no respectable argument against a new voting system. Advocates of this use the heavily loaded description, electoral *reform*, when what they mean is electoral *change*. For the sake of brevity, I rest my case on the odd events which have occurred under Germany's proportional system. The smallest party there, the Free Democrats, has had a share in government constantly since 1969: this though they have sometimes experienced difficulty in reaching the five per cent threshold of votes required to win any seats in the Bundestag. In 1966, after they brought down Ludwig Erhard's Christian Democratic government, a working party on electoral systems recommended that Germany should adopt the British method, first past the post, to prevent such actions in future. Because the parties could not reach agreement, this did not happen.

But the conclusive event, in my view, came in 1982, when the Free Democrats executed another *volte-face*. During the life of a parliament, they abandoned their coalition with the Social Democrats, and teamed up four days later with the Christian Democrats. The Free Democrats' leader, Hans-Dietrich Genscher, Germany's almost perpetual Foreign Minister, justified this by a famously cynical dictum: '*Eine Wende ist notwendig.*' (A change of direction is necessary.) Necessary in whose judgement? The voters'? No! In the view of the leader of the party which came only third in all post-war German elections.

When Labour raised PR, so late in the campaign, and for no better apparent reason than that Charter 88 was holding 'a day of constitutional action', the party's message became blurred. This was aggravated when Neil Kinnock, anxious to avoid making PR in Westminster elections an issue involving loyalty to his leadership, refused to say which way he leaned. The weekend after John Major told me he was disappointed with the public reception for his campaign on the constitution, this bungled operation enabled him to revive it.

This was the election when I, like many others, became disillusioned with opinion polls, though neither commentators nor politicians could afford to ignore them. Tory insiders warned me as early as January that their private polls showed the public polls were consistently overstating Labour support by several percentage points. Even before the campaign began, William Waldegrave adumbrated an interesting theory, in the course of predicting, with what later seemed like clinical accuracy, that the Tories would avoid a hung parliament by about twenty seats. It proved to be twenty-one.

The theory was that it was remarkably difficult to dislodge a Tory government in what was a very conservative country. He did not think this reflected any particular credit on his own party, but called in aid of his argument what happened in 1964 and 1974. Even after the Profumo affair, the refusals of Iain Macleod and Enoch Powell to serve under Alec Home, and the limitations of Home as an electioneer, the Tories had only lost narrowly in 1964. In February 1974, when Ted Heath had put out the lights for reasons that ordinary people could not understand, they again had only just lost.

The fallibility of opinion polls became obvious during the 1992 election. I am not an expert in polling, and I confess to having been torn in my reactions during the campaign. The BBC's election coverage would have been incomplete without some account of the polls, which appeared in newspapers day after day. Politicians and their spin-doctors talked to me as much about the polls as they did about policy.

But the Corporation had suffered a bad experience in its *Election Night* programme in 1987, when it used a system that was only in part an exit poll. John Birt, later to be Director-General, joined the BBC just at that time, but since election plans had already been made, he did not involve himself. The projection at the beginning of the election results programme proved disastrously wrong, to the delight of Conservative critics of the BBC. One of John Birt's first acts was to enlist academics to conduct an enquiry. In 1992, our projection – based this time on a proper exit poll – was not notably more accurate. It seems to me, in retrospect, that the conclusion is inescapable: some people simply do not tell the truth to pollsters, perhaps because they believe they ought not to be asked how they intend to vote or how they have voted.

After much earlier panic, some of it poll-induced, I noted a significant gain in confidence at Conservative Central Office in the final week. The blip in their poll standing a week earlier – and who knows whether or not it represented anything real – allowed them to warn Tory defectors that a protest vote for the Liberal Democrats risked letting Neil Kinnock and Labour in. About that time, their reports from the constituencies had encouraged them to believe John Major was getting across on taxation, recession, a 'disunited kingdom' and – an issue which was to cause him much anguish after his victory – Europe.

50

CLOUDS AND SILVER LININGS

I retired as political editor of the BBC in the autumn of 1992, just before my sixty-fifth birthday, though I continued to broadcast and write as a freelance, from Westminster and elsewhere. One of my discoveries about even partial retirement was that the use of logic and instinct now had more often to replace day-by-day contact with politicians as a means of judging events. I have yet to discover whether or not this is a sufficiently reliable guide. An intriguing test of this is the attempt to bring peace to Northern Ireland, a subject which has interested me, because of my origins, for the past thirty years.

In the midst of many other troubles which engulfed John Major within six months of his election victory, he decided that we would make yet another effort to achieve a settlement in Ulster. Indeed, some admirers hoped this might salvage his much criticised leadership: people who were generally hostile to him would be more inclined to give credit for a patently well-intentioned attempt to solve a problem they did not understand.

As this book has not revisited the Irish question since Chapter 17, when I described the collapse of the power-sharing executive of 1974, we must now make a final expedition to Ulster. Almost forty years ago, interest in a broader politics caused me to leave Belfast and finish up at Westminster. While I was working full-time at the House of Commons, I followed Irish developments as best I could from there. After I retired as political editor, I became an even more distant observer. But when trouble erupted at home, I could never avoid looking back in sorrow at the country of my birth. Again, this is not a history of events, but 'as it seemed to me', at the time and since.

The second half of the modern Irish crisis centres around the Anglo–Irish agreement of 1985, negotiated between Margaret Thatcher and the then Taoiseach, Garret FitzGerald. But the story recommences much earlier, after the violent overthrow of the 1974 administration. I still regard this as the last, best hope of permanent peace in Ulster, because it addressed not peripheral issues, including relations with the Irish Republic, but the kernel of Ulster's quarrel: how two peoples with conflicting national loyalties could live together in their small province, and govern their lives jointly and fairly.

By acknowledging that this power-sharing must take place within the United Kingdom, for so long as that was the wish of the majority of its people, the settlement was in tune with political reality. Contrary to what British and Irish newspaper readers might deduce, opinion polls showed that power-sharing within the United Kingdom was the only solution which commanded support from a majority of both Protestants and Catholics. But Westminster and Dublin politics have made the conundrum more complicated than that.

With the tragic irony which has often afflicted Irish affairs, the Protestant extremists who led the assault on the power-sharing settlement in 1974 actually encouraged the trend in London attitudes which they feared: an ambiguous, not deeply held, but pervasive feeling that the ultimate solution might be an all-Ireland one. After the strike succeeded, some at Westminster regretted that the Sunningdale settlement had included an 'Irish dimension', since this helped to destroy the remarkable internal agreement between Northern Unionists and Nationalists to bury ancient enmities and work together.

But in the Irish Republic's domestic politics, no politician could afford to exclude the Irish dimension, since this would leave him open to attack by opponents. Successive British governments went along with this imperative, because if they kept Dublin at least acquiescent in their policies, they reduced criticism there, as well as in the United States.

This particular international dimension was an unnecessary and essentially frivolous complication to an already impossible dilemma. It was one which only a nation whose political class has lost self-confidence in its handling of Irish affairs would have tolerated. Geoffrey Howe hints in his memoirs that someone — presumably from London — actually prompted President Reagan to enquire anxiously of Margaret Thatcher whether she was going cool in the negotiations for the Anglo–Irish agreement. I find that bizarre, even improper.

On Ulster, Irish Americans have combined atavism with considerable ignorance. A peculiarity of the Irish diaspora is that American immigrants of Ulster Protestant origin — a huge migration, under religious persecution, in the early years of the American colonies — have totally assimilated in American life; while Irish Catholics, most of whom arrived after the potato famine a century-and-a-half ago, have retained their identity, despite all the influences of the American 'melting pot'.

The Boston Irish, the political master race of Massachusetts – who asserted their ethnic separateness when the state tried to bus black children into their areas in the cause of educational equality – nevertheless feel themselves to be still oppressed, clinging together for mutual support. The liberal economist, J.K. Galbraith, though a political ally of the Kennedys, had a sardonic comment on the inhabitants of their Boston Irish base:

> They would remain a bruised and exploited people, nature's underdogs, as an ample and sometimes excellent literature can confirm. No other race withstands success so well.

In the decade after 1974, successive Northern Ireland Secretaries attempted political initiatives. Some of these foundered on their own contradictions, others were undermined by continuing violence. Dublin never fulfilled its repeated promises of greater cooperation on security, including extradition of wanted terrorists to Ulster or England. British ministers talked about this with two voices: in private they constantly complained to journalists like myself; in public they said matters had improved, on the principle that half a loaf was better than no bread, and that Dublin would help less if London seemed publicly ungrateful.

Yet in 1978 came a leaked British Army intelligence report, which must have given the IRA more aid and comfort than anything before or since. This said that victory over the IRA was impossible while the Republic provided 'the classic safe haven so essential to any successful terrorist movement'. It pointed particularly to freedom from extradition for crimes committed in Northern Ireland. Everybody knew what was wrong, but they could not agree on how to put it right.

On one press visit to the Republic, soon after a mass escape of convicted terrorists from the Maze prison, near Belfast, I was assured by a senior Garda officer that his force's intelligence about the IRA was so good that they would have all the escapees back in custody soon. Sadly, this proved to be misplaced optimism, both about their probable capture, and the attitudes to extradition of courts in the Republic and the United States.

Ambiguity was the small change of Anglo–Irish relations in the bleak eighties. At the instigation of John Hume, leader of the Northern nationalists, Dublin convened a New Ireland Forum, which reported in 1984. Only nationalists took part. Its recommendations were either for a unitary Irish state, federation or confederation, or joint authority between London and Dublin. All three were unacceptable to the British government, as well as to Unionists.

Before the Secretary of State, Jim Prior, gave his response in the House, Dublin asked to have advance sight of his statement. When Irish ministers read an early draft, they complained that it was too negative, and begged that something positive be inserted. Prior obliged, but was astonished later to see that the inserted paragraph was the only one referred to in the government statement from Dublin.

The Anglo–Irish agreement of 1985 was hailed at the time as yet another 'historic breakthrough'. If Britain had the equivalent of an Académie Française, 'historic' is one word which might usefully be banned, or rather left to await the judgement of history. The agreement established an inter-governmental council between London and Dublin, with Irish ministers regarding themselves as guarantors of Northern nationalists. Ironically, in view of events ten years later, one of the arguments used in favour of the agreement was the need to save the electoral support of John Hume's SDLP from incursions by Sinn Fein.

After the agreement was signed, Geoffrey Howe, who as Foreign Secretary took great pride in it, invited me to a lunch for the retiring Irish Ambassador in London, Noel Dorr, who together with the British Cabinet Secretary, Sir Robert (later Lord) Armstrong, played a decisive part in the negotiations. The atmosphere of complacent triumph in the speeches was reminiscent of Bernard Shaw's Professor Higgins: 'We did it!'

The trouble was that it had all been done without the consent of Eliza Doolittle. London had acted without effectively consulting the Ulster majority, while the SDLP had been kept fully informed by Dublin. A more certain recipe to induce the ancient Irish political tactic of boycott could not have been imagined. The Unionist MPs at Westminster resigned their seats and fought by-elections, winning all but one of these. For years, Unionist politicians refused to meet British ministers, and politics locally went back into the stalemate from which they had emerged when John Hume ended *his* boycott.

The process of consultation within Whitehall about the agreement has produced much retrospective criticism. Comments in volumes of political memoirs published in the nineties give an odd impression of how the British government approached what was proclaimed to be an historic agreement. Nigel Lawson complains that the Cabinet was faced with a *fait accompli*, and that only Margaret Thatcher, Geoffrey Howe, Douglas Hurd and Tom King knew in advance what Robert Armstrong had negotiated. Lawson regarded the agreement as 'a political liability', and wondered how any objective observer could think otherwise.

Many of his colleagues, including Tom King, according to Margaret Thatcher and Geoffrey Howe, seemed to share these doubts, and when her own memoirs appeared, they contained a strangely disillusioned conclusion:

> Greater support by the nationalist minority in Northern Ireland or the Irish Government and people for the fight against terrorism were not going to be forthcoming. Only the international dimension became noticeably easier to deal with . . . it is surely time to consider an alternative approach.

Margaret Thatcher has always had a distant view of the Northern Ireland problem. It was one of the few subjects on which she seemed willing to give the Foreign Office and the Whitehall mandarinate their heads. When Douglas Hurd was Northern Ireland Secretary, he suspected her primary interest in the subject was the welfare of English soldiers – a proper preoccupation, but not a sufficient one.

John Major provided an 'alternative approach', though perhaps not the one which the Thatcher memoirs implied. This is a story which has not yet reached its conclusion. Any initiative which produces a suspension of violence by both the IRA and the Protestant paramilitaries is worth the effort put into it. At worst, it has saved lives during the period of ceasefire, and made the existences of ordinary people in Northern Ireland more tolerable. At best, peace becomes a habit which it is too difficult for either set of paramilitaries to break.

What is not so easy to detect is the logic of the 'peace process'. One possibility, a benign one, is that the IRA has grown tired of violence, that the original message which the British government claimed to have received through secret channels nine months before the Downing Street Declaration was genuine. This said that the conflict was over, but that the Provisionals needed Whitehall's advice about means of bringing it to a close.

Sinn Fein vehemently denied the existence of any such message, and Gerry Adams said: 'Nothing could be further from the truth. The capacity of Republicans to engage in struggle is totally undaunted. If the IRA wanted to surrender, they would simply surrender.' Earlier, for good measure, he had said that the British people must 'sue for peace'.

All this was said before the ceasefire, and it may not be as gloomy as it sounds. Any Republican leader who advocated giving up the armed struggle without achieving any of the IRA's objectives would be accused of dishonouring those who had died in that struggle, not to mention their victims. He would be in danger of assassination by his own side. The benign explanation of the ceasefire therefore has some life in it.

The malign version is that which is believed by fearful Ulster Protestants, and sedulously purveyed by some politicians and commentators on both sides of the argument. This is that London has given the IRA secret assurances that moves to Irish unity are a question of 'when', rather than 'if'.

This is where I must rely on logic rather than information. In the period before and since the Downing Street Declaration, there has been what must surely be deliberate ambiguity in the use of the phrase 'self-determination'. Anybody who has read any Irish history from the 1920s knows that this fundamental democratic concept means different things to different people. After all, it was because of disagreement about which area or areas in Ireland had to have this right of self-determination that Lloyd George strove to square the circle, through the partition which accompanied Irish independence. It was for endorsing this arrangement that Michael Collins (leader of the old IRA, which won the South its independence) was assassinated by more irreconcilable Republicans, the progenitors of Fianna Fail.

Most commentary on the Major–Reynolds agreement showed scant understanding of this distinction: when Unionists talk about self-determination, they mean by people within the present boundaries of Northern Ireland, and indeed that appears to be the guarantee enshrined by London and Dublin in the Anglo–Irish agreement of 1985, as well as in the Downing Street Declaration of 1993. But when Republicans and at least some Nationalists speak of self-determination, they mean for the island of Ireland as a whole.

Acceptance of the latter definition might satisfy the IRA, but its result would probably be an outburst of violence involving many more in the Protestant population than have supported the UDA or UVF. Logically, permanent peace in Ireland will depend on how that difference is resolved. Or, perhaps more probably, left semi-permanently unresolved, as it was between 1921 and 1969.

EPILOGUE

Precisely three months after the Conservatives' fourth election victory, and John Major's first, a senior ex-minister invited me to go for a drink in Annie's Bar. He said: 'I want to be conspiratorial.'

Although myth says otherwise, Annie's Bar, the only hostelry in the Commons where MPs and journalists can buy each other drinks, is not an ideal place for conspiracy. A politician who is not an habitué stands out like a sore thumb, and might just as well climb to the top of Big Ben and shout across Parliament Square that he's 'up to something with the media'.

But like myself, this man was moving to the end of his full-time career at Westminster, and was giving his long-standing opposition to the European project a final airing. I could see he wanted to be mischievous. As we settled at a table, the quizzical looks of old lags at the bar did not deter him in his indiscretion.

He began by denouncing John Major as a mere tactician, a leader with no vision. The economy was spinning out of control. Because of higher unemployment, public spending would rise. Interest rates were really remaining high because of Britain's membership of the Exchange Rate Mechanism, but ministers would say this tightness was aimed at reducing inflation. Yet with such a weak labour market, wage inflation was no problem.

The government need not assume, he said, warming to his task, that recent generations of new Tory MPs were 'gents', who would do what they were told out of loyalty, as their predecessors had done. He had advised young Euro-sceptics that they could risk rebelling without endangering their careers, for when the European row was over, the whips would want to bind up wounds, and would be looking for able young rebels to promote.

His jeremiad continued into our second half-pint. The government was going to have a dreadful two years, and he was by no means certain that it would win the next election. This was a surprising confession from even a discontented Tory, so soon after John Major's victory. At that time, Labour's fourth successive defeat had created a widespread – and foolish – view that John Major would inevitably remain Prime Minister until the millennium.

What was remarkable was the speed with which the political mood changed. In another three months after that conversation in Annie's Bar, and within six months of the Prime Minister's election victory, his imminent demise became almost as fashionable – and foolish – a prediction. In my last few months as political editor of the BBC, politics had entered a new febrile phase. But the issues were old ones: the failure to achieve economic recovery; tax increases (Conservative ones, this time); and Europe.

The obvious turning point in John Major's fortunes was 'Black Wednesday', 16 September 1992, the day when Britain had to leave the European Exchange Rate Mechanism. This combined the explosive issues of economic disarray and Britain's relations with Europe. During Margaret Thatcher's long reign, the Parliamentary Conservative Party had become much more right-wing and Euro-sceptic. To many new MPs, the ERM combined the vices of being both European and an interference with the purity of their market forces ideal.

Like Labour in the eighties, the Conservative party was in an ideological period. That ideology, whether right, wrong, or indifferent to the welfare of the nation, was profoundly dangerous for the unity of the party, the comfort of its leader, and its pride in winning more elections than it loses.

Much ministerial blood had already been spilt in the disputes over Britain's entry to the ERM, which played a significant part in ending the careers of Margaret Thatcher, Geoffrey Howe and Nigel Lawson. Now, just when even Euro-sceptics like Norman Lamont, Michael Howard and Michael Portillo were prepared privately to defend Britain's membership, the pendulum swung and hit the Prime Minister and his Chancellor on the backs of their heads.

My pocket diary for 1992 – a handsome, leather-bound book, embossed 'Maastricht: Europe, 1992', which I carried that year in place of the usual utilitarian BBC model – records my attendance at Harrogate all that week, for the Liberal Democrat Assembly. But that was my intention rather than what happened. Within two days of our arrival in Yorkshire, reports of sterling's difficulties drew many of us political reporters back to London. Black Wednesday is almost the end of our story. But first we must examine the events which led up to it.

This Conservative roller-coaster ride, coming so soon after election victory, diverted me from keeping as close an eye as I would have liked on the opposition. But a change in the Labour party's fortunes was the other new element in British politics. Neil Kinnock never became Prime Minister, indeed never held government office at all. He took over leadership of his party when many people believed it to be in terminal difficulties. Yet as the most single-minded party manager in Labour's now almost century-long history, he put it in condition to be a contender for power again.

Although Labour lost in 1992, Kinnock's mathematical achievement then was a remarkable one. In 1983, at the height of the Alliance's popularity, Michael Foot gained only twenty-seven per cent of the national vote, just two per cent away from a demoralising third place, behind the Alliance. The third force in British politics has declined steadily from that high-water mark. In 1987, Kinnock raised Labour support to thirty-one per cent, compared with the Alliance's twenty-three. But the Alliance could still claim that it was in second place in 228 of the Conservatives' 375 seats, sixty-three per cent of the total, and in many places had a better chance of defeating Tory MPs than the official opposition.

By 1992, any prospect that the Alliance's successors, the Liberal Democrats, might replace Labour as the principal opposition party had evaporated. Their national vote fell from twenty-three per cent to eighteen, and their number of MPs, at 20, represented a net loss of two, compared with Labour's increase of 42, to 271. Nor could the Liberals any longer argue that they were principal challengers to the government in more constituencies than Labour. The number of Tory seats in which they were now in second place had fallen to forty-three per cent. The next election was clearly going to be more of a Conservative–Labour battle than any since 1979.

John Smith took over the leadership from Neil Kinnock with over-whelming support, but few illusions. He once wryly said to me that a career at the bar provided two valuable lessons for politicians: it taught them that they had to work with some strange people, and that they sometimes had to handle very odd briefs. His own instincts were those of a traditional Labour man representing a deprived area of Britain. He was a strong believer in redistribution of wealth, and believed that Labour would have to stand and argue a case on taxation, and that the public would respect them for this.

He said this to me before the 1992 election, when the Conservatives made his shadow budget, which acknowledged the need for higher taxes, their principal target. At our last talk before his death, which took place after Kenneth Clarke had confirmed Norman Lamont's imposition of VAT on domestic fuel, and imposed other tax increases, John Smith's mood had changed. This was partly because of his experiences during the election. But he also said sternly that working people had now suffered enough heavy extra taxes, and he was not going to add to the burdens of what he unselfconsciously called 'our own people'.

Now leader of the opposition, and with the Conservatives badly enough damaged by devaluation and other reverses to make the prospect of a Labour government more likely, he took a sober view. Labour would finance its social programme – education, health and social welfare – out of increased economic growth. I recalled that this was what Gaitskell had said in 1959, but Smith added a rider: 'If we can't get growth, we can't have the programme. That is a truism about government.'

A couple of years earlier, when he was awaiting his certain election as leader of the opposition, we met one day by chance, in the corridors of Westminster. It was a sunny summer day, and John asked me to come out on the terrace for a drink and a chat. It has always been one of my favourite places at Westminster, with a lively background of river traffic on the Thames, and Westminster Bridge as a reminder of how different London must have been even in Wordsworth's day.

He was in relaxed mood, but bubbling with ideas about what he would do when he took over from Neil Kinnock. An abiding theme, in this and other conversations, was restoration of the role of the family in British society. He remained a Scots Presbyterian, and was depressed at the thought of unfortunate single mothers, isolated with their children in tower blocks in his own and similar constituencies. They must have nursery schools that would enable them to get back to work. That would be better for them and for their children, and would take them off benefits.

At our last meeting, in the spring of 1994, he was convinced the Tories had miscalculated the damage they had inflicted on themselves by forgetting what they had promised at the election, about taxes and recovery. He remained hopeful about the future of the British economy, arguing that half the public deficit was caused by unemployment. He therefore put production of more jobs at the heart of his programme.

John Smith's natural optimism about his political fortunes was increased by a belief, which he expressed to me that spring, that the Conservatives were now facing the problem which had destroyed Labour's chances in the eighties: internal faction. He was planning for a general election in 1996, he said, though 'in my bones I feel it will be before then'.

Long before the time came to fight that election, John Smith was cruelly cut down by a heart attack, and thus became, in the most absolute sense, another of Labour's generation of lost leaders. After the 1992 defeat, not only Neil Kinnock, but his deputy Roy Hattersley and Gerald Kaufman had retired from the front bench. They joined others in their political generation in the Callaghan government, including the three younger members of the SDP's Gang of Four, David Owen, Shirley Williams and Bill Rodgers, who would not hold government office again. Opposition politicians had paid a heavy price for the divisions they were unable to heal.

Apart from the general election of 1992, Maastricht and the ERM were the high points of my final year as political editor of the BBC. Maastricht came at the end of 1991, four months before John Major's election victory, though its echoes reverberated through his post-election term. The European Council which took its name from that Dutch town was held in freezing December weather. My abiding memory of it as a broadcaster was that, because of security restrictions, John Simpson and I had to deliver our reports while standing on a large table. Television journalism is a funny old trade. The explanation of our bizarre perch is that the camera required a backdrop of the twelve flags of the European Union, displayed outside the headquarters building, but that viewers must remain oblivious of the high wire fence which separated us from them.

So we stood on the table. This seemed to be on the direct route of an icy blast from the Russian steppes, which had swept across the North German plain to us. Often, in the ways of live news, we had to wait on the table for a long time, our earpieces playing goobledegook to us, minds slowly freezing up. In one memorable interview, John Simpson reached a point where he wanted to mention Norman Lamont. The cold was too much for memory or patience, and he referred to 'the Chancellor of the Exchequer, whose name, for the moment, eludes me'. We all sympathised, and regarded it as a stylish piece of broadcasting. As it turned out, in the cruel world of politics, it was not a name we had to remember for much longer.

After the long drawn-out end to the Maastricht summit, the Prime Minister recorded an interview with me at 3.30 in the morning. He was ebullient about his opt-outs from the Social Chapter and from further moves towards full Economic and Monetary Union, and triumphantly claimed that this was 'game, set and match for Britain.'

The trouble about this was that the other eleven countries had thought they were all on the same side of the net. Specifically, many European politicians, of widely different political colours, could not see how free trade would be allowed to survive if capital within the Community simply flowed to the cheapest labour markets. Workers were also voters, and the spectre of protectionism always lurked at the politicians' shoulders.

Three hours and a brief sleep after that interview, I was back at the conference centre, waiting to report on Breakfast Television. Sitting outside the studio with me was the Portuguese Foreign Minister, Joao Deus Pinheiro, who was also to be interviewed. He had just taken over for Portugal's term as President of the EU, and in our few minutes together, he revealed how much his and the other nations resented the opt-outs. He concluded menacingly that Britain would never get off with anything like this again.

His intention then was not to say anything so undiplomatic on British television. My report came first, and he probably heard that and the recording of my Major interview before he went on air. Whether one or other of these provoked him or not I cannot tell, but when the Portuguese minister reached the studio he left Nicholas Witchell in no doubt of the antagonism to Britain that John Major's claimed triumph had provoked. It was a harbinger of trouble to come, at home and abroad.

The ashes of Britain's ERM demise have been raked over often enough. When the pound weakened in the late summer of 1992, Whitehall suspected that German unhelpfulness stemmed from a hostility which began at Maastricht the previous December. Others criticised Norman Lamont for failing to take up an offer to realign sterling within the ERM. This would have been taken as a political defeat, but on nothing like the scale of the panic-stricken September days which preceded and followed Britain's exit and devaluation.

Just a week before Black Wednesday, I discovered in a talk with Paddy Ashdown how reluctant opposition politicians were to risk being regarded as unpatriotic by saying anything which might bring the pound down, though they mostly believed it was over-valued. Ashdown was convinced that a straight devaluation would force Norman Lamont's resignation. That seemed probable to me too, but it was not what happened.

When the devaluation did finally take place, Downing Street offered the television networks interviews with John Major. Advance briefing left me with an impression that their principal aim was to calm political nerves, especially those of Conservative MPs, who were dispersed during the long summer recess. Clearly interviewers had a duty to dig deeper beneath the surface than that. This was a major reverse for the government and for Britain, and we were the first to have an opportunity to question the Prime Minister about it.

The other broadcasters, Michael Brunson of ITN and Adam Butler of Sky, conducted their interviews before me, because their networks had earlier bulletins. Each took much longer than the five or six minutes the press office had tried to insist on. I pegged on at the Prime Minister for a full fifteen minutes. He was not pleased, saying to me afterwards that what he disliked was the chance this gave us to choose parts of the interview which suited our agenda, rather than what he was trying to get across. I assured him that I would take a personal part in the editing for all bulletins, and I would try to ensure it was fair.

What caused this sharp exchange was not just my determination to take whatever time I thought was needed, but also one question I decided had to be asked. Clearly Norman Lamont's standing, like that of any Chancellor who has to devalue, was seriously undermined. The Prime Minister dismissed suggestions that he might ask Lamont to resign. I then put the inevitable question: was he not retaining Lamont in post simply because his own reputation was so tightly bound to that of his Chancellor?

It was not a question I enjoyed putting to a man I found personally congenial and friendly. John Major is quite a different character from the public image that has been pinned on him, that of a grey man, without intellectual or emotional depth. One of the ludicrous aspects of modern journalism is that commentators or other artists who have little personal acquaintance with politicians decide they are grey, wear their underpants outside their shirts, or even trousers. The caricature often has no connection with reality.

Major is a lively, sometimes amusing, but always tough and combative politician, who takes a highly personal view of his battle with opponents and the media. Prick him, like Shylock, and he bleeds. When I put the question about his personal position, he took about ten seconds to respond. During this time, words came from his mouth, but no clear meaning. Like any competent performer, he kept speaking while he assembled his thoughts. Then he said, with great force, that anybody who knew him would reject my suggestion that he would retain Lamont merely to preserve his own position. The necessary question had been asked; the inevitable answer given. Nine months later, when Norman

Lamont was dropped, I thought my question had been justified, though I regretted the resentment it so obviously caused.

The devaluation provoked a decline in the Prime Minister's standing which, since his election victory in April, had seemed unchallengeable. The anti-European Right of the Conservative party and its supporting press soon converted 'Black Wednesday' into 'Golden Wednesday', and claimed the new, lower parity had launched an economic recovery. But though indicators might turn benign, interest rates fall, and City analysts and the Treasury keep detecting the green shoots of recovery, the 'feel-good factor' which affects voters seemed to be infinitely delayed.

This public scepticism about economic recovery was the dangerous backcloth to John Major's unpopularity. During a tightly fought election, the Conservatives had promised that recovery was just around the corner. They had warned that a Labour government would make tax increases inevitable, and prolong the recession. Soon they themselves were putting VAT on domestic fuel, raising National Insurance contributions, failing to index allowances against income tax, reducing mortgage tax relief. The government had concluded that the only way to fight clear of its economic problems was to ask people to accept reductions in their living standards.

I was nearing the end of my eleven years as political editor. The party conferences in the autumn of 1992, enlivened by Britain's exit from the ERM, were my swansong, and my successor, Robin Oakley of The Times, took over after that. The BBC had invited me to spend two afternoons a week at Westminster, to give commentaries on their Westminster Live programme. This also enabled me to keep in touch with political friends and acquaintances, and to collect material for the political sketch I had given for several years in On the Record at Sunday lunchtime.

The outlet for my written journalism, the Listener, had died long before the election, when the BBC decided it could not sustain its respected magazine any longer. New Statesman and Society offered me a column. I informed my bosses, but by the time the mysterious processes of consultation had taken place, and I was told that John Birt, the new Director-General, was not happy that I should take up the offer, my first column was already advertised in the paper. The NSS's increasingly right-wing counterpart, the Spectator – which I had written for, in its earlier, liberal phase in the late fifties, when Ian Gilmour was proprietor – had become almost a house journal for many BBC staff, so I did not feel any sense of guilt.

I continued these activities until this book demanded my full-time attention. The Statesman column gave me greater opportunity to stand back and look at politics, and the BBC also commissioned me to prepare a television film on unemployment, which someone archly called 'Cole on the Dole'. By the beginning of 1993, I became aware that the government's unpopularity was more serious than in earlier economic down-turns. In part, this was because it was the second recession the Conservatives had presided over. It was also different in its effects. For the first time, articulate middle-class people, especially in the south and midlands, discovered they were now in the 'sackable classes'. They complained more audibly than people who were all too used to unemployment.

We filmed in a depressed housing estate in Newcastle-upon-Tyne, a mining district of Yorkshire, and a part of Hertfordshire which had been hit by redundancies in the aircraft and general engineering industries. It demonstrated to me, yet again, the value to a political journalist of getting away from Westminster occasionally, for it was not until two years later, in January 1995, that I saw reflected in a public opinion poll the feelings I detected during work on that film.

In this real, often harsh world, absence of the feel-good factor no longer seemed surprising. Too many people had either lost their jobs or were afraid of doing so. Almost everyone knew somebody – children, family or friends – who had faced redundancy. Not only miners and factory workers, but company directors, accountants, solicitors, architects and other professionals found themselves on a scrapheap from which they could see no exit. Economic statistics and theory both seemed far removed from what was happening.

I wondered whether ministers had wandered into a new, and dangerous hazard: that in curing one disease, they provoked another, like a doctor who gives excessive drugs for an ingrowing toe-nail, and causes his patient's hair to fall out. They were living in an uncharted world anyhow, for the deregulation of financial markets and the onset of the information revolution had made national economies even more unpredictable, and uncontrollable, than before.

It was an irony that a government which preached the ultimate wisdom of markets has seen its European exchange rate policy, a central plank of the economic platform on which it had been elected, undermined by young men in red braces shouting into telephones. The severe blow the money markets had administered to the Prime Minister and Chancellor had echoes of the way in which trade union activities had undermined elected governments in the seventies. But most commentators regarded markets, unlike trade unions, as a force of nature.

The cause of many of John Major's troubles was the changed nature of employment. Ever since Margaret Thatcher's early days, her more dogmatic ministers had two obsessions: to create a deregulated labour market; and to assert that British manufacturing industry was in inevitable decline. They almost relished their belief that the future lay in services.

Now these two policies were demonstrating their downside. For those made redundant, the wages in deregulated, non-unionised service jobs – security guard, van driver, supermarket stacker; worse still, commission-only salesman of insurance or double-glazing – were so close to the benefit level of a family man that he sometimes asked himself: 'Why work?' More alarmingly, in areas of chronic unemployment, and especially in inner cities, this 'why work?' syndrome was in danger of running through successive generations of the same family. It was what I had seen happening in Ulster, and it contributed to the troubles there. In Britain as a whole, it also swelled the cost of welfare benefits, undermining the public finances.

A second hazard emerged in the constantly deferred hopes of recovery in the retail trade and in the housing market. Although the indices said recovery was well under way, people no longer behaved as if they believed this. Apart from those actually without jobs, too many others feared for their future, because they were in part-time work or short-term contracts. Even in the two industries in which I had myself worked for half a century, journalism and broadcasting, short-term contracts were now commonplace. These may suit managers, but are not well thought of by mortgage-lenders.

The implications for the demand side of the economy were obvious to everybody except blinkered eyes in Westminster and Whitehall. People with non-existent, perilous or low incomes were reluctant to spend what money they had. A subjugated labour market might seem like good supply-side economics, but it did not revive markets for goods, services or houses.

The arrangement I had made with the BBC, as well as with my other client, the *New Statesman*, was that I would convince my long-suffering wife Madge I had really retired by stopping work at the end of May and not resuming until the party conferences in October. I have always disliked the hot and often humid months of June and July at Westminster, and this seemed a good time of the year to travel more, and read a few books. But it had an uncovenanted effect on my judgement of that summer's political developments.

During 1993, Westminster was dominated by the alarums and excursions of the Maastricht legislation. With a small majority, and a substantial, and ever more disaffected group of Conservative rebels, the

Government had a hard time. This combined with by-election reverses to create an atmosphere of chronic crisis. In the few newspapers I read abroad or in brief periods at home during that late spring and summer, the future of the Prime Minister was a subject of obsessive discussion.

Away from the Westminster hothouse, I found the excited state of opinion about John Major's chances of retaining his job bewildering. The dangers were difficult to take at face value, because the rational incentive for Tory MPs to seek another change of leader was not present. First, to do this twice within two or three years would look whimsical. Second, the public would scarcely accept again that a change of leader meant a change of government. Third, if the steam behind the revolt was discontent over Europe, no alternative leader who was likely to be more Euro-sceptical was in evidence. Finally, my judgement of John Major's character was that he was not the kind of batsman who would 'walk' before the umpire's finger was raised so decisively as to brook no argument.

But when I went to the Tory conference at Blackpool in October, I discovered this was not just a case of my newspaper colleagues taking in each others' gossip. The receptions each evening at which I met ministers and other MPs were buzzing with speculation about the Prime Minister's future. Soon I was as deeply into these discussions as I would have been in my former job.

Yet logic still said that a Tory MP, calmly judging his own and his party's prospects, would not be well advised to take part in a conspiracy to remove another leader. In 1994 similar turbulence recurred, in part because John Major's 'Back to Basics' slogan was left looking faintly ridiculous by a series of sexual and financial scandals affecting ministers and Conservative MPs.

Just as in Harold Macmillan's day I believed that sex was less important than economic difficulties in deciding whether he would hold on as prime minister. I could not believe that John Major would sink in a bog of Conservative sexual sleaze. Only if by-elections and opinion polls remained unprecedentedly bleak into the last eighteen months of the parliament would a challenge to his leadership be a rational, rather than a mere emotional reaction by Conservative MPs. And by then it might be too late anyhow.

With the detachment which semi-retirement had brought, I mused about the shambling uncertainty with which Tory backbench MPs now criticised their leader, without doing anything effective to remove him. This contrasted with what Walter Bagehot, in the last century, admiringly quoted 'a cynical politician' as saying about them: 'By Jove, they are the finest brute votes in Europe.' Bagehot went on to adumbrate his 'principle of parliament', obedience to leaders:

> Change your leader if you will. But obey Number One while you serve Number One, and obey Number Two when you have gone over to Number Two. The penalty for not doing so is the penalty of impotence. It is not that you will be able to do no good. You will be able to do nothing at all.

John Major's troubles were aggravated in May 1994 by a defeat in the elections for the European parliament. These had now turned into the British equivalent of the American mid-term elections, and provided voters with a chance to kick the government. Interesting as this extra electoral test might be for domestic politicians, I was disappointed that Strasbourg had not succeeded in bridging the democratic deficit in Europe. The theory in the seventies had been that once direct elections were introduced, these would give MEPs authority to win more power. An elected parliament would take actions which would be of interest to ordinary people, and thus at last force press and broadcasting to report its activities.

But national governments were too jealous of their power to surrender much of it, and as the eighties turned into the nineties, the peoples of member countries seemed less, rather than more interested in the European parliament. The gloomy circle was complete: no popular interest in events at Strasbourg until it won power over policies which affected people's lives; no power conceded to it by governments until their citizens insisted on this.

Meanwhile, authority in Europe lay with the council of ministers and twice-yearly summits of the heads of state and government. These haggled on in private, drawing further and further away from the voters of Europe, and crushing the last sparks of European idealism beneath the wheels of the horse-traders. Yet finance and business were ever more Europe-wide in their activities, so that individual governments were deluding themselves in believing they could have independent economic policies. The European Union was affecting more and more aspects of people's lives, yet their governments seemed not to know how to make it seem less remote.

The stunning blow to Labour of John Smith's death in May 1994 produced a respite in the constant speculation about John Major's future. Attention now turned to the election to choose his new Labour challenger. Even in Edinburgh, after a deeply moving funeral in the Smith family's Church of Scotland parish, the rumour was beginning that Gordon Brown, whom I thought of as John's natural successor, might stand down in favour of his friend Tony Blair. The leadership election which followed was conducted with a civility that has not always attended such events in the past. Bill Morris, leader of the transport workers, asked me to preside at his union's hustings at Westminster, where Tony Blair, John Prescott and Margaret Beckett presented their cases and answered questions. It was the one brief interruption of my work on this book, for I had decided to avoid all engagements. I subsequently declined a suggestion that I should take the chair when the three candidates moved round Britain for the Labour party's own hustings.

I already knew much about what Tony Blair thought Labour needed to do if it was to be elected, for we had talked often, before and since the 1992 election. He had been one of those urging John Smith to 'take on' the party, by reforming its structure. Smith took this advice in the conference debate on 'one member, one vote'. Blair believed Labour needed a mass membership, which would keep MPs more in touch with the people who elected them. He saw his party's problems as arising from its recent status as a 'coalition of minorities'. This had created similar electoral problems for the American Democrats and the German Social Democrats. Without mass membership, he maintained, Labour would not get close enough to ordinary people to win power, and therefore to help the minority who were poor and unfortunate.

The problem for Tony Blair was how well he could combine this determination to keep Labour close to the people who were likely to vote for it with a radical agenda which would distinguish his party from its opponents. He began his leadership with instincts to achieve the second objective as well as the first. Even while Margaret Thatcher was still Prime Minister, Blair was worried that Labour was not being radical enough; was not, for example, establishing itself as a party which believed in sensible public spending.

He argued that a party of the right might just get off with 'riding the opinion polls', but a party of the left must lead public opinion. His own suspicion in the summer of 1990 was that while the eighties had been the period of tax-cutting, the nineties might be a time when people realised they needed to do more things collectively. This fitted in with his friend Gordon Brown's belief that Labour could only achieve support for policies of redistribution if it rekindled a spirit of community.

Long before John Major and Tony Blair faced each other across the despatch boxes as leaders of their parties, Blair used to ruminate on their contrasting political experiences. He first came to know Major when the future Prime Minister was the Treasury whip, and he himself joined Labour's Treasury team. The fact that this was just ten years earlier is a reminder of how quickly the political generations have moved on.

Blair deduced from his own experience that young politicians often come to Westminster without a well-developed set of beliefs to guide them. He had known only that he was a Labour man, but it had taken the years in opposition for him to reflect on what exactly he thought most important. Because John Major had been in office almost from the outset of his parliamentary career, he had not had the same time to work his way to a set of beliefs against which he could make day-by-day decisions. Before the 1992 election, Blair detected a Prime Minister who was torn between the views of Chris Patten, his party chairman, and Norman Lamont, his Chancellor and leadership campaign manager.

This was, of course, a comforting view for a political opponent. Since then, John Major has been singed by the fire which burns constantly at the summit of politics; and Tony Blair is now himself experiencing the strains of a similar lonely exposure. As the Prime Minister's troubles with his party rumbled on throughout the parliament, he clung to the posture he had adopted since succeeding Margaret Thatcher in November 1990, and which won the 1992 election for him.

In that contest, with Labour still not acceptable to enough voters, he squared the circle: preserving enough of Thatcherism to hold the Tories together, and to make sense to voters of the previous thirteen years; while engineering enough of a break with her final years to save himself from foundering on her electoral unpopularity.

That served for the 1992 election, but as John Major's own poll ratings slumped, and stayed low, the question left hanging in the air was whether this was more than a staging-post. Would it save the Conservatives again? With Europe as a constant threat to the unity of his party and government, he did not feel strong enough to tell them, or the voters, that Thatcherism was dead; perhaps that the eighties obsession with ideological certainty was dead; and that 'Majorism' – a word he wisely eschewed – simply meant doing the best a Prime Minister could in difficult circumstances. 'Circumstance' is a word with a good Tory pedigree. Indeed, it has continuing resonance for pragmatists of every political loyalty, perhaps for every politician who wants to win power in a democracy.

Yet to proclaim the death of ideology is, to most politicians, a danger-ous act, since it may seem close to admitting that principle in politics is dead. This is not so. There is a vast area for political action between obsession with declarations of ideology – whether confirmation or abolition of Labour's Clause IV, for example – and the opposite: simply asking the C2s, the voters most obviously up for grabs, what they want, and promising, implausibly, to give it to them.

In the real world, in which most ordinary voters do not devote every waking hour to political thought, a party only succeeds by convincing people that what it believes the nation needs is close enough to what they themselves really want. This means grasping what are settled and justified popular concerns, rather than mere passing whims or prejudices, and seeking means to satisfy them. Not the old, cynical: 'I am your leader; I must follow you.' But certainly not: 'I have a doctrine which tells me what is good for you, and mere events cannot alter it.'

To call this an ideology may seem grandiloquent. Rather it is the politics of democratic principle. During the nineties, in search of a surrogate ideology, politicians and commentators adopted as a common conceit 'the Big Idea'. Parties flirted with everything from Citizens' Charters and 'Back to Basics' to constitutional reform through Bills of Rights or new voting systems; even, heaven help us, provision for arts, sport and charities through the National Lottery. (When this was launched in 1994, I came across a radio script I wrote in 1984 about George Orwell, whose famous novel of that name had the 'proles' devoting much of their energy to quarrels over *their* National Lottery. *Absit omen!*)

I set out my own ideas for a Big Idea in the *New Statesman* in February 1994. Despite the then fashionable preoccupation with non-economic subjects, I argued that no politician who expected to be taken seriously could wander on the periphery of public concerns, and dodge the obvious issue: the growth during recent recessions of a substantial under-class, and the consequences of this for the rest of us. Oddly, both the principal party leaders at that time, John Major and John Smith, had spoken strongly to me about the malign effects on British life of our class-ridden society. 'Class', it seemed, has become more, not less import-ant since the brain-death of Marxism.

My definition of the problem facing political leaders in Britain was this:

How does a government respect the rights of individuals to do the best they can for themselves and their families, and yet nurture collective provision that will not just build the roads and keep them safe, but also relaunch the postwar assault on underprivilege and poverty in education, health, housing and work?

There was an age of optimism after the second world war that assumed social problems could be tackled. This flowed naturally from the belief that since all social classes had recently contributed to a desperately narrow victory over evil, all deserved the fruits of victory. The optimism, and the spirit of fellowship which went with it, evaporated with the economic failures suffered by both Conservative and Labour governments from the late fifties onward. It has taken us a long time to admit how chronic Britain's economic decline has become. Our collective reaction to that decline has been non-collective: to look after Number One.

Individualism as an ideology has a destructive downside. For Conservatives, it obstructs their traditional concern for 'the condition of the people'. For socialists, it engenders nervousness about arguing the case for collective action, lest that should lose the votes of those who have come to feel that the less politicians intervene in our lives, the better. So we plough on through the litter, crime, violence of the housing estates, avoid walking alone after dark, complain about hospital waiting lists, inadequate schools, and the growing number of people in their fifties who will never work again.

If that passage seems gloomily apocalyptic, readers should remember that I am sixty-seven. For all of us, the age of youth – in my case, the immediate post-war period – often leaves memories of a golden era. The personal and the political are difficult to separate. Yet as an unashamed supporter of – even apologist for – politicians and the political process, I am convinced that there are profound dangers if Westminster and Whitehall seem to stray too far from the anxieties which concern the public, and pursue private obsessions.

The skill of politics, surely, is to discern what are the problems that people believe make their lives less comfortable. The skill of leadership is to work out policies for solving these. Not pandering to public opinion, but giving it a lead. Sometimes this may require the politician to tell the voters frankly why something is not possible – why there cannot be better public services without higher taxes, for example. The dominance in all the political parties of the new sciences of presentation has not encouraged that honest democratic process.

Before political friends gather at the steps of my pulpit to shout abuse, let me confess that several more books might be devoted to the causes of the worrying separation which now exists between politicians and the public. The inadequacies of the media in which I have served for half a century would be among these causes. There is something in Tony Benn's complaint that communication lines between the British people and their parliament have been disrupted.

The faults are by no means all on the politicians' side, or even the media's. The public also need to work harder at understanding politics if they are to be wisely governed. They get the newspapers and television programmes they want, rather than those which would best serve their interests. It would be sad if a population which grows bored with politics gets only the politicians such apathy deserves. In the period during which I have observed British politics, I believe the public have always been better served than that.

BIBLIOGRAPHY

Baker, Kenneth, *The Turbulent Years: My Life in Politics*, Faber and Faber, London, 1993

Benn, Tony, *Diaries*, Hutchinson, London, 1989–94

Callaghan, James, *Time and Chance*, Collins, London, 1987

Castle, Barbara, *Diaries*, Weidenfeld and Nicolson, London, 1984

Clark, Alan, *Diaries*, Weidenfeld and Nicolson, London, 1993

Cole, John, *The Poor of the Earth*, Macmillan, London, 1976

Cole, John, *The Thatcher Years: A Decade of Revolution in British Politics*, BBC Books, London, 1987

Crosland, Anthony, *The Future of Socialism*, Jonathan Cape, London, 1956

Crossman, Richard, *The Diaries of a Cabinet Minister*, Hamish Hamilton and Jonathan Cape, 3 vols, London, 1975, 1976, 1977

Hetherington, Alastair, *Guardian Years*, Chatto and Windus, London, 1981

Howe, Geoffrey, *Conflict of Loyalty*, Macmillan, 1994

Ingham, Bernard, *Kill the Messenger*, HarperCollins, London, 1991

Jenkins, Roy, *A Life at the Centre*, Macmillan, London, 1991

Lawson, Nigel, *The View From No. 11; Memoirs of a Tory Radical*, Bantam Press, 1992

Owen, David, *Time to Declare*, Michael Joseph, London, 1991

Taylor, Geoffrey, *Changing Faces, A History of the Guardian 1956–88*, Fourth Estate, London, 1993

Thatcher, Margaret, *The Downing Street Years*, HarperCollins, London, 1993

Wilson, Harold, *The Labour Government, 1964–70*, Weidenfeld and Nicolson, London, 1971

Wilson, Harold, *Final Term*, Weidenfeld and Nicolson, London, 1977

INDEX